2/11

THE STATE OF SEX

The State of Sex is a study of Nevada's legal brothels that situates the nation's only legal brothel industry in the political economy of contemporary tourism. Nevada is part of the "new American heartland," as its pastimes, people, and politics have become more central to the nation. The rise of a service and leisure economy over the past 60 years has propelled sexuality into the heart of contemporary markets. Yet, neoliberal laws in the United States promote business but limit sexual commerce.

How have Nevada's legal brothels survived, while the rest of the country criminalizes prostitution? How do the brothels operate? Who works in them? This book brings social theory on globalizing economies, politics, leisure consumption, and emotional labor in interactive service work together with research on contemporary prostitution and sexual commerce. The authors employ an innovative, multi-method sociological approach, combining historical analysis of how the brothels came to be with over a decade's worth of ethnographic research on the current state of the industry.

Barbara G. Brents, Ph.D., is Associate Professor of Sociology and Faculty Affiliate in Women's Studies at the University of Nevada, Las Vegas.

Crystal A. Jackson, M.A., is a Ph.D. student in the Department of Sociology at the University of Nevada, Las Vegas.

Kathryn Hausbeck, Ph.D., is Senior Associate Dean of the Graduate College and Associate Professor in Sociology at the University of Nevada, Las Vegas.

CONTEMPORARY SOCIOLOGICAL PERSPECTIVES SERIES

Edited by Valerie Jenness,
University of California–Irvine
and Jodi O'Brien,
Seattle University

This innovative series is for all readers interested in books that provide frameworks for making sense of the complexities of contemporary social life. Each of the books in this series uses a sociological lens to provide current critical and analytical perspectives on significant social issues, patterns, and trends. The series consists of books that integrate the best ideas in sociological thought with an aim toward public education and engagement. These books are designed for use in the classroom as well as for scholars and socially curious general readers.

Published:

Political Justice and Religious Values by Charles F. Andrain

GIS and Spatial Analysis for the Social Sciences by Robert Nash Parker and Emily K. Asencio

Hoop Dreams on Wheels: Disability and the Competitive Wheelchair Athlete by Ronald J. Berger

The Internet and Social Inequalities by James C. Witte and Susan E. Mannon

Media and Middle Class Moms by Lara Descartes and Conrad Kottak

Watching T.V. Is Not Required by Bernard McGrane and John Gunderson

Violence Against Women by Douglas Brownridge

Forthcoming:

Gender Circuits: The Evolution of Bodies and Identities in the Technological Age by Eve Shapiro

Transform Yourself, Transform the World by Michelle Berger and Cheryl Radeloff

Sociological Storytelling by Sarah Fenstermaker and Nikki Jones

Also of Interest From Routledge:

Sex For Sale: Prostitution, Pornography, and the Sex Industry, Second Edition, by Ronald Weitzer

The Handbook of Sexuality Related Measures, Third Edition, edited by Terri Fisher, Clive and Sandra Davis, and William Yarber

The Feminist Theory Reader: Local and Global Perspectives, Second Edition, edited by Carole McCann and Seung-kyung Kim

THE STATE OF SEX
Tourism, Sex, and Sin in the New American Heartland

*Barbara G. Brents,
Crystal A. Jackson, and
Kathryn Hausbeck*

Routledge
Taylor & Francis Group

NEW YORK AND LONDON

First published 2010
by Routledge
270 Madison Avenue, New York, NY 10016

Simultaneously published in the UK
by Routledge
2 Park Square, Milton Park, Abingdon, Oxon OX14 4RN

Routledge is an imprint of the Taylor & Francis Group, an informa business

© 2010 Taylor & Francis

Typeset in Minion by RefineCatch Limited, Bungay, Suffolk

Library of Congress Cataloging-in-Publication Data
Brents, Barbara G.
  The state of sex: tourism, sex, and sin in the new American heartland / Barbara G. Brents,
  Crystal A. Jackson, Kathryn Hausbeck.
    p. cm.—(Contemporary sociological perspectives)
  Includes bibliographical references and index.
  1. Prostitution—Nevada.   2. Brothels—Nevada.   3. Sex oriented business—Nevada.
  I. Jackson, Crystal A.   II. Hausbeck, Kathryn M.   III. Title.
  HQ145.N3B74 2010
  306.7409793—dc22   2009030856

ISBN 10: 0–415–92947–4 (hbk)
ISBN 10: 0–415–92948–2 (pbk)
ISBN 10: 0–203–86025–X (ebk)

ISBN 13: 978–0–415–92947–9 (hbk)
ISBN 13: 978–0–415–92948–6 (pbk)
ISBN 13: 978–0–203–86025–0 (ebk)

To everyone who has ever sold or traded sex.

To everyone who has ever sold or traded sex.

CONTENTS

SERIES FOREWORD

This innovative series is for all readers interested in books that provide frameworks for making sense of the complexities of contemporary social life. Each of the books in this series uses a sociological lens to provide current critical and analytical perspectives on significant social issues, patterns, and trends. The series consists of books that integrate the best ideas in sociological thought with an aim toward public education and engagement. These books are designed for use in the classroom as well as for scholars and socially curious general readers.

The State of Sex draws on over a decade of ethnographic work and a multi-method sociological approach to provide a comprehensive analysis of Nevada's legal brothels. At the macro level, Brents, Jackson, and Hausbeck utilize sociological theory on globalizing economies in general, and the leisure economy in particular, to situate modern-day legal brothels as sites of well-institutionalized sexual commerce. Along the way, they demonstrate how historical, institutional, political, and legal contexts shape the social organization of sex for sale. Likewise, they explain how and why legal brothels survived in select Nevada counties while the rest of the country criminalizes this form of sexual commerce. At the micro level, they provide an insightful empirical analysis of the protocols and practices *within* suburban and rural brothels. The focus is on how women come to work in Nevada's brothels, the social relations between brothel workers and those who own and frequent brothels, and the emotional work that accompanies—and in some sense constitutes—labor in brothels. Combining these macro and micro analyses in a seamless and creative way, *The State of Sex* ultimately advances an innovative way of understanding the sale of sexualized leisure in the "new American heartland." It is a way of understanding that includes compelling lessons about the dynamics of gender, class, and racial inequalities; indeed, the book is ultimately about how almost every element of the brothels—from marketing to performing the labor—reproduces *and* challenges traditional conceptions of masculinity and femininity as well as what constitutes appropriate sexual activity. Understood in this way, this book is first and foremost about the socially constructed nature of sexuality, gender, and market activity in a global economy. It is also, simply put, an interesting and valuable read about the changing contours of the world's oldest profession, both historically and in the modern moment.

Valerie Jenness
Jodi O'Brien

PREFACE

In 1998, we were flying from Las Vegas to Reno in one of our first visits to a northern Nevada brothel. Sitting in front of us on the plane was John Ensign, the Republican U.S. Senator from Nevada, quietly but intently reading the *Las Vegas Review Journal*. In that newspaper, and in just about every paper in the country, people were reading lengthy verbatim excerpts from the just-released Kenneth Starr report on the Clinton–Lewinsky scandal, including details about acts that may or may not count technically as sex. If we ever wondered about the importance of our research, that scene stopped us cold. When the President of the United States was caught in an illicit sexual relationship with a young intern named Monica Lewinsky, sex was thrust into the public arena in ways that would have been unimaginable just a few years earlier. Or maybe it just highlighted how important sex was already becoming in our culture. Clinton's affair was a public backdrop for the next ten years of culture wars over the meaning of appropriate and inappropriate sexual behavior, and where to draw the line between the public and private aspects of sex.

What we anticipated would be a titillating adventure flying across Nevada to interview people who sold sex in brothels suddenly took on new significance. We were going to the places where politicians, movie stars, truck drivers, miners, tourists, and crane operators had purchased sex for decades. Did they know something about sex in our culture that would help explain the hoards of news crews and Congressional panels grilling the President of the United States and his once intern about their sex lives?

That was more than a decade ago. In the ensuing years, thanks to the commercial sexual dealings of former Louisiana Republican Senator David Vitter and former New York Democratic Governor Elliot

Spitzer, prostitution as political scandal repeatedly has made national and international news. At the same time, Nevada's gambling resort destinations, and the economic growth that industry has fostered, have gone from being seen as peculiar to being so mainstream that Nevada held one of the first 2008 presidential caucuses. The state is increasingly recognized as a barometer of future urban economic trends across the country. Gambling, in some form or another, is now legal in most states in the United States. The mainstreaming of certain sex industries like strip clubs, pornography, and adult toys is almost old news to the national press. Academic research on sexuality, gender, and commercial sex has exploded. All of this has made very clear to us that the answer to what is happening to American sexual culture requires us to look at the complex interface between politics, economics, gender, and sexuality.

This book is the result of a long collaboration. When we began, outsiders knew precious little about the Nevada brothels, and we were outsiders. Save for a few journalistic accounts of life in brothels and the brothels' place in Nevada history, the burgeoning field of academic research on the consensual adult sex industry had largely overlooked, or dismissed outright, America's only legal prostitution industry. We might have too, had it not been for some savvy and intelligent women who nudged us in this direction, and for living in Las Vegas where the culture of the community is steeped in women's bodies and sexuality.

As for each of us, the journey has been a bit different. . . .

In 1992 Gayle and Lisa wanted to write a paper on prostitution for a sociology class on feminist theory and research that Barb was teaching. Gayle was a women's studies major and mother who had returned to school after raising a family and building a career. In a large intro class she took with Barb the previous semester, she happened to sit next to a woman who was an escort. Her newly gained sociological imagination was triggered; she was intrigued. Lisa was a young sociology major also pursuing a certificate in women's studies. Gayle called up Fran, the owner of what was then Fran's Star Ranch near Beatty, and drove for an hour and a half to interview three sex workers. They also interviewed nine escorts and seven erotic dancers. For those two, the experience was eye-opening. In their class presentation, they enthusiastically reported that they were surprised to find that the workers said it was all about the money! Another newly enlightened feminist male student presented a paper on cocktail waitresses at the Rio Hotel & Casino, then in the midst of a lawsuit for management-set weight requirements. The three students battled. He said waitresses and sex workers didn't complain about their work because they were suffering from false consciousness. Gayle countered, "If the workers said they meant it, aren't you just putting your opinion on them?" At that time, Barb was not that far out of graduate school. Her training was in political sociology. She had written a dissertation on social security. She knew little about these debates except for what she read and witnessed after a few short years living in Las Vegas; but she was hooked. Barb, Gayle, and Lisa took the paper and presented it at the American Sociology Association conference in 1993. At that time, there was almost nothing written about the brothels in Nevada.

The following year, Kate arrived at UNLV as an Assistant Professor in Sociology. She had written a dissertation on feminist theory and the cultural phenomena of so-called "post-feminism." One of the things that most amazed her when she first moved to Las Vegas was how public and open apparent illegal prostitution is in southern Nevada. It was not just the billboards and the handbills, the websites and the back pages of free weekly newspapers; it was evident in the small interactions between strangers on the street. By the end of her first semester at UNLV, she had been propositioned for prostitution three times: once in a convenience store buying Tylenol late at night; once while stopped at a red light in her car; and once walking down the Strip with friends. In every instance she thought she looked like a professor, albeit one shopping, driving, strolling; and in each case a stranger thought of her quite differently. It was clear that these instances were far less about her, and far more about the cultural climate of Las Vegas. So when she first began looking for research, writings, and photos of the legal brothels, she was startled to find that they were fairly invisible and did little advertising, while the sex industry in Vegas was thriving and very visible. Her personal experiences, her feminist consciousness and academic interest in the intersection between gender and culture, as well as this somewhat surprising inconsistency, led her to ask the core questions that help anchor this book.

After numerous articles, and several years, husbands, and kids, there seemed to be something else to say. Enter Crystal. In 2003, Crystal was a nascent feminist and a nascent social scholar, sitting in an undergraduate women's studies class, defending strippers against classmates who were saying awful things about them. She knew, in her heart and head, that her friends who worked in strip clubs, or as scantily clad cocktail waitresses or nightclub hostesses, or who engaged in casual sex for a night of VIP treatment and free drinks at a nightclub, were not making bad decisions that would haunt them forever; they were not bad mothers, or damaged, abused women, nor were they engaging in unsafe sexual practices any more than other sexually active women. She was surprised by the vehement verbal attacks—the semester up until then had been full of camaraderie as the students had found a space that fostered their feminist and social consciousnesses. She had loved being surrounded by people who "think like me," who were critical of sexist billboard advertisements in the city, who were upset by racist teachers, who hated being treated differently based on gender or sexual orientation or ethnicity or religion. But on the issue of sexual expression, particularly a commodified sexual expression, young feminist solidarity melted into contentious debate. Crystal began working with Barb and Kate in 2003 when she began the Ph.D. program in sociology at UNLV.

This book is thus the result of over a decade's worth of scholarship, collaboration, and activism, looking and relooking, thinking and rethinking. It would not exist without all the relationships that happened along the way. We have gained entreé into an international community of scholars and activists who explore sexual commerce. We have talked to workers in brothels, independent sex workers who strip, who sell sex, or who are high-end escorts; brothel owners, strip club owners, policemen, county officials, state legislators, scholars, and advocates on all sides of the debates. As advocates/academic pundits, we have offered testimony to city boards, business groups, and the Nevada state legislature. We have offered our support to local and national sex workers' rights organizations. Each of us has explained herself, again and again, to curious academics, feminists of all persuasions, industry workers, family members, and friends. We have grown from all of this.

So to the countless number of people who helped us every step of the way, from initial thoughts to entering the field, from those who shared their lives with us to the final preparation of this book, we thank you. You all know who you are, and we do too. We are very grateful.

And in no particular order, we would like to thank several of you by name or organization.

First, and most importantly, thanks to those whose experiences and lives we have tried to describe. Especially for those who work in the brothel industry, we owe you a debt of gratitude. We wish we lived in a world where we could list every one of your names with no fear that anything we have said will come back to haunt you. Until then, we dedicate this book to you, and to everyone who has ever sold or traded sex for something.

For introducing us to the world of brothels, thanks to those in the industry, especially George Flint, the Nevada Brothel Association, the Sin City Chamber of Commerce, and the brothel owners and managers who welcomed us into their businesses. Our special thanks to our friends and colleagues in the sex workers' rights movement, especially the Sex Workers' Outreach Project (both here in Las Vegas and nationally), the Sin City Alternative Professionals' Association, and the Desiree Alliance.

Thanks to all those who wittingly or unwittingly helped us in our travels to understand sexual commerce in Nevada: Denys Coyle and the Border Inn in Baker, Nevada, Valerie Huyge, Robert Miller, Stephanie Pleasants, Kent Hamilton, JoNell Thomas, John Galliher, Rich Serrano, Allen Lichtenstein, Gary Peck, the ACLU of Nevada, Betsy Fretwell, Patrick Caffrey, Jim Geffert, and Rich Reich.

Thanks to those who provided all sorts of assistance, doing interviews, transcribing tapes, conducting literature reviews, helping with coding, and who, by doing so, could not help but give us insights into what it all means: Tina Winninger, Chrissy Nicholas, Josette Letizia, Marshall Smith, Katy Gilpatric, Cheryl Radeloff, Candice Seppa-Arroyo, and Lynn Wolfe from the Department of Sociology. Thanks to Gene Moehring for sharing relevant literature on the history of Nevada, and to Ellen Rose for her early enthusiasm and support. The beginning of this research was funded through a UNLV College of Liberal Arts Research Award in 1997. Over the years, the UNLV Department of Sociology allowed research assistance and course reassignments; thank you.

In particular we would like to thank those who provided invaluable edits and critiques of entire drafts and chapters in the various stages of writing: Laura Agustín, Teela Sanders, Ron Weitzer, Myra Marx Feree,

Susan Lopez Embury, Bob Fisher, Amanda Brooks, Sara Miles, Guy Rocha (who knows everything about brothel history), Marcia Gallo, Lynn Comella, Ann McGinley, David Dickens, Jenny Heineman, Allison Heard, and especially Jackie Maloy. Thanks to the Huntridge Writing Group who read early drafts (some read many drafts) and held lengthy discussions with us, including Jennifer Keene, Robert Futrell, Anastasia Prokos, Carol Mason, Lois Helmbold, and Matt Wray. Many, many thanks to Val Jenness. And special thanks to our anonymous reviewers for their insights and assistance.

For providing sanity and support throughout the process, we extend heartfelt thanks to the Department of Sociology Sex Group, including Chrissy and Jenny mentioned earlier, and also Suzanne Becker, Deo Mshigeni, Jennifer Reed, and Sarah St. John, and the students in sociology of the sex industry class in Spring 1997 and Fall 1998.

And finally, thanks to our families for their patience, understanding, and encouragement, even when they did not quite get what we were writing about or why we are so passionate about all of this.

Barb needs to thank her family for keeping her eyes on what is important, Michael Pawlak, Sydney, Abby, and Greta Pawlak; her dad, Walker Brents, Jr. and mom, Lorna (who is undoubtedly shaking her head from the great beyond); brothers Walker and Barry Brents and their families, Jane and Jack Pawlak, and all my cousins, aunts, second cousins, and anyone else who was either intrigued or confused by our chosen studies. Thanks to Dee and Johnny Wirth who helped make this all worth it.

Crystal extends thanks to her family and friends: Thanks to my unwaveringly supportive parents, Paula and André, and my fabulous sister, Rachel, for always keeping me in check. Thanks to Desirée, "the unit," and my close friends, especially those who grew up in Vegas and those who support or participate in our city's sexualized commerce.

Kate would like to thank Mom and Bud, Dad and Rosemary, Maggie, Erik, Douglas, Mike and my whole Korgan family, for all their understanding, support, laughter, and encouragement over the years. Thanks, too, to all the friends and colleagues who have traveled along the long and winding road with me, especially Elena Howe, Kasey Baker, JoNell Thomas, Katy Gilpatric, Jon Wynn, Luis Gurri, Allen

Shelton, Andy Harper, Nicole Rogers, Kerie Francis, Andrew Ramsay, Joe Schoenmann, Hal Rothman, Richard Beckman, and Ron Smith. Most especially, thanks and so much love to Jonah Jakin Schoenmann and Todd Korgan, my two big loves.

1
INTRODUCTION
The State of Sex

Let's talk about gaming, 24-hour availability of liquor, quickie divorces, all the things we do here in Nevada. We have been very successful at this because we recognize one overriding issue, and that is that one man's morality is another man's pleasure . . . Now because of my background in tourism, I've been asked many times over the years, by hotel owners, business people, even elected officials, "What can we do here in Ely to bring more tourism in?" And that question has only really one answer. It doesn't matter who's asking it, or where they're from. And that is you have to offer people something that they can't get at home.

Phil, Ely citizen, at a public hearing on their legal brothels

For years, brothel prostitution has been Nevada's dirty little not-so-secret secret. Nevada is the only place in the United States with legal prostitution.[1] Nevada is also one of the top tourist destinations in the world, with an economy dependent on the millions of tourists who come into the state to indulge in legalized gambling.[2] In a country where prostitution is criminal everywhere else, Nevada officials cringe every time the press mentions the state's legal brothels. Legal brothels operate in only ten rural counties, not in the large resort cities of Reno and Las Vegas. Nevada's brothels look nothing like the ultra-modern, upscale strip clubs, adult nightclubs, or ultra lounges in the big city, chic, mega casinos. At most, around 500 women work in 25 to 30 legal brothels scattered throughout the state in small towns and along remote highways.[3] The locals staunchly defend the existence of their brothels, so much so that despite state level animosity, in the past ten years no state legislator has dared try to shut down the industry.

Why are these brothels still there? On the face of it, the answer is clear. Nevada built a tourist industry on turning deviance into leisure. Nevada had legal gambling before any other state in the United States. From that they built some of the largest resorts in the world, exploiting the seemingly ever-growing appetite for fantasy, indulgence, sun, and sin. Amid the slot-machines and roulette tables, scantily clad cocktail waitresses and topless showgirls tantalize tourists. Outside, pictures of strippers are splayed across billboards, and hawkers hand out free fliers filled with color photos of mostly nude women. Called a "triumph of globalized postindustrial capitalism," Nevada's resort cities, Reno and Las Vegas, excel in packaging glamor, spectacle, fantasy, adventure, and sexuality.[4] Las Vegas is particularly successful, luring 37 million visitors a year, with the promise that you can "be anyone you want to be" and "what happens in Vegas stays in Vegas."[5] The state's tourism thrives on selling an image of boundless sexual possibilities. Legal prostitution seems to be an added bonus.

Despite this, the casino industry prefers to market just the allure of sex and has always opposed the state's legal brothels. State and tourist industry leaders feel they walk a fine line between constantly shifting consumer tastes for and against sin and deviance. Sex as a commodity exposes people's worry that private intimacies in a public market can harm human relationships.[6] We associate a host of images with prostitution—crime, women's exploitation, immorality, and disease. In the face of this, it is not that obvious why these brothels persist.

Yet the symbolic importance of Nevada's legal brothels keeps growing, underscored by the popularity of an ongoing series of documentaries by HBO TV, *Cathouse*, about one legal brothel, the Moonlite Bunny Ranch outside of Reno. The mayor of Las Vegas, the largest city in Nevada, keeps trying to stay ahead of the changing market for sin and discusses legalizing a red light district downtown. An executive from the Hard Rock Hotel and Casino came out publicly in favor of some form of legal prostitution in Las Vegas. As criminalizing prostitution does not seem to slow the trade in the urban areas, both politicians and resort leaders privately wonder if some form of legal prostitution might not be a good thing.

The rising importance of tourism and sexual commerce is all part of broader social changes happening in a post-industrial consumer economy. Across the globe the sex industry comprises an ever-larger portion of a rapidly expanding tourist industry. In an economy with widening income disparities, the wealthy and the not so wealthy seek escape and adventure in their leisure time, and the poor find jobs providing it. This has meant more sexual consumption, from strip clubs to sex toys to digital porn beamed to a cell phone. Men remain the major consumers, but women are the fastest-growing consumer segment of the adult industry.[7] Newspapers and magazines report on the numerous ways the sex industry is going from seedy to stylish—*Hustler* magazine has a storefront on Sunset Drive in Hollywood, and porn stars like Jenna Jameson are reaching superstardom. The right to choose one's pleasure competes with fundamentalist religion to dominate the morality of the age. Concerns about an increase in trafficking, political sex scandals, debates about the freedom of women working in the sex industry, and the ever-constant debates about morality continue to fuel battles over the place of the sale of intimacy and sexuality in consumer culture.

No state in the United States has been as successful at capitalizing on these social changes as the state of Nevada. Between 1997 and 2007, Nevada has grown faster than any other state in the U.S., drawing rural Midwesterners, urban Californians, and immigrants from Asia and Latin America to cheap housing, plentiful jobs, and business opportunities that spin off its success as a global tourist destination.[8] This state of sex, Nevada, is thus an ideal place to start looking at the conditions of commercial sex today. Although sex has been bought and sold for centuries, something potentially different is happening in today's consumer society. What can Nevada, one of the fastest-growing states in the country, the epitome of a tourist leisure economy, and the only experiment in legalized prostitution in arguably the most advanced industrialized nation in the world, reveal about sexual commerce? What does prostitution look like when it is legal? How do broader social inequalities of gender, class, and race affect brothel prostitution?

Do the particular political, historical, and social circumstances in which prostitution occurs influence what prostitution ultimately is? What can we learn from Nevada about how private intimacy in a public market-place affects human relationships? To answer these questions, we examine the basic social relations and social institutions that characterize sexual commerce in Nevada's legal brothels—the political and economic settings, its business organization and labor strategies, and the people who work in it.

MAPPING THE TERRAIN OF NEVADA'S BROTHELS

While we like to think of Nevada's rural brothels as remnants of the Old West, the reality is much more complex. Nevada's small desert towns appear as American as apple pie—homes with picket fences, small businesses, churches, schools, and gas stations clustered along a main street. For those people who know just where to go, brothels are found in nondescript buildings, houses, or trailers, identified by the smallest of signs naming the Stardust, Mona's, or the Shady Lady Ranch. The idea of sex for hire seems out of place on streets that feel more like a set from the 1960s Andy Griffith Show than postmodern twenty-first-century communities.

Yet Nevada's brothels exist in what some argue is currently one of the most dynamic and dramatically changing regions of the country. Nevada is a part of what a Brookings Institution study calls the "New American Heartland" as its economy, people, and politics are becoming more central to the nation.[9] In contrast to its history in Old West industries like resource extraction, the entire Intermountain West has seen surprising population and employment growth in the past 20 years, spearheaded by a global economy no longer based on natural resources, but on "traded" industries—businesses that sell products or services to other regions and countries.[10] These include hospitality and tourism, as well as information technology, and knowledge creation. Nevada's transformation to a mature service economy has been nothing short of phenomenal. The availability of jobs in the tourism industry has spurred the fastest-growing population growth in the country.[11] People have poured into the West from the original Sunbelt states of California, Texas, and Florida. And these populations have also become much more diverse: the foreign-born population in the region has quadrupled since the 1970s, mostly with immigrants from Mexico and other Latin American countries, but also from Asia and Europe. The Brookings Institution called Las Vegas the most important face-to-face business-networking venue in the country thanks to its convention business. The Brookings Institution study concludes: "Contrary to its current marketing slogan, what happens in Las Vegas often does not stay there, but instead influences global commerce."[12] These dynamics have also impacted the rural regions of the state.

This dynamism extends to the state's politics. The politics behind this growth is also representative of trends in the rest of the United States. The West has been known for its libertarian political culture since the turn of the century, an opposition to central government, and a belief in the rights of individuals to make their own personal and economic decisions. Nevada politicians have always generally encouraged private enterprise over social support, imposing few restrictions on businesses. Indeed the politics that allowed brothels to exist well into the twentieth century and beyond World War II were quintessentially libertarian. However, since the 1970s, political institutions across the globe, not just the American West, have embraced neoliberal economic policies supporting free markets, decentralized and small government institutions, low public spending, and low taxes. This kind of political economy has encouraged a proliferation of a wide range of businesses to meet market demands, including sex-related businesses.

While neoliberal economics is akin to libertarianism, Western libertarianism has an awkward relationship with socially conservative "values" politics. Where economic neoliberalism sets the sex industry free, social conservatism seeks to shut it down. Nevada has a history of fighting attempts by the rest of the nation to regulate its morals, be it gambling or sex. Today's culture wars fuel a resurgence of anti-prostitution, anti-sex industry politics in many places in the world. This resurgence is often led by the same conservative groups who espouse free market business policies. However, in Nevada, the new middle America, neoliberal opposition to central government and a belief in individual free choice extends to morals regulations. Western libertarianism is inflamed by the hypocrisy and inauthenticity of government attempts to "shove their values down other people's throats."[13] Some analysts argue that this reflects a "market morality," a value system emphasizing the freedom to choose one's lifestyle via consumption patterns inherent to consumer culture. Seen in this light, Nevada's social libertarianism portended current trends.

Nevada's geography has played a major role in the politics, culture, and economy of the state and is important to understanding the brothel industry. Nevada has among the most densely populated cities as well as the most sparsely populated rural areas. Two cities anchor opposite ends of the state: the Las Vegas metropolitan area with more than two million people in the south, and the Reno area with just under 400,000 in the north as of 2008. Las Vegas and its surrounding area constitutes one of five Western "megapolitan" corridors, dense urban regions where a relatively large territory is linked by overlapping commuting and employment exchanges. The remainder of the state's population is spread out across more than 100,000 square miles. Most of the rural counties have fewer than six persons per square mile on average, compared to the national average of 79.6 persons per square mile. In fact, seven counties average approximately one person per square mile.[14]

Nevada's geography is fairly typical of the dry mountainous western United States. The eastern slopes of the Sierra Nevada mountain range cradle the Reno/Carson City metropolitan area in the north. Las Vegas and southern Nevada are part of the Mojave Desert and receive less than five inches of rainfall a year on average. Much of Nevada is literally the dry, cracked remains of a giant mud puddle. Low desert basins are broken by fault lines along the edges where the bedrock is pushed up into mountain ranges. Northern Nevada is higher and cooler than southern Nevada; it gets more rain, and sustains some livestock grazing, irrigated pastures, and agriculture. While resource extraction is no longer Nevada's main industry, mining is still important for many rural towns. One of the world's most productive gold mines is in northern Nevada, near Elko and Carlin. A chunk of land the size of Rhode Island in the south-central part of the state houses the nation's nuclear testing range. Indeed, more than 85 percent of Nevada's land is federally owned, either by the Bureau of Land Management, which leases the land to ranchers, farmers, and mining interests, or by defense and military installations.[15] Also, the intermittent mountain ranges sustain outdoor recreation.

Brothels emerged in the mining towns of the mid- to late 1800s, but their persistence into the twenty-first century is directly related to the growth of tourism. The dramatic population growth in the past

30 years has had a profound effect on the industry. Not surprisingly, the largest brothels are clustered as close as they can get to the boundaries of the counties containing the biggest resort cities. In the past 20 years these brothels have become more suburban than rural. Suburban brothels are the biggest houses, with up to 80 women contracted at any given time, and are often the most profitable. About an hour's drive from Las Vegas, the Chicken Ranch and The Resort and Spa at Sheri's Ranch skirt the township of Pahrump in Nye County, a rural community that has seen its population grow 321 percent between 1990 and 2006.[16] The two brothels are out on Homestead Road, once a dirt road that at one point was miles outside of town; now several housing developments creep closer. On the other side of Pahrump, nearer Amargosa Valley, is Mabel's Whorehouse and Cherry Patch II. About 20 minutes' drive east of Reno along Interstate 80 there has been the Mustang Ranch (now the World Famous Mustang Ranch), the Old Bridge Ranch (closed in 2008) and the newer Wild Horse Ranch. An hour's drive from Reno, just east of Carson City, are the Moonlite Bunny Ranch, Miss Kitty's (now the Love Ranch), the Kit Kat Ranch, and the Sagebrush. (See Appendix A map.)

The smaller rural brothels are located progressively further from the two main population centers. In the past 20 years, six rural brothels have operated beyond an hour's drive up Highway 95, a mostly two-lane highway that links Las Vegas in the south to Reno in the northwest.[17] The tiny southern Nevadan towns along this corridor survive from sporadic mining and some agriculture, but mainly from federal and military projects, and the tourism that the highways bring. Brothels in the southern part of the state are mostly in trailers located outside city limits. Located along the highway, Angel's Ladies, which closed in 2007, sits three miles outside of Beatty (two hours from Las Vegas); the Shady Lady Ranch is a half hour north of Beatty. Just under a four-hour drive from Las Vegas, and five hours from Reno, are the Cottontail Ranch at Lida Junction and Billie's Day and Night and Bobbie's Buckeye Bar in Tonopah, though these are now closed.

In the northwest part of the state, still along Highway 95 but closer to Reno, a number of brothels have existed, though all but one are now closed. About three hours south of Reno, the Wild Kat Ranch remains open in Mina but the Playmate Ranch in Hawthorne is currently closed. The Lazy B Ranch and Salt Well's Villa near Fallon and under two hours from Reno are also closed. These brothels are often non-descript, with little more than a sign and a few cars in a gravel parking lot (large enough for semi-trucks to pull in). These brothels, for all their sparse traffic, are often the only businesses for miles.

In the northern part of the state, brothels are in older, more established small towns along the four-lane Interstate 80, which connects San Francisco, California, in the west to Salt Lake City, Utah, 750 miles east. Most of these towns are between a two- and five-hour drive from Reno. Over the past 20 years there have been five brothels in Winnemucca, My Place Bar and Brothel (now closed), Simone's de Paris (closed), Villa Joy, the Pussycat Ranch, and the Cozy Corner—now the Wild West Saloon. There have been two in Battle Mountain (Calico Club, now Donna's Battle Mountain, and the Desert Club, now closed), two in Carlin (Sharon's Place and the Dovetail Ranch), four in Elko (Mona's Ranch, Inez's D&D, Sue's Fantasy Club, and No. 1 Geisha—also known as CharDon's and the Mona Lisa), three in Ely (the Stardust, Big Four, and Green Lantern, now closed) and two in Wells (Donna's Ranch and Bella's Gentlemen's Club).

Nevada's Brothel Laws

There are approximately 36 licensed brothels in the state, with about 25 to 30 operating at any one time. Nevada's brothel regulations are highly decentralized.[18] Brothels are regulated at state, county, and city levels. Relatively few state laws exist, but those that are on the books restrict prostitution to licensed brothels located in counties with fewer than 400,000 residents. The laws zone brothels away from main thoroughfares, churches, and schools, often relegating them to the outskirts of town.[19] Up until a state Supreme Court ruling in the summer of 2007, Nevada outlawed advertising (although internet advertising had not been subject to much legal scrutiny), including recruitment of new workers. (Appendix B shows Nevada County brothel laws and income.)

The Nevada Administrative Code contains health and testing policies. These codes require customers to wear condoms. Prostitutes are to be tested for sexually transmitted diseases including HIV, syphilis, gonorrhea, and chlamydia before they can be employed and periodically after employment. No testing is required for customers.[20]

The majority of brothel regulations occur at the local level, by either the city or county, depending on which body has been designated by county law as the regulating body. These local-level licensing codes further regulate the brothel industry, and their ordinances vary somewhat. Potential owners are required to pass strict background checks to receive a license. You cannot get a license if you have ever been convicted of a felony or drug charge, theft, embezzlement, or a crime involving the use of a deadly weapon, or if you are judged "contrary to the health, welfare, or safety of the City [County] or its residents." You also cannot hold a license if you have ties to any illegal business, or if you have "associates who the Board considers to be inappropriate for the operation of this privileged business."[21] According to local officials and owners, there has long been a fear that, as with gambling, prostitution may be dominated by the mob or other organized "undesirables."

All brothel licenses are non-transferable, and site specific. County and city laws typically spell out precisely how many licenses there may be at any one time. Officials have the power to revoke licenses for any reason and are free to impose other regulations at will. Officials can essentially enter a brothel, investigate, and even revoke a license for "any cause harmful to the health, safety and welfare of the general public" (as in the county codes of Churchill, Carlin, Elko, Lander, Mineral, and White Pine).

Brothels do not hire women as employees but as independent contractors. All counties require prostitutes to have a work card issued by the local police or sheriff's office. In most cases these are the same cards issued to all hotel and casino employees. They identify workers by legal name, require minimal background checks and a fee, and must be renewed periodically. The majority of counties will not issue work cards if an applicant is under 21 (though in a few counties the minimum age is 18), or has been convicted of a felony or drug charge. In some counties, these cards and their background checks do not identify the place of employment. In other counties, cards must show the place of employment.

Given that Nevada is the only place in the country with legal prostitution, there has been surprisingly little empirical research on how Nevada's legal brothels actually work. Some of these have been quite critical, particularly of the treatment of women. Most of the studies have commented on the informal rules that often worked to keep women isolated and stigmatized. Few laws have meant local

authorities have lots of leeway and many times treat brothels and workers in discriminatory ways, unlike other businesses.[22] Other studies
have relied on these to make the case that legalized prostitution as it
was practiced in Nevada was often little better than other forms of
regulation.[23]

Yet given the relative failure of policies criminalizing sex workers to
eliminate or even slow prostitution there has been no recent broad-
based, in-depth empirical research on Nevada's system of legal prostitution. For years, sex worker rights organizations have been highly
critical of Nevada's legal brothels for allowing workers little flexibility.
Nonetheless, a few sex worker rights organizations are beginning to
look again at practices in at least some legal brothels as an option that
might work for certain sex workers.

SITUATING PROSTITUTION: CONTEXT MATTERS

Among scholars, the question of whether prostitution is right or wrong
has quite often clouded empirical examinations of how prostitution
actually works.[24] Most studies have been rather micro; that is, they
have looked at the background and motivations of individuals entering prostitution. The most intense debates have been by feminist
academics who focus on how the industry as a whole affects women.
Unfortunately, the debates have been extremely polarizing. One side
has argued that prostitution is inherently patriarchal, exploiting
women as a class for the benefit of men.[25] The other side has argued
that prostitution represents a potential flowering and empowerment of
women's sexuality.[26]

As a result of these debates, often referred to as the feminist sex
wars, by the mid-1990s there had been a major rethinking within
academic feminism about prostitution. Scholars have begun to move
beyond essentializing prostitution; that is, seeing prostitution as one
monolithic, unchanging institution. Studies now examine how larger
social dynamics affect the various forms prostitution may take.
Scholars like Wendy Chapkis, Johanna Brewis and Stephen Linstead,
Ine Vanwesenbeeck and Teela Sanders use concepts from studies
of labor to look at similarities between selling emotions in the sex
industry and the traditional service industry.[27] Most recently, scholars
across the globe such as Ryan Bishop and Lillian S. Robinson, Kamala

Kempadoo, Jo Doezema, Julia O'Connell Davidson, Patty Kelly, and Laura Agustín are situating prostitution in the context of a globalized culture and economy, examining its effects on workers, including how race, ethnicity, class, and immigration create different experiences for different sex workers. For example, scholars have studied the various ways global migration patterns and trafficking impact prostitution and laws about prostitution.[28] Studies have broadened to include men and transgender sex workers, male clients, and policing tactics undertaken to curtail clientele.[29] Several studies are analyzing the spread of neoliberal politics and how it affects the regulation of prostitution.[30] And several studies have begun to investigate the geographies of sex work and the significance of place.[31] Recent studies have examined the relationship between the growth of global tourism and prostitution. The impact of global tourism is far from uniform, spurring a variety of forms of prostitution as well as having different effects on sex workers.[32] Prostitution is not just one thing that affects all workers in the same ways; context also matters.

Today's consumer culture has altered the social relations around selling sex. Over the past 50 years, a globally integrated economy has created new products and new forms of labor, and has placed consumption as the central dynamic of culture. Tourism has become the world's largest employer, and even non-tourist industries increasingly sell fantasy, relaxation, and memorable experiences. Some analysts have argued that our very relationships are transformed as intimacy and even self-identity become fleeting, temporary, and flexible, based on how and what we consume. If, in this context, workers, businesses, and consumers all become more adept at buying and selling human emotions, what does this mean for prostitution? Have any of these dynamics changed the nature of the traditional gendered, racial, and class inequalities that frame prostitution? Have any of these dynamics changed the nature of prostitution itself? Nevada's legal brothel industry is an excellent site to study how we have come to consume sex in late capitalism.

RESEARCHING THE BROTHELS

This book draws on more than ten years of qualitative fieldwork in Nevada's brothel industry. Our research has several aims and so relies on several sources of data. Our interest is as much in the politics, history, culture, and organization of brothels (Chapters 2, 3, and 4) as the experiences and practices of sex work itself (Chapters 5 and 6). Thus our data came partially from ethnographic data gathered from formal interviews and observations we made in visits to 13 of 26 brothels between 1998 and 2002, including the Mustang Ranch, Old Bridge Ranch, Moonlite Bunny Ranch, and Miss Kitty's, all around Reno; the Cozy Corner in Winnemucca; the Calico Club in Battle Mountain; Sharon's Place in Carlin; Mona's in Elko; the Stardust and the Green Lantern in Ely; Angel's Ladies in Beatty; and the Chicken Ranch and Sheri's Ranch in Pahrump. Since that time we have conducted numerous unstructured interviews and observations in subsequent visits to brothels, at brothel-related events such as conventions, public meetings, celebrations and parties, and at public debates on brothels. Our interviews with people who were professionally or politically involved in some aspect of the brothel industry, such as politicians, lobbyists, and lawyers, as well as with brothel owners, managers, bartenders, and of course, working women, offer an insight into how participants actively give meaning to their experiences with the brothel industry. We have worked to gain a deep understanding of the internal social relations within and among the brothels.

These interviews and observations generated more questions on the external social relations between the brothels and the state, other businesses, and local citizens. For this aspect of our inquiry we built on the ethnographic data with analyses of historical and contemporary documents, websites, media stories, newspaper articles, laws, policies, and programs regarding the state's brothels. Our discussions of the context and history of brothels in Chapters 2 and 3 rely heavily on this secondary data. Much of the history of brothels is assembled from references to brothels in published research on Nevada's history generally and the few books and articles written about Nevada's brothels by historians. Discussions in Chapters 4, 5, and 6 are contextualized and cross-checked with these data as well. We also collected data from county sheriff and city police departments, county and city tax assessors, and other regulatory bodies. These data gave us a reliable picture of regulatory practices at the local level.

Between 1998 and 2007 we conducted semi-structured, open-ended interviews with eight regulators including two city mayors (one representing a small town in northern Nevada, one representing a large city in southern Nevada), two vice police officers in southern Nevada, two city police officers from northern Nevada, and one county district attorney from northern Nevada. These interviews lasted from half an hour to two hours each. We have spoken informally, on and off the record, with four state legislators from southern Nevada.

We interviewed 13 current and former brothel managers and owners between 1998 and 2002. Nine of the brothel owners or managers were from northern Nevada, and four were from southern Nevada. We interviewed management of the two biggest brothels, Sheri's Ranch outside of Las Vegas and the Moonlite Bunny Ranch outside of Reno. These interviews were conducted in person and on site. We interviewed the head of the Nevada Brothel Association, Geoff Arnold, and the organization's lobbyist, George Flint, a number of times, most recently in 2007. Over the past ten years, we have had countless informal discussions with activists both for and against brothels, with customers, and with other managers and current and former prostitutes.

Gaining entrée to the brothels was not as difficult as it first seemed it would be. Owing to the stigma surrounding even legal brothel work, we initially relied on gatekeepers like George Flint to help provide access to brothel owners. His influence, for example, allowed us access to the then-open Mustang Ranch. But the vast majority of our contacts were made independently and outside of these more formal channels. We first cold-called all of the brothels operating across the state in 1998 to set up interviews. The majority of the persons answering the phone indicated it was best to just call when we got into town, and in subsequent years we took that tack. Sometimes we were unable to reach the owners of the brothels to set up interviews during the time we were in town. Three brothel owners refused to grant access, claiming journalists love to paint dismal pictures of the brothels. With these few exceptions, most brothel owners were very open to allowing UNLV researchers into their businesses, and spent several hours giving us tours, participating in interviews, introducing us to other owners, and encouraging the women to speak to us. One owner allowed us to spend an unsupervised night in the brothel (with no expectation of working). In all cases, owners left the room when we interviewed the women.

In Chapters 4, 5, and 6 we use data from semi-structured interviews we conducted with brothel sex workers and managers to gain insights into work and life at a brothel. Owing to the great interest in interviews with prostitutes, we provide some detailed information below about how the interviews were conducted.

We conducted semi-structured, face-to-face interviews with 38 prostitutes between 1998 and 2002. (See Appendix C for a list of women interviewed.) Each of these lasted from half an hour to two hours. In all, we interviewed 23 women at five large, suburban brothels, and 14 women at smaller or mid-sized brothels in more isolated rural areas. We interviewed one woman over the phone who had experience working in several of the brothels. Most of the interviews took place in the brothels in northern Nevada. Less than an hour's drive outside of Reno, we interviewed ten women at the Moonlite Bunny Ranch near Carson City, six women nearby at Miss Kitty's, two at the Mustang Ranch, and two at the Old Bridge Ranch. Moving across I-80 east from Reno, we interviewed one woman at Sharon's in Carlin, one at the Calico Club in Battle Mountain, and four at Mona's in Elko. On the east side of the state, we interviewed four women at Green Lantern in Ely. In southern Nevada, we conducted three interviews with women at Sheri's Ranch in Pahrump and four interviews with women at Angel's Ladies in Beatty.

The majority of interviews were arranged in advance with the permission of the owners, but there were a few cases where we simply stopped by the brothel and were able to speak with whoever would talk to us. Only one owner who agreed to speak with us did not want us to speak to the women in her brothel. She spent several hours giving us a tour and allowing us to interview her. She was a former worker herself and then co-owner of the brothel. Her business partner owned another brothel across the state where he let us interview women in his brothel.

Most of the interviews took place during visits to the brothels in the afternoons, when business is slower. The managers would ask around to see who was interested in talking. Often at the conclusion of the interview the women would tell us that another woman wanted to talk to us and would take us to her room. Sometimes the interview would be interrupted with the arrival of a potential customer. If the woman we were talking to did not get chosen by the customer she might return to the interview, or we might move on to another woman.

We tended to be very open about how individuals wanted the interview conducted, so in three cases we interviewed two women at once. In one case all four workers talked to us at the same time in the parlor. In most of the small brothels we were able to interview everyone who was currently on shift. The larger brothels like Sheri's Ranch and Moonlite Bunny Ranch tended to be busier, and it was harder to talk to a large percentage of the women who were working.

Our interviews included open-ended questions on how they began working at the brothels, the meanings of work and workplace practices, their attitudes toward sexual service labor, why they chose to work in the brothels and the sex industry generally, and what working at the brothels meant in their personal lives. We asked very broad questions to allow workers to talk about things they felt were important, and tried to avoid exoticizing or stereotypical questions that assume sex work is aberrant, unnatural, or unhealthy. The interviews were all conducted in women's rooms at the brothels or, on a few occasions, in the lounge area, always without management present. Some of the managers, owners, and other interviewees gave us permission to use their real names. We identify all sex workers using pseudonyms.[33]

During the interviews we conducted in 2000, we also collected 25 surveys assessing demographic information, occupational history, and attitudes toward work from prostitutes in three of the large brothels: the Moonlite Bunny Ranch and Miss Kitty's, both outside of Reno in northern Nevada, and Sheri's Ranch outside of Las Vegas. Some of the surveyed women were also interviewed, but not all. To ensure anonymity, the surveys were not marked with identifiers and so we cannot correlate surveys with interviews.

We analyzed all the interviews with the sociological understanding that how our participants talk about the brothel industry reflects the ongoing interaction between their beliefs, how they think outsiders judge the brothels, and their interpretations of daily life in the brothels. How women construct the work and their lives tells us more about the depth of the cultural tropes of "prostitute" and how they produce order in their everyday lives than about the actual details of their lives. As with most ethnographers, we are not necessarily seeking a truth against an independent standard to determine whether or not the participants are truly exploited or truly empowered. We are most interested in how they see and describe their lives.

What the women talked about the most, then, revolved around explaining their work in a way that contrasted with how they believed most people viewed the industry. We think this is one main reason why they were so anxious to talk to us. They seemed to want to share, with an interested and sympathetic audience, how this work was or was not like what they felt everyone else thought it to be.

Since our interviews, many of the brothels have closed, reopened, and closed again, been bought and sold, changed owners and even reverted back to their original owners, giving testament to the great flux in the industry, particularly with the smaller brothels. As of 2009, only a few of the owners we interviewed remain. Currently there are 25 open and operating brothels, though this number has fluctuated up and down since we began our research over a decade ago. We write knowing that much of the ownership and brothel names will be out of date, if not already, then soon.

We use the phrases "sexual commerce," "commercial sex," and "sex work" to refer to the sale of sex in the brothels. These terms are also used when referring to other forms of sexual labor in today's marketplace, including lap dancing, adult film performances, phone sex, and other exchanges involving paid sexual performances or activities. We realize that there is an important debate about whether sex in this sense is or is not wholly and simply labor. Our use of these alternate terms does not exclude the potentially profound inequalities that surround the social relations of selling sex. Recognizing the symbolic importance of the term "prostitution," we are very judicious in our use of the term in this book. We use the term "prostitution" to refer to the institutions organized to sell sex acts in the public marketplace as distinct from other forms of sexual commerce. In addition, Nevada laws use the terms "prostitute" and "prostitution," so we use these terms to reflect the only legal construction of this form of commercial sex in the United States. We are aware that the term "prostitute" often signifies criminality, deviance, victimhood, or a master status, and so when we refer to women working in the brothels we refer to them as workers and to what they do as work. In this way, the theoretical framework driving our research is grounded in the women's lived experiences to most accurately describe the nature of the activities and people in the brothel industry.[34]

The Brothel Industry Uncovered

This book is organized to look at social relations at the individual and institutional levels so that readers will understand the complexities of such a contentious business. The first half of the book looks at history, politics, economics, and culture. The second half looks at the businesses, practices, and people in the brothels.

Chapters 2 and 3 discuss the contexts of Nevada's brothels. In Chapter 2 we look at work by other scholars and analysts discussing broader changes in the economics, culture, and politics of contemporary consumer societies that impact commercial sex across the globe, and in Nevada as the symbolic state of sex. We also look at research on how identity, consumption, and labor are affected by the growth of a leisure service industry. We look briefly at previous prostitution research that centers on the problematic relationship between sex and the public market.

Chapter 3 examines the politics, culture, and economics that have shaped the development of a legal brothel industry in Nevada since the late nineteenth century. We examine why Nevada has legal brothels and not any other Western state with a similar history. In the first part of the chapter we look at how the mining booms from the late nineteenth and early twentieth centuries laid the groundwork for prostitution's relationship with local leisure economies. There was a diverse array of sexual leisure services in the state's early economy. The wide array of leisure economies later turned into the foundation for Nevada's tourist industry. We argue that gender and class struggles played a role in narrowing the scope of commercial sex into today's regulated brothel industry. In the latter half of the chapter we discuss how brothels became institutionalized.

In Chapter 4 we describe Nevada's brothels as businesses and examine the organization of brothels as they make sex into something that is for sale. We analyze the internal operation of the brothels from ownership to marketing to management and workplace relations. Brothels, like other tourist-based leisure industries, must manage shifting consumer tastes away from routinized acts to a desire to consume individualized fantasies. The way they manage these is similar to other businesses, but is also acutely impacted by gender stereotypes and inequalities.

Chapter 5 looks at how women come to work in the brothels. We look at women's paths into the brothels as consequences of labor dynamics in a growing leisure economy. Brothels draw women with diverse backgrounds, from service industry workers seeking more income to illegal workers seeking a break, to career sexual entertainers. Suburban brothels are increasingly drawing workers with more resources who can capitalize on more upscale leisure consumers. Since legal brothel workers are independent contractors on short-term contracts, workers in a brothel almost always work in other venues as well, whether illegal or other legal forms of sex work, or the service industry at large.

Chapter 6 looks at brothel labor itself. We examine the various ways women workers negotiate private intimacy and emotions as public commodities. Like in other service, leisure, and tourist industries, as brothel workers move toward selling individualized experiences and fantasies rather than an assembly-line of rationalized acts, the women's practices reflect a range of approaches for managing body and emotional interactions and their own sense of self. Ultimately, this means that the experience of labor in brothels varies widely. Indeed, some workers in suburban brothels are approaching their labor in ways that value both body work and emotional connections. There are certainly some workers among all the brothels whose approach challenges conventional ways we think about emotional labor and authenticity.

In conclusion, Chapter 7 details how we understand the sale of sexualized leisure, and how our conclusions translate into ongoing policy debates. First, we conclude that we can no longer understand prostitution as any one thing. Context matters. The basic social relations and institutions characterizing Nevada's legal brothels are surprisingly similar in form and function to non-sex leisure industries. Today's new global economy has created a context that affects the forms prostitution takes. Legal brothels in Nevada should be understood primarily as leisure businesses in a contemporary consumer society.

Second, brothel prostitution is highly affected by the dynamics of gender, class and racial inequalities. The brothel industry capitalizes on heterosexuality and reproduces the same class and ethnic inequalities that pervade other service industries and mainstream businesses generally. Almost every element of the brothels, from marketing to performing the labor, reproduces some very traditional conceptions of appropriate masculinity and femininity, and even of what constitutes appropriate sex. At the same time, brothels fracture our idea of what sex is. Commodifying sex means that sex is constructed as many things, varying combinations of physical acts, but also including varying emotions and attitudes. The women who "sell sex" profit from the transgressive nature of the act, and in so doing create sex as something both special and private, and publicly commodified. If sexuality, gender, and market activity are socially constructed ideologies, then brothels are sites where meaning can be renegotiated by the people involved.

2

CONTEXTS OF SEXUAL COMMERCE

A global service-based consumer economy has profoundly altered the social relations around buying and selling sex. From fertility rituals in the temples of ancient Egypt, Greece, and India, to today's global sex work "circuit," the contexts surrounding what we now regard as prostitution have changed.[1] History, culture, and place impact the meaning, the organizational setting, and the actual exchanges involved in prostitution. Even within similar settings, how women conduct sex work varies greatly.[2] Thus, our examination of the Nevada brothel industry begins with a look at scholarly debates on recent changes in today's society and how these impact sexual commerce, in particular the development of the leisure and tourist economy in the United States and its relationship to the state of sex in the contemporary marketplace.

THE GROWTH OF THE LEISURE ECONOMY

Industrialized societies are in the midst of a dramatic shift in the organization of production and consumption that is transforming the way we live and interact. After World War II, production of durable goods moved mainly to poorer countries while the United States and much of the West have since developed an economy driven by services, leisure, and cultural products. Consumption, rather than production, drives a global late capitalist economy.[3] We live in an increasingly globalized world, one with greater economic integration and interdependence of countries, cities, and towns, involving an increased circulation of goods, capital, ideas, and people. These changes have affected social relations such as what and how we consume, the way we work, our politics, and even our very sense of ourselves.

A key part of this new consumer economy is the consumption and production of leisure. From restaurants to recreation to travel, the development of a leisure economy has been an essential pillar of U.S. consumer capitalism since the 1920s. Since the 1960s, travel and tourism have taken center stage in this new economy in local and international settings. Travel and tourism is the world's largest industry. It employs nearly 8 percent of all workers worldwide, and produces 9.4 percent of the world's gross domestic product.[4]

There are several consequences of a leisure-based economy. In the late twentieth century, activities that had been components of private or familial relationships—such as cooking, cleaning, childcare, education, and companionship—are more likely to be purchasable services. We are now negotiating the lines between public and private activities, and between intimacy and the market. Much of what we sell in a service economy is relationships. The growing markets for leisure have blurred these lines even more. From the pampering of a spa package, to the exhilaration of an adventure tour, to the friendly bantering of a poolside server to seeing locals make custom goods by hand, workers sell travelers convincingly authentic experiences in the form of "entertainments, spectacles, happenings and distractions."[5]

Buying and selling these kinds of relationships are not just part of global travel. Local markets are also driven by practices we commonly associate with tourism that took hold beginning in the 1970s. These new services are "touristic" in nature.[6] Touristic services are images and experiences that explicitly contrast with consumers' normal, mundane, everyday worlds of home, work, and community. Touristic services sell escape, spectacles, adventure, fantasies and personalized interactions. For example, people retreat to a neighborhood sports bar or shopping mall.[7] Local industries increasingly sell various types of experiences, such as themed adventure, spectacle, fantasy, voyeurism, and even transgression, rather than durable goods or services with predictable outcomes.

This globalized leisure economy is highly unequal, and its growth exacerbates class, gender, and racial and ethnic inequalities.[8] From informal sales of local goods to maid services to an international sex tourist industry, today's transnational service economy is exploiting inequalities within a country, and between wealthy and disadvantaged nations. People with more disposable income travel more often, more easily, and more widely at the same time as being able to consume touristic experiences without going far from home. People with limited means are more likely to labor in the service industries that provide leisure experiences for others to consume. They may also be consumers of local services and leisure themselves, and may also travel, but face more hurdles and restrictions to do so. A global leisure economy has necessitated a more mobile workforce at the bottom of the class ladder, yet richer countries impose punitive immigration policies, and restrict travel and work permits and visas.

The growth of a leisure economy exacerbates even the symbolic markers of inequality. The move to spectacle and excitement to sell leisure services is strategically accompanied by a move to "upscale": to create a setting, mood, and/or set of activities that reflect upper-class styles and settings.[9] Marketing class means emulating characteristics of the class immediately above the target clientele. Luxury travel, for example, advertises an illusion of wealth to draw in large numbers of middle-class travelers. They sell a sense of being part of the upper-class elite.

The leisure economy encourages the consumption of gender and ethnicity as markers of difference between worker and client; the ethnicity and gender of a worker are part of the purchased experience. Women, who are seen as a source of cheap labor, make up the majority of service industry workers today. Women are also tapped as "naturally" more adept at the emotionality of service work and stereotyped as a more docile workforce, better at pampering and catering to a customer's needs. Their participation in service industries globally has grown tremendously as the industries have developed.[10] In the United States, poor women—disproportionately women of color—labor in the lowest paying and least recognized service sectors, like home caregiving or cleaning services, while white women dominate in better paying or more respected service jobs. Globally, it is largely women of color who are the targets of microcredit programs in Third World countries. In the United States, it is largely women who have been swept up in the rise of a "racialized service economy."[11] Tourist and leisure industries capitalize on dominant forms of heterosexual masculinity and do so in ways that encourage objectifying women as part of the experience. These experiences often rely on exotic, romantic myths about the simplicity of poverty or mysterious foreign locales in ways that stereotype people of color.

The growth of a global leisure economy also transforms our sense of place. Global transportation and communications connect us with more and more places. Those places we call local are expanding. As localities become more connected, even traditional categories of rural, urban, and suburban are changing meaning. Before World War II, there was a more definitive rural/urban split in terms of people, economies, and markets in the United States. But today, being "rural" in a geographic setting does not mean that industries and people are isolated from local, state, and economic structures writ large. The mythology of the rural/urban divide plays into our understandings of tourism, work, leisure, and consumption. We assume rural areas to be fairly homogenous in culture and ethnicity, enclaves of low- and middle-class white people. But rural areas can be quite diverse in ethnicity and class, and include immigrant populations, and can depend on tourism, to some degree, for economic stability.[12]

How Work is Organized

In this new consumer economy, the organization of work is changing. The highly rationalized large factory assembly-line is disappearing, replaced by individual service industry workers in smaller decentralized workplaces. There are fewer long-term, stable jobs available. Service industry jobs pay far less than traditional manufacturing jobs. Workers today tend to move from job to job, city to city, or even country to country in search of better pay, with little chance of advancement.

Workers today are also likely to be employed part time or self-employed, responsible for how, when, and where they perform tasks, and the results of these tasks. Many businesses, particularly those providing services, are contracting with consultants, freelancers, or independent contractors for services. More and more, jobs as diverse as taxi cab driving, entertainment, law, personal services, and sex industries like strip clubs and escort agencies are performed by independent contractors. Hiring independent contractors instead of employees places the burden of financial responsibility on the worker and not on the business. Healthcare, materials for work, retirement, job protection, and other benefits that used to be taken care of by employers are now symbols of a bygone industrial era. Independent contractors' income is more dependent on the service they provide, unlike an hourly or salaried employee who receives a regular, steady paycheck. The contractor has to save, has to calculate and set aside money for quarterly estimated taxes and social security, has to plan for retirement, and has to prepare for low earning periods.

In this kind of employment, workers are expected to self-motivate and act more autonomously than their factory counterparts. As the service industry becomes more touristic, rationalized outcome-oriented approaches to management have given way to more decentralized, flexible supervision with employees being hired to sell uniqueness, variety, and individuality.[13] This has had a number of important consequences for how we understand employer–employee relations and indeed, the nature of the labor process.

How employers control the work process has changed in a number of ways. Studies of management show that even for factory work, force was rarely the main mechanism employers use to control workers. In understanding power and control, research has looked at both the structure of work as well as at the relations and actions of individuals within that structure.[14] Workers use various strategies to both resist and comply with management demands. Likewise patterns of exploitation and control are also framed by gender and race relations. A boss may be controlling a worker's action, but so too are the norms and distinctions that frame what constitutes gender and race.[15]

In a service economy control is all the more complex. With service work, workers must also attend to the expectations of customers and clients. This decenters chains of command, adds more potential sources for exploitation, and complicates the structures that impact power at work. Research finds that worker loyalty can flow to either customer or boss in the course of many jobs.[16]

Until recently, research on traditional service work, in particular sales and fast food, has examined how management has tried to rationalize and control how workers provide services by applying assembly-line principles to their workplaces. This is evident in the use of scripts, employing formulaic routines and interactions, deskilling jobs, and exerting significant control over the service exchange environment.[17] But rationalizing services has proven much more difficult than organizing an assembly-line, especially in an era of increasing consumer demand for individualized experiences. Predictability and sameness are not as profitable in a leisure economy as individualized service, even if it is an illusion of a tailored customer service experience. In order to package service as spectacle, adventure, experience, and fantasy, research finds that managers are encouraging service workers, especially in middle- and upper-class leisure industries, and professional and semi-professional jobs, to engage in more individualized interactions and complex negotiations with their customers. Since scripted, carefully monitored interactions do not sell, managers hand over more control to interactive service workers to provide intimate, personal, and unique interactions. Thus leisure service work has become more decentralized, autonomous, and employee directed.[18]

Debates about the benefits of flexible work and decentralized management are almost as polarizing as debates about prostitution. Independent workers are depicted as either more at the mercy of self-interested business owners or as completely empowered to choose the time, manner, and place of work. The reality is that some of these contingent jobs do allow considerable flexibility, autonomy, and freedom from monotony. Others may be more tightly controlled, with little freedom, and involve dangerous tasks. Some flexible workers may be skilled and highly trained, but many come from secondary labor markets with low skills, low pay, high turnover, and few avenues for advancement. Research is increasingly finding that it is the contexts around these forms of labor rather than the kind of job itself that matters. The amount of power and control individuals have, political agendas, and corporate responsibility all impact job satisfaction and outcomes. People work for a variety of personal, economic, and cultural reasons, limited by larger inequalities of class, citizenship, gender, race, ethnicity, and so on. Some people work to increase their standard of living, others to pay off debt or secure financial footing; others work for survival or for their children's welfare. Feminist economists have long held that having multiple job opportunities may help women establish their value within households. Having a job to fall back on in times of financial hardship, or when there is discord or danger in the home, grants a woman more power in household decisions.[19] All of these changes in the organization of work can have important consequences for how we understand both the organization of sex work and control and potential exploitation of sex workers.

Self and Emotions on the Job

In a consumer-based economy, the nature of labor is changing as well. Workers in service jobs who interact with customers sell, to varying degrees, emotions, performances, and human connections. Virtually every job that requires interaction with the public or customers requires workers' emotional labor. Evoking emotions has been critical to the work of more traditional service workers, such as restaurant servers, sales people, flight attendants, childcare, and fast-food workers.[20] But in the growing leisure economy, adventure, unique experiences, skilled care, fantasies, and interactions with others are themselves a commodity. Leisure industries rely especially on a degree of authenticity, including friendliness, companionship, competency, and empathy, as elements of commodified service. In this context, selling feelings, human relationships, and even intimacy become more critical to successful commercial exchanges.

Since Arlie Hochschild first examined "the commercialization of feeling" in airline attendants in 1983, subsequent studies have found that almost every job involving interactions with customers has emotional demands. Emotional labor, as Hochschild defines it, is the knowing use of certain skills that incorporate one's voice, gestures, body movements, or facial expressions to manage one's own emotions and to tap into a customer's emotions. Emotional labor requires acting, reconciling the performance of emotions with one's "true" emotions and self-identity. Hochschild identified two ways in which workers managed their emotions to match the job requirements. They employed what she called surface acting, displaying emotions that they really did not feel, like acting friendly when they were really angry at a customer. Or they managed their feelings through deep acting, making an effort to more authentically feel the emotions required by the job.

Since Hochschild, studies have extended our understanding of the complex performances entailed in emotional labor in two ways: first, the extent to which this emotional labor affects the power and well-being of individual workers, and second, emotional labor as a skill that adds value in today's service economy.

It is commonplace for service jobs to require that workers display good cheer and empathy even when frustrated, and enthusiasm even when bored. The financial success of many service workers depends on meeting clients' expectations of "good service." How does this pressure to perform affect a worker's psychological well-being? Hochschild felt that the commercialization of feeling requires workers to estrange themselves from their real selves. This inauthenticity in interactions eventually leads to varying degrees of anxiety, identity confusion, frustration, exhaustion, self-alienation, and burnout. Indeed, the question of authenticity—faking versus changing one's true feelings—became central to understanding the effects of emotional labor.

However, recent research finds workers and consumers are increasingly experienced at negotiating the lines around authenticity, intimacy, and the market. Just because a job requires a lot of emotional labor does not inevitably result in psychological distress. Extensive research on a variety of service occupations is finding that emotional labor is not uniformly alienating or inauthentic. Displaying positive emotions at work and even deep acting (an effort to truly feel the emotions demanded by the job) can be satisfying and give workers a sense of accomplishment. Researchers find that interactive service workers in a variety of occupations employ myriad practices and strategies for dealing with burnout and alienation. And the amount of burnout or alienation they experience varies significantly, even within similar job categories. The issue is not so much the nature of the job as the ability of workers to respond to the emotional demands that matters.[21]

Doing emotion work often requires performing traditional gender norms. Feelings are gendered in the sense that women are assumed to be "naturally" emotional or better nurturers than men, and are expected to do this kind of labor with little compensation. Yet one of the key conclusions that Hochschild and successive studies made is that emotional labor is a labor-intensive skill that produces value. The performance of gender and sexuality can therefore add value to a commodified exchange in both non-sexual and sexual service industry jobs.

Yet, workers providing this kind of emotional labor are consistently under-rewarded.

Consumer society has potentially changed our experience of self. We have always thought that there is a stable character that guides actions through an entire range of different situations one encounters in everyday life. In the cultural psychology book, *The Saturated Self,* Gergen claims that in today's postmodern world we have no single, true, core self to center the rest of our experiences; we can easily call up any number of selves depending on the situation and context. Gergen argues that the fast pace and complexity of postmodern culture and late capitalism generate so many interactions and disconnected relationships that our self is saturated, leaving little recognition of a core self, or little allegiance to a singular, unchanging, version of the self.[22] This has profound effects on how service workers produce the range of identities and emotions required of them in the leisure economy; how they negotiate the need to sell themselves; and how sex workers, as a subset of these service laborers, think of themselves and manage their work. In a context where the very notion of a core self is changing, selling services is more about crafting selves and negotiating fluid and flexible emotional boundaries than about selling a "core" of one's "self."

As the experience of selfhood changes, so too does the context for providing emotional labor. Indeed, research on leisure economy workers such as adventure tour guides suggests that they easily accept incongruities, feel little anxiety over their shifting identities, and embrace their multiple selves.[23] Research on tourist industry workers is especially telling in showing that "authenticity" in this sense may be becoming less important. Even in a study of fast-food and insurance workers, sociologist Robin Leidner argues that worker and client "must negotiate interactions in which elements of manipulation, ritual, and genuine social exchange are subtly mixed."[24] Leidner examines how routines in fast food require workers to inject attributes of authentic humanity, friendliness, consideration, and personal attention into interactions. Workers must motivate themselves to keep up their enthusiasm. Leidner quotes Tom, an insurance salesperson: "You have to learn to read people, to figure out what they want in a salesperson, and BE that person."[25] The service industries are requiring more personalized and convincing emotional labor when selling even the most mundane products and services. When the exchange is more intimate or the experience sold is supposed to be more intense, the emotional demands on workers are even greater.

The body is also increasingly part of the service economy both as looks become an important part of image, and as bodily labor becomes an important job. Many places of employment put pressure on more workers to remake their own image in ways that not only involve performing emotions, but also includes aesthetic labor, self-branding, and personal style. Aesthetic labor refers to using the attributes of one's body to "look good and sound right" for the job.[26]

Obviously jobs such as fashion modeling make the body the key source of value, and women must conform to dominant standards of beauty.[27] But everyone from airline attendants, waiters, and bankers to data processors and image consultants also manage body and image. For some workers, aesthetic labor is largely about gender, managing one's body to "conform to a conventional, heterosexual image of masculinity and femininity."[28] Several studies that focus on jobs in the tourism, hospitality, and retail sectors argue that for workers, the presentation of the body should be understood among the variety of techniques and skills that make up emotional labor and the strategies to manage identities.[29] These studies, taken together, demonstrate that a wide variety of service industry jobs (both sexual and non-sexual jobs alike) are requiring manipulation of body, identity, sexuality, and emotion. Emotional labor scholars conclude that it is important to look at the specific organizational environment and individual practices.

Likewise, labor on others' bodies is increasingly central to post-industrial global economies. In leisure economies, employment as beauticians and barbers, coaches and personal trainers, childcare workers, yoga instructors, massage therapists, and tattooists is increasingly prevalent. An aging population increases the need for all sorts of medical professionals, occupational and speech therapists, mortuary workers, and workers dealing with body fluids and wastes. Bodily labor as well blurs further the lines between public and private intimacies, and complicates our understanding of self, body, and sexuality.[30]

A Culture of Consumption

These changes in economic structure, industry, and work parallel similarly massive shifts in cultural practices. As late capitalist consumer culture blurs the lines between public and private life, our notions of self and social relationships, gender and sexuality, politics, and morality are being transformed.

Consumer culture is changing the way we think about ourselves. The quest for goods and services is as much a quest for lifestyle, including relationships and identity, as to meet basic needs. Goods designed to be short-lived in style and substance, along with the temporary nature of purchased services, create throw-away or temporary values, at a cost to "stable relationships and attachments to things, buildings, places, people and received ways of doing and being."[31] Late capitalism has reshaped identities into fragmented and mutable consumer-based individualistic lifestyle options.[32] Instead of seeing ourselves in fixed, traditional categories of social class, ethnicity, gender, or sexuality, we can now invent and reinvent our own storied biographies, social identities, and personal characteristics in fluid and flexible ways, in relationship to our patterns of consumption. Negotiating boundaries of self between work and home, private life and public space, intimate or family relations and professional relations, or interacting with strangers is less about maintaining a centered single self than about "crafting selves" and moving between them.[33] In this context, the notion that there is a stable, core, authentic, or "real" self is seen by many as a relic of past times.

Our meanings and understandings of authenticity are also being altered. In modern industrial societies the concept of authenticity has been central to the evaluation of emotions or the quality and genuineness of people and relationships. In our public lives, authenticity has long been an important criterion for evaluating the degree of fulfillment or alienation we experience in the workplace and in civic society. In today's late capitalist consumer economy, turning experiences into things to be bought and sold means that commodified services must be reproducible, predictable, and recognizable, but they must look and feel as if they are not. The connection between images of human relationships, emotions, and commercially available products, services, and spectacles has intensified. As Guy DeBord and Marshall McLuhan philosophized, we live in the "society of the spectacle" where "the medium is the message."[34] Few people believe that buying Nike sneakers will make them an Olympic athlete, or wearing Victoria's Secret lingerie will transform them into a supermodel.

Whether it is real or illusion doesn't matter. Consumers expect that identities, emotions, and relationships will be connected with products or services. Consumers expect to be treated with friendliness when they go to a restaurant, with professionalism and understanding when buying a home; they expect to be pampered and treated like royalty when they travel. Whether or not the interaction is genuine is irrelevant to most consumers; it is the feeling and the experience that matters.

Several sociologists argue that masculinity and femininity are themselves performances or negotiations that come into existence as people interact. In a sense, commodified leisure activities are one site where gender is both expressed and created through social interactions. The active processes of reifying and transgressing gender are part of the everyday relations and businesses of a global leisure economy. The consumption of leisure and distraction often occurs in highly gendered settings, such as bars, health clubs, spas, shopping boutiques, and strip clubs and other sexually oriented businesses. These places promote certain performances of both masculinity and femininity that are likely to be quite different from how either the buyer or seller may act in other public and private spaces. These may be quite stereotypical versions of manhood or femininity, and the workers involved may not consider those attributes to be parts of their identities. In addition, masculinity and femininity vary across social class, race, and ethnicity. Thus performances of gender differ considerably based on social categories and sites of consumption.

In some ways, late capitalism liberalizes sexuality. Consumer culture is accompanied by a market ethos that encourages connection, intimacy, and pleasure. Products and services that ease the way for these experiences flourish. This ethos celebrates relationships for relationship's sake, largely unburdened by pressures related to reproduction, economic necessity, traditional norms, or even gendered role expectations.[35] Consumer capitalism, with its emphases on ephemerality and temporality, has spurred a culture that tends to value pleasurable sensation itself as much as more durable relationships, and recreational over relational sex, or even the blending of both. Fluid, non-marriage bound constructions of sexuality are more commonplace today than perhaps ever before. The purchase of intimacy—in casual social exchanges and in explicitly physical, sexual ones—is easily accessible, relatively affordable, and within the norms of everyday consumption in both public and private spheres.[36]

As a result, today there is greater social acceptance of gender equality and sexual pluralism in certain countries. Attitude surveys in the United States and Great Britain tend to show that the average citizen is more accepting of sexual diversity and the quest for sexual pleasure in late capitalist culture. Various surveys in the U.S., especially among urban populations, show a greater tolerance of pre-marital heterosexual sex, casual sex, and serial relationships since the 1980s and greater tolerance of gay sexuality.[37] Over the past 50 years we have witnessed an increasing acceptance of women's sexual agency, tolerance toward sex outside of marriage, more open conversation about sexual pleasure, and heightened awareness of homosexuality, bisexuality, transexuality, and transgenderism in the general population.[38] This all challenges cultural traditions that explicitly link sexuality to marriage, reproduction, and family. Further, traditional scripts that dichotomize genders between an active, aggressive male sexuality and a passive female sexuality have developed to include more diverse opportunities for intimate relationships, family forms, alternative sexual communities, and explorations of desire and sexuality, including commercial options. Traditional sexual identities like gay and straight are increasingly challenged by pansexual, transgender, bisexual, and queer identities.[39]

Social actors in late capitalist global economies have transformed the public and private spheres. In the United States, trends track a 60 percent increase in single-person households; an increase in divorce, remarriage, and non-nuclear families of all sorts from female-headed households to blended families and step-families and other "alternative lifestyles"; declining birth rates; relatively easy access to birth control; and the cultural presence of feminism, and gay and lesbian rights. These trends toward sexual pluralism have taken private discourses and practices of intimacy and pushed them squarely into the public marketplace. In other words, sex is central.

Despite these liberalizing trends, social anxiety around the specialness of sex and discrimination against those who embody sexual diversity continue to affect people's lives.[40] Social pressures to conform to monogamy are strong. The sexual expression and activities of youth are ignored or sanctioned. While sexual diversity seems to be increasingly tolerated by large segments of society, heterosexuality is still dominant and binary gender dichotomies of male and female remain entrenched. There is increasing polarization among groups on these issues, and in the United States, the divides tend to be tied to intersections of social class, ethnicity, urban/rural geographies, political and religious affiliation, and age. These splits are evident in cultural debates over moral issues related to sex, sexual orientation, gender identity, marriage, abortion, and family. As we document a liberalization of sexual attitudes and gender scripts, it is clear that traditional roles, practices, and values help define what is considered normal and acceptable. We are in the midst of a major reconsideration of gender, sexual attitudes, and practices. These changes are best understood in conjunction with changes in other realms, such as labor, leisure, commodity culture, and the self.

Along with transformations of identity, authenticity, gender, and sexuality, the ubiquity of consumer culture has also resulted in a fragmentation and pluralization of politics and values. Identity has been politicized and our sense of self is tied to market niches where we find comfort or thrills. Social movements coalesce around a complex gender politics, sexuality, ethnicity, desire, and commercial selfhood, and have entered the political arena to impact cultural beliefs and practices. The current popularity of sustainability and marketing "green" business is one example of how community organizing, business, and government regulation intersect in a way that appears to generate socially responsible and environmentally sound endeavors (though dependent on who you ask).

Fragmentation and decentralization have also spilled into philosophies of governance. The growth of neoliberalism in the years after World War II has meant that throughout the world, governments have designed policies that encourage businesses to flourish by removing bureaucratic rules seen as constraining industry. Late capitalist consumer culture fosters a climate of deregulation that has removed safety nets for those people unable to benefit from the shifting economy.[41]

Finally, late capitalist consumption has also encouraged a kind of free market morality of choice that replaces traditional religious moralities with more liberal, market-based moralities. Protective regulations and social supports have given way to the notion of individual responsibility and individual liberty. In this climate, freedom becomes the ability to choose one's lifestyle and one's patterns of consumption.

Choice itself becomes the new moral principle of our age, the arbiter of our highest values. With respect to personal relationships, intimacy, and the leisure industry, this means that complex personal relationships can be bought and sold via orderly, less ambiguous, contractual arrangements within the market.[42] Although buyers must beware, there have never been more opportunities to purchase human relationships, feelings, and pleasure than the global marketplace offers today. While there is certainly no universal consensus about which choices are appropriate or best, there tends to be consensus about the value of choice in the marketplace itself. The ability to freely purchase all kinds of goods and services has injected free-market liberalism into personal morality, and resulting shifts in relationships and intimacy have created significant controversy and fodder for media, politics, and government. This rhetoric of the free market and individual freedom is spreading to the regulation of morality and sexuality. In general, compared to the 1960s, the obscenity, sodomy, and anti-pornography laws that once constrained sexual behavior and consumption are increasingly overtaken by the laws, ethics, and morality of the market: the contract and the principle of free choice.[43]

THE STATE OF COMMERCIAL SEX IN LATE CAPITALISM

In today's cultural and economic context, sexuality—among other emotions—is squarely in the public eye through advertising, entertainment, news, and political debates. Arguably, sex is more central to today's economy than at any previous point in history. Yet sex is widely considered to be among our most private, emotional, physical, and psychological human intimacies. In its ideal form, it is supposed to be the deepest human connection and the most authentic expression of the self. Thus, sex as a commodity challenges the lines we construct between public and private intimacies. To some social theorists, sex as a commodity represents a postmodern challenge to modern constructions of the self and authenticity. To others, it helps demonstrate that the lines between public and private, between economic value and personal life, were never as rigid as some believe. As such, questions about the purchase of intimacy become central to the analysis of sexual commerce.

Since the dawn of the twentieth century, pundits and

businesspeople have recognized that sex sells. Indeed, sex has helped drive the growth of consumer culture. Mainstream popular culture, art, and advertising have become more sexualized. Media analyst McNair has labeled the social promotion and acceptance of sexualized looking and voyeurism as "striptease culture." Non-pornographic advertising, movies, television (and their celebrities), clothing, and accessories all experiment with representations and parodies of porn. "Porno-chic's" avant-garde cultural forms mimic the hard, glossy images of porn, but are culturally acceptable as entertainment, fashion, or art. And businesses that sell sexualized services, sexual aids, devices, and education, and even sex, are thriving. As sex continues to sell more and more products, services, and leisure, it becomes more central to our economy and more integral to our cultural forms and social interactions, especially in the marketplace.[44]

The sex industry is a term we use to refer to enterprises that sell explicitly sexual products, contact, services, or practices. In the globally integrated consumer economy, the market for sex as a commodity has intensified. International tourism and business travel have helped to spur the growth, as have the expansion of the internet, the ease of mail order commerce, the diffusion of computer and video technologies, and shifts toward market liberalization. Exact statistics are difficult to find and often unreliable, in part due to the difficulty of deciding exactly which products, services, and exchanges should "count" toward sex industry statistics, and in part because of the often still marginalized nature of parts of the industry where there is no consistent counting of irregular, criminalized, or stigmatized forms of sexual commerce. However, by any estimate, it is clear that since the 1990s the sex industry has grown tremendously in both formal and informal economic and cultural sectors.

Worldwide, the sex industry was worth "at least $20 billion a year and probably many times that," *The Economist* estimated over a decade ago in 1998. In that same year, a study by the United Nations' International Labor Organization found that of the four countries that report statistics for the sex sector—Indonesia, Malaysia, the Philippines, and Thailand—between 800,000 and a million people receive payment for sexual services. The sex industry generates between 4 to 13 percent gross domestic product in these countries.[45]

In the United States the sex industry is arguably bigger than the

NFL, NBA, and major league baseball combined, generating as much as $14 billion annually. In 1997, there were more than 100,000 adult websites, and profit estimates for online porn range from $50 million to $2 billion per year. Today, there are more than a million and a half adult websites. An industry report estimates that in 2005, 957 million pornographic adult films were rented or bought from retail stores. The biggest market share growth is in cable pay-per-view via satellite and cable television in homes and hotels. Most of the profits from porn belong to mainstream corporations like AOL/Time Warner, AT&T, Marriott, Hilton, Westin, and GM. The live sexual fantasy and inter-actions found in strip clubs also contribute to the growing sex industry. It is widely estimated that there are 2,500 to 5,000 strip clubs operating in the United States, and that average profits range from $500,000 to $5 million per year per business. Rick's Cabaret, which owns 13 strip clubs throughout the country, reported profits of $6 million in 2007. In 2005, the entire erotic dance industry in the United States brought in approximately $2 billion.[46]

The sex industries have not only grown; many have done so in ways that make adult sexual commerce more mainstream in look, content, and audience. In large U.S. cities, the seedy-looking strip clubs and adult stores with blacked-out windows are being displaced by much larger, more high-end sex shops and gentlemen's clubs with bright signage and limo or car service. In Britain, "peep shows, erotic films, and lap dancing bars have become an accepted part of night-time, and to some extent, the day time entertainment industry."[47] In Ant-werp, Belgium, a high-end "super-brothel," decorated by super-star architects and designers, caters to both a local and global leisure elite who want to consume this type of experience. In this context, even direct sexual services including indoor prostitution are becoming increasingly tolerated and visible. Prostitution is moving away from the streets and to the yellow pages and internet. As these businesses become more visible and mainstream, the business practices and work within them are becoming more routinized, and many look more and more like other service and leisure industry jobs. Adult businesses have to become more businesslike to attract more conventional employees, customers, and investors.[48]

Legal adult businesses have grown tremendously since the 1980s. These companies seek to attract more affluent customers by developing reputations for cleanliness and classiness. Upscaling often translates into a broader profit margin. Adult video and erotic dancing have remained legal businesses, and experience a relatively large amount of support from the general public. High-tech sex toys, lifestyles in adult/entertainment/club industries, and sexual subcultures are increasingly part of high-end market niches where consumers have plenty of disposable income. As the sex industry has become more mainstream, it has also begun to attract many female customers. Women have been the fastest-growing market for adult videos for the past several years.[49]

At the same time, working-class venues remain small and some are dropping prices. They tend to attract workers who have less social capital and are potentially more subject to poor working conditions. The mainstreaming of the sex industry is as much about social class, race, and ethnicity as it is about liberal attitudes toward sexuality.

This trend relies on contradictory impulses. On the one hand, the industry maximizes profits by drawing in a wider variety of customers and tapping high-end markets. On the other hand, the adult sex industry also markets transgression. These outlets for sexual desire are pleasurable and exciting because they are beyond the bounds of mainstream culture. The obvious irony of commercial sexual enterprises today is that their growth and successes risks killing the thrill of indulging in the taboo.

Government regulations are contradictory. On the one hand, neoliberal policies have allowed many forms of adult entertainment and products to flourish legally. On the other hand, politicians remain very squeamish about visibly supporting sexual commerce. The mainstreaming of the sex industry has spurred a backlash among religious, fundamentalist feminist, and other conservative groups. Governments find themselves having to balance the cultural trends toward liberalization with this backlash. In many ways, anti-sex industry interests paradoxically help maintain the sense of taboo that commercial sex depends on to market its service. As we will show in this book, this has been the case in the Nevada brothel industry. Even though the sale of sex in the state is legal and regulated, the owners have tried to lay low politically over the years, which has also helped to cultivate an aura of mystery and intrigue. However, the trends toward mainstreaming and upscaling mean that some owners are becoming more visible.

Prostitution in Late Capitalism

How have all these changes in late capitalism affected the practice and organization of prostitution itself? Given the centrality of sex to our culture and economy, and the growth and mainstreaming of the sex industry, is it accurate to say that the sale of sex may be becoming more like other service industries in both organization and the nature of the work? The commodification of service has several implications worth exploring to set the stage for understanding Nevada brothel prostitution.

Recent research has argued that there are distinct similarities between interactive service workers and sex workers with respect to the experience of commodifying emotions. Research has examined emotional labor among erotic dancers and found both similarities and differences between their experiences and those of service workers in mainstream segments of the leisure economy.[50] Research on prostitutes themselves shows that exploitation in the prostitution exchange is notably similar to emotional labor in other service work.[51]

Much of the debate about prostitution revolves around the idea of the authenticity of the exchange, and the implications of selling one's identity or "self." As we have shown, selling one's "self" in the form of relationships and emotional labor in the marketplace is done more frequently today in all kinds of service work. Research on the performance of sex work also shows that, as with the selling of other personal services, the selling of sex can be dehumanizing (as human relationships become all about economic exchange) and liberating (as when new forms of exchange become possible and manageable for larger numbers of people). These debates have gendered connotations as well: sex work, though diverse in gender and sexuality of both worker and client, is largely undertaken by women, and the focus of debates tends to be on heterosexual services with women workers and men clients.

Consumers themselves have seemingly contradictory notions regarding the "genuineness" of the relationships they are purchasing. Research on why men seek street prostitutes shows that clients are interested in sexual practices to which they otherwise have little access and desire the transgressive qualities of a more public street exchange. Some clients want to avoid the responsibilities and emotional attachments of conventional relationships. Some may seek unambiguous pleasures of commercial sex. Elizabeth Bernstein calls this "bounded authenticity," and she argues that customers recognize that the line between intimacy and the marketplace is blurred. Prasad argues that a market morality in neoliberal societies encourages consumers to seek the ease of market exchanges for sex over more traditional relationships.[52]

These issues get right to the questions surrounding intimacy and the market. Many scholars argue that a society that increasingly tears down boundaries between intimacy, sexual bodies, and commodity exchange necessarily reproduces traditional gender inequalities that exploit, objectify, and oppress women. This argument is built on basic assumptions that the interaction between buyer and seller is gendered and is therefore unequal, and that the basic relationship between owners or managers and their workers is inherently exploitative.

However, research on customers, and prostitutes' attitudes toward their work, seem to indicate that with increasing cultural acceptance of the sale of sex and sexuality, the very stigma that has marked prostitution may be decreasing. Some sellers of sex are less likely to think of themselves within stigmatized categories of "whore" or "prostitute." Due to the sexualization of late capitalist culture, some sex workers feel less stigmatized. This is partly attributable to the new ways in which we create identities. Both buyers and sellers of sex potentially recognize that the intimacy and interactions of their exchanges are negotiated on a commercial playing field, and involve multiple and varied performances of gender and identity.

In addition, the nature of the "product" that is sold in prostitution may be changing. In some places, there is evidence of a decline in street prostitution and an increase in workers using the internet. Some argue that this increased demand for the fantasy of sensuous reciprocity is replacing the desire for quick, impersonal sexual release. Bernstein found that in San Francisco, for a variety of reasons, prostitution is moving indoors, and more middle-class consumers are seeking longer, more holistic experiences in a sexual exchange.[53] Customers seek a variety of specific sexual pleasures and practices. Some seek brief liaisons. Others may desire a more pampered service or an experience built on warmth, friendliness, intelligence, and compassion as much as physical appearance and physical contact.[54]

In a study of strip clubs as homosocial touristic spaces, Katherine Frank has found that men are not buying sexual arousal, but relaxation.

This includes the ability to engage in stereotypical masculine behaviors (and perform masculine identity) with no repercussions (where a man can be a man) in an uncompetitive environment free from the pressure and expectations of relations with women. Strip clubs provide a masculinized form of entertainment where customers can escape "to a world where masculinity, companionship and the spectacle of female bodies can be purchased."[55] What they purchase is a very gendered form of leisure and escape from an everyday world of work and home. They perform a type of masculinity in a sexualized scene to establish intimate connections with dancers, not necessarily to be sexually gratified. In a study by Danielle Egan, regular customers, for the most part, did not come to the strip club to purchase sexual release and they did not see themselves as seeking prostitutes, ever.[56] This makes clear that a very different set of dispositions is driving a market for direct sexual services than the market for sexualized services like erotic dance or pornography, including an expanded understanding of erotic experience and elevated expectations for sexual fantasy, style, and scene.

CONCLUSION

Taken together, these approaches to leisure consumption and labor can provide a rigorous frame for analyzing the wide variety of contemporary forms of prostitution. The very dynamism of late capitalism and the growth and diversification of global sex industries, intertwined with larger global leisure economies, means that it is no longer instructive to see prostitution as a static entity consisting of, as Jane Addams put it in 1917, " 'victims of White slavery' who need to be rescued from immoral people and forces."[57] It is imperative that we think beyond familiar tropes when trying to understand prostitution and sex workers today in the very specific historical, economic, cultural, and social contexts in which commercial sex is exchanged. Location, gender, social class, and ethnicity all intersect to inform experiences of labor and consumption. While prostitution may be the oldest profession, the context in which it occurs has changed, and this change potentially affects what it means to sell sex. Examining the persistence and morphing of gender and class inequalities in consumer culture will help us understand the position of sex industries within broader social institutions.

In this chapter, we have shown how the characteristics of late capitalist economies, including the expansion of consumption of services and leisure, permeate social life. This economy spurs a sexualized culture and the sale of sex. Prostitution in late capitalism, more so than at the turn of the nineteenth or twentieth centuries, exists in a culture and climate where economic and social relations have increased a market for sex, where the sale of sex is more commonplace, where more and more human relations are bought and sold in growing service and leisure economies, where workers are more likely to routinely negotiate multiple selves, and where feminism has challenged inequalities in gender relations. Late capitalist culture has transformed the very notions of sex and identity, fracturing both, and opening both to heightened commodification as products that may be bought and sold in the global marketplace.[58]

3

THE MAKING OF NEVADA PROSTITUTION

Without tourism it is likely that there would be no legal brothels in Nevada. Without legal brothels it is likely that there would not be the kind of tourist industry that exists today. These two statements seem strange on several fronts. Anyone who has spent time in the majority of Nevada's rural brothels would probably see very little in common between a globally interconnected cosmopolitan tourist center in Las Vegas and these small, converted trailers, blending into the desert background in tiny towns miles and miles from the nearest resort. Likewise, if you pay attention to the at-best wary tolerance between the resort industry and the brothels, you might conclude that the tourist industry grew in spite of the brothels, or that the brothel industry grew in spite of the tourist industry.

However, when you look at Nevada's history, it is clear that prostitution was a key and very open component of the state's developing leisure industry until the 1950s. In about the mid-twentieth century, professional promotion of tourism in Nevada focused on selling sexuality in urban areas, not selling sex per se. This focus on sexuality instead of sex left independent working women with less control over sexual commerce. Framing all this was a market morality that foreshadowed the development of late capitalist culture in the rest of the nation, and indeed, globally.

In this chapter we will make two main points. First, brothels were a key part of the development of Nevada's tourist economy. Second, there was a diverse array of sexual leisure services in this early tourist economy. But these various sexual services were gradually channeled into one venue—brothels. This occurred through gendered and class struggles over who ran businesses, who was politically connected, and the rise of the casino industry.

Prostitution in Industrial Societies

We know that prior to industrialization, women who were paid for sex played very different roles in society. They played key roles in religious practices in ancient Mediterranean cultures and India. In pre-modern cities including Moscow, Shanghai, and Paris, courtesans were important components of elite culture, providing mannered and educated companionship as much as sensual pleasures to men in a society dominated by contractual marriages.

Once industrialization began, prostitution changed. Cities filled with newly mobile working classes, freed from the traditions of the agricultural extended family. Across Europe, Asia, Africa, and South America in the years after 1800, cities became a site of economic and social development in new ways. Historian Timothy Gilfoyle points out that urban industrialization meant that for these newly mobile working classes,

> ... men delayed marriage and patronized prostitutes in exceptional numbers. Industrialization and economic transformations created a ready supply of migratory, independent, low-wage earning women, many of whom viewed prostitution as a viable economic alternative to poverty. Not only were these male and female subcultures unprecedented in scope, but they were embedded in popular, modern, consumer cultures that countenanced new behaviors of sexual expression and purchase.[1]

These workers helped create a new leisure economy of dance halls, movie theaters, cafés, burlesque, cabarets, and brothels. These businesses provided an array of services appealing to desires for escape and relaxation, crafting a market for services that helped separate the spheres of work and play. These created new job opportunities for women. As modern cultures and industrial economies dramatically changed social, economic, and political relations, so too was the business of prostitution affected. Prostitution expanded. As industrial factories focused on efficiency and mass production, a new market for quick, reproducible sex opened, which was demanded and supplied by middle- and working-class men and women. In France, for example, one historian argues that industrial-era brothels provided "taylorized coitus" and "conveyer-belt" sex where women saw 30–50 clients a day.[2] The working-class market emphasized more sexual offerings. The courtesan experience of domestic companionship didn't disappear.

At the same time, the developing urban industrial upper class was crafting its sense of itself against both aristocratic decadence and the laboring working classes. Bourgeois concerns about morality, religious virtue, appropriate gender, and nationalism led to new ways of regulating sexuality in the market. In some sense, the regulation of the body became part of the work of growing modern states. The industrial age dawned with increasing anxieties about the body and all sorts of proscriptions for appropriate and inappropriate public and private behaviors. Emerging bourgeois elites looked with disdain at working-class and immigrant culture, seeing their forms of leisure as degenerate and immoral. At first, these decadent leisure businesses were regulated and zoned to corral public disorder, and prostitutes were targeted for open and notorious behavior. From the 1870s to the turn of the twentieth century, many cities in the U.S., including most western cities on the frontier and more urban Midwestern cities like St. Louis, New Orleans and St. Paul enacted systems of licensed brothels which included mandatory medical examinations, red light districts, and restrictions on mobility. Even as late as the 1950s, laws in Britain, China, Argentina, and in various localities in the U.S. and Japan regulated the public disorder of prostitution through zoning, medical and brothel regulations. This created boundaries between poor vice districts and "respectable" upper-class neighborhoods.[3]

By the turn of the twentieth century, powerful Victorian-era social movements encouraged the development of regulatory regimes that blended Christian and nationalist ideologies; notions of bourgeois manners, self-control and civility ideals of the companionate, pro-creative, nuclear family, and notions of men's and women's appropriate roles as family members and as citizens. These laws targeted working-class women and, by emphasizing public health and safety, they established prostitution as a crime of morality rather than an issue of public disorder. Prostitution itself became a crime and the prostitute herself became the symbol of women's fall from grace. Russia in 1917, Argentina in 1936 and 1955, France in 1946, China after 1949 and the U.S. by the 1920s either ended regulation or criminalized prostitution altogether.[4] Sexual commerce now had a different relationship to mainstream culture.

WILD WEST BUSINESSES AND MINING CULTURE: THE LEISURE ECONOMY IN NEVADA, 1900 to 1940

In the eastern half of the United States the industrial economy was taking hold. There was a different economic dynamic that drove development in the western half of the United States. Men and women of all races and classes had been moving west toward less settled areas in search of jobs and opportunities. But it was the discovery of gold in California in 1849 that fueled a massive migration of mostly white settlers from the eastern United States to the western frontier. The sparsely populated, dry, desert region between the Rocky Mountains and California became altogether different, thanks to the gold and silver rush. In the following 80 years, this migration fueled an economy built on a massive extraction of natural resources. In the towns that grew up around mining a bustling economy developed of working men who sought leisure activities after work and women who saw opportunities to provide services.

This was especially true for Nevada, whose vast deserts and harsh climate discouraged many from settling for long. The first gold rush brought 40,000 people to Nevada by the 1860s, and enough promise of riches to catapult Nevada into statehood in 1864 before it had reached the proper population threshold. The first boom between 1860 and 1880 occurred in a vein in the northern part of the state, in the foothills of the Sierra Nevada due east of San Francisco. This boom brought the Pony Express and a criss-cross of railroad and supply towns that later developed a nascent civic infrastructure, which led to the more stable small towns of today—Reno, Carson City, Winnemucca, Ely, and Elko. Nevada became the number one contributor to the United States' gold and silver stocks in the years following the Civil War.[5] When that vein ran out, an economic slump hit the state and the population declined dramatically. But a second gold discovery in the southern part of the state spurred a mining boom between 1910 and 1930. This one centered in Goldfield, and from that sprang Las Vegas as a supply and railroad town.

Nevada's first large towns were these boom towns. Virginia City exploded after silver was discovered in 1859 to become a sophisticated city with a population of 25,000 in less than 15 years. It was the largest city between San Francisco and Denver at its peak, and the largest city in Nevada until the turn of the twentieth century. It was brimming with restaurants, brokerage firms, clothiers, and saloons. Some 30 years later the second mining boom centered in the southern Nevada town of Goldfield. Goldfield's population rose and fell from one tent to 20,000 people and back to 5,400 between 1903 and 1910. In 1905 it had 162 brokerage firms, 27 restaurants and nearly 60 saloons. Even after its decline, Goldfield in 1910 was still the second largest city in Nevada. It fed the tiny supply town of Las Vegas, whose population would not pass Goldfield's peak until after World War II. Even Reno, which became Nevada's largest town in 1900 in between mining booms, would not get to a population of 20,000 until 1940.[6]

From these boom towns came the economic, cultural, and political infrastructure that has framed Nevada's development. Boom towns were populated by large numbers of single men who came as waged miners, in addition to entrepreneurs of both genders who established service businesses around the mines. It brought together European immigrants as well as African Americans, Chinese, and native Paiutes. Up through the 1960s, Nevada politics were dominated by men and a few women who made their fortunes in these towns.[7] What they learned of business and success they learned from the free-spirited culture and entrepreneurial economy of boom towns. Virginia City, for example, became an industrial city with urban sensibilities, and a large service industry grew within it. Boom towns embodied fast urbanization, quick decline, and a play-hard culture; they were able to grow quickly because of entrepreneurship, and an influx of migrant workers in dangerous work. Fast growth meant a haphazard infrastructure and inadequate healthcare. Waged miners had high mortality rates from disease as well as mining accidents, but wages were also relatively high, and money was plentiful. The towns' predominant occupations meant that there were large numbers of single men. In 1860 in Virginia City, 5 percent of the population was female. As the town grew to 11,319 residents in 1870, 31 percent, or 3,505 of these, were women.[8]

Saloons, Vice, and the Boom Town Leisure Economy

Saloons and sexual services were anchoring service businesses in Nevada's early mining towns. Indeed, saloons were a key component of newly urbanizing cities throughout the United States. In 1915, New York had one saloon for every 515 persons, Chicago had one for every 335, and San Francisco had one for every 218 people.[9] Saloons were even more prominent in mining towns. Deadwood, South Dakota had one for every 60 residents; Leadville, Colorado one for 85; and Goldfield, Nevada one for 135.[10] Saloons in these mining camps were often the first businesses to be established, and they frequently served multiple purposes as bar, hotel, general store, restaurant, post office, barber, general gathering place, stage coach station and sometimes even became the church, funeral parlor, or operating table.[11] In a climate where single waged miners and speculators worked in dangerous, high-paying work, an economy of escape prospered. Besides providing general infrastructure services to the town, the saloons provided services that catered to escape—drinking, gambling, dancing, theater, and prostitution—and so developed strong economic and political power.

Prostitution, gambling, and drinking were mainstays of the economy.[12] From the perspective of eastern visitors it was a climate rich in vice, a fact that became the subject of much embellishment by a variety of writers. Mark Twain wrote ten years after living in Virginia City:

> Vice flourished luxuriantly during the heyday of our "flush times." The saloons were over-burdened with custom; so were the police courts, the gambling dens, the brothels, and the jails—unfailing signs of high prosperity in a mining region.[13]

Thus "vice" established a culture of escape and became a symbol of prosperity, framing the service businesses not just in Virginia City, but in many boom towns throughout the state.

Femininity and Sexuality in the Mining Towns

Many women were able to capitalize on the undeveloped infrastructure in mining towns and worked as seamstresses, servants, saloon keepers, and boarding-house operators. Studies of census records and diaries in mining towns also show women working as miners, cattle ranch owners, traveling entertainers, and typesetters. Petrik argues that women entered more traditionally male fields in pioneer communities for several reasons: higher divorce rates, large age differences between men and women, shortages of women, and poorly developed schools and churches (the power base of women at that time).[14]

While the majority of women who came to Virginia City came with their spouses, many single women came to boom towns to work as prostitutes.[15] By 1870, the height of Virginia City's prosperity, prostitution was the most commonly listed occupation for women. Census records show 157 women who listed occupations did so as prostitutes.[16] In addition, there is evidence, although we do not know the numbers, that many women worked in multiple jobs, including as part-time prostitutes or saloon girls. In Paula Petrik's study of Helena, Montana, a mining town similar to those in Nevada, many single working-class women were also "proprietor-prostitutes," both running a saloon and providing services themselves.[17]

The provision of sexual services in Virginia City had many forms, and women in these settings worked independently out of dance halls and saloons. Many made a good living mostly dancing with men, providing entertainment for miners after a long day at the mines. Other women worked out of different venues. They rented two-room houses or worked in a block of "cribs" (one-room shacks) on D Street just below the main commercial corridor. Others owned or lived in brothels in two-storey parlor houses across from the Virginia and Truckee Railroad Depot.[18]

Archeologist Alexy Simmons identified distinct class differences in these venues. At the top tier were self-employed white women renting the small houses on D Street. These houses, she found, were decorated with lace curtains and rocking-chairs, and were heated with a small wood box stove. They usually owned their own furniture, including mahogany beds, fancy bedspreads, and rugs.[19]

At the second tier were brothels, which were two-storey parlor houses with cooking and dining facilities. The public rooms were furnished more lavishly than other venues. A probate inventory of Jessie Lester's brothel on D Street and Sutton Avenue found that the two parlors were furnished with chandeliers, lace curtains, carpets, two sofas, and ten chairs. Upstairs there were five bedrooms with spittoons, water pitchers, linen window shades, carpets, beds with springs, and wool or horsehair and wool mattresses. The women lived in the basement. Archeological research on other western brothels found women's personal belongings including cosmetics, birth control devices, musical instruments, board and card games, paraphernalia for alcohol and opium use, clothing, and frequently, toys and children's artifacts. These brothels were occupied mostly by white women.

At the third tier, a block of saloons toward the end of C Street stood next to cribs occupied by Chinese and Native American prostitutes. In the 1870 census, all but nine of the Chinese women who lived in Virginia City were prostitutes (although research by Sue Fawn Chung indicates that the census enumerator of 1870 may not have understood the role of the second wife[20]). Three of 26 African American women were recorded as prostitutes.[21]

Virginia City, like other cities of the time, had its share of venereal disease and drug use. A study of Storey County hospital patients during the 1800s found that the majority were being treated for venereal disease. Among prostitutes' biggest problems were venereal disease and drugs, the same drugs that plagued upper-class white women at the time.[22]

Like Virginia City, Goldfield, whose peak occurred between 1906 and 1911, also had a thriving prostitution industry. Women here also worked in a wide variety of service jobs as well as running several stores, restaurants, dance halls, and hotels. The brothels were licensed and legal. A constable recalled that nearly 500 women worked in a legally zoned red light district for dance halls and brothels at one point, making it practically a "city onto itself [sic]."[23]

Gender in this context was different from the developing Victorian ideology of women's proper place that pervaded the more urbanized eastern United States. According to historian Sally Zanjani, there were "certain indications that Goldfield women had a tough fibered streak that differentiated them from the submissive hand wringing model of Victorian womanhood that still prevailed in much of the country."[24]

James Scrugham, early governor of Nevada, wrote the following about women in the mining camps in a report of the Comstock Lode in 1935, almost 60 years after the fact.

> Prostitution flourished, as in all camps, and courtesans promenaded the streets slowly, decked out in gay dresses and showy jewelry, and drifting about with the restless tide which set to and fro throughout the city . . . In towns without wives they substituted. The camps were not for wives. They just couldn't put up with the roughness. Hell, many camps didn't have water. I don't know when it was that Virginia City, for example, first got flush toilets . . . The miners, some coming in from a day in the drifts, some coming in from months of prospecting, hands calloused, boots worn, having smelled only sagebrush and sweat, living like Indians, why, the poor bastards knew the one place they could get a welcome, a smile, a bed with springs, clean sheets, the smell of perfume, was the crib. So the cribs were the place . . . Come evening, the card-sharp and the blacksmith took the same walk down the street of whores. The girls understood; they played the phonograph, and they had pictures on the walls.[25]

This account illustrates one politician's understanding of gender and prostitution in a mining economy. Prostitutes provided men with escape from the danger of the mines. They gave men the missing comforts of home as well as sexual services. They were, as he characterized it, "rougher" wife replacements. The account creates a distinction between women who were proper "wives" and women who were rougher prostitutes. While the above account represents a romanticized image of prostitution, it does reveal a different ideology about gender and sexual services than the Progressive-Era ideologies that were developing in the eastern United States at the time. The actual conditions of working prostitutes varied far more than these accounts indicated. Yet, these accounts indicated at some level a respect for the place of prostitution in mining economies. They were not the same as the "good, proper wives," but they had a certain status. As one historian reports, "thus, a small company town with all the traditional and 'acceptable' societies and fraternal orders of the day found no great moral dilemma in the existence of its numerous saloons, gambling halls and brothels."[26]

We may never know exactly what wives or other women actually thought of sex workers.[27] As discussed above, we do know that many women worked in several jobs, and some included selling sexual services in the mix. Zanjani reports one incident in Goldfield where a scandal of sorts erupted. A number of wives were also working part-time as prostitutes. One local resident noted that the husbands did not mind because, "In the code she wasn't cheating if she collected for it."[28]

There are also indications that acceptance of this "tough fibered streak" in women extended into an acceptance of labor rights for prostitutes. While there to organize miners in Goldfield, the Industrial Workers of the World (IWW) sought to organize stenographers in brokerage houses and prostitutes in Rhyolite and Goldfield. In 1905 there was an attempt by several prostitutes to impeach the Justice of the Peace, the district attorney, and a policeman for collecting illegal fees. The IWW attempted to plead the case of the prostitutes in their national periodicals, and some claim the prostitutes were organized into Goldfield's local No. 77. In 1906, some prostitutes in nearby Rhyolite distributed a card with a reference to unions which read, "The Unique and Adope Concert Halls are Unfair Houses and we request all union men not to patronize." Certainly the Victorian-era ideas of women's asexual moral purity and their proper place being limited to home had not fully infiltrated western boom town culture.[29]

The Local Politics of Vice

Mining camp politics clearly supported a coexistence with vice. There were institutional constraints preventing much social regulation. Early residents were not tied to a local community, and people moved frequently between mining camps for opportunities. Camps were slow to get churches, which often provided the institutional framework for social regulations. City planners, to the extent that there were any, dealt with vice by zoning. The goal was to better order municipalities— a well-planned community was supposed to promote public health, safety, morals, and general welfare. Mining towns, including Virginia

City, Carson City, even Goldfield, passed zoning laws containing saloons, entertainment, and prostitution to certain streets in the city. When the Las Vegas township was laid out in 1901, one block was designated the "vice" district and allowed the sale of alcohol: Block 16.

While local politics reflected a coexistence with vice by regulating social order, politics at the state level was more susceptible to lobbying from national social movements and the federal government concerned with regulating morality. At least part of the reason the Nevada territory was carved out of the large Utah territory in 1861 had to do with attempts by Utah's Mormon government to impose moral constraints on mining towns that were seen as out of control.[30] As Nevada gained statehood, most of the state's economic and political elite (which also included many Mormons up through the 1960s) came from the mining towns of Virginia City, Goldfield, and Tonopah. That Nevada politicians cut their teeth in these mining towns is critical to understanding the persistence of prostitution in the state. Those entrepreneurs who were able to amass fortunes and political power developed a gender ideology that, while still somewhat traditional, accepted women as workers, and saw prostitution as more an issue of control than of morality.

National politics after the Civil War—middle-class Victorian ideals, the social purity movement and early twentieth-century Progressive-Era politics—were increasingly concerned with regulating and controlling immoral behaviors, particularly those of immigrants and women.[31] While Progressive-Era laws controlling women's behavior were spreading throughout the country, there were few signs that these laws were having much of an effect in Nevada.

It is not that Nevada was untouched by the moral reform movements that were sweeping the nation. Nevada's first territorial governor was a federal appointee who tried to encourage laws controlling vice, but often came up against resistance from locally grown legislators. During Nevada's first ten years of statehood, battles were fought over alcohol, gambling, and prostitution. Against the wishes of some early governors, Nevada legislators legalized gambling except for a period between 1909 and 1915. Various state laws during the end of the nineteenth and beginning of the twentieth centuries responded to national concerns with prostitution, defining it as a moral problem. In 1887, state law forbade brothels within 400 yards of a school or principal street. In 1903 the state legislature outlawed brothels within 400 yards of a church. A year after the U.S. Congress passed the abolitionist Mann Act and Bennett Acts prohibiting interstate and international traffic in prostitution, Nevada state law prohibited an individual from placing women in a brothel, or men from habitually visiting a brothel. In 1913 Nevada state law prohibited pandering, living off the earnings of a prostitute, and advertising. In 1923 the Nevada legislature passed an act mandating county licenses for amusement, entertainment, and recreation businesses.[32]

But these policies seemed to be minimal concessions that legislators who grew up around prostitution would make to appease reformers who tried to match the mood of the rest of the country. Nevada lore is filled with stories of locals who resisted the laws. Rather than close their brothels, the town of Austin moved their red light district out of the range of a school in 1911.[33] Citizens in Riepetown declared another street as their Main Street rather than move the saloons. Citizens in Searchlight moved the school away from a brothel. The 1923 licensing bill spurred probably the most serious efforts to clean up prostitution. But locals consistently resisted. Historians characterized Nevada's mining captains, railroad magnates, and cattle kings: "They all had the same agenda. To keep the government from taxing or regulating them."[34] This same anti-government mentality often spilled over to other forms of social regulation.

Progressive-Era politics also spurred a number of company-owned mining towns in Nevada, which paradoxically, helped promote prostitution. From the mid-1800s until the 1930s, many companies set up towns to house and sustain workers in industries where the work site was often isolated. This was especially true for mining. Nevada had a good share of company towns, where the homes, stores, recreational facilities, and schools were owned and managed by the company. Many of these, especially during Nevada's second mining boom in the early 1900s, were also influenced by Progressive-Era ideologies about controlling workers' morality. Companies kept a tight grip on social life in the confines of the town.

In reaction to the tight social grip, a thriving service industry based on vice and escape would develop just outside of these towns. During a copper boom in the early 1900s, the Nevada Consolidated Copper Company built two towns, Ruth and Kimberly, in White Pine County in the central northeast corner of the state. These two towns were just outside of Ely, and a small but stable stagecoach stop and post office were established in the 1870s. By 1907 Riepetown had sprung up outside of Ruth and Kimberly, not surprisingly anchored by a collection of saloons, gambling houses, as many as four dance halls, and a number of cribs. The town thrived while the mines were booming. Even Ely, which established a vice district during these years, found saloons and prostitution bulging at the borders, according to newspaper reports from that time.[35]

Newspapers reported continuous battles between the company towns of Ruth, Kimberly, and Ely, and the workers, residents, and business owners in Riepetown. The mine owners along with civic organizations, ministers, and schools were highly critical of the disorderly, lawless vice in these towns. But the timing of their opposition coincided with labor union organizing. Attempts to shut down the saloons and gambling halls began at about the same time as the Western Federation of Miners and other unions made Riepetown their headquarters. Unions had practical reasons for locating in Riepetown. Company towns not only wanted to control workers' moral behavior, they also wanted to prevent unionizing. In 1909 the White Pine District Attorney tried to shut down the dance halls by invoking a recently passed Nevada law prohibiting dance halls on the main street. Riepetown businessmen, (reportedly including one "legitimate businessman," 16 saloon owners, and numerous people running cribs or renting rooms for prostitutes) resisted and designated the town's main street as Pheby Street, two blocks south, "in order to work the least hardship on property owners, some of whom have dance halls on the main street." In 1911, the Industrial Workers of the World came to Ely to organize, and they too set up shop in Riepetown, finding the saloons an hospitable place to organize. National IWW leader C. E. Mahoney was even elected mayor of Riepetown. A few years later, federal agents arrested several citizens of Riepetown on white slavery charges. Kennecott Copper bought many of the mines beginning in 1915 and continued to pressure county officials to close the saloons, but it was not until Prohibition in 1919 that the saloons were shut down and the towns dried up.[36]

In 1919 the moral fervor reached a point where reformers were able to pass a bill prohibiting the sale of alcohol throughout the United States. Nevada steadfastly resisted, and as with the rest of the nation moved the consumption of alcohol underground.

Prohibition and a rising number of zoning laws had a major effect on Nevada prostitution. The places where women could work independently dried up. In dance halls, the line between prostitution and other sexualized work was often blurred. Providing a variety of entertainment for men in saloons and dance halls had allowed some women independence. Earlier, social purity reformers had been able to pass laws policing women's access to liquor, and by the 1900s women were barred from drinking in saloons in many locales. As more laws to contain vice were passed, business owners were in the best position to negotiate or lobby for exemption or change. As the example of Riepetown shows, laws went along with business and property owners' needs, and independent women had little power. Increasingly, independent prostitutes lost the political clout to fight zoning, licensing, and other containment ordinances. Brothel landowners not only had clout, they often espoused a rhetoric of containment and the dangers of unregulated prostitution. Consequently, their brothels continued to profit.

Nevada Turns to Tourism

In the early 1920s, Nevada hit a serious mining slump again. The state lost population, the boom towns dried up, and only the supply towns that were serviced by major railroads survived. Goldfield's population shrank to 700 and Virginia City's to 600 in the 1930 census.[37] Meanwhile, the rest of the nation was entering a period of unprecedented economic boom at the same time as Prohibition was spurring a strong underground economy. Advances in mass production spread consumer goods and new forms of leisure consumption to the masses. In fact, Prohibition coincided with the institutionalization of vacations, paid leave at work, and mass consumption of leisure activities.[38] Throughout the country, the economic growth of the 1920s contributed to a surge in tourist resorts in out-of-the-way locations like Hot Springs, Arkansas, and Palm Springs, California. Over the next 90 years, Nevada's foundational culture of escape for the workers—drinking, gambling, and women—was transformed into the state's economic base of tourism and play for middle-class consumers.

Nevada's tourist industry, at least initially, derived partially from the nation's fascination with the Old West. Jackson Lears writes that an increasingly urban society developed an almost cultish longing for an authentic self, one born of physical experience.[39] The erotic longing that came with this was as much a part of the sexual story of the nation as the Victorian era's suppression of open sexuality. In the midst of the 1870s and Victorian cultural restrictions on sexual expression, a number of writers developed an interest in the cultural representations of the Old West.[40] Bret Harte and Mark Twain lived in and wrote from Virginia City, Nevada—the heart of Nevada's first mining boom. They were among the first to spin tales for a national audience of a lawless, rugged West where whores with hearts of gold cared for rowdy prospectors.[41] In later years, Pulitzer Prize-winning Harvard historian Bernard DeVoto wrote of Virginia City's courtesans: "They drove through the streets reclining in lacquered broughams, displaying to male eyes fashions as close to Paris as any then current in New York."[42]

So when Nevada did capitalize on this interest in tourism, it did so in two ways. The state appealed to the nation's longing for those experiences denied by bourgeois culture. State businesspeople and certain politicians framed this in the rhetoric of the Wild West. By the 1920s, Reno, a supply town founded in 1878, had become Nevada's largest town with a population of around 12,000 people. City leaders began to recognize that tourists from the East Coast and California could become significant contributors to the state's economy. During the 1923 mayoral election, prostitution and its potential boost to tourism became a campaign issue. Edwin E. Roberts, a former Congressmen running for mayor, campaigned on a platform to keep Reno's reputation as a wide-open gambling center and to turn Reno into the "playground of the world." Roberts handily won the election. Over the next ten years, Roberts led the campaign to loosen restrictions on gambling, divorce, alcohol, and prostitution. Declaring that "I don't believe in Prohibition or any kind of reform that takes from any man or woman their right to find happiness in their own way," Roberts and the city council in 1923 passed an ordinance establishing a red light district on the north shore of the Truckee River between Center and Second Streets. This district became known as the Reno Stockade. In 1931, Roberts helped convince the state to legalize gambling, and they shortened the already brief residency requirement for divorce from three months to six weeks. "You cannot legislate morals into people," said Roberts in a 1931 mayoral campaign speech,

> You can't stop gambling, so let's put it out in the open. Divorce
> is the only solution when marriages are unhappy. And if I had
> my way in this Prohibition year, I as mayor of Reno, would
> place a barrel of whiskey on every corner, with a dipper, and a
> sign saying, 'Help yourself, but don't be a hog.'[43]

These decisions helped cement Nevada's image as a hedonistic playground. Shortly after the decisions to legalize gambling, shorten the residency requirement for divorce, and tolerate prostitution, a *Los Angeles Times* editorial called Nevada a "vicious Babylon" and the *Kansas City Star* called Reno a combination of "Sodom, Gomorrah and Hell."[44] At the same time, this increased the nation's fascination with the Wild West. During the 1930s and early 1940s, a number of the nation's best writers moved to Virginia City. From there they filled the pages of the *Saturday Evening Post, Ladies Home Journal, Gentlemen's Quarterly*, the *New Yorker, Gourmet, Town and Country*, and *Life* with articles that created our current myths about the wild and woolly West, and romanticized its legendary soiled doves. As James and Raymond argued in *Comstock Women*, "the West came into vogue."[45] The Virginia City mining district became fashionable once again and the town doubled in size. The 1940 movie *Virginia City* by Warner Brothers raised national attention. The West was painted as a place of wonder, legend, and inexhaustible abundance. Divorce and bohemian freedom drew more writers from metropolitan areas after World War II. It was not unusual to meet Saul Bellow, Joe Liebling, Salvador Dali, or Robert Caples at the Virginia City Delta Saloon. Arthur Miller's experiences while waiting for a divorce at a ranch on Pyramid Lake north of Reno in 1956 influenced the movie, *The Misfits*. These writers were fascinated by drunks and prostitutes. The legend of a middle-class prostitute, Juila Bulette, was rewritten to describe an elegant and beloved madam. Lucius Bebe and Charles Cleeg's writings made the prostitute famous. Television series dating from the 1950s such as *Bonanza, Have Gun Will Travel*, and *Paladin* all rose from and fostered these images of Nevada's western essence.[46]

Nevada capitalized on these images, and while easy divorce and gambling attracted most tourists, open prostitution played a significant part in the images of the Wild West. Max Miller, a San Francisco writer, wrote in the 1920s on the tourist draw of the cribs that made up Reno's red light district, the Stockade: "They are about to observe what they always have longed to see, flesh, glistening and raw, spiced and diademed. They are about to visit the Isle of the Sirens—and not be arrested for it."[47] The Reno Stockade, at its height between the 1920s and 1940s, had a total of 150 prostitutes in as many as 80 cribs lining the north bank of the Truckee River. The Stockade drew local ranchers and miners, but it also drew a healthy tourist trade from all over the United States. The Stockade also drew women from all over the country who wanted to escape increased repression of the ability to sell sex. They hung their names on the doors of tiny cribs and worked in three eight-hour shifts for sometimes $2 a customer (about $25 to $30 today). At one end there was a dance hall with a band where women would dance with customers before retiring to the cribs. The women had weekly exams for venereal disease and paid $2.50 in rent as well as paid a fee for meals at a nearby dance hall and restaurant.[48]

Another small supply town was finding that tourism played a key role in its survival and growth through the 1940s. Las Vegas was founded as a railroad junction in 1905 and prospered as a supply town for the mines in Goldfield, Rhyolite, and elsewhere in southern Nevada. Just five years after its establishment, its population shot from a few dozen to 950 in 1910. By 1930, after the mining slump decimated the towns that fed it, the population of Las Vegas had grown to 5,100, making it the second largest town in Nevada.[49]

Las Vegas grew from the increasing commodification of the Wild West and the growing leisure economy that developed in the rest of the state. Early on, speculators recognized the value of vice. The original plan for the town in 1905 restricted the sale of alcohol to one district, and in doing so de facto designated a vice district. The plots in Block 16 (on North 1st between Ogden and Stewart) achieved the highest prices at auction. Five years later Block 16 had six hotels and 11 saloons. By 1911, Las Vegas had a known population of eight prostitutes whose address was "Block 16, occupation none, borders, unrelated," according to the census in 1910. During Prohibition, Las Vegas saloons were turned into boarding-houses (and kept selling booze anyway), and prostitution grew even more.[50]

Some of the most powerful men in the state had financial interests in the thriving sex trades. William J. Graham and James McKay, operators of the Bank Club, Reno's biggest casino in the 1920s and George Wingfield, former Goldfield mine owner and now a banking magnate, all had financial ties to the land that contained the cribs in the Reno Stockade. All three men came from the mining camps at Tonopah and Goldfield, and had a history with brothels. The Reno Stockade was a big money maker. One unidentified writer estimated that in the 1930s the restaurant alone brought in $214,000 a year.[51]

Federal–State Relations and the Politics of Vice

As the federal government began to play a larger role in the economy, it began to invest heavily in Nevada. From the beginning, while many an entrepreneur made a fortune in Nevada, economic life in the state was still at the behest of entities with large amounts of capital, from national mining companies to the national railroads. The placement of the railroads determined which mining camps would grow into towns and which would die out. Speculation allowed fortunes to be made quickly and fostered a free market spirit among local businessmen. But economic stability in the state did not come until the federal government began to play a much more active role in the economy during the Depression. From the huge reclamation projects of the 1920s, to the Hoover Dam—the single largest government project in the 1930s—to land grants for ranches, to the massive federal military spending in World War II, Nevada developed the infrastructure necessary to sustain larger populations. Nevada was a major benefactor of Roosevelt's New Deal building projects (starting in 1933). In all, the federal government pumped $19 million for the Hoover Dam, and another $4 million for infrastructure into southern Nevada from 1930 to 1939.[52] With this economic power, the federal government also tried to use its leverage to control what it considered to be the out-of-control morals in the state. Early on, however, just as Progressive-Era laws regulating vice and sexuality had little effect on the state other than to elevate the value of vice, the federal government's economic power only made the product Nevada was selling more valuable.

In 1929, the construction of the Hoover Dam brought thousands of workers to the Las Vegas area, who together had an average monthly payroll of $500,000, just as the Depression was hitting the rest of the country. The construction firms built a company town called Boulder City, close to the dam and some 30 miles away from Las Vegas. Just as the mining companies had done years earlier in northern Nevada, these firms severely restricted vice, outlawing gambling and prostitution within the city's borders, and so Las Vegas flourished as the provider of vice. The boarding halls and dance halls of Block 16, like the Double O, the Arcade, the Star, the Jazz Club, the Arizona Club, the Pastime, and the Honolulu Inn, served up booze, women, and gambling. The workers were not the only consumers. In 1932, 100,000 visitors came to see the dam; two years later, 300,000 came; and in 1935, 500,000 came.[53] Between 1936 and 1941, New Deal spending slowed, the dam was completed, and many dam workers left. But a growing tourist trade and southern California's interest in gambling, and the fact that reformers were cracking down on illegal gambling at about the same time, spurred a number of hotel and theater chain owners to buy property along what would later be known as the "Strip" on the Los Angeles highway just south of town. In 1941, the first of a new breed of luxury hotel/resorts, the El Rancho, opened just outside the Las Vegas city limits. The following year, the Last Frontier opened. These hotels carefully recast the theme that downtown Las Vegas had made work, the "Old West in Modern Splendor." The Last Frontier even installed the bar they had bought from the Arizona Club downtown. As interest in gambling grew, prostitution remained Las Vegas' number two tourist attraction.[54]

While gambling was officially legal, prostitution was not officially sanctioned in laws. It became increasingly contested in the growing urban areas. Local reformers in Las Vegas and Reno made several attempts over the years to close down or move the districts, but there was always a subtle resistance by the town boards and city councils, and apathy from the majority of the population. The most significant response always came when the federal government pressured them to control prostitution. In 1929, federal officials asked the city of Las Vegas to get rid of Block 16 so that they could build a post office downtown. Local property owners resisted. The local newspapers wrote not about the vice or morality of the activities on the Block, but about the morality of complying with the federal government's request if it were not legally binding.[55] The Block was not moved, and the post office was built anyway. In 1936, Fannie Ryan, the wife of a prominent state senator, led a charge to close Block 16. Her efforts ultimately failed and an article in the July 9, 1937 edition of the *Las Vegas Evening Review Journal* signaled the end of the attempts to close it down:

Figure 3.1 Open prostitution was a key component of Las Vegas' early tourist industry. Above are sex workers at Las Vegas' Arizona Club, Las Vegas, Nevada, 1931 [Nevada State Museum, Las Vegas (Winthrop Davis, photographer)]. Courtesy of UNLV Special Collections.

> Las Vegas's number 2 tourist attraction (gambling, of course, still ranking number one) blossomed forth in all of its semi nude glory again last night when the girls of the famous Block 16 deserted their places behind the thin board partitions and took up their customary nightly vigil in the doorways and windows of the North First street resorts.[56]

Throughout the 1930s, various containment ordinances were passed which had the effect of controlling independently working prostitutes. In 1932, an ordinance was passed in Las Vegas banning men and women from loitering on the streets. Other ordinances kept women out of bars and behind partitions, and in an important ordinance portending future brothel policies, Las Vegas mandated that prostitutes live on Block 16. The justification had to do with health tests and a desire to prevent women living elsewhere who had not been blood tested for venereal diseases from coming into the district.[57]

Racism also marked the city's relations with prostitution. Racial discrimination in Nevada caused several commentators in later years to call Nevada the "Mississippi of the West." In the 1910 census, four of the eight prostitutes listed were black and one was Hispanic. Meanwhile, the rest of the population in Las Vegas was 90 percent white.[58] In a *Las Vegas Evening Review Journal* news story on April 27, 1934, Frank McNamee was quoted saying, "we've rid the city of the colored bootleggers and now we are going to start in on you girls." The city began charging black prostitutes with vagrancy. The city also began to encourage separate facilities for whites and blacks, and soon after issued a liquor license to a property owner to establish a "colored annex."[59]

World War II and Prostitution Politics

Throughout the country, it was World War II that dealt the final blow to the open prostitution that remained in urban areas. Combined efforts of military officials, public health campaigns, and social purity campaigns during the years prior to the 1920s had successfully transformed the image of prostitution from a problem of social disorder to a sexual and moral problem with prostitutes themselves. As a result, prostitutes were seen as responsible for posing a physical and moral menace to young soldiers. During World War I, federal authorities successfully closed most red light districts near military bases across the country, and they remained closed thereafter.[60] However, most of the West continued to resist ideologies controlling vice, and prostitution persisted in the interwar years.

The U.S. entrance into World War II changed all this. The federal government again sought to control prostitution by invoking the fear of venereal disease. In July, 1941, the U.S. Congress passed the May Act prohibiting "prostitution within such reasonable distance of military and/or naval establishments . . . needful to the efficiency, health and welfare of the army and navy."[61] In addition, the federal government began a rather difficult attempt to impose national morals on local Nevadans who had profited greatly from providing those vices.

The federal government chose Nevada to house several military bases, most south of Reno, near Tonopah, and north of Las Vegas. Lieutenant General J. L. DeWitt of 9th Army's Western Defense Command made the broadest interpretation of the May Act when, three weeks after Pearl Harbor, he asked Western governors to close all local "vice resorts."[62] His letter said nothing about venereal disease, but talked about "a constant danger that these places may be employed as agencies of subversive and disloyal elements in our midst." The Washoe County district attorney immediately closed the Reno Stockade. Two smaller brothels outside the official district, the Cottage and Green Lantern, defied military orders until the federal security agency pressured city and county officials to padlock them. Elko commissioners tried to ignore the ban, but backed down quickly when Wendover Air Base just across the border in Wendover, Utah threatened to declare the city off-limits.[63]

According to historian Eric Moody, most brothels in the small towns went underground during World War II. Virginia City saloons kept civilian clothes in back rooms so that military personnel could slip out of uniform and go to the brothels on D Street, according to Gordon Lane, a Virginia City resident. Virginia City was by now down to 400 to 500 people, but it still had five brothels operating.[64] Beatty circulated a petition in favor of brothels, stating, "after all, there isn't much to do in Beatty, we haven't television, we don't have a radio station."[65] Winnemucca passed an ordinance prohibiting brothels anywhere in the city during the war, but "the line" of brothels operated anyway off and on, according to old-timers. Tonopah resisted, but eventually closed 12 of its 13 brothels, although many argue that they still had a healthy business servicing soldiers. Wells passed an emergency ordinance agreeing to "curtail the spread of venereal disease to members of the armed forces of the United States sojourning in said city or in the neighborhood."[66]

Las Vegas strongly resisted shutting down Block 16. Las Vegas Mayor Howell C. Garrison was quoted in the *Las Vegas Evening Review Journal* of October 11, 1941 saying, "Closing of Block 16 will bring about an undesirable situation in Las Vegas. Were it within my legal power to do so, I would not approve the closing order."[67] The *LV-Boulder City Journal* wrote that "the police ... were alarmed and unhappy about the closing [of Block 16]. They knew that streetwalkers would again become a problem, that venereal disease rates would probably go up, and that the city's families would be subject to attacks."[68] In June, 1942 the city finally passed an ordinance prohibiting prostitution in a one-mile radius around the city, ending legal support.

It is important to point out here that the May Act did not end prostitution; it temporarily ended overt government sanction of prostitution. Prostitution continued throughout the state. In Las Vegas and Reno, the police were much more consistent in their attempts to enforce the law. But in towns near military bases, the brothel districts continued to serve the new influx of soldiers, just as the saloons kept liquor flowing during Prohibition.

Gaming, Girls, and Sun: The Resort Industry and the Institutionalization of Legal Brothels, 1940 to 2000

The contemporary brothel industry established itself in the landscape of Nevada's tourist industry. By the 1940s, Nevada was poised to capitalize on the changing postwar moral landscape, and its leisure economy exploded into a bustling tourist industry. During the 1950s, Las Vegas rewrote its image from an Old West town to marketing "classy" leisure including chic images of scantily clad women. At the same time, the federal government continued to exert moral pressure on Nevada through two mechanisms. Several large Cold War military projects were proposed in the state under the proviso that prostitution be shut down. Second, federal hearings on gambling and organized crime threatened the growing resort industry. State and local officials and businesses had much to lose if the revenue sources from tourism and from military spending were lost. In the face of these two forces, there emerged a different ideology about gender that shunned working-class images of open sexuality.

Under federal pressure, the growing casino industries sacrificed open prostitution to make gaming look legitimate. The brothel industry developed in the rural towns in a way that wrested control away from independently working women. Rural/urban battles over class-based images of gaming and women resulted in the state almost inadvertently legalizing brothels in the late 1970s. The AIDS scare in the 1980s further institutionalized brothels as the state strengthened HIV testing laws and allowed brothels to successfully market themselves as safe havens from disease-rampant sex.

Sexual Liberation, Social Class, and Tourism

World War II was a huge economic boon to Nevada. Military bases brought soldiers to the area, eager to consume leisure activities just as the miners had done years before. The populations of Reno and especially Las Vegas skyrocketed. Las Vegas' population went up 200 percent, from 8,422 in 1940 to 24,624 in 1950. Tourism to the West exploded. Nevada drew five to seven million tourists in 1945; 20 million in 1950, and 50 million by 1960. Gross state gaming revenues broke just over $27 million in 1945, and by 1956 they hit $120 million.[69]

Nevada's small towns drew on Old West images to bolster the sagging mining economy and build an economic base out of tourism. Reno drew on the divorce and gambling trade and was initially the most well known of destination resorts in the state. In the one year period after World War II, Nevada granted 20,000 divorces, around the same number as the state of New York.[70] Nevada politicians scrambled to retain wartime federal investment, securing a number of Cold War military contracts. By around 1947, gaming passed mining as Nevada's number one industry.[71]

Las Vegas had already developed cachet in the nation's fascination with Hollywood's glamor and their sexually liberal lifestyles. In 1939, the Las Vegas Chamber of Commerce spent $500 to capitalize on Ria Langham's divorce from Clark Gable and drew a surprising amount of national attention as they advertised Nevada's liberal divorce and marriage laws along with gaming.[72] At the war's end, in a move few cities had tried, the Las Vegas Chamber of Commerce instituted a media campaign to market Las Vegas itself as a product to consume. Over the next few years, the Chamber and various advertising firms recast Las Vegas, de-emphasizing the Old West theme and instead emphasizing, as historian Eugene Moehring puts it, "a desert paradise—the ideal getaway for those embracing the new, permissive morality popularized during World War II."[73]

They appealed to the modern consumer in a marketing scheme that very explicitly linked glamor, sexuality, and the luxury-seeking tourist. They constructed a seductive, classy vision of women, and sex appeal became the selling hook for the new resorts. The Las Vegas Chamber of Commerce sent a steady stream of glossy prints of young women in swim-suits on Lake Mead, at golf courses, and by swimming pools to newspaper and magazine editors. Resorts had the Flamingo-ettes, Texas Coa Girls, and Desert Inn Beauties. In this view, it was not sex itself that was for sale, but sexuality linked to glamor and escape. Jeanie Malone, former Desert Inn Beauty, explained, "We were not there for that purpose. We were there to decorate the casino. And some of the girls were very good at the game–which was to get the guys to give you the chips without going to bed with them."[74] In 1945 Las Vegas spent $84,000 on publicity, more than any other U.S. city. As historian David Schwartz says, "By the late 1940s, Las Vegas was inexorably identified in the public mind as a landscape of sexual possibility." *Business Week* carried a headline in 1950 about Las Vegas: "Sin and Sun Pay Off. Reporting most rapid growth of wealth in a single community in the nation's history."[75]

In the postwar years, novels, magazines, and movies grabbed and ran with the image of Las Vegas, assisted by the Chamber of Commerce's propaganda machine. Las Vegas played into that same postwar image of masculinity that spawned the rise of the Playboy empire—the idea that any man, married or not, can have the girl or sexual adventure of his dreams.[76] In 1952, Frank Sinatra and Dean Martin bought shares in the Sands Hotel, and by 1960 the era of the Rat Pack was in full swing.[77] In the postwar years the federal government developed a military gunnery range 60 miles north of Las Vegas and in 1951 began testing nuclear bombs. The "secret" tests were themselves quickly marketed to boost tourism, even marrying images of sexy women and atomic bombs. The Las Vegas News Bureau prodded journalists to cover the tests by day and Las Vegas by night.[78]

However, these newer images of women transformed the city's approach to prostitution. The images of "classy" women showed upper-class, white, young women who did not openly sell sex. They sold possibility and sensuality, but not sex. It is a classic paradox that the use of images of women to sell sexuality meant the end of open prostitution in the urban tourist centers.

Ending Prostitution in Nevada's Urban Areas

While Reno's famous Stockade was shut down during World War II, a few brothels outside the district remained open. In 1948, Mae Cunningham, a madam who ran a brothel known as the Cottage on the outskirts of Reno before the war that managed to stay open, hired six maids, a cook, a housekeeper, and 11 prostitutes and set up the Willows on 900 E. Commercial Row. The Willows was actually in Reno, a few blocks closer to the train station than the old Stockade. The city attorney filed suit to shut down the Willows as a public nuisance, the only legal recourse, since state law did not forbid brothels. On March 7, 1949 the Nevada Supreme Court ruled that brothels were a public nuisance, citing the 1861 adoption by the Nevada Territory of English common law. After this ruling, Clark and Washoe county commissioners enacted ordinances that made prostitution explicitly illegal. The Cunningham decision was the key case in defining the legal status of Nevada brothels for the next 20 years, and it was used against a number of brothels in the urban areas. Brothels no longer enjoyed full official support as they had in the past.[79]

In the south of the state, the newly rising casino interests in Las Vegas felt that the fresh "classy" vision did not mesh with legal prostitution as embodied in Block 16. In 1946, after wartime restrictions against prostitution were lifted, the Las Vegas Chamber of Commerce assembled gaming owners together with medical and school officials to discuss the future of the block.

William J. Moore, executive director of Last Frontier Hotel, reported the conclusions of the group to the local newspaper: the city should close Block 16 and not designate another district because of its effect on tourism.[80] Max Kelch, president of the Chamber of Commerce, said, "If prostitution were allowed to return, it would nullify all the good advertising and publicity work the J. Walter Thompson company had done for this area."[81] Powerful Mormon and Catholic leaders also joined the call, citing not morals, but the image of the town as it might affect tourists. The paper reported that prominent Mormon and head of the local Boy Scouts Bryan Bunker said that prostitution only gave Las Vegas a "black eye" at just the time when promoters were spending thousands of dollars to project a positive image to tourists.[82]

The local newspaper, which had been supportive of legalized prostitution, now came out against prostitution, stating both health and economic reasons. This view was not without opposition. A few days later, the Las Vegas Junior Chamber of Commerce voted by a narrow margin to support legalized prostitution. They argued that it could, as it had in the past, draw tourists.[83] In the end, those against prostitution won. Las Vegas followed Reno's lead and officially disavowed legalized prostitution for good. Las Vegas' few brothels moved to the outskirts of town on the highway to Boulder Dam. Las Vegas closed its last openly operating brothel in the mid-1950s.

However, the closing of open brothel districts in the major cities did not end prostitution in the state. Rather, World War II and the growth of tourism just changed its form—further confining prostitution to organized businesses restricted to certain areas, and eliminating opportunities for women to work independently.

The Mob

Another force contributed to the end of open prostitution in the urban areas: the growing role played by organized crime in the city. Las Vegas', and to a lesser extent Reno's, reputation as a resort destination for transgressive yet classy entertainment was both fed and tainted by the image of organized crime in Las Vegas. Again, conflicts with the federal government fed the rebellious nature of the state. Prostitution in the second half of the twentieth century would now be seen in a different light.

Since the state legalized gambling and changed fiscal laws to benefit the rich in 1931, Nevada primed itself, knowingly or not, to benefit from the rise of crime figures who had organized during

Prohibition. After Prohibition ended, and as other states cracked down on gambling, casino owners, bootleggers, and gambling hall owners came to Las Vegas in force. At the Depression's end, when banks were loath to gamble on risky propositions, when the Syndicate was looking for legitimate outlets for a rising drug trade and vice money, when average operators were looking for a more welcoming place to gamble, and Nevada was looking for gambling investors, Nevada became the promised land for organized crime. Money from shady sources came to town in droves. When that money was combined with loans from Mormon banks, the founding casinos of Las Vegas and Reno took off, fueling a half century of boom for the state.

Thus during the 1950s, when Congress appointed the Special Committee to Investigate Organized Crime in Interstate Commerce, better known as the Kefauver Commission, gaming interests thought the end was in sight. Although the focus was on organized crime, the Commission concentrated on what it felt was the heart of organized crime—gambling. The Commission conducted investigations from May 1950 to 1951. While the Commission was probably best known for elevating the Mafia to mythical status, it successfully shut down most gambling operations throughout the rest of the country. These efforts further drove gambling businesses to Nevada.

The Commission saw an opportunity in Nevada's open vice, and in November, 1950 the Commission-made a much publicized visit to the outcast state. Unfortunately, their high profile, nine-hour investigation into Las Vegas did more to bolster Las Vegas' rebel image than it did to uncover crime. But it did make Nevada officials paranoid and eager to rid themselves of any image of vice that might be detrimental to that of a resort destination. In 1955 the state established a gaming control board, and published the infamous "Black Book" listing 11 individuals with Sicilian-sounding names who were prohibited from entering Nevada brothels.[84]

Over the next two decades, the resort cities and the casino industry further distanced themselves institutionally from prostitution. Throughout the 1960s, Nevada again fought for legitimacy. The Federal Bureau of Investigation, the Internal Revenue Service, the Bureau of Narcotics, the INS Alcohol and Tobacco Tax Unit, and the Department of Labor intensely scrutinized the state's gambling industry. Meanwhile, Nevada's prime competitor, Cuba, shut down all gambling in

1961, so the state became the major player as a world tourist destination for gambling.[85] This made the stakes for the continued existence of a gaming industry much higher for tourist and leisure business owners, and for the state itself.

Whether it was the federal government's continued military investment in the state, or the threats to interfere with gambling, economic interests in the state certainly felt a pressure to both clean up the image of gambling even while marketing its transgressions. The effect of all this was the scapegoating of legal prostitution. State officials, urban politicians, and casino owners saw prostitution as an obstacle to the mainstreaming of gambling, as well as a blight on the classy tourist resort image.

The Urban/Rural Divide

There was no move to eliminate prostitution in the rural areas. The casino businesses were not directly threatened by prostitution further away from cities. After the Cunningham decision, Dr. R. H. Caples, the state health officer, sent a letter to all 17 county district attorneys asking them to close the remaining brothels as public nuisances. However, most rural DAs and county commissioners interpreted the decision as giving them "local option" and ignored the order. So strong was support for the brothels in some areas that ten days after the nuisance ruling in 1949, State Senator Aaron V. Tallman of Winnemucca authored a bill to grant local option to counties and cities to license brothels. The legislature quickly passed the bill by a strong majority in both houses. Las Vegas Air Force Base protested, arguing that such a bill would still be in violation of the May Act. Governor Vail Pittman vetoed it, saying that this support of brothels "can only be regarded as a condonation of a condition that has been repugnant throughout successive generations." In response, over the next several years, most counties passed ordinances legally stipulating that brothels were not nuisances to avoid the nuisance charges.[86]

This is not to say that the rural areas were untouched by concerns about prostitution. Indeed, established brothels had to devote increasing resources to staying in the good graces of city officials. Winnemucca passed ordinances outlawing brothels everywhere except the Line. After a shooting, Tonopah closed its red light district near the main streets in 1951, and its one remaining brothel moved to the outskirts of town. Many towns followed suit, either confining brothels to the red light districts that had evolved over the years, or forcing them to the outskirts of town.[87] This meant that the capital needed to operate prostitution businesses increased yet again. The historical evidence seems to indicate that up until the 1970s, most of Nevada's brothels were owned and/or operated by women. The more institutionalized brothels became, the fewer women were in charge.

Throughout the 1950s and 1960s, the rural counties cared little about the federal government's perception of the state as vice ridden, since brothels occupied a relatively larger proportion of their economy. Prostitution in the rural areas was still so firmly entrenched that in 1951 Clark County District Attorney Roger Foley told a *Time* magazine reporter that "he was helpless to combat organized vice unless citizens were willing to make complaints and county law-enforcement officers would direct the complaints to him."[88]

Nine years later, in 1960, Nevada Attorney General Roger Foley demanded that all 17 of Nevada's district attorneys give him a report on the status of prostitution in their counties. No one obeyed. According to a newspaper, one told Foley to "act more like an attorney and less like a general." The Nevada District Attorney's Association passed a resolution telling Foley he had overstepped his authority. Rural district attorneys continued to take the official position that they had to have a complaint before closing a brothel.[89]

In Winnemucca, a Baptist minister put enough pressure on Humboldt County District Attorney James Callahan that Callahan went to the County Commission for permission to close the Line, a street of five brothels just below Main Street. The Commission refused. Callahan arrested all five brothel madams for running businesses "for the purposes of lewdness, assignation and prostitution." A jury of 11 men and one woman took 11 minutes to judge the first brothel madam, Irene Roy, not guilty. The city dismissed charges against the rest. "Hell, everybody was hoping they would find them not guilty," former Winnemucca mayor Felix Scott told reporter Doug McMillan. Following his failed attempt to get the rural areas in line, Foley gave up his campaign. The Baptist minister who initiated the whole sting lost his day job at a local lumber yard.[90]

McMillan reported similar stories in Elko. In response to

complaints in 1964 from an Elko Baptist minister, the Reverend Arthur Blessitt, Police Chief Dan Taelour responded publicly with a statement saying he thought prostitution might exist in town, but, "I can't verify it." District Attorney Joseph McDaniel said in the *Nevada State Journal*:

> I won't say whether there is or isn't prostitution in Elko. I'm sure that if there is, there's no one in Elko is going to be surprised. Our position is the less said the better, and when the point comes when the majority of people don't want it, I'm sure it will be eliminated.[91]

The Conforte Lightening Rod

Several of these conflicting trends are best illustrated in the story of Joe Conforte, probably the best known of Nevada brothel owners.

> To the old-line Nevadans who resent federal intervention in any form, to these western sons and daughters who have elevated their frontier independence to a religion, Conforte is a combination Robin Hood and Godfather IV.[92]

Joe Conforte first came to rural Nevada in a wave with other bootleggers, gamblers, ex-cons, and organized and independent crime figures, after being run out of Los Angeles in 1955 for arranging sexual services out of his taxi cab. Conforte convinced Sally Burgess, the proprietor of Sally's near Fallon Naval Air Station, to help run Triangle River Ranch in a trailer on the border of Washoe and Storey County. A few years later they got married. Over the next 20 years, Conforte opened brothels throughout the state, including in Beatty and Montgomery Pass between Tonopah and the California border.[93]

The desire to legitimize Nevada gaming to the federal government, along with Conforte's Sicilian heritage and heavy-handed style, drew the attention of local law enforcement. From 1958 until 1981, Conforte was subject to a string of arrests throughout the counties in which he operated. As with other brothels throughout the state, whatever charges law enforcement came up with were either dropped or reduced to small fines in court. The most-told stories are his battles with Bill Raggio, the district attorney in Washoe County between 1958 and 1970. Joe Conforte and Sally Burgess located their Triangle Ranch brothel in a mobile trailer at the border of Storey, Washoe, and Lyon counties, allowing them to move the trailer into whichever county was more hospitable. Raggio was able to get Conforte sent to prison in 1959 for trying to extort him and for income tax evasion. In March, 1960, acting on a court order that declared the Triangle Ranch a public nuisance, Raggio set fire to Conforte's Triangle Ranch.[94]

When Joe got out of prison in 1966 he bought the Mustang Bridge Ranch in Storey County. The Mustang made Conforte famous. He upgraded the brothel from a trailer to a gated group of trailers. There were 40 to 50 prostitutes on duty at each shift, and it serviced 200,000 customers a year.[95] Conforte launched a public relations campaign of sorts, donating money to churches, Boy Scouts, and charities. He gave away hundreds of turkeys during the holidays and supported anti-drug campaigns. He also made contributions to the campaigns of local officials and, to help win voters, he built Lockwood, a low-rent trailer park near the Mustang Ranch. The trailer park provided a nice cadre of voters when election time came. In 1971 Conforte claimed, "I'm accepted here now just like any other businessman. I even get invitations to make speeches at the Lions and the Kiwanis."[96]

Legalization

The year Conforte bought the Mustang, Carson District Court Judge Richard Waters ordered Conforte to close the brothel as a public nuisance and to repay Storey County a total of $5,000 in five monthly installments of $1,000 to offset the costs of patrolling the River District to make sure houses stayed closed. Conforte paid the total fine but continued to pay the monthly cost of patrolling, and kept the brothel open. Three years later, Storey County District Attorney Robert Berry finally advised Storey commissioners that they needed an ordinance to make the $1,000 a month coming in legal. On December 5, 1970, two lame duck Storey County commissioners, Lowell "Buzz" Goodman and Martin Rosso, voted against the commission chair and passed by two to one an emergency ordinance legalizing prostitution within a 500-foot radius of the old Mustang Bridge, some 40 miles east of Reno on Interstate 80. This was the first brothel-licensing ordinance in the nation. In January, Sally Burgess arrived at the Storey County Courthouse in Virginia City with $3,000 cash for the Mustang Ranch's first quarterly license payment.[97]

Conforte began helping other brothel owners to lobby county commissions to legalize their brothels. The main reason they were successful was financial. By transforming loosely codified "fees" into legal licensing charges, the monies they collected from brothels became more stable and legal. The $18,000 legal yearly licensing fee Conforte paid in 1971 accounted for one-fifth of the county budget, paying the salary of the sheriff and a few part-time employees.[98]

In Las Vegas, the Clark County District Attorney and the County Commission began to consider legalizing a brothel outside Las Vegas. Supporters argued that it would reduce the number of streetwalkers who were becoming more visible on the Strip. Gaming and convention leaders in Las Vegas organized against it, reportedly arguing that legalized prostitution could hurt their family appeal. Las Vegas Convention Authority Chair Wes Howery said, "One thing we are fighting in booking conventions is the image of Las Vegas. If we legalize it, it would really hurt us."[99] Responding to a fear that local Las Vegas leaders might cave in and allow brothels again in the city, the increasingly powerful gaming interests lobbied state representatives early in 1971 to prepare a statewide law to ban brothels.

The gaming industry in Nevada was in the midst of another major transformation. The state passed a law allowing public corporations to own and operate casinos. The Howard Hughes Corporation was buying casinos from the mob in Las Vegas at a dizzying pace. Newspaper articles in the *Las Vegas Review Journal* in 1970 and 1971 reported a growing convention industry. The growing marketing machine was trying to craft an image of Las Vegas that comforted tourists and made gambling look mainstream. On the one hand, as one state senator said, "Casino owners want prostitution around but want to control it themselves in their own hotel rooms." But making gambling mainstream was also about fighting the old image of a mob-owned Las Vegas. Gaming and other interests charged that it was the mob-connected Joe Conforte who was behind the brothel proposal and had actually likely bribed the County Commission. As now Nevada Senate majority leader Bill Raggio (Conforte's old nemesis) said, "We were anxious to take care of Clark County and a problem we had with a local racketeer, Joe Conforte."[100]

Rural legislators fought the brothel ban. One of the more powerful members of the State Assembly represented Lyon and Storey counties outside of Reno, which had some of the largest brothels in the state and whose county coffers benefited the most from legal fees. The urban legislators did not yet control the legislature. Thus, a compromise bill was passed easily in the Senate banning brothels only in counties with populations over 200,000, at that time excluding only Clark County, home of Las Vegas. In the Assembly, rural legislators tried to kill the bill entirely by referring it to the agriculture committee. But on February 25, 1971, the bill passed the Assembly and was signed into law. For the first time since 1923 the state legislature had addressed the legality of brothels. Nevada Governor Mike O'Callaghan simply told *New York Times* reporters, "the less said the better."[101]

The statute never directly empowers counties or incorporated cities to license brothels. Deciding this, in fact, was highly contentious. It was not until 1980 that the Nevada Supreme Court ruled that a county with a population of less than 400,000 could actually regulate and license brothels, effectively establishing a pattern of "local control" in brothel regulation.[102]

In their book on the passage of the 1971 statute, *Morals Legislation without Morals*, Galliher and Cross state that economics was the main motivation behind the bill. They argue that Clark County's opposition to brothels was not a moral one. Rather, the opposition came from what was seen as an economic need to maintain an image amenable to tourism. Further, they argue that the opposition to brothels was about building Las Vegas convention business and maintaining a "family" image. From our research, we have found that cleaning up Las Vegas' image was also about social class as much as it was about gender—that is, maintaining a middle-class image of sexual liberation. Classy-looking sexualized female bodies are helpful to Nevada's tourism, while blatantly selling sex, as Galliher and Cross argue, is not.[103]

The rural counties' support of brothels was also about economics. Prostitution provided a large revenue for rural counties. Galliher and Cross quote a Las Vegas circuit judge who said, "In one sparsely populated county, the red-light house is the biggest employer; in another it is the second biggest employer."[104] But it was also about the working-class basis of support in the rural areas.

The 1971 prostitution law spurred several counties to pass licensing ordinances. Many counties held elections, and supporters of brothels won more often than not. In 1970, Churchill County had made brothels illegal, but in 1974, conflicts between the Fallon Naval Air Station and local residents sparked a re-vote. County Health Officer Dr. Darious F. Caffaratti alerted residents to a rising venereal disease rate, and suggested to county commissioners that legalizing prostitution was a good way to keep Fallon Naval Air Station's sailors away from local girls. Fallon Naval Air Station Commander Captain W. B. Mucie denied his men were promiscuous. Local resident Dorothy Beale Cann collected 1,000 signatures to put the matter to a vote. Several church groups failed to hold the vote up in court, and the legalization referendum was passed 2,367 to 1,795.[105]

A few counties were less inclined to codify their practices until much later. In 1974, Bill McDonald, City Attorney of Winnemucca, justified their reluctance to pass licensing ordinances.

> The county's been here since 1861, and the town—the houses—came along eight to ten years later. The feeling is that they've always been here so why close them . . . There's been talk about licensing the houses as a revenue measure, but what we pick up in taxes we'd probably lose in charitable contributions. They're steady supporters of the Boy Scouts and the church raffles.[106]

In 1975, Lincoln County opened its own pandora's box. Lincoln County was the next closest county to Las Vegas on the other side from Nye County. Officials encouraged a county-wide referendum that they hoped would close the two brothels, Judy's and Sheri's Ranch, then operating near the Clark County line 80 miles from Las Vegas. The vote was 675 to 671; the brothels won by a narrow margin. Recognizing the potential windfall, three more brothels tried to move to town. Kitten Creek Ranch burned to the ground as soon as it opened. Rumor had it that the other brothel owners did it. Three years later, the body of the former owner of Judy's was found in a gravel pit with a bullet in her head. At around the same time, a cab driver was murdered. In the scandal and melée that followed, the Lincoln County District Attorney pushed another referendum to a vote, which this time came down against brothels 823 to 467. The remaining brothel owners collected signatures for a third ballot initiative in 1982, but it failed three to one. Businesses in Caliente and Alamo lamented the loss of the brothel industry in their towns.[107]

Beverly Harrell, the madam who ran for State Assembly in 1973, had been operating the Cottontail Ranch at Lida Junction in Esmeralda County on federal Bureau of Land Management (BLM) land. In 1967, she received special approval from the BLM and the County Commission under the Small Tract Act of 1938 to continue operations. In 1971, nationally syndicated columnist Jack Anderson broke the news to the nation that the BLM and Secretary of the Interior Roger Morton was a brothel landlord. Morton immediately took action to evict, arguing under the Cunningham case that the brothel was a public nuisance. For two years, Harrell responded that there was no one to offend in Lida Junction, since her brothel housed the only residents. On November 17, 1973, District Judge Roger Foley Sr. denied her claim, saying, "just because prostitution has been declared illegal in Washoe and Clark does not make it legal in other counties."

Harrell fought back. In June, 1974, she moved her mobile trailers 2,000 feet on to private land. Then she announced her candidacy for the Nevada State Assembly. Her platform promised to fight for government funds for a mill where small-time miners in the area could process their ore profitably. She promised an education campaign against venereal disease. She promised to fight to open large tracts of BLM land in Nevada to other agencies, a very popular plank. She won the primary easily, but she lost the general election to a veteran politician, Don Moody, former Mineral County Commissioner, by 122 votes.[108]

The Nation's Eye on Legalized Prostitution

Nationally, Nevada's image teetered between that of a state to be envied for its open vice and that of a state to be reviled for its corruption. The passage of the 1971 state law linking county population and legal brothels opened a media feeding frenzy. Joe Conforte was thrust into the national limelight. The *New York Post*, the *New York Times, Rolling Stone, Look* magazine, *Newsweek*, and *Time* all followed the sex wars in Nevada. In *Look* magazine, Gerald Astor reported:

Indeed, Nevada seems to enjoy an abundance of harlots, with girls, unbothered by cops, cruising big hotels, and houses–legal, tolerated and unlawful–operating full blast. Currently, Conforte and his associates hope to open up Las Vegas, which still seems to prefer bar hustlers and call girls to legitimized prostitution.[109]

The nation was bemused by the shady characters who were accepted in Nevada. Over the next several years, articles pointed out that Joe Conforte was considered an accepted businessman. Magazine writers highlighted brothel owner Beverly Harrell's run for State Assembly. In October, 1979, Nye County Sheriff Joni Wines, who was embroiled in controversies surrounding a brothel arson, posed for a photo for *Us* magazine holding a World War II Thompson submachine-gun in her hands with the headline, "A machine-gun toting grandma tames her wild west town." The following week, *New West* magazine had a full-page cover photo of Joni Wines and two deputies, characterizing Nye County as a place "where many of the men come when they feel burned out by Las Vegas and many of the women come in the company of a pimp." A short five months later, on Febuary 5, 1980, Wines was recalled.[110]

Not long after Storey County legalized Conforte's brothels, Irene York, madam of a Lovelock brothel, La Belle, tried to move it closer to Reno at a site two miles closer to town than the Mustang. The license was denied. "I was afraid if we allowed another brothel operation, there might be some kind of argument and someone might get killed," former Storey County Commissioner Clint Salmon said later. York went to court claiming Storey commissioners were supporting a monopoly. Carson District Judge Frank Gregory ruled that commissioners had the right to do so. In 1973, the State Supreme Court agreed, saying a brothel license, like a gaming license, is a privilege, not a right.[111]

While the media loved to play up the Wild West image, there was, on occasion, actual violence in brothel politics. Lincoln County lost its brothels due partly to violence stemming from inter-brothel competition. Burning down brothels, whether it was by the local district attorney or other brothel owners, must have at times seemed more effective than using legal means. Clearly, though, the battles seemed more intense the closer they were to large cities.

One of the more infamous brothel-burning cases was made famous by Jeanne Kasindorf in her book, *The Nye County Brothel Wars* (1985). The book tells of how Walter Plankinton opened six trailers as the Chicken Ranch in Nye County in 1976 for $60,000.[112]

According to Plankinton, when he went to Nye County District Attorney Peter Knight to introduce himself, Knight told him that running the brothel would cost $75,000 and five percent of his take. When Plankinton refused, officials did everything they could to shut his brothel down. On June 10, 1978, after a court ruling in his favor, his brothel burned to the ground after county firefighters failed to arrive on the scene. Two years later, in December, 1980, the owner of the Shamrock brothel in nearby Lathrop Wells, Bill Martin, was convicted of arson, but no one could confirm what most suspected, that Nye County officials gave the orders.

Before the fire, and as part of the effort to shut down the new brothel, in Spring 1977, Nye County Commissioners declared the Chicken Ranch a public nuisance. They did so in spite of being able to collect only 30 signatures from the public in a county of 1,000 residents, and in spite of already having three brothels in the county, Fran's Star Ranch in Beatty, Bobby's Buckeye in Tonopah, and the Shamrock in Lathrop Wells. Plankinton filed suit.[113] In 1978 the State Supreme Court said that by implication, the law that made brothels illegal in Clark County repealed the common law rule on public nuisance. Counties officially now had local option. District Judge Stanley Smart from Fallon accused the state of confusing the issue by refusing to legislate brothels one way or the other. Too much authority rested in local governments.

> The particularly unfortunate part is that people come to feel– and I am not implying that there is any truth to this anywhere– that those who are in a position of authority, whether it is the county commissioners or the District Attorney, are making their decisions as to who should operate and who should not operate for improper reasons, including allegations of receiving payoffs and everything that goes with that. This is an unhealthy situation and it is one that should not be allowed to continue in this state. And I would certainly hope that the legislature would do something about it. I agree with the argument that the 1971 state law did, by implication, repeal the common law. On that basis, it is the order of this court that a permanent injunction be entered, perpetually enjoining the defendant, Nye County, for seeking to abate the operation of the plaintiff, Walter Plankinton, of a house of prostitution.[114]

Bill Raggio later lamented that if legislators had known they were making brothels more legal, they would never have passed the Clark County law.[115]

Even the right of counties to vote on the brothel issue had to be adjudicated in court. Judy Kuban and Lorraine Helms, the two madams who lost brothels when the Lincoln County referendum was passed, argued that the Plankinton decision meant that Lincoln County could not deny brothel licenses. In 1980 the State Supreme Court said the voters did have a right to prevent brothels from being legalized in their county. This also gave counties the right to regulate brothels in whatever manner they deemed suitable.[116]

Unlike Lincoln County, the media attention and arson convictions failed to convince Nye County voters that they should ban their brothels. In 1980, Nye County voted 2,300 to 1,200 in favor of brothels in an advisory ballot question, "Do you favor legalized prostitution in Nye County?"[117]

A short six years later, Walter Plankinton sold the Chicken Ranch he had bought for $60,000 for $750,000 to Western Best, a partnership of Kenneth R. Green, an ex-pharmacist and Marin County real estate broker, and Russ Reade, a former schoolteacher.

In the following years both Conforte and local brothel owners individually lobbied county commissioners to get brothel-licensing ordinances in 11 of 17 counties. Each county created its own unique ordinances which essentially legislated its existing practices.

Meanwhile, throughout the 1970s, Conforte continued to be investigated by Washoe and Storey County grand juries.[118] By the 1980s, Conforte's surveyors included the Federal Bureau of Investigation. In 1981, he fled to Brazil to escape charges of income tax evasion. While Conforte was in Brazil, Raggio pushed a state bill to shut down the Mustang Ranch. It barely passed the Senate Judiciary 4 to 3, but was defeated in the Senate 11 to 9. In December, 1983, Conforte came back to town to testify against Judge Harry Claiborne on bribery charges. He had cut a deal to have his tax evasion charges reduced and other charges dropped in exchange for testimony on the case. These charges against Claiborne were later dropped, but Conforte was able to stay (Claiborne was later convicted and served time in an Alabama prison). The following year Conforte was arrested in Reno for buying a 17-year-old a drink. Tiring of the battles, that year Conforte tapped George

Flint to form the Nevada Brothel Association so that the brothels could lobby for favorable brothel laws and to add an air of legitimacy to the business. Conforte's days of openly operating the Mustang were over.[119] At one point in the 1980s, the U.S. government actually took control of Mustang. Conforte fled the country to avoid arrest for tax evasion and is believed to be living in South America. After years of battle, in 1998 the FBI successfully implicated Mustang ownership in income tax violations, and in 1999 the Mustang Ranch finally closed its doors for good.

The Nevada Brothel Association, AIDS and Brothel Entrenchment

The nationwide panic around AIDS actually helped institutionalize the brothel industry in Nevada. By the mid-1980s, the battles around brothels were in a delicate balance—the urban gaming industry opposing brothels, and the rural politicians supporting it. The population of Las Vegas again nearly doubled between 1970 and 1980, from 273,000 to 460,000.[120] Between 1978 and 1985, Las Vegas and Reno legislators introduced various forms of bills to ban brothels, but these never gained enough support to get out of committees. As a Fallon assemblyman said of a 1985 bill introduced by a Clark County legislator, "The publicity would have gone nationwide again, focusing on a problem I don't think exists. The rural legislators feel that prostitution is not a problem in our areas."[121]

During the summer of 1985 Nevada felt the impact of the growing AIDS epidemic. After the death of celebrity Rock Hudson, brothel owners believed that patrons were increasingly confused about the safety of prostitution. Sagebrush Ranch brothel owner Jim Fondran said on October 2, 1985, the day Rock Hudson died of AIDS,

> Business dropped off in all brothels … In general, people didn't know whether it was safe or unsafe to go to legal houses. With all the publicity that prostitutes can spread AIDS, people assumed that included legal prostitutes in Nevada. They were lumping us with illegal street prostitutes who are intravenous drug users.[122]

The first policy action came from the Nevada State Health Division (NSHD), which in spite of the fact that the national Center for Disease

Control (CDC) had not determined prostitutes to be "high risk," recommended testing for legal prostitutes. The *Las Vegas Review Journal* reported that one NSHD member was convinced that HIV and AIDS would shift its initial trajectory from at-risk populations such as gay men, IV drug users, and hemophiliacs to the heterosexual male population through prostitution. With state-sanctioned legalized prostitution, it was their duty to take action immediately.[123]

In March, 1986, in spite of still inconclusive evidence linking prostitutes to the spread of HIV/AIDS, the State Board of Health passed regulation, through the Nevada Administrative Code, which required mandatory pre-hire and subsequent monthly HIV testing as a condition for employment and obtaining a county work card. HIV-positive women could not get a sheriff-issued work card for the brothels.[124]

By the fall of 1986, pressure began to mount in three areas. First, opponents to the brothels became more vocal, arguing that the testing policy was ineffective and full of avenues for evasion since there was no monitoring, there were different rules in different counties, and the state had no consistent means of enforcement. A group calling themselves the Committee to Abolish Brothels had formed to elect legislators who were anti-brothel. Opponents drafted legislation to close the brothels. Even a long-time supporter of the brothels, Assembly leader Joe Dini (D-Yerington), told the newspaper prior to the start of the session, "This AIDS thing has gotten a lot of people worried." They anticipated a battle in the coming session.[125]

Second, the brothel owners got together for the first time in the spring of 1985 and decided to form the Nevada Brothel Association (NBA). Conforte himself, recognizing that his style of ownership may be a thing of the past, asked respected and established wedding chapel lobbyist George Flint to help form the Nevada Brothel Association. By 1986, 22 owners had joined, and they had registered a lobbyist, Flint, to begin work during the upcoming 1987 legislative session.[126]

Third, San Francisco was in the midst of a divisive battle over closing its bathhouses. State officials, watching the growing national news coverage, feared similar battles over Nevada's brothels, and the effect on Nevada's tourist industry if the brothels made similar national headlines.

In the fall of 1986, a new state health administrator, Larry Matheis, made a case to the governor for tightening regulations rather than shutting down the brothels. He recalled,

> My argument internally with the governor, the attorney general and others was that we were being irresponsible not to take a look at whether or not there should be a public health oversight of what was going on. At a practical level and political level, if a tourist or a group of tourists visited a legal brothel in Nevada, contracted HIV, went back to another state or went to another country, then reported that they got HIV in a legal brothel in Nevada, it seemed to me that we as a state were partially responsible.[127]

Governor Richard Bryan was not enthusiastic about opening "a can of worms." Matheis recalled later that he had to walk a fine line between those who wanted to see the industry gone and those who wanted to keep brothels. There is little evidence that Matheis was a strong supporter of brothels. But as a state bureaucrat he was motivated by a desire to protect the liability of the state, not eliminate (or save) an industry. Said Matheis,

> What I was trying to do was exclusively address the public health issue and what the state's responsibility was to public health. I was not engaging in a religious debate. I was not in the business of judging morality. I was not in the business of determining if it should be legal in the state. Neither was I in the business of endorsing behaviors that people chose to engage in. It wasn't my role to do any of those things, but it was my role to find a way to get the best possible public health solution.

On the one hand, Matheis said, "We were not going to be able at any time to be a 100 percent confident of 100 percent coverage." Thus there was a policy case to be made for shutting down the brothels. On the other hand, "Once we accept that Nevada's allowed it legally to be engaged in large parts of the state, we can't bring certain safety, but we can certainly bring safety within some predictable level." Matheis also began to work very closely with the Nevada Brothel Association.

> They were a hard sell, in the end they became very strong supporters of what we had done. They were the most skeptical.

> In the end they saw that this could actually save the industry, probably from the one thing that scared them the most. I think they've always thought that they could beat moral arguments, but they couldn't beat a public health argument.

Matheis convinced brothel owners to enact a voluntary condom policy. While a few owners joined in, others were reluctant. A few owners realized that condom use was a wise business move to reassure the public, but they could not enforce universal adoption of a condom policy. In January, 1987, appearing with the Nevada Brothel Association, Matheis introduced a policy requiring mandatory condoms to the State Board of Health. Several months later, this became part of the state administrative code as well. Several owners agreed to cooperate voluntarily with the state law requiring condoms before it went into effect on January 1, 1988.[128]

In later interviews, public health policymakers admitted that they chose to address brothels before other risky behaviors and that they chose to institute testing of prostitutes before other HIV prevention policies. Larry Matheis argued that the state had to have an immediate visible response even if it was largely ineffective in stemming the spread of HIV/AIDS. Policymakers perceived the need to act to preclude public fears from draining valuable state time, resources, and personnel from other aspects of the epidemic. Said Matheis,

> Dealing with HIV/AIDS, we had to take off the table something that was not a big part of the issue. Brothels were not a major source of risk to the public, but it was the kind of issue that could get in the way of dealing with it ... Especially when people are afraid, when they are uncertain, they try to find a way to re-characterize the subject into something they are comfortable with.[129]

Matheis repeatedly noted the symbolic nature of the AIDS testing policy, pointing out that while brothels were probably not the source of transmission of AIDS to heterosexuals this response fit the public's historical perception of disease-spreading prostitutes. By playing on the public's perception, the state lowers both its fiscal and political accountability. Said Matheis:

If we hadn't responded, I think we would have had this huge public campaign issue about legal brothels in Nevada and their tremendous risk to the public as a diversion from addressing the issues of HIV and AIDS.

In essence these policies shielded the brothel industry from attack during the AIDS panic, and effectively protected the state's tourism industry. The testing policy was, by all accounts, ineffectual and, at first, merely symbolic. Subsequent policy changes, including the condom policy, made the approach to preventing the spread of AIDS more effective. Since then, no employed prostitute has tested positive for HIV or AIDS. The condom policy was actually made with the assistance of the brothel industry. While the policy was against their short-term interests by potentially driving customers away, it was in the long-term interests of the industry. This cooperation signaled a significant shift in the attitudes of brothel owners, their relationship with government, their own organization, and their political power as a group.

Solidifying Brothel Legitimacy

The AIDS crisis legitimated the legal brothel industry in Nevada in a number of ways. First, it forced the brothel industry to become more politically astute, utilizing their professional association and putting on a more legitimate, businesslike face. Second, it bureaucratized and rationalized oversight of the brothels in a way that quelled public fears about the spread of disease. Owners began to change the image of the "pimp" from that of an unscrupulous brothel owner to one of a modern businessman. From World War II until the 1980s, the brothels had mostly been run by former madams or men well schooled in running vice and illegal prostitution. Brothel opponents would often bring up information about murders, bribes, bomb threats, burglaries, and holdups—all emanating from "criminal elements" in the brothels.[130] Conforte, former owner of the Mustang Ranch, in many ways epitomized the old school, whose informal methods of lobbying earned him labels of "mob connected" and "racketeer."

By the mid-1980s, more mainstream businessmen with experience in construction or real estate were beginning to buy brothels as investments, creating partnerships. Nevada Brothel Association lobbyist Flint was easily able to convince the newer owners of the largest brothels that they needed lobbying power. The spokesperson and president elect of the NBA, Russ Reade, was the relatively new co-owner of the Chicken Ranch outside Las Vegas. The fact that Reade was a former school-teacher added a more legitimate face to the industry.

Further, Reade himself took a proactive stance toward the AIDS crisis. In February, 1986, he became the first brothel owner to require condoms in his own brothel, and he convinced several of the other owners of large brothels to follow suit. His public face, and these "good faith" efforts on the part of some business owners, helped take the wind out of opponents' sails in the crucial 1987 legislative session.

Reade allowed the Center for Disease Control to test women working in his brothel as part of a study beginning in 1986 on sero-prevalence and risk factors for HIV in prostitutes.[131] In July, 1987, just in time for the conclusion of the 1987 legislative session, these results were released. Reade also persuaded brothel owners to help fund a UCLA study of sexually transmitted diseases (STDs) to be conducted at the Chicken Ranch, examining records of STD test results starting in 1982. In August, 1990, Reade appeared with Dr. Gary Richwald of UCLA's School of Public Health on CNN's *Larry King Live* to publicize results of this study. These studies found no sero-transmission of HIV and a level 1 percent positive gonorrhea rate.[132]

This move successfully mobilized the AIDS issue for the brothels. The contrast between the legal brothels where tourists were "safe," and illegal prostitutes who were the real "murderers," as portrayed by supporters of a bill making it a felony for illegal prostitutes to be found HIV positive, left the brothel industry in an extremely good position. Between 1987 and 1989, there were further attempts to close the brothels, but they did not publicly use the AIDS panic as a justification.

In late 1987, after the legislative session ended, newspapers reported an effort on the part of the gaming industry to lobby legislators to shut down the brothels. The rationale: brothels hurt Nevada's image. Lobbyists James Joyce and Sig Rogich, powerful voices for the gaming industry, claimed that brothels were hurting efforts to diversify the economy. But Governor Bryan replied, "To be perfectly honest, I have never heard any concerns on any of my trips . . . There is no question that prostitution invites considerable commentary by the national media as far as Nevada goes." The state's economic development director was more circumspect in explaining the image problem:

There is no way anybody can say it helps, and I think any rational person would see, that in terms of attracting the new businesses that we are seeking, that it hurts ... We are left with that one uniqueness in all the country. It has all sorts of prurient attributes to it that make it a high visibility kind of issue ... I make no moral judgments on it. There are very good arguments for legalized prostitution. But the point is that no state in this nation has it, except us. And it's not like we are California. It is not likely we are seen as trend setters. We're seen as an anachronism.[133]

In May, 1988, Steve Wynn, owner of several large casino projects and a huge force in gaming politics, wrote a letter to Governor Bryan saying simply,

We have outgrown legalized prostitution. The existence of brothels in Nevada is just one more item that out-of-state media people use to denigrate the quality of life in Nevada. Although we could engage in a lofty dialogue about how prostitution is going to be with us anyway, I think the argument misses the point altogether. The point is that it is not good for Nevada's image to have wide open, legalized "cathouses" and the sooner we put that image behind us the better we will be.

The governor replied:

As you know, this is an issue that has been debated for years. The six counties that have legalized prostitution support the right of local control and cite prostitution as a source of revenue vital to the health of their economies. The issue of outlawing prostitution has arisen in several past legislative sessions. Each time it was defeated. As you may have read in recent news, the legislature does not appear to be expressing much of an appetite to outlaw prostitution in the 1989 session. Until the legislature sees fit to act on the matter Nevada counties with legal prostitution will still have the option of local control.[134]

The last attempt to legislate against the brothels was in 1989, and that bill could not get out of committee. Newspaper articles cite the two arguments Wynn made for wanting them closed: the legal abuse of women and the image of legal prostitution projects outside of Nevada.

Other state senators again argued that there were more important battles to fight. Senator Dina Titus, D-Las Vegas, said she did not support a brothel ban because she believed in local control. "Besides, there are bigger battles to fight," she said. "Where does O'Donnell [the state senator introducing the brothel bill] stand on day care and child support?"[135]

Since then, there have been no attempts to introduce legislation to ban brothels. In 2005 and 2009, the legislature briefly considered various taxes on brothels, a move supported by the brothel industry. These did not pass. Nevada's stalemate in some ways continues. While there are still opponents to having legal prostitution at all in the state, at the same time visible entities such as the mayor of Las Vegas and the Hard Rock Casino have publicly expressed desires to open brothels in Las Vegas.

CONCLUSION

From boom town saloons to a tourist industry capitalizing on images of the Wild West, Nevada's leisure economy was built around open prostitution. Women worked in a variety of contexts—from owning saloons and brothels to working as dancers, entertainers, and prostitutes, both independently and for others. Up until World War II, Nevada did not regulate the sex industry as a moral problem, but rather to control order, establishing vice zones and red light districts. In the eastern United States, Progressive-Era laws criminalized prostitution, and eventually drinking and gambling, as part of larger efforts to control working-class and immigrant behavior throughout the early twentieth century. Victorian gender and sexual ideologies did not take hold in Nevada or other western states in the same way they did in the rest of the United States. Women workers eventually lost much of their mobility and flexibility through Progressive Era-inspired regulations that seeped through. But there remained a different gender ideology around sexuality in the West than elsewhere. Although there was constant pressure from national sources to control morals, this often ended up feeding the nation's fascination with vice in the state. Nevada, by the 1930s, recognized that sexual and hedonistic fun was a marketable component of the state's developing tourist economy, and prostitution became, as one commentator said, Nevada's number two tourist industry, second only to gambling. Here the choice to consume, rather than religion, spirituality, or justice, defined freedom for Nevada's citizens and its tourists. It is the subsequent development of and dependence on this tourist industry that differentiated Nevada from the rest of the western states, and allowed it to retain legal prostitution.

In the years after World War II, the state's tourist industry grew dramatically. As southern Nevada businesspeople and politicians began marketing sexualized images of women, the image of the prostitute worked against the new promotion of Las Vegas as a middle-class tourist destination. "Classiness" meant sexually alluring women, but not open prostitution. In order to make gambling look legitimate, the casino industry distanced itself institutionally and officially from the sale of sex. While there is much evidence that the casino industry simply wanted to control prostitution on its own terms, these images of class certainly helped eliminate open prostitution in growing, urban areas. Efforts by casino owners and local officials in the 1970s to outlaw brothels met with strong resistance from rural county governments, and in fact resulted in the law which technically legalized the brothels.[136] Rural areas had, and still have, a strong economic interest in maintaining brothels.

Understanding Nevada's legal prostitution today is impossible without understanding its roots in mining, and later, in tourism. While Nevada's legal brothels are unique, in many ways the industry grew in a political, social, and economic culture that is increasingly part of the landscape across the United States today. Neoliberal politics has put regulations that protect a free market ahead of policies that regulate moral behavior. A growing service industry has positioned tourism as one of the largest industries in the world. Late capitalist culture encourages a morality of choice in consumption and acceptance of some sexual diversity. Yet, open prostitution remains highly contested in urban areas. The history of class, race, and gender in Nevada provides an important context for understanding the brothel industry today.

4

THE BUSINESS OF SELLING SEX

How do Nevada's legal brothels operate today? The state has undergone dramatic demographic changes since brothels became legal. The entire arid western United States between the Rocky Mountains and the coastal ranges has grown three times faster than the national average since the 1990s. Nevada grew 49.5 percent in the 1990s and continued to be the fastest growing state in the country between 2000 and 2007.[1] Most of this growth has occurred around the urban areas, especially Las Vegas. However, these demographic and economic changes have had a huge effect on brothel operations.

This chapter examines how gender, class, and the dynamics of place play out in the operation and organization of Nevada's brothel businesses today. In particular we look at location, ownership, marketing, day-to-day functions, relations between managers and workers, women's mobility, and women as independent contractors.

Rural Places, Modern Businesses

Although brothels are legal only in the remote, sparsely populated areas of the state, these brothels cannot be understood as simply rural businesses. The entire state, including rural areas, has been affected by an increasingly globalized tourist economy. We call the largest brothels located near the urban centers of the state suburban brothels. Suburban brothels are located across the county borders near Las Vegas and Reno, usually 30 minutes' to an hour's drive away. They have been in rural counties, but as these metropolitan areas have grown, they increasingly find themselves in the suburbs. These houses tend to have more women working, and bring in a more diverse clientele. The women who work here tend to have bodies that better fit the dominant but narrow Western standards of beauty. Being closer to populated resort cities means that these brothels also tend to draw in more tourists. The more isolated rural brothels that are located progressively farther from population centers often have from two to five women working. These may be along remote highways or in small towns.

On the one hand, the brothels operate in towns whose politics, relationships, and gender, class and race dynamics are typical of rural areas. The jurisdictions governing brothels are typically made up of three- and four-person county commissions or city councils. Citizens have face-to-face relations with both elected leaders and local businesses, including the brothels. The customers who keep the brothels operating generally labor in traditionally masculine industries like mining, farming, and construction. For the most part, as mining and construction businesses open and close in small towns, locals accept brothels as relatively stable businesses. Local citizens tend to support brothels' right to exist.

This acceptance has been based on the fact that brothels are relatively hidden, low key, and "don't bother anybody." Many of the local ordinances and informal rules reinforce this fact. For years, brothels could not advertise. Brothel licenses are privilege licenses, meaning local officials can enter properties at will. Business codes allow emergency closures for vaguely defined "health" reasons. Local norms may require workers to limit activities in town, and rules that require workers to live at the brothel during their contract stem as much from the desire to keep brothels concealed as from health concerns. The manager of the Old Bridge Ranch conveys this sentiment: "We want everyone to know we are open, but we don't want the public to hear about us." Hy Forgeron, Lander County District Attorney, told us that in small towns like Battle Mountain, brothels work best when they do not rock the boat. Forgeron explained that while rural Nevada is relatively conservative compared to Las Vegas and Reno, brothels are part of the local tradition.

> The local governing bodies here, I think are more vulnerable to individual opinion, simply because of the size of the communities that they regulate, and the people that they will run into personally going to pick up their mail at the post office. They are not at all insulated from people that live in the community . . . You may look at that as kind of a contrast, there happens to be a conservative rural body and still license a brothel, well it happens, but it's still touchy . . . they are going to keep the brothels because they are tradition. But they don't want to be known for that . . . If you tell them [local government] up front, I want this 100 by 100 foot neon sign and this palatial establishment, they are going to be less receptive . . . I really think that the more restrained they are the better their future is going to be.

In towns where everybody knows everybody else, brothel owners and managers have to make sure they are part of the local culture in order to foster goodwill and acceptance. Many brothel owners donate scholarships to local high schools, buy jackets for fire departments, donate uniforms to sports teams, generate funds for local families in need, participate in local parades, carnivals, and holiday festivities, and run other town events. By supplying little league teams with uniforms, organizing the 4th of July parade, and making regular donations to the local Rotary Club, several brothel owners have become respected community members. Brothel workers must maintain a delicate balancing act as well. Even though some workers return to the same brothels year after year, most come and go. And none of the workers are integrated into the community. The workers in the brothels are rarely from the small towns in which they are working, and are more likely to be strangers than the customers, coming to the towns from all over the United States.

Community members we spoke to support workers' right to work, but they also had very gendered notions of proper behavior for working women. One local female resident of Ely captured the tenor of support workers have in town:

The girls, when they come downtown, are probably the most polite, courteous women in this community. They keep their manners on, their verbal manners, and they spend a great deal of money in this community, and I don't think we have the right to tell them that they can't work.

On the other hand, small town Nevada is not the same as small town U.S.A. There is legal gambling in downtown Ely and throughout the state. Towns across the entire state of Nevada, not just the urban centers, have always relied at least partially on tourists coming to the state to gamble.[2] Nearly every small town has a casino or two that anchors their tourist economies. Outdoor recreation has spurred a growing tourist industry in some of the most remote places in the state. Many of Nevada's small towns market their outdoor activities, such as hunting, hiking, biking, and increasingly capitalize on the market for outdoor, western adventure tourism and cultural entertainment. The National Cowboy Poetry Gathering brings 10,000 people to Elko each winter, and the Burning Man festival in the Blackrock desert north of Reno attracts nearly 35,000 visitors. Art galleries, espresso shops and brewpubs like the Ruby Mountain Brewery in Elko are replacing the rugged, working-class saloons and diners. Over the past 20 years, wealthy people from across the United States have been purchasing ranches near popular areas offering fly-fishing, mountain biking, skiing, and rock climbing in various parts of the state. This means that rural Nevada is enmeshed in an economy that relies more and more on the diversity of strangers coming to town.[3]

Rural Nevada, like most of the West, has been predominantly white, but new residents are more racially diverse. A mix of retirees, wealthy young adults, and professionals in various service industries from the Sun Belt states of California, Florida, and Texas are moving to small towns, especially around Elko.[4] In addition, in 2006, 19.7 percent of Elko County's population was Hispanic, the highest of any rural county in the state. Storey County has the smallest Hispanic population, 5.1 percent. In Winnemucca, 10.4 percent of the population is foreign born.[5] Many working-class seasonal employees on the ranches around Ely come from South America. Immigrants from a number of countries come and go as mining employment expands and contracts. Brothel workers tell us that they sometimes do not speak the same language as their clients. For example, one worker said that during one week she entertained two Croatian truckers and a couple of Hispanic men.

As a result, these towns' interconnected economies are progressively engulfed in a larger, global tourist culture, complete with economic shifts toward service-based leisure businesses. They are certainly not as racially diverse as the urban centers of Nevada, but more so than many rural areas across the country. The "outsider" is a valued consumer of local tourist and leisure businesses. At the same time, some towns face challenges adjudicating between the comfort zones of locals and the diverse cultures of newcomers and tourists.

The suburban brothels have been most affected by these dramatic changes. Suburban brothels have always been able to capitalize on the millions of tourists coming into the metropolitan resorts of Reno and Las Vegas. But in recent years suburban areas are seeing dramatic population growth—between 1990 and 2006 the town of Pahrump, outside of Las Vegas, has seen its population grow by 32 percent. Suburban brothels have been able to support up to 80 women working at a time, and have more capital to respond to changes in the market. In recent years these brothels are seeing a sophisticated male tourist who is willing to spend more money on entertainment. But a growing global tourist industry is affecting all of the brothels: the way brothels are owned and structured, the way they market themselves, how they are managed, and how sex is sold.

RUNNING THE SHOW: BROTHEL OWNERSHIP

Where brothels used to be owned by individuals who had come through the sex industry ranks, the brothels have gradually shifted hands to small businessmen coming from outside the sex industry, and even to corporate partnerships. Years ago, George Flint, head of the Nevada Brothel Association, used to speak about the two different kinds of people who owned brothels: the traditionalists and the squares. He does not talk much about this divide any more.

Traditionalists were owners who came from within the sex industry —they either used to work as prostitutes or managers, or they came from a family who did. They may have been involved in the industry in other places where it was illegal or at least quasi-legal. The owners and managers of the Old Bridge Ranch, for example, were relatives of Sally

Conforte, a long-time madam who helped run the Mustang Ranch next door. Sally was married to Joe Conforte, who, before coming to Nevada, ran illegal prostitution in California. Fran's Star Ranch near Beatty was run by former sex worker Fran York. Back before the brothels were legalized, Flint explained that brothels were "traditionally a woman's business." Insiders considered it inappropriate for anyone but a woman to own or manage a brothel. Traditionalists often had experience running an illegal or quasi-legal business, which meant they knew when to lay low. They were acquainted, if not experienced, with methods of working with local government officials when the law was not always on their side.

According to Flint, squares were owners who had not run a sex business before. They came to brothel ownership from legal, usually non-sexual industries. They saw brothels as a business investment. Flint often reiterated that the scariest thing about squares is that they want to run the brothels like a regular business. Flint said Joe Conforte told him that these new people run brothels as if they are selling cough drops and they do not understand "the delicateness, the sensitiveness, the tenuousness of it." At least until the mid-1990s, the brothels were for the most part run by the traditionalists.

Ten years after Flint made these statements it is difficult to find a brothel that is not owned by a "square." The men and women who had been running the brothels for years are retiring and being replaced by a new breed of owners who see the brothels as being like any other small business. Many brothel owners have come to the brothels from diverse industries such as contracting, teaching, and real estate. Individual small business-men and -women still own most of the rural brothels, but are less likely to come from within the business. A retired couple from Oregon bought Fran's Star Ranch when York retired and changed the name to Angel's Ladies. A former owner of a small printing franchise, Jim Walker, bought Mona's in Elko and the Stardust in Ely from traditionalists who had run the businesses for years. Geoff Arnold, a former small business owner, bought Donna's Ranch in Wells from Helen Smally who had run brothels for nearly 50 years, legal and illegal, throughout the United States. Says Arnold,

> One of the things that has happened since then is you get this corporatization happening. I'm a good example. I come in, clean it up and say, "hey this is the way you ought to run a

business. And you ought to be honest about your books, and you report your income, and do 1099s. And we ought to teach the girls to file tax returns and all those things." And then the industry starts to change.

Nevertheless, this newer breed of brothel owner still has some of the cultural influences of days gone by. The brothel owners, particularly those in very rural areas, do not want to cause a debate to resurface on a local or state level. Many owners are still fiercely independent. Patricia, manager of Sharon's Place in Carlin, proudly talked about how her son was well integrated in the town. Charlie Kendrick grew up in Nevada and worked for ten years as an accountant at the Sands Hotel in Las Vegas. He and his former wife Sharon, who grew up in Carlin, decided to build Sharon's Place. Charlie knew the game from the beginning, says his mother. "He knew the Mormons; he knew all the people he needed to know to go down to the city and get his license. Otherwise they might not have had him," said Patricia Kendrick. "The Mormon Church wanted him, the grandmothers wanted him, and the senior citizens wanted him. They knew what we were, and like I say, Sharon was born and raised here." She added, "Everybody loves Charlie."

There is even a slight trend toward monopoly today. In 2007, a couple bought all five of the brothels on "The Line" in Winnemucca and today own the only operating brothels in Humboldt County, Villa Joy Ranch and the Wild West Ranch. They bought My Place from Barbara Davis who owned it from 1977 to 2007, and the Pussycat Ranch from Sylvia Binder who owned it between 1989 and 2004. My Place and another of the five brothels, Simone's de Paris, were torn down. The Pussycat Ranch is closed for a remodel. The owners had plans to build a much bigger brothel on one of the closed brothel sites, though the economic downturn that began in 2008 seems to be preventing that from happening.

The biggest brothels rarely have single owners, and these co-owners employ managers rather than manage themselves. Kenneth Green and Russell Reade became the first partnership to own a brothel, Western Best Ltd., when they took over the Chicken Ranch in 1982. Green is an entrepreneur from northern California, Reade a former schoolteacher. Reade became one of the first male managers, and ran the ranch up until several years ago. Green and Western Best Ltd. have been trying to sell the Chicken Ranch for the past several years at a price tag of $5 million, and only partnerships or corporations have been bidding.[6]

With this kind of corporate capital investment, large, suburban brothels are diversifying. Because brothel licenses are privilege licenses, owners and financial backers are protecting their investments by spreading financial risk. Moonlite Bunny Ranch owner Dennis Hof recently opened Dick's Roadhouse, a $2 million, 6,000 square foot restaurant less than a mile away from his brothel in the Reno area.[7] The newest owners of Sheri's Ranch are corporate owners who have a diverse array of holdings in sex industry and non-sex industry businesses. Among the owners is Chuck Lee, a car dealer and retired police officer from Las Vegas. He teamed up with Resort Entertainment Companies (REC) and purchased The Resort and Spa at Sheri's Ranch in 2001. Their corporation also owns two legal strip clubs in Las Vegas, Sheri's Cabaret, and Seamless. Sheri's Cabaret is a traditional mid-sized strip club on the industrial corridor off the Las Vegas Strip. The Cabaret uses the same logo and name as the brothel, making clear the connection. In December, 2005, REC hired Las Vegas Strip ultra-lounge designers and opened Seamless in Las Vegas, a large, upscale, ultra-modern gentlemen's club (a strip club) and swank afterhours ultra-lounge (a dance club with expensive drinks and reserved VIP areas) with $20 million state-of-the-art lighting and a unisex restroom. This level of capital investment is unprecedented in any company also owning a brothel.

As traditionalist brothel owners retire, there is more turnover among owners. The Kit Kat Ranch in Carson City, like many brothels in the state, has been closed and opened several times, passing from corporation to corporation three times between 1986 and 2004. According to the Kit Kat website, in 2006, it was purchased by a mother-and-daughter team, Sheila and Jacie Caramella. On the website, the Caramellas stress that they had no experience in the brothel industry prior to their investment in the ranch and that they were not, and are not now, brothel prostitutes themselves.[8] With the severe economic downturns of 2001 and 2008, Flint says he is seeing a kind of survival of the fittest that hits both overextended large brothels and the tiniest of the smaller rural brothels.

MARKETING LEGAL SEX

Broader economic and demographic changes have forced brothels to change how they market their two major customer bases: tourists and locals. For years, the bread and butter, so to speak, of the brothel industry have been locals, including mostly white, working-class customers, a mix of truckers, miners, construction workers, and ranch and farm hands. Locals are employed or residing (even if temporarily) in the area, and/or pass by frequently. However, this group is becoming increasingly racially and ethnically diverse.

Using low-key and inconspicuous methods of marketing, brothels have appealed to a traditional working-class masculinity by combining a sexualized home away from home with a kind of tongue-in-cheek humor and masculine, slightly bawdy, slightly kitschy decor. Brothels have marketed to this group by selling their product as discrete sex acts often chosen from a menu. The half-hour half and half (which begins with oral sex and moves on to vaginal sex) has been the most common service purchased, and remains so today. But in response to the growing tourist market and changes in male consumption, some brothels are marketing a more sexualized experience, a fantasy.

With the changing economy and a progressively more diverse tourist base, many brothels have recognized the potential to appeal to a different kind of masculinity, the more urbane, modern male customer potentially willing to spend larger amounts of money in a single visit. These middle- and upper-class men can spend thousands or even tens of thousands on an evening. In response, some brothels, especially suburban brothels, remodeled to create a classier décor. And while most brothels still retain a low-key profile, remaining quiet and avoiding publicity, there are pressures to change this approach. A few suburban brothels are adding services that specifically reach out to more mainstream audiences, like a sports bar and a non-brothel hotel. Suburban brothels have been better positioned to capture this market, but even rural brothels have tried to position themselves to net some of the new client base.

Publicizing a Concealed Business

Keeping brothels hidden and out of the public eye has not just been part of brothel culture, it has been enforced by law. When brothels

Figure 4.1 Like many brothels along highways, Donna's in Wells on busy Highway 80 relies on truckers for business as well as local ranchers, and increasingly tourists. Author photo.

were legalized, it became illegal for them to advertise. It was a violation of state law to advertise on public streets or highways or anywhere that prostitution is illegal. All but one of the counties had additional prohibitions on advertising within the county or city. Many counties still limit the size and placement of signs marking brothel buildings. One county mandates that they be marked as "Guest Ranch—Men Only."[9] This meant that brothels could not do any of the advertising or marketing that other legal businesses take for granted, including placing want ads for workers in two of the most populous counties in the state, Washoe and Clark. Most brothel owners have accepted and even embraced this. The manager of Old Bridge insists, "No publicity is good publicity." They operate under the notion that customers do not like to be seen, or even have it known that they go to brothels, and the public does not need to be alerted to the presence of brothels. If they are too visible, owners fear their licenses could be pulled, or the entire industry could be made illegal.

As a result, brothels had to be relatively creative in how they advertised. For years, many had the philosophy that they were marketing to customers who, like themselves, wanted to be inconspicuous. They relied on guidebooks and word of mouth that attracted mostly working-class travelers. The technique worked well to keep these customers returning. They hit the market for kitsch and sold witty menus, hats, T-shirts, and coffee mugs or gave away matchbooks with the brothel name, logo, and address. Most of the suburban brothels have gift shops where they sell promotional items like T-shirts, hats, shot glasses, and ashtrays. Brothels also use promotions to advertise their services, holding concerts and coordinating with other local events like car shows. Some brothels have offered discounts to firefighters working on wildfires nearby, a free $50 gift certificate for a customer with a driver's license from a neighboring state, or free gas cards in times of economic hardship. When Citizen's Band (CB) radios were popular in the 1970s and 1980s, many brothels relied on these to attract highway visitors. Truckers still use the CB, and rural brothels closest to Interstate 80 in northern Nevada often require workers to take shifts on the CB, broadcasting sexy invitations to truckers to stop by for coffee, showers, and relaxation.

Today's suburban brothels are in a position to spend more money on creative forms of publicity. For example, they have more funds than their more isolated rural counterparts to hold various events, sponsor charity fundraisers, and generate out-of-state recognition and media exposure by collaborating with other businesses. The Chicken Ranch and Sheri's Ranch outside of Las Vegas are members of the Las Vegas Sin City Chamber of Commerce.[10] The Chicken Ranch has effectively branded itself. The name of the ranch came from a brothel by the same name in Texas which inspired the 1978 Broadway play *The Best Little Whorehouse in Texas*. Shortly after the brothel was bought by Kenneth Green and Russ Reade in 1982, the AIDS scare of the 1980s prompted the owners to hire a public relations firm, Fisher and Associates. Together they worked with state officials to establish better health-testing rules and publicized a UCLA study on sexually transmitted diseases in the brothels. The public relations firm's strategy has been to help them provide "discrete, tasteful, and conservative" marketing strategies, according to the firm's owner.

Like much of the adult industry, the brothel industry began to take advantage of the internet in the late 1990s, and this allowed them to reach a wider audience. Customers were the first to use the internet, developing list serves and message boards where they archived information on the location of the brothels and posted reviews and advice. Initially, the brothels themselves did little for fear of violating the advertising ban. In fact, in 1997 the city of Elko and Churchill County wrote into their ordinances language specifically prohibiting advertising within their jurisdiction via computer. Donna's Ranch in Wells still has a paragraph on their home page that reads,

> This site is clean, classy, tasteful and amusing! Although our trademark Donna's Girl is a "hot babe," she is only a cartoon drawing. As there is plenty of smut on the Net already, there is none here. There's also no advertising. As long as we continue to have no pornography or solicitation, then this site has the approval of the local authorities and the Nevada Brothel Association.[11]

A few other brothels went so far as to experiment with selling real time online videos of women in the brothels, but we cannot find any brothels that do this today. Over 90 percent of the brothels open today have a website. The larger brothels close to Las Vegas and Reno especially rely on them to centralize communication with workers, set appointments, display who is available for the month, and advertise various events. Sheri's Ranch, the Chicken Ranch, the Mustang, and the Sagebrush Ranch websites have video tours or free videos of the women. On the Sheri's Ranch website, a customer can reserve a bungalow and arrange for complementary limo service to take him from Las Vegas to Pahrump. The larger, more suburban brothels like Sheri's Ranch, the Chicken Ranch, and the Moonlite Bunny Ranch have the most elaborate, technologically advanced websites that are professionally designed.

Pressure to be more visible is mounting in some ways, and this has been most evident in the approach taken by Dennis Hof, owner of the Moonlite Bunny Ranch. Hof has used some particularly creative ways to advertise his business, despite apprehension on the part of his peers in the industry. Hof's very visible media strategies make colleagues in the industry nervous. Hof, Air Force Amy, Brooke Taylor, and other women currently working at the Moonlite Bunny Ranch are often featured on the Howard Stern radio show and several TV talk shows and morning shows. The Moonlite Bunny Ranch is also the subject of the ongoing HBO series *Cathouse*. His "bunnies" have appeared in a variety of adult films and pose in *Playboy* and *Hustler*. Hof also openly promotes himself as a brothel owner. He appeared on Fox News during the 2008 presidential election, publicly endorsing libertarian Ron Paul for the Republican Party presidential nomination. He offered a discount to anyone using their Bush Administration stimulus check (sent out in 2008) to purchase a party, and encouraged them to sign a thank-you note that would be sent to the President. Hof also markets voyeuristic transgression by making sure to tell any media personality or interviewer who will listen that "everybody comes here—every rock star, athlete and a few politicians that you'd love to know about but I can't tell you."[12] In thumbing his nose at the dominant lay-low approach of the rest of the industry, Hof told one reporter, "A high-profile approach brings higher-quality girls and better-quality customers."[13]

In 2006, after years of official brothel industry resistance to making any waves, the Nevada chapter of the American Civil Liberties Union convinced Bobbi Davis, owner of the Shady Lady in rural Nye County (about two and a half hours north of Las Vegas) and two local weeklies, *Las Vegas City Life* and West Wendover's *High Desert Advocate*, to challenge the state's advertising ban. According to newspaper reports, Davis was motivated because "I live outside a town that has 1,100 people in it. We don't want the locals, we want the tourists." *Las Vegas City Life* wanted her and other brothel owners to advertise with them. As one of the city's alternative weeklies, the paper ran plenty of risqué ads for local strip clubs and outcall agencies featuring scantily clad women. The papers were motivated as much by the desire for more profits as by the desire to protect free speech, according to editorials. *High Desert Advocate* publisher Howard Copelan told reporters, "I have a right to deny ads myself, but the state doesn't have the right to tell me what I can and cannot advertise as a legal business."[14]

In August, 2007, the court ruled it was unconstitutional for state statutes to ban advertising in Nevada counties where brothel prostitution is illegal. The Nevada Brothel Association and several brothel owners, both large and small, were not pleased. They feared high-profile ads could ruffle the feathers of state politicians and possibly lead to a new law outlawing brothels, a perpetual fear. Now brothels can advertise throughout Nevada, including in Clark and Washoe County. Although State Attorney General Catherine Cortez Masto has appealed the decision in the U.S. Ninth Circuit Court, a few advertisements have popped up across the state in local alternative newspapers. Ads for two Nye County brothels, the Shady Lady Ranch and the Chicken Ranch, have appeared in *Las Vegas City Life* and on mobile billboards around Las Vegas. These ads still reflect a discreet approach. Advertising "VIP treatment at working man's prices," the Shady Lady Ranch ad is not racy or even very sexy. The ad pictures a couple fully clothed in Old West garb. An ad for the Chicken Ranch features their logo, a drawing of a pair of women's legs hatching from a broken eggshell. Advertisements for strip clubs or escorts in the same section of the paper contain much more explicit wording and illustrations.

Rural Marketing Trends

One of the ways in which smaller rural brothels have attracted nomadic working-class men is by marketing themselves as a sexual home away from home. Several brothels offer services that they call the "comforts of home." Angel's Ladies, near Beatty, encourages truckers along Highway 95 to come in and shower or even to just buy a souvenir. The manager told us that developing a repeat customer required some breaking in. The website for the two Winnemucca brothels, Villa Joy Ranch and Wild West Saloon, advertises "overnight parking, free showers, free wi-fi in all parking lots, and free breakfast" for truckers. Other brothel owners told us they did not find it useful to give anything away for free. Most of the suburban brothels do not offer many free amenities.

The décor of many rural brothels' parlors is like a slightly masculine version of a grandmother's living-room. Those we visited in the late 1990s saw décor reminiscent of the 1970s, with shag carpet and dark paneling offset by comfy couches and worn, wood coffee tables. The only difference is that the pictures on the walls are a little more risqué than one might imagine of a stereotypical grandma's house. At the time, many brothels also loved to cover the walls with satirical signs alluding to the transgressive nature of their business, like "max speed limit 69 m.p.h."

Bars in the rural brothels serve important functions in attracting working-class men. Several of the brothels we visited in the northern part of the state had quite busy bars in the evening, full of ranch hands or miners getting off shift. These brothels do not allow in women who are not contracted with them for fear that they may be angry wives or girlfriends. As a result, these brothels become very masculine hangouts. Working women frequent the bar area trying to get customers. A few brothels do allow women as bar customers, and these bars have become another drinking option in town, regardless of whether customers want sexual services or not. In other brothels, the bars discourage drinking without purchasing services because they do not want to become the local hangout. But they do recognize that alcohol often provides "liquid courage."

On the outside, the aesthetic of the small, rural brothels is usually simple and plain. All the smaller brothels along southern Nevada's highways are trailers with various amounts of decoration and embellishment. Two small brothels lie outside of Las Vegas, Mabel's Whorehouse and the Cherry Patch II. The Cherry Patch sits right next to a truck stop at the intersection of U.S. Highway 95 and local Highway 160 in Amargosa Valley. The Cherry Patch has life-sized alien bodies painted on the fence (a reference to Area 51). There is even a spot to snap a photo with room for tourists to place their heads on the alien body. These establishments, including the truck stop, are all owned by the same person.

In northern Nevada, the small town brothels are frame buildings and old homes, some going back to the turn of the twentieth century. Usually there is little signage out front; in the daytime it is hard to tell what these businesses sell. Often there are parking lots large enough for truckers to pull in. At night, lighted signs or a single red light give away their mission. Now that the advertising ban is gone, the brothels may expand signage to bid customers to enter, but almost two years after the ban was overturned, the lack of signs remains.

Rural brothel owners depend on tourists and recognize that this type of client may be the newest source of profit. In Elko, for example, the busiest seasons for brothels coincide with hunting seasons, mountain biking events, and other outdoor events. For years, many of these brothels have capitalized on the nostalgia for the Old West, and have marketed to tourists using these themes with names like The Old Bridge Ranch, Kit Kat Guest Ranch, Donna's Ranch, or the Stardust Ranch. Even today, the Old West is a marketable image to more upscale tourists. In 2002, the Dovetail Ranch was remodeled to look like an old log cabin building. One owner told us he bought a rural brothel in Elko because of its Old West feel.

> I like Western movies and stuff like that and there's prostitutes working in the saloons and the brothels of old time. You know they have the old back bars and that kind of thing. That's kind of the way Mona's is and it appealed to me.

The rural brothels also market to tourists, or at least touristic impulses, in other ways. The majority of women who work in the brothels are white. However, there are demands for women of other races and ethnicities. Brothels often promote Asian women in stereotypical, exoticizing ways. Inez's D&D in Elko has for several years marketed itself as a brothel with all-Asian women. The Dovetail Ranch in Carlin has occasionally marketed itself as a house with many Asian workers.

To our knowledge, there is no explicit attempt to target specific ethnic groups as customers in marketing. In truth, non-white customers can often be subject to discrimination. While no woman told us about discriminating against anyone personally, women and managers

Figure 4.2 The five brothels in Elko are clustered in a neighborhood just off Main Street. Here you can see Mona's and Sue's Fantasy Club. Just around the corner are the others. Their signs are relatively small and look nothing like venues for sexual commerce in the larger resort districts. Author photo.

Figure 4.3 Sharon's Place in Carlin, like many brothels, was originally a single trailer that has since been expanded. Author photo.

Figure 4.4 Rural brothel owner Charles Kendrick displays some of the artwork adorning the parlor and bar area at Sharon's Place. Many rural brothels were adorned with kitschy and joke signs. However, Sharon's and a number of other brothels have since remodeled their interiors to look classier. Author photo.

did disclose stories about other women who refuse to serve black men. One brothel worker in a rural brothel told us,

> Like I know some girls that won't do black guys. I know a lot of girls that won't. They'll still take them back to the room, but raise their price, you know, so that they don't feel bad. You know, then if they say they can't pay it then, "Oh, well I'm sorry, you know, choose another lady." I don't know many that have done it often. But, I have run across that. And I asked one girl, "Why won't you?" And they're like, "because, you've got a whole bar full of cowboys that are white, they might not want you because you did a black guy."

Another woman mentioned that she knew women who would not have sex with Asians, or with Middle Eastern people, or with Hindus. She said a brothel may have a diverse clientele, but some women just refuse to entertain anyone who is not white.

By and large, the traditionally masculine down home or kitschy style is giving way to a more stylish and contemporary look as brothels try to reach more tourists. More and more rural brothels are starting to remodel to upscale décor to attract tourists who are willing to spend money, a move which will further exclude poorer migrant workers, usually people of color. The Wild Kat Ranch in Mina, halfway between Las Vegas and Reno, typically houses only three to four women. Yet its website boasts a newly remodeled hot tub, dungeon room, bar, and an above-ground swimming pool. Still, its paneled walls and a parlor-like living room maintain the small town feel. The Stardust in Ely added their hot tub room in the late 1990s. Carlin's Sharon's Brothel and Bar has taken down its toilet seat photo frame and now its website advertises photos of a classier, more refined-looking setting. Before it closed in 2007, Angel's Ladies added what they called a fantasy room—a separate trailer in the back with relatively new carpeting and bed covers.

Suburban Marketing Trends

Compared to other Nevada brothels, the larger suburban brothels have always had a higher volume of customers, a large percentage of whom are tourists. They have always been able to market toward more diverse tourists. These brothels are slightly more upscale than their rural counterparts. The parlors are accented with masculine, heavy furniture. The suburban brothels have had money to remodel, and in recent years have changed their décor and added services to entice a higher class and more mainstream tourist. Several of the larger brothels have invested in renovating their facilities, moving away from western or homey interiors to more stylish, chic, and even elegant aesthetics. The Sagebrush Ranch near Reno, for example, has a 360 degree virtual tour online of their bar and parlor that shows a newly remodeled mahogany bar with lots of seating and granite countertops. Suburban brothels now have hot tub rooms, specially decorated or themed rooms, and dungeon rooms to build their fantasy atmosphere. A few brothels are experimenting with having small erotic dancing clubs. One even advertises an espresso bar.

Brothels are also expanding the extra services they offer. Many suburban brothels offer free round-trip transportation or limo service from Las Vegas to Pahrump (Sheri's Ranch, the Chicken Ranch) or in the Reno/Carson City area (the Kit Kat Ranch, Moonlite Bunny).[15] Most suburban brothels' websites now openly welcome couples and swingers, and a few express a willingness to accommodate single women. Rather than marketing the "comforts of home," these brothels appeal to urban tourists who are used to a more sexualized mainstream culture and who are seeking a brothel "experience."

The Resort and Spa at Sheri's Ranch

The transformation of Sheri's Ranch into the Resort and Spa at Sheri's Ranch is a prime example of these trends.[16] Sheri's started in 1982 as a small trailer home with a few wings added later to accommodate more rooms. In January, 2001, Chuck Lee, along with some other investors in Resort Entertainment Companies (REC), bought the ranch. The new corporate owners spent $7 million in renovations. They completely redesigned the interior, added a hotel and sports bar, and built several 800 square-foot private bungalows. The tall two-storey whitewood clapboard building now boasts two large entrances, one to the sports bar, and one to the brothel parlor. The owners increased the number of rooms and redid the parlor with a new upscale look—white couches sit on dark finished wood floors, accompanied by a fireplace, a curio cabinet, sleek coffee tables, tasteful nude paintings interspersed with

Figure 4.5 Sheri's Ranch in Pahrump is an example of the upscale, open look suburban brothels are adopting to attract more mainstream tourists as customers. Author photo.

landscapes, a crystal chandelier, and a large piano. They built separate fantasy bungalows with themes such as a Roman bacchanal, the Middle Ages, an African safari, and the psychedelic 1960s. The hot tub party room décor was sponsored by Budweiser beer. Budweiser has helped sponsor other brothel events and public concerts. The brothel also added new amenities for workers, including a pool, a gym, a facial spa, a full beauty salon, and a computer room.

Sheri's also follows another suburban brothel trend, expanding to include non-brothel services. In Sheri's case, this is designed to appeal to mainstream customers who are not necessarily seeking a sexual experience. Sheri's opened two non-sexual businesses in and near the brothel. A separate ten-room, non-brothel resort hotel with a heated pool and waterfall, volleyball court, and spa was added to the property. The non-brothel resort hotel markets itself to semi-adventurous couples who want to spend the night "at a brothel" without necessarily purchasing any sexual services. The hotel does not allow prostitution in those rooms, but the brothel is a short walk across the pool area.

In addition, Sheri's Ranch is home to a sports bar. A customer can enter the sports bar without having to enter the brothel. Inside, customers will find cozy booths, big-screen TVs, and a full menu of food and drinks. On a spring weekday in 2008, we found the bar filled with businessmen, elderly couples, and local men and women having lunch. There has been talk of adding a golf course or even some kind of housing development on the grounds.

The goal of the new owners was quite explicit: to attract a new market by targeting mainstream consumers. According to a newspaper article, the main goal in remodeling Sheri's Ranch was to "draw the mainstream attention that the Nevada brothel industry has always avoided ... [the new owner] wants the brothels to be seen as just another business in the community."[17] Sheri's has tried to accomplish this in several ways. For example, most brothels maintain the feel of transgression by making a customer ring a buzzer to a locked front door to gain entrance. (This also serves, managers feel, to protect customers against angry wives or girlfriends.) The doors at Sheri's are always unlocked. The business welcomes a wide variety of people through its doors, not just potential clients. For example, both men and women are welcome. Unlike other brothels where only paying customers or bar patrons are allowed in, here organizations or curious people can get a tour of the facility. For a few years in the 1990s, Sheri's offered long brothel tours to associations like Elderhostel and the Red Hat Society (organizations for seniors) or Las Vegas tour groups; at one time they averaged three prearranged tours a week. Today, women, senior citizens, and groups of friends can eat and drink at the bar; the working women mingle in the bar with men who are alone. In 2004, the brothel held a golf tournament and raised around $7,000 for the local Pahrump Senior Center. Sheri's Ranch continues to host public events through professional organizations such as the Sin City Chamber of Commerce.

Moonlite Bunny Ranch

In the northern part of the state, individual entrepreneur and brothel owner Dennis Hof casts a wide marketing net in a different way. Hof is appealing to a more mainstream tourist, but he also seeks to cultivate the customer who desires a unique sexualized experience.

His Moonlite Bunny Ranch and Miss Kitty's (now the Love Ranch) are each designed to appeal to a different client base: the Moonlite Bunny Ranch is for the man with more money to spend who seeks a sexual fantasy, and Miss Kitty's is for the working-class man.

Hof bought the Moonlite Bunny Ranch in 1993 and a nearby brothel, Miss Kitty's, shortly after. The two brothels, which both started out as small trailer homes, are located just outside of the state capital in Carson City, and within an hour's drive from the resorts at Lake Tahoe and Reno. In 1999, the Moonlite Bunny Ranch's infamous nearby competitor, the Mustang Ranch, closed due to federal tax fraud and racketeering charges against the owner. Hof decided to fill the void and began a high-profile marketing strategy. In the past several years, Hof has been able to get a few adult movie stars to work at his brothel, and now he markets the Moonlite Bunny as a sexualized fantasy land where you can sleep with your dream adult film star or a "bunny" who is featured on the *Cathouse* series.

Over the past ten years, Hof has expanded the Bunny Ranch to 35 rooms that can accommodate more than 50 women. He continues to remodel the Bunny Ranch, most recently in 2007 to change the façade and the parlor. The exterior is a one-and-a-half-storey façade, tan with white trim and large, stained oak, frosted glass doors. Hof got

Figure 4.6 Suburban brothel owner Dennis Hof points out some of the additions he was planning on making to the Moonlite Bunny Ranch. The property also has a spa and horses that the workers can ride if they wanted. Author photo.

rid of a high, imposing fence and now, like the Chicken Ranch, the building is separated from the parking lot by a four foot white decorative wrought-iron fence. The parlor now has two crystal chandeliers, red velvet couches, and leopard print carpeting. It has a six foot-high humidor, fireplaces, and a pole for dancing.

Hof has increased the size and function of his bar over the years. While there is no separate entrance, at the back of the parlor under a neon sign is the "Bunny Bar." One has to pass through the parlor to get to the bar, but one can proceed to the bar without a line-up. There is also a gift shop with souvenirs, Bunny Ranch T-shirts, golf towels, DVDs, and various adult toys. That Hof encourages a wide range of visitors is evidenced by a sign at the entrance from the highway that advertises the Bunny Ranch's 24-hour gift shop, "Free-Tours, No Sex Required."

When Hof describes what distinguishes the Moonlite Bunny Ranch from other brothels, it is not just an updated and classier façade. He is trying to sell a sexualized experience. This push has two components: branding the Moonlite Bunny Ranch, and balancing appeal between mainstream impulses and the transgressive aspects of his business.

Hof proclaimed, "I'm single-handedly trying to sanitize this vice." His method includes shifting attention from the "bread-and-butter" working-class male customer and luring the more urbane, wealthier male tourist or worker, willing to travel and spend more for a sexualized fantasy. He organizes his brothels to be interactive and personable. Hof argues that at both his brothels, he is able to get more money from customers by approaching the service they are buying as more of an experience rather than just routine sex acts.

Employing adult film stars adds to the sexualized fantasy atmosphere of the Moonlite Bunny Ranch. Customers may spend upward of $10,000 to party with their favorite adult actress or *Playboy* Playmate. Hof shared the story of a man "that drove half way across the United States to lose his virginity to [adult film star] Sunset Thomas because she was his favorite."

Hof also sees himself selling quality. He explains,

Moonlite has a mentality that the girls believe they're worth the money . . . When you can look somebody in the eye with conviction and say, "great, you know, I understand oral sex, I am the best at it, and it's gonna be five hundred [dollars]," perception is reality. If you can build a perception that you're the best sexual partner in the world, and the experience that I'm gonna have with you is gonna be the ultimate experience, well, then it is.

Hof astutely summarized the Moonlite Bunny marketing strategy to Rita Cosby of MSNBC, stating: "Our brand has gotten so big because of the notoriety we get because of our HBO show and Stern and all the different people that promote us, then we're able to sell the brand right here, the Bunny Ranch brand. It's hip. It's fun."[18]

Hof uses the name recognition of many of the female workers; the women with previously established reputations in adult film use Hof for mutual promotion. Long-time worker Air Force Amy has been featured on *Cathouse* and is one of the Bunny Ranch's most well-known stars. The online gift store even advertises Air Force Amy hot sauce.

However, Hof has not let go of the bread-and-butter clientele. His second brothel, Miss Kitty's, markets to customers with less disposable income. "There are clients that are spending tens of thousands and there's guys that are spending hundreds, and I want it all." He says, "Just 'cause he can't afford a porn star charging a couple thousand dollars for a great sexual experience, doesn't mean that he shouldn't have a good sexual experience." In 1999, the Cyber Whoremonger Club, an organization for brothel enthusiasts that votes annually on the best brothels and workers in the state, voted then Miss Kitty's the best cathouse in Nevada, and awarded the Courtesan of the Year and Sweetheart of the Year awards to two workers there, Nikita and Dusty, respectively. Dusty, a top earner with a private room at Miss Kitty's, said, "it was very good for advertisement, those kinds of titles."

While Hof's and other suburban brothels undoubtedly get a more diverse clientele than some of the smaller, isolated brothels, the same racial dynamics seem to still be at play. The front webpage of the Moonlite Bunny features several "bunnies." The only featured visibly non-white bunny is Maya Love, an Asian woman whose main photo shows her pictured in a Chinese-looking wrap dress brandishing a sword above her head. Women of color, besides Asian women, are rarely given feature spots on any of the suburban brothel websites. There are several African American women, and a few Latina women, buried in later pages, but the top sellers tend to be white or Asian women.

How Sex is Sold

In addition to these changes in ownership, marketing, décor, and non-sexual amenities, brothels are also changing the nature of the sexual services they offer. The party is always a combination of particular sex acts and interactions. In this section, we discuss the various elements in the process of selling sex in the brothels, and highlight how these correspond, or do not correspond, to the trends toward more adventure, escape, and fantasy fulfillment in the service industry broadly.

Most brothel experiences go something like this. An interested customer drives to one of the 25 or 30 brothels currently licensed in the state. In most brothels the customer rings a doorbell. The doorbell usually signals the women on shift to come to the parlor. A manager, host, or hostess will greet the customer, bring him into the parlor and ask, "Would you like to meet the ladies?" If the customer agrees, the women will stand shoulder to shoulder in a line-up, dressed in an array of lingerie or club wear, with their hands behind their backs, and introduce themselves one at a time. A customer may then select the woman with whom he wants to "party," or he may go to the bar, if there is one, for a drink before choosing. If he goes to the bar, the women will come up individually, spend a few minutes chatting, and then let another woman approach. At some point, the customer chooses a woman and she will give him a tour of the facilities. The tour is an opportunity for the two to get to know each other and to get a sense of the options for the party. They then proceed to the woman's room where they will begin negotiations for time, acts, and money. In most houses, management will listen in on these negotiations through an intercom. Once they reach an agreement, the woman will "book" the money by bringing the money to the main office. Many brothel managers then set a timer. Before the money is booked, the woman gives her customer a "dick check," a visual inspection of his genitals, looking for any signs of disease. If there are none, she books the money and the party begins. After the allotted time, management will usually knock on the door or otherwise indicate that it is time to renegotiate. If the customer is done, they return to the parlor. The worker can decline a customer, or "walk" him, at any point if negotiations do not work out, or if she is concerned about anything she sees in the dick check.

Brothel managers and workers have traditionally attempted to rationalize the provision of sex as far as possible into contained standard choices for customers to make. Line-ups, prices based on time and acts, and timers are all techniques that rationalize sexual service provision. Nevertheless, managers and workers also recognize that the service they provide cannot be entirely rationalized. While women are fairly skilled at controlling the timing of customer orgasms, there has always been disagreement around whether the "get 'em in, off and out" mindset is the most desirable or profitable for workers and management. The women who can earn the highest per party price often cannot run their party in an assembly-line fashion, and provide much more than bodily gratification. We will discuss this in more detail in Chapter 6.

As brothel businesses today change with changing customer tastes, demographics, and potential markets, this issue becomes even more important. Studies of clients of New Zealand's and Australia's various sites of quasi-legal prostitution find that customers seek something more than simple physical release, complaining about prostitutes who make little effort to "disguise the commercial nature of the interaction."[19] Today's sexual tourist demands experiences of escape, relaxation, fantasy fulfillment, and intimacy.[20]

As Dennis Hof says, "At the millennium, sex is more about fantasy and role play than it is about penetration. [. . .] We push that at the Ranch. Our motto is 'Not Just Sex—An Adventure.' We want to create that adventure."[21] As he told us, "I don't want that mentality, that mentality of some of these brothels still, and of the Mustang, which was definitely what you call a trick and travel mentality—'come in, get it up, get off, get the fuck out'."

Suburban brothels provide settings for longer, more date-like experiences that include a variety of services. The Chicken Ranch sells private bungalow packages that can include massage options, and in-house dates complete with catered dinners. The Moonlite Bunny Ranch online menu includes the regular array of sex acts, but also includes additional options like overnight stays, what is labeled as a "girlfriend experience" or a "porn star experience," dinner dates, and opportunities for out-dates. The New Mustang Ranch in Storey County offers on-site and off-site date options so that the customer can "enjoy the perfect date for dinner on the town, dancing, gaming, skiing or sight-seeing." The private bungalows at Sheri's Ranch can be purchased with a package that may include a complementary steak and lobster dinner and a bottle or two of champagne.

Getting Started: The Line-up, Bar, and Appointments

The line-up is one of the most basic ways brothels rationalize the purchase of sex. The line-up has historically been the single mechanism that customers use in choosing with whom they will party. It has evolved into a highly scripted event. The women stand in a line, smile, and keep still until their name is called by the house manager or host, or until it is their turn to introduce themselves. They may then step forward and say their names and a quick comment, or shift their posture in acknowledging the introduction. They may not make any additional moves. In most cases, the women must keep their hands behind their back. They must show up for the line-up dressed in an "appropriate manner," which usually means nipples and pubic hair are covered. It all happens very quickly. After each woman in the line has had her introduction, the customer is then urged to choose which woman he would like to be with. The shift manager urges a customer to make a selection. In some cases, he is urged more strongly than others. In some brothels, he may opt out of the decision and if there is one, proceed to the bar. In the smaller rural brothels that have no bar, he must choose out of the line-up.

At this level the initial sale of sex is organized as if picking a product off the store shelf. The women are on visual display. Many owners and managers, particularly those in the rural brothels, view the line-up as the most efficient way to move customers through the brothel. Many a manager has talked about the frustration of having a customer who cannot or will not choose and the skill it takes to move the overwhelmed customer to a choice. The line-up is one of the more interesting mechanisms for rationalizing the sale of sex and has become ingrained in brothel organizational culture.

The line-up also means that the initial interaction, especially for the first-time customer, is heavily focused on the body and bodily presentation and less on the emotional and experiential services that are part of the sale of sex. The line-up was created under the assumption that the most significant selling point of a worker is her body. Even entrepreneur Dennis Hof acknowledges, "The guy's mind is a computer, and he's looking at height, weight, age, hair color, legs, breasts, and it's all physical, okay? It's totally physical."

While the body is very much what is being displayed here, the women also know that hooking a client is about more than just their bodies. As a result, one of the women's biggest complaints during our interviews concerned what is called "dirty hustling."

Emili, who works at Sheri's Ranch, explains what is forbidden in a line-up,

> like not showing breasts, not showing pubic hair in the line-up, not doing anything like that, ya know. Waving or blowing them a kiss, or winking your eye, or anything. I mean, there's nothing like that. You stand there and you can basically introduce yourself, "hi, I'm so and so, or hello, good afternoon" or whatever. But that's basically all it is. Your hands are behind your back and you just stand very still and you don't speak back to them.

Dirty hustling is any activity which is perceived to give any one woman an "unfair" advantage. The interesting thing about the norms of the line-up is the contradictory messages about what women see as key in selling their services. On the one hand, they know the body is important. On the other hand, interactions and exchanges are equally important. Women are not even allowed to take a sneak peak at a customer waiting for a line-up for fear the customer might see them. Emili continued, "A lot of times that one teeny bit of familiarity is enough to get you picked, because they've seen you first."

Emili articulates that since all a woman has in the line-up are her smile and eye contact, "you have to be able to hypnotize. If you can get that eye contact, you have to be able to hypnotize them back." The idea that you can hypnotize with eye contact and a smile means that connection is a significant part of what is being sold in a brothel.

For these and other reasons, owners and managers are slowly moving away from exclusive dependence on the line-up. Many owners say it is just too degrading for the women. Patricia, manager of Sharon's

Place, declares, "I wouldn't have my dog working in a line. I feel like, a) you're a piece of meat, and b) it causes dissension among the other girls." Dennis Hof admits the line-up is "a little bit degrading . . . it's like the Chinese butcher shop when you're hanging up the meat and he says, well let me have that one over there, that chicken over there. That doesn't fit with my mentality."

Sharon's Place uses a photo album and a menu when a customer comes in. A customer picks a girl from the book and she is called from her room. Once the customer meets the worker, he may choose to party with her, or he may decide to choose another woman. The manager makes clear that she will not let a customer change his mind more than once. This works well in a small brothel. Especially if a customer comes in when many of the women may be sleeping, the photo album prevents every woman from having to make every line-up. It also completely eliminates the dirty hustling problem. But in some ways, this even further eliminates anything beyond the body that can influence a customer's selection.

Managers also recognize that many customers are intimidated by a line-up and will send reluctant customers to the bar, so that they can have a drink of, as they characterize it, "liquid courage." Crystal, the manager at the Stardust, told us that if a customer does not pick a woman from the line-up, she instructs the woman who has booked the least that day to sit at the bar with him.

Workers and managers in suburban brothels see customers' reluctance to choose from a line-up as indicative of a changing dynamic in commercial sex. Many brothels rely more and more on their newly expanded bars to allow customers to get to know women before choosing to party with them. Alexa Albert describes the process at the Mustang Ranch in the early 1990s, whereby if a customer refused the line-up, the women would one by one approach the customer at the bar to try to persuade him to party with her.[22] At Sheri's Ranch in Pahrump outside of Las Vegas, a customer can request a line-up, but he can just as easily bypass it and enter through the separate entrance to the bar. Owners and managers estimate that around 50 percent of business comes from parties initiated at the bar. The owners of Sheri's Ranch and the Moonlite Bunny Ranch believe that the informal, fun atmosphere of the bar fosters the sale of sex. This is a significant shift toward less rationalized and more individualized interactions.

Dennis Hof is the most explicit in talking about what motivates his desire to move away from a line-up. He markets the experience of the Moonlite Bunny Ranch as like "a single's bar except the odds are real good." Hof believes the business of selling sex is not just about picking bodies, but about picking personalities. Hof feels the customer "doesn't want to go to the room unless he feels close to you, or feels like you're friends, or there's some inner personal action going on there, okay?" While men look at women and initially size up their looks,

> the sexual experience is much more than physical. You know, it's verbal, it's that interaction okay? So, in a line-up situation, a girl that is young, attractive, or has big breasts or something will tend to get picked all the time. It creates a tremendous amount of rejection for everybody. I mean can you imagine standing up, 40, 50, 60, 70 times a day and having guys looking at you like this? Guy comes in standing there looking you over, can you imagine what that feels like? The girls start smarting off. And the guy says, "well I don't know if I can make a decision." And I say, "well imagine that, uh huh." It's just a silly concept.

The Moonlite Bunny Ranch still has women line up for customers entering the brothel to introduce themselves. But the Bunny Ranch encourages client–worker interactions in the bar area, and personalized exchanges. Jane, who works at the Moonlite Bunny Ranch, says,

> Part of my day is spent working the bar and just kinda hanging out talking to people. I don't get picked out of a line-up a whole lot, so I have to work the bar if I want to make any money. And a lot of people will just go with me because they like my personality.

Hof believes that relying less on a line-up is more profitable, and customers will spend more money if they receive individualized service. "By eliminating the line-up, I've got a willing buyer and a willing seller. The guy is sold on the fact that they've got the right personality. I've also expanded my base of employees [to] more than just young girls competing against each other."

Suburban brothels are also increasingly relying on appointments and reservations. Their websites are designed to accommodate online reservations in ways similar to making hotel reservations. Since websites have pictures, customers can rely on a "virtual" line-up to choose women with whom to party. Many sites provide women space to say something about themselves, and the sites have message boards for customers and workers to communicate publicly. Sheri's online reservation system allows you to choose a fantasy bungalow, your fantasy package, and a woman with whom to party, all online. As websites are expanding, we would imagine that return customers will rely heavily on online reservations or message boards, especially to prevent a wasted trip to a distant brothel. Several of the more established brothel workers market themselves directly on the internet. The top-earning women have their own websites that list their events and appearances, any adult films they star in, and merchandise. Many include calendars that show when they will be on contract at various brothels. The sites have links to the brothel websites where customers can make online reservations. Particular women are featured on various brothel websites, and can be emailed directly through that website. When Air Force Amy was working in both southern and northern Nevada, her own website (www.airforceamy.com) gave her schedule in both locations. However, she uses the email of the brothel where she is currently on contract. Many women also maintain a visible online presence in various blogs and chats, and can use that to refer customers to brothels' online reservation system.

Negotiations and "The Party"

"The party" refers to a set of discrete acts that are packaged, labeled, and sold within a negotiated time. Since workers are "independent contractors," brothels are not supposed to set prices for them, although some houses do have informal house minimums. Consequently, each woman must negotiate her own prices with each individual customer. By the time the customer is in the room, the woman will have shown him special areas like the hot tub room, any themed party rooms, the VIP room or suites, or a dungeon if there are any of these. The small talk along the tour has given the worker a chance to ascertain if this is the customer's first time, where he is from, and what he does for a living. It also serves to give the worker a chance to figure out the customer's financial situation, whether they are likely to become a regular, and if they live close by.

Brothels often somewhat jokingly present souvenir-like menus of services, without prices listed. Some women create their own menus to use as a starting point in negotiations. The menus are often parodies of restaurant menus with appetizers, entrees, and desserts. Negotiating prices as time and acts imposes some structure on the party. Higher earning women at the suburban brothels tend to make sure that their menu includes opportunities for role play and "spontaneous" sexual expression, which bring in a higher price.

Jackie at the Calico Club, a small rural brothel in Battle Mountain that caters mostly to truckers and miners, comments, "I'll say the most common party is half and half, and they'll be like, you know, 'start off with a blow job and end with sex.' But you only get to come once. And then usually they go, 'okay that sounds good'."

Workers at all the brothels, including suburban brothels, almost always price even the most expensive parties based on acts. We interviewed Bretney at the Moonlite Bunny several years ago in 2000: "Girls charge anywhere from $600 to $2,500 an hour ... I have sold $1,500 'cos that's what I charge for just sucking cum, anal, multiple penetration, multiple orgasm."

Rationalizing a longer fantasy experience is difficult. A clue to how this is done comes from Air Force Amy, one of the top earners at the Moonlite Bunny Ranch. She advises potential customers in the "frequently asked questions" section of her website,

> The following party could very likely cost $1,000 and can be negotiated for more or less, and could likely include all of the following: Friendly conversation, visiting in the parlor, touring the facilities, libations, strip tease/sexy lap dance, shower together or romantic Jacuzzi or bubble bath, view XXX videos, foreplay/full contact sensual massage, breast sex, oral sex, intercourse with various positions, cunnilingus or 69, one ejaculation, souvenirs, condoms, lube, oils, lotions, sex toys. This party could last anywhere from 30 minutes to an hour.[23]

This party is quite full of scripted events, and can last for a fairly short period of time. While Amy refuses to be specific on her website, there is room for negotiation. She also specifies that unlimited orgasms can be negotiated for an additional price. However, she adds a little further down that, "Extended parties (4 hrs +) are offered at a much-discounted rate, depending on activities. i.e. 24 hrs at $10,000 = less than $500 an hour." According to her website, she even has a party available "wherein you can do anything you want for as long as you want and as long as you can for one price. The only rule is—no naps." Friendly conversation and a romantic Jacuzzi session are listed as services right along with cunnilingus and one ejaculation.

If for any reason a customer and a worker fail to reach an agreement, all the women we talked to, whether in suburban or rural brothels, said they were free to "walk" the customers any time they chose. Celeste, a worker at the Green Lantern, a rural brothel in Ely, affirmed, "We are independent contractors; we have the right to refuse anybody for any reason." Misty, another worker at the Green Lantern, added, "We can stop them here, we can stop it at the bar." Celeste explains, "Of course that doesn't mean in some houses you aren't going to take some heat over it." But Celeste indicated that she was always able to convince any member of the staff, including parlor maids, cashiers, or whoever she spoke to that she was not going to party with anyone whom she thought would be a problem.

Dennis Hof talked about his philosophy:

> You don't party with anyone you don't want to. You don't do any sex act that you don't want to, and you don't do it for any less than you think it's worth. Okay? So the guy comes in and we don't care what the problem is. If the girl thinks the guy is too tall, too short, too black, too white, too skinny, too fat, too rich, too poor, don't even explain to us. Just stay away from the guy.

Hof says he asks that the women not be rude, but rather just introduce them to a "friend," another woman on shift. For Hof, allowing women to have this power is about smart business as much as it is about respect for women. "So with doing that, you have girls that will come to work for you that wouldn't normally come to work in prostitution."

Once the service and pricing have been agreed upon, the woman collects the cash or credit card, and will then either leave the customer in her room and give the manager the money or she will bring the customer to a payment center to pay. In a large brothel she goes to a booth, office, or operation center and pays the money to the manager.

In a smaller brothel, the operation center is likely the kitchen. The manager will take the payment and record it in any one of a number of ways, and then set a timer, depending on the negotiation. We have seen everything from a kitchen timer next to a three-by-five card with the woman's name on it to an elaborate wall system of hanging cards to a white board and marker. In most houses, the manager keeps track of time. The office knows when the customer's time is up and he needs to either leave or renegotiate and pay again.

Safe Sex

One of the major selling points that brothels use to justify their legal existence in Nevada is the issue of safety: protecting the physical safety and sexual health of both the workers and the customers. Safety is often a mixture of health-related, management-related, and symbolic practices.[24] First, the brothels are widely recognized for business practices that promote women's safety such as mandatory condom use, monitoring via intercoms, payment procedures, and panic buttons. Yet often brothel surveillance practices serve two goals: they protect women, and protect profits for women and owners. Second, the legal nature of the brothel offers a unique form of protection for the women against bad customers and against arrest. Local police are allies of the brothels. Unlike street sex workers, the brothels can rely on local law enforcement as a back-up in the unlikely case of trouble. Third, the workers also engage in particular safety practices, from training each other (no formal training is provided by the house) to their visual examination of the men's genital area for health risks.

During the AIDS panic of the 1980s, brothels gained some legitimacy in the state by proactively helping to establish mandatory condom-use policies, and by instituting health testing for sexually transmitted infections (STIs) for the women. Thus they promote themselves as safer alternatives for customers than untested illegal sex workers. These practices, however, mark the women as potential carriers of disease and are really aimed at protecting men's health.

Although the women are subject to rigorous health testing, the "dick check" is the only mechanism for scrutinizing the client's health—a little discussed but critical element in keeping the women healthy and in control. Once a customer goes back to the room, the woman conducts a "dick check" after negotiations but before any sexual activity. She washes off the customer's penis in a "peter pan" and looks for visible signs of STIs. The women often discuss symptoms and safe sex.

Ruby at the Moonlite Bunny describes the dick check:

> Look for anything abnormal. You know what an ingrown hair looks like. You know the difference between herpes and an ingrown hair because of where it is. You look underneath their balls, between their legs, and you just give them a really good once over. You're looking for any kind of warts. You're looking for any kind of herpes, shedding skin. You check the tip to make sure that the fluid coming out is clear, and that's the kind of best dick check you can do. You also can get them in front of a black light and some things will show up.

Sometimes a customer does not pass the dick check. Workers then engage in a bit of education, describing symptoms and safe-sex practices with the man. Many women told us that they will sit and talk to a customer for a while before they send him back so that he will not be embarrassed returning to his friends too early. Again, women emphasize their freedom in determining who they will accept or reject. If a customer has a visible health problem, they can turn him down. Some women told us that they may refer a customer to another woman who is comfortable partying with a customer with certain symptoms.

There are also many mechanisms that protect women from physical violence. In most brothels, negotiations are monitored through an intercom in a central location. Most managers listen to negotiations and turn off the monitor once negotiations are complete. They say they do it for two reasons: to prevent theft, and safety. Owners identified a fear of employee theft as the major reason for using intercom systems to listen in on negotiations. One owner worried about losing out on the house cut: "You have 10 percent of the ladies that will try and rip you off seven ways to Sunday."

But both owners and workers recognize that listening to negotiations also protects the workers from customers. One manager told us that they listen in even "while she's bringing that money up to the office we continue to listen. Sometimes the customers get a little bit nosey and want to start looking in drawers and everything and we have a loudspeaker in every room and if we hear that then we yell at him over the loudspeaker." Another owner was firm that the intercom primarily "is about our safety concern. The house listens in on every negotiation."

Owners and workers both feel that the most likely time men may get angry or violent is during negotiations. The house can hear if the client gets unruly or abusive during the negotiation and interrupt if needed. A manager said, "If a girl is unsure of a customer she might ask you to listen, for security. Or, instead of turning on, I would walk out—this is such a small house—I'd walk down the hall and listen."

One worker expressed that she was reassured by the practice of management listening to the negotiation: "Say for instance you get in there, and ya know, they start right away climbing all over you . . . it's like wait a minute, you haven't shown any cash and you don't have free reign until there's an exchange made here. Okay?"

Collecting money before the service is provided is another way to ensure safety. That the credit card and cash are not in the woman's room ensures that the client does not try to steal money. Bob, owner of a small northern Nevada brothel, explains the rationale behind the practices of collecting money from the customers.

> The idea there is to get the money out of the room so that there's no attempt on the man's part at some point to be physical or forceful to regain his money. So it's sequestered away where he can't get at it. And then she puts down how much and the time, like 25 minutes or ten minutes or however long she's going to be and then brings it to the bartender and then we log it and set the timer.

The room timers allow the house to keep track of who is working when and who is running over time and might need management intervention. But managers are also responsible for letting both the client and the worker know the party is over. Says Bob,

> Then it's our responsibility to end the party. You want to eliminate the lady from any of the decisions in the process so that she is sheltered from any browbeating or coercion from the gentleman's part about more time or anything. She's put in a position to be able to say to the gentleman, "Oh you're the best I've had all day or all week or all year and I'd love to spend the

next hour in here with you, but these SOBs I work for are going to come pounding on the door and we're going to get in trouble unless either we leave the room or we talk more money." We encourage the lady to put the burden on us. And then she's their buddy and we're the bad guys.

All the brothels we visited had emergency call buttons in each bedroom. When pressed, these panic buttons would either link to a direct intercom in the office—formal or makeshift, depending on the brothel—or ring a buzzer that could be clearly heard by the madam, management, or another employee. In most brothels, the buttons are located at the head or side of the bed. These buttons are a major source of security for most of the women we interviewed, and many pointed them out as their direct link to help should an incident occur. A worker explains, "You push the panic button once and you have immediate rescue." Owners discuss using them as a back-up system in case other mechanisms fail.

No woman we talked to had ever actually used the panic button. The panic buttons seem to be more of a symbolic mechanism for protection against danger. A few workers expressed concern about the location of the button, or explained how they consciously positioned themselves to have easy access to the button. The only worker we interviewed who had experienced a violent customer pointed out that "panic buttons are a joke . . . usually they're across the room, but if you can get across the room you can get out the door."

Moreover, the women act as each other's safety net, as experienced or established prostitutes train new workers, and a house full of women provide security for each other. Women new to brothel prostitution, called "TOs" or "turn-outs," are shown the ropes by established workers who offer job training in the form of crash courses in the hallway that include tricks of the trade, and "sexpert" advice. Sharing skills can mean everything from how to put on a condom to how to provide dominance services. And peer training also promotes an element of safety. New turn-outs are shown how to use the mirrors on their walls to monitor a customer's movements from several angles and how to use something near the bed, like an ashtray, as a weapon. Further, having experienced workers explain that if a customer became violent, the women will "beat the dude all the way out to the gate" is reassuring.

Brothel owners have a clear interest in maintaining their image as law-abiding, trouble-free businesses in order to keep their licenses and maintain good relations within their communities. The owners we interviewed ensure this by making it policy to call the police at the slightest hint of trouble to send a message that they do not tolerate bad behavior. One owner explained, "The whole name of the game is control. But that control also makes us get along pretty well with the sheriff's office." As another owner said:

> You can be too late, but you can never call him [the sheriff] too early. So if they have the slightest hint of a problem, they call the sheriff. If they ask the guy to leave and he says, "I'm not going to," they say fine, I'll call the sheriff. They don't even argue with him. They just call the sheriff, and usually by the time the sheriff gets here the guy's already left. So all we do is give the sheriff's deputy a cup of coffee and send him down the road.

A policeman, who was not entirely supportive of prostitution, explained the difference between enforcing prostitution in the brothels versus on the streets:

> And it's like anything else, once you're in law enforcement you sort of have to enforce the laws. And we come in and part of what we do is just make sure everything is going okay . . . Because a lot of times you get patrons that go frequent other bars and get a little bit on the intoxicated side they want to come into here. They want to raise hell at the last minute. So you know, I think we look at it more on that aspect. The girls are working just like anybody else . . . The ones we look for are the lot lizards or the ones that are out soliciting over the CB at the truck stops. Those are the ones that are doing it illegally and those are the ones that we get mostly concerned with.

In practice, most brothels report that they very rarely need to involve the police to control customers. One policeman who was paying a check-up call to a brothel told us, "We don't get very many calls here at all. The last two or three years there's been next to nothing."

These mechanisms work in guaranteeing women's safety. Of all the women we interviewed, no one save one woman had a story about an act of violence she had experienced, or had heard of another woman experiencing. This one woman had been working in the brothels for nearly 16 years, and that was the only violent incident. Most of the women who had worked in other forms of illegal prostitution said that safety was one of the main reasons they came to the brothels.

Further, the set-up of the brothels makes client anonymity and easy exit difficult. During a shift, the behavior of the customer is being assessed as soon as he walks through the door, before the actual paid party. The brothel provides a houseful of people just a flimsy door away from the monetary exchange and sexual interaction.

In effect, the legality of the brothels underpins the safety mechanisms exercised in the industry. Being legal lends a symbolic and material legitimacy and authority to the business, with all the rights (police protection) and responsibilities (house rules to protect health and body) that accompany it. On a sociopolitical level, legality requires a level of transparency and responsiveness to the constant public scrutiny of the local community, police, and policymakers. The function of legality seems to have severely reduced the factors of systematic violence assumed to be a part of sexual commerce.

MANAGEMENT AND WORKPLACE RELATIONS

Contracts and House Rules

Like laborers in more and more service industries, workers in the brothels are independent contractors. In most service work, employers are motivated to hire independent contractors because it makes them exempt from many workplace regulations and payroll taxes. Independent contractors, such as women working in erotic dance clubs, are supposed to work flexible hours and follow looser workplace regulations than workers in employee/employer businesses. The contractor essentially rents space in the club or brothel in exchange for working in an existing venue where clients come.

Contracts between the brothel and contractor are negotiated individually and specify hours, shifts, and for those with a residency requirement, length of employment. We found that brothels commonly require first-time contractors to work some minimum, usually from ten days to three weeks, although smaller brothels in isolated areas offer more flexible arrangements. Sheri's Ranch has a minimum of one week and a maximum of three weeks. The websites for smaller brothels, like the

Shady Lady Ranch in southern Nevada, and the Villa Joy Ranch and Wild West Saloon in northern Nevada, advertise a special 14-day contract. Once a worker has proven herself from the perspective of the manager, these contracts may become more flexible.

On top of the contract, each house has rules that specify working hours, how and when workers may come and go from the premises, shift rules, room and board charges and requirements, fees and fines, grievance procedures, and income splits. House rules can also specify meal hours, dress requirements, rules on personal property, and other expectations. Most of the brothels require contractors to pay the brothel 50 percent of the amount negotiated with a client. Until she sold My Place in Winnemucca, Barbara Davis' was the last brothel left that took only 40 percent for the house. Women usually pay room and board on top of that. They often have to tip bartenders, cleaning staff, cooks, taxi and limo drivers, and other brothel staff. At Sheri's Ranch, workers pay room and board of $46 a day (as of 2008), which includes all meals (including a 24-hour soup and salad bar and beverage center), housekeeping services, a workout room, a tanning bed, a computer room, and a lounge.[25] Some brothels waive room and board if a woman makes no money in a particular evening, or if she does exceedingly well. Workers also pay for the required medical testing, any body management like hair and makeup, and clothes or other goods from mobile businesses that frequent the brothels.

Smaller rural brothels have varying hours and some close for part of the evening. In many cases, a middle-of-the-night client may roust the night manager and whoever may be on night shift out of a nap. Many of these small brothels have what they call an "early girl" who is on call if someone visits during slow hours in the morning or afternoon. The brothels in Elko and Ely actually close between about 4 a.m. and noon, and most women work the busiest shifts at night.

All of the suburban brothels are open 24 hours a day. Most require women to work an 8- to 12-hour shift. Troy Regas, a manager at the Old Bridge Ranch outside of Reno, explained that when the women are working their shift, they are required to make every line-up. They may be excused if they tell the floor maid (for example, if they are eating), but management has to know where the women are.

Sheri's Ranch is one of the few brothels that requires women to work 24-hour shifts under certain circumstances, which is one of the strictest policies in the industry. In 2006, the manager told us that ladies have three minutes from the call to be lined up on either side of the parlor in full makeup, hair, shoes, and clothing. If there are more than 20 women working, they work 12-hour shifts, and they do not have to make a line-up when they are not on shift. If the house falls below 20 women, then everyone is on 24 hour shift all the time. They may be fined $50 if they miss a line-up.

This 24-hour shift was a part of Sheri's Ranch management rules, even during the ownership prior to the remodel. Manager Ray Slaughter defended the practice, saying that if there were shorter shifts, the women would complain about who would get the better shift. Ray maintains that if he could think of a better way, he would.

> So what you could do is the girls who make two thousand go to bed. And then the ones that didn't make any money, they have all the opportunity to make the money. But then they start fighting among themselves, you know, so, "if she's gonna get in the line-up I'm gonna get in the line-up," and so there's no way to keep a perfect peace. Believe me, I've done it for ten years.

Other staff members at Sheri's Ranch had their own perspectives on the 24-hour shifts. As Penny, the cook, said, "That's what kinda makes this one different from the others, I guess the philosophy there is, all your girls make the line-up then you have less chance of losing a customer because you know that they have your selection." A few of the women workers get through this practice by comparing it to having a baby, "like when you have an infant and you know you're getting up and you're nursing, you just learn to sleep whenever there's a moment, when you train your body that way."

Women's Mobility

The majority of brothels in Nevada are very different from other service industries in one main respect. In many brothels, workers are required to live at the brothel, a practice known as "lockdown," and it is one of the more controversial brothel practices. In recent years though, this is starting to change, and suburban brothels in northern Nevada permit women to leave the premises after working a shift, instead of staying on-site for the duration of their contract. Brothel operators who continue to practice lockdown gave us several reasons for doing so. The most frequent justification is health. Owners fear that women may have unprotected sex outside of the brothel after having passed a mandatory health test. Thus they threaten to spread disease to customers. Many owners cite local health codes, saying every time a woman left a brothel she would have to be retested. However, we were never able to verify the exact regulations, and assume it is a matter of interpretation, something likely worked out informally between local authorities and brothel owners. Still, it is worth noting that not a single woman we spoke to wanted to gamble with their health or their livelihood by having unprotected sex outside of a personal relationship. A few owners also admitted that limits on mobility help to ensure that women do not set up dates outside of the brothel and cut out management altogether.

While most brothels allow women to come and go at will while not on shift, even if they reside at the brothel they must usually notify managers of their whereabouts. Other brothels impose even stricter rules. These restrictions on mobility go beyond the bounds of typical independent contracts. Local police and/or sheriff's offices used to issue a set of written rules governing where and when women may be seen in town. However, since the 1990s, governing authorities have eliminated these rather archaic and probably unconstitutional written restrictions.

The smaller brothels in more isolated towns tend to be more lenient. Managers who require women to live at the brothel have, in a few cases, become much more flexible with the rules, depending on the trust that has developed between owner and worker. Celeste, who works at a small brothel in Ely, explained that the lockdown at her brothel means "you can leave, but you won't have a job when you get back. When you leave you have to be chaperoned by a bar manager." On the other hand, a manager of a brothel near Beatty told us that women with cars can make runs into town for up to four hours if they want, as long as staff know where they are and someone is covering the floor in case a customer comes. If they do not have their own transportation, the manager may drive them.

Most managers told us they let women go where they want when they are not on shift as long as staff know where they are. They always added a caveat—if they are caught in town at a bar being rowdy, making trouble, or being too visible, they will get that privilege revoked.

Thus, we suspect that lockdown practices vary significantly from town to town owing to a combination of management proclivities and local informal norms.

For a brothel of any size, keeping track of independent contractors is a balancing act. This is especially true for rural brothels who may not have customers for several hours at a time. At Angel's Ladies, the white board in the kitchen tracks the shifts of about ten women. When we were interviewing women there, the board was tracking the whereabouts of four women who were in residence. The rest on the board were either on vacation or planning to return soon, and the board recorded the dates they were expected to return. Angel's had several acres of surrounding land, including a large swimming pool built from a natural hot springs, a vegetable garden, and a small barn. Janet, the manager, told us that the women often go for long walks or hang out at the pool. When they do, they have to mark it on the board. They can go to town for four hours at a time, and the manager told us it is usually to go to the store, the clinic, or the post office.

While brothel workers seem subject to unduly strict rules on mobility, in interviews with us, workers were less concerned about mobility than other aspects of the job. Most of the women working in the rural brothels come from outside the area and often outside the state. Staying at the same place where they work is a practical and inexpensive option for some women coming from out of town. Small towns provide less anonymity—a new woman in town will be noticed. She may not want to be identified as the new prostitute in town, so staying at the brothel gives some protection for workers.

Emili says that staying at the brothel does bother her, "I'm used to being home every night. I'm used to working out everyday in my pool. I'm used to being there and at least seeing them [my children] when they're sleeping, whether it's before I go to work or when I get home." Some women told us that the lockdown was just one of those things you put up with for the money.

Several owners are very critical of these restrictive practices. One of the owners of a small rural brothel is incensed over the practice of lockdowns at other brothels. "I don't know where this thing is coming from about if the lady leaves the house she has to be retested. That would essentially destroy their business and it's a pretty stupid idea." He believes this probably violates legal independent contractor rules.

This owner blames restrictions on mobility for causing a shortage of brothel workers. He considers the lockdown to be one of the biggest hurdles to finding new women to work in the brothel industry. Lora Shaner managed Sheri's for a number of years and wrote the book *Madam: Inside a Nevada Brothel* about her experience. She told us,

> If I owned a brothel, I would let them work their shift and go home, and come back the next day . . . When they're here for three weeks at a time, they get antsy. They begin to feel like it's prison. It's not good for their morale. It's not good for business, instead of smiling brightly they're frowning, looking at the floor, tired.

In the past ten years, several of the largest suburban brothels have ended this practice. Larger brothels in northern Nevada, in both Storey and Lyon County, allow the women to go home after their shift if they want. Some of these are the same brothel owners who, five years earlier, had told us they could not by code let women go home. The decision to change was largely a financial one. Troy Regas at Old Bridge explained to us that he could work 50 women in a 30-room house because people could double up. They could work 12-hour shifts, stay open 24 hours and have workers pick the days when they want to work. Some brothels charge women a shift fee when they go home while not on shift. The management also made the decision because of competition for good workers. Many realized that their best workers could easily choose to have more flexible hours by working legally in dancing and adult movies or by working illegally.

The suburban brothels have also become flexible in the kinds of contracts they negotiate with workers. Regas told us that his contracts are very flexible and can be altered by Yvonne, one of the managers:

> Let's say they want to adjust it [the contract] somehow. Well, when they work that out with the lady who does that, they just write it in and they initial it, and that's that. So you know it's as flexible as they negotiate with Yvonne. So if they come in here and they say, "Hey you know Yvonne, blah blah blah, I got to work day [shift] this day, and swing [shift] this day," she'll work it all out. She'll sit down with them and then she'll pencil them into the boards and that's that.

Dennis Hof also promotes flexible shifts at both the Moonlite Bunny Ranch and Miss Kitty's. Dusty, in her forties, a high-earning worker at Miss Kitty's, explained: "most of the girls work 12- to 14-hour shifts and I work an 8- and 10-hour shift and can basically come and go. I appreciate it. He [Dennis] knows I'm a single mom, and so if I come in and get a specific amount booked, I can go."

Brothel workers Lani, 19, and Alice, 19, specifically mentioned the freedom to come and go at the Moonlite Bunny Ranch as one of the things they liked best. Alice said, "Well if I don't wanna come to work tomorrow, I don't come to work tomorrow. If I want to take three weeks off, I take three weeks off." Lani reiterates, "Exactly, if you ever want to go home an hour early, you just ask them. Tell them 'I'm gonna go home an hour early,' give them your reason and they'll be like, 'okay see ya later.' " Alice added, "If I want to go run and go tanning, I can go tanning, if I wanna get my nails done, I go get my nails done." They both contend that the Moonlite Bunny offers a preferable work arrangement, "The other brothels you have to stay in the house until it's time to go. This place is really cool. They're really flexible. It's really cool."

Because of the stigma surrounding prostitution, it is very important that we make the point that in none of the brothels where we interviewed women did we see anything leading us to believe that a woman could not terminate her contract with the brothel if she so wished. The women are technically bound by the same contracts and relations of employment as any other independent contractor, although in practice some brothels seem to stretch the rules. Women negotiate many of the terms of their contract. If they need to leave before the contract is over, owners do not force or coerce women to make them stay. If they violate the lockdown or other terms of the contract, they will probably not be rehired. A woman may face transportation problems in a remote brothel if she does not have her own vehicle. But no woman who we interviewed ever expressed that she was concerned about being able to leave, nor did anyone tell us about others who were concerned about being forced to finish out a contract. It is not in a brothel's business interests to have a woman working who does not want to be there. Troy Regas, manager of the Old Bridge Ranch, explained:

> If a girl comes to me and she says, "Hey I want to go home,"
> I don't tell her, "Hey you've got to stay here, you've got a

contract." I say, "Well you know, you're not tied here, but just remember that you know the way we do business here, if you can't keep up your contract, we won't let you come and sign another contract."

Dennis Hof spells it out in terms of profit:

> It takes 250 to keep 50 working. I mean these girls fly in from all over the country. I mean, when you come in here, if it's your desire to come in and work every month, you come in the first of the month and you say I'm staying until I make $5,000, and maybe it's two days maybe it's ten days. Then you leave and that's okay, we don't care. We don't care at all, this is like a hotel for us. All this is like a hotel and you're booking names and places and all that. I want to stay three days, I want to stay seven days, I want to stay twelve days. OK? We let them do whatever they want to do. And that's why they come back to us, and that's why they work, 'cos we let them do it.

Managing the Brothel

Simultaneously running a workplace and housing is a big challenge for owners and managers. Managing a brothel could be described as running a sales center while having to supervise a workforce of unpredictable size, under a variety of different contracts. In many ways we found that the relationship between management and brothel sex workers is similar to workplaces where managers oversee a flexible independent labor pool. At the same time, running a brothel is also like running a dormitory. Brothel workers may be diverse in terms of class, race, and culture. Women work in close quarters under conditions of intense competition. The women tell us that this breeds both close familial relationships and intense disagreements. Since managers oversee both work time and personal time, in the day-to-day life in a brothel, managers and workers get to know each other in a very different way than in other service businesses. Add to that the dynamics of an all-female labor force, mostly male consumers, and the stigma of sexual labor, and we begin to see the unique gendered dynamics of the brothel industry under the larger umbrella of a service economy.

Brothel managers and owners are acutely aware of the stigma

surrounding their business: the stigma of being in a sexualized industry, and the stigma of women's exploitation. A female manager of a small northern Nevada brothel railed against what she perceived to be the gossip of some women in town, contending that she keeps a respectable business and does not even allow customers to curse.

> What do I care what people on the outside say?! If a door is locked, people on the outside are sure there's all sorts of things going on in here. The women downtown have the class of striking dock workers and mouths to match. And I can tell you a lot more goes on down there than they'll ever see in a brothel.

Another brothel owner made the case to us that prostitution in sixteenth-century France and England gave women political clout. "Prostitution really opened the door for the original liberation of women." One manager said everybody thinks "we're in sex orgies, and that's totally, totally untrue." He admitted that when he first started the job, "it was a novelty, you know, seeing half-naked girls, as my head's going around all the time. But now it's just like looking at furniture, you know, like being a gynecologist."

Every owner and manager we talked to stressed that they approach the brothels as a business and that, as part of the business, women are workers who deserve respect. Dennis Hof asserts, "This is a business. A legal business, and the people in it should be treated with respect okay? Me, the girls, everybody." Ray, who managed Sheri's Ranch said, "You know, it's a business and we treat it like a business. I love the girls, you know, and I get along with them."

However, the owners do sometimes have contradictory ways of dealing with management issues. How owners and managers frame the problems of the business and talk about the workers reveals the complexities of gender, power, and the workplace. Witness this contrast of talking about what is essentially the same set of problems: Ginger, who managed the Calico Club in Battle Mountain for ten years, described the women who work for her, "They're independent as hell. They don't listen to anyone. If we listened to our mothers, we wouldn't be in this business." Dennis Hof, owner of the suburban Moonlite Bunny Ranch, put the issue this way: "What we can't have is a house full of unmotivated girls that are not able to achieve their goals and have us not achieve ours." Both are talking about the challenges of supervising workers; one characterizes it as a personality trait, the other character-izes it as a business issue of matching rational ends and goals. In many ways, this is the major tension in running a brothel.

For example, the main issue for owners is profit, but they are totally dependent on how much the women negotiate for and earn in a shift. The owners articulate their concern as altruistic, a concern about women earning money for themselves, but owners' profits are clearly at stake. Patricia Kendrick, who helped manage Sharon's Place in Carlin, said: "Any girl with any brains could knock down at least $52,000 a year minimum." Bob, manager at the Calico Club, said, "For a woman who's got her head together . . . if she's treating it all like a job, she's making $55,000 a year. And that ain't too shabby." We heard comments like these from quite a few managers, particularly in smaller brothels.

Some management styles micro-manage the women as a way to keep the workplace efficient and orderly. Many smaller brothels have fairly extensive systems of fines for not making line-ups or shifts and for not being fully dressed or in proper makeup. Conversely, suburban brothel owners tend to rely on other methods to control the work environment. They weed out the "problem" workers. Dennis Hof says,

> The success of the Bunny Ranch is rather than having real hard core rules and laws for the minority, we treat everyone as if they're gonna do things properly, and then we eliminate the minority. In other words, if you have 150, 200 girls, and only 10 percent of them, 15 to 20 girls are butt-heads, alcoholic, drug addicts, socially don't fit, then all the rules are made for every-body. Well, why make it such an environment when all you have to do is get rid of the 15 or 20?

Ray Slaughter echoed Hof's sentiment in a slightly different way. He talked about doubling the business since he began managing Sheri's Ranch in the south:

> Yea, you know, sound business principles, and run it like a business. And, you know, keeping people happy, that's a tough tightrope to walk around here. But we don't allow any trashy people out here. Some of these girls are, you know . . . whether she's a crack addict or a street whore or whatever, and we get rid of them right away.

Suburban brothels can afford to simply replace any woman who is not working out, or who, in their words, is that 10 percent of "trashy people," because they have a larger pool of workers on staff and a larger pool of potential new contractors.

Many brothel owners talk about trying to help low-earning women be more profitable before they fire them. Managers at the larger brothels indicate that for some the problem is simply inexperience. Troy Regas at the large suburban Old Bridge Ranch said:

> We'll try to like help them. And it could be a problem with their negotiations. We'll come in and we'll try to tell them, well there's better ways to negotiate. There's you know . . . and try to give them advice, which sometimes is like criticism, but everybody needs a little.

Ray Slaughter recalled when Emili first came, after getting into debt working long hours as a hostess at a chain restaurant and at a gas station.

> She was so new, she didn't do well at all here about the first five days she was here. She was about ready to call it quits, and then the girls got a hold of her, started teaching her, you know, how to negotiate, how to present herself, and how to talk to people. And she's really shy, you know. She's done very well ever since.

Many owners and managers also struggle with women who socialize too much on the job instead of concentrating on work. Many owners of large and small brothels lament workers who do not take their jobs seriously.

> You motivate them by telling them, you know, you girls, this is serious stuff. And we want you to make your money, then get out of here and go have some fun. And, if that's all you want to make, then make it quick and go lay on the beach. Go do whatever turns you on. Go to Europe. Go back to Kansas City and play with your children and have a good life with them. Do whatever you want. While you're here we want you to be focused, and the reason you're here is to make money. This is not, this is not the place to look for your social environment, although they do.

In the large suburban brothels competition is intense, and when women do not make money they are simply asked to leave. This is especially true when there are women waiting for a space to open up at the house. Suburban brothel managers can afford to be much more bureaucratic in their approach. Dennis Hof put it this way:

> We're looking at the numbers all the time, just like any other commission business. You're looking at numbers and you talk to people and you say "excuse me, what's going on in your life? You know, last month you were here for two weeks and you booked $35,000, made $17,000 for yourself. This month you've been here for ten days and you booked $4,000. What's happening?" "Well, I'm arguing with my boyfriend, and I got this." "What can we do to fix it? You know, why don't you go home? Why don't you go see him, get this thing worked out, when you're ready come back. Okay?"

Ray Slaughter, at Sheri's Ranch, explained:

> They stay here a week and if they haven't booked then I'll tell them Friday, "look you're not doing it, sorry but it's not working out." So, that happens, you know, that happens occasionally. They go to line-up, they get dejected and they get depressed and they're hanging their head and looking at their feet on the line-up. And they're never gonna get picked doing that, you know. So it's showbiz.

Likewise, although the Moonlite Bunny Ranch is flexible with women's contracts, Hof expects women to honor their commitments, and if they do not then he will not bend the rules for them.

> Now what we don't do is if you say, "I'm coming in on the 1st and I'm going to be there for nine days." First comes in, "uh my dog's sick, uh I'll be there tomorrow. Uh, I missed my plane, uh my kid's got a cold, okay?" I say, "okay, okay, that's fine, fine." Finally you get there on the 7th, okay? That room's been empty all that time. So you come in, and you go to work and we don't say anything to you. Now it's time for you to go home. You say, "Excuse me, let me talk to you, next time you want to come here, you just show up. If there's a room we'll give it to you. If not, you're gonna have to sit in a hotel until it's ready,

because I'm not blocking a room out for you because you showed me that you're not responsible."

Yet Hof argues that his system works because he gives a substantial amount of freedom and respect to the women.

> So, if a girl doesn't want to give a blow job, a working girl, then she shouldn't have to. If she doesn't want to get on her hands and knees she shouldn't have to. If she doesn't want to do anal sex she shouldn't have to. And it's been tremendously successful, 'cos what the girls do is they end up partying only with guys they want to party with and they only do things they want to do, and they only do it for the price they want to do it. Now, with that being said when you give them that latitude, guess what? They probably do about 99 percent of what the guys want to do with the girl that they want to. But if you tell them, "you're gonna fuck every guy that comes in here, and you're gonna do everything that he asks you to, and you're gonna do it for the house minimum price," it just creates that environment that I don't want any part of.

Conversely, rural brothel owners have a much more difficult time simply breaking contracts with workers who do not follow the rules. As one small brothel owner observes, "As the ladies become more and more scarce, we are forced essentially to give them more and more leeway and let them do things that you would not have normally done."

Misty, working at the Green Lantern, assesses women's relationship with management:

> Managers will do everything they can to keep you here, because you're money for them ... They're not going to make no money if they have no girls and they try and please you. They're not going to break the rules for you, but if they can help you, if they can make you happy, they'll do that.

One of the biggest issues for brothel owners is the question of women who have pimps. The number of women who come to work in the brothels with pimps is unknown. Few of the women we talked to mentioned pimps, but we did not explicitly ask. When writer Alexa Albert explored the Mustang Ranch in the 1990s, she reported that most brothel prostitutes have pimps. But the women we interviewed, as we will show in the following chapters, also talked about changing pimps or dumping pimps and coming to the brothels.

The term "pimp" itself is controversial. At a basic level, "pimp" refers to a boss who manages your business, someone who brings in customers and takes care of the work environment and is paid for it. Pimps have historically been constructed as violent, controlling men who lure women into sex work, emotionally and physically control them, and take all their income. The image often has racist connotations (Jewish men in the late 1800s, or black men in contemporary culture), and the men are pictured as living off the earnings of a prostitute. The reality of an intimate or management relationship is often much more complex than popular portrayals.[26]

The owners and managers of Nevada's brothels frequently face accusations from media that they are themselves pimps, at the same time as they see the affects of abusive pimps on their workers. As a result, there is a deep antagonism between male managers who control women's sexuality in the legal workplace and those men who control women's sexuality in illegal sex work.

Hence, owners do not like pimps. Geoff Arnold, owner of a brothel in Wells, thinks that though some of his workers have pimps, the brothels play a liberating function. Arnold explained:

> Although one of our purposes is to get 'em away from the pimps because it is so disruptive inside the house. The damn pimp is calling all the time and whenever he calls, she's crying or she gets upset . . . One of the jobs of the madam, and she's 73 and all the girls call her mom, and the guys call her mom, but she is a mom to those girls and she helps keep them straight. And one of the things is to take them under her arm and say, "Honey, you need to stop sending money to that asshole."

The legal brothel industry in Nevada can be an escape valve for those women who are coerced to work illegally by a pimp. The owners often told stories about how they helped women get away from abusive pimps. A small brothel owner suggested that legality is the path to freedom from a pimp:

> By coming into a legal brothel, and we have had a couple of these cases, she is now doing something which is legal, so he

cannot use that as a force over her, and he is the one that is illegal. So if a lady with an abusive pimp comes into the house, and he shows up, he's the one that goes to jail. She's perfectly legal. She's basically in the clear. So it is a way to peel that influence off, if and when it's necessary.

Hof seconded this idea:

> When you legalize this business, these girls don't need a pimp. They don't have to have a pimp. I'm not their pimp. I'm their friend, I help them make money. We work together.

None of the brothel owners liked to contract with women who have pimps, and suburban brothel owners in particular do not like to employ women who obviously have pimps. Hof asks questions about women's experiences with a pimp or pimp families in the interview process because "we don't want that stuff, you know, we just don't need it. And it makes for a nice environment." Lora at Sheri's Ranch also feels that "there's no comparison between a brothel prostitute and one on the street, there's no comparison at all, even though some of these girls do have pimps, they [the pimps] don't come here, to beat them up, believe me, they just don't."

Said Ray Slaughter facetiously,

> Oh, if they come out here I'll deal with 'em. In a New York second I'll deal with them. Couple of them told me they were gonna come out and play pool one night. Bring 'em on out here. Yeah right, yeah. You know, we don't allow them on the premises at all. And they know better than to come. And if they did come, we'd get rid of the girl right away. And she'd never be welcome back here again.

However, owners and managers recognize that there are complexities in the relationships women have with pimps. Bob calls it "a very strange psychology." He continues,

> And it's not, "Hey, ho, you leave me alone; and I'll beat the shit out of you." There is some degree of that . . . somehow, there's a very deep emotional relationship there. And this is why you get these working girls that come in that have come off a pimp, and they're not allowed to have a good time. They cannot have

an orgasm in the room. That's verboten. You know, and usually you can't kiss. You can go screw but you can't have a good time. And you can't let him kiss you because, "That's for me."

Some brothel managers expressed a more nuanced understanding of care and monetary support. One female manager of a small brothel contends, "To me I don't care if they're married or whatever. If somebody is at home and they're not working, or putting in money, that's a pimp . . . 98 percent are supporting somebody else. That is, they say they were with somebody else and you know boyfriend or husband." Hof similarly underscores this notion of what living off the earnings of a sex worker can mean:

> Family's a great pimp. They are wonderful pimps because the mother that disowned her when she got into prostitution, who now they've patched things up, who's watching her baby, will think nothing of calling up and says, "uh you're baby needs to go to the doctor. You better send me $2,000 by Thursday, 'cos I'm going to the doctor, okay? And you better send me $2,000. This baby needs clothes, this baby's starting school, you know I need $1,000, I need $1,500, I need this money tomorrow. We've got to pay the rent. I don't have the money to pay the rent. Okay?" They're wonderful pimps.

Not only do owners and managers differentiate themselves from pimps using the legality of brothels as the crux of their argument, they also judge other brothel managers on a fairly taboo issue, having sex with women working in the house. Geoff Arnold, who owns the Donna's Ranch in rural Wells, said:

> One of the things that I have seen that differentiates between the places that are really good and well run and the ones that are kind of slovenly is whether or not the owners are doing the girls. I mean, ya know, I don't really understand how an owner could get away with doing the girls, you know? But some of them do. Not very many, I'd say out of 30 houses there's maybe three.

The owners we spoke with constantly contrasted their own approach to management against these three. These three, who were never named, were held up as the ones who also search women, or lock up women's belongings, or withhold payment. Crystal Burns, a part owner of the Stardust, talked to us a great deal about how her previous experience as a former working woman herself makes her a better quality manager. For her, one of the major issues is owners having sex with the women, and for her it is a respect-for-women issue,

> But I'll say one thing, I'm for ladies rights. I am an owner and I'm an expert now. I go for women's rights. I don't go for the shit that you lock up keys not giving your money and all that crap . . . Do you think the owners treat the workers the same as would be treated as any other business? No! Absolutely not! Because they can get away not doing it, and word that the bosses fuck around the ladies, fool around with the ladies, in different houses [gets around]. Mix business with pleasure without paying money.

For most of the male owners, avoiding sex with the women is just good business sense. Sex is first and foremost a commodity in this environment. As Ray Slaughter of Sheri's Ranch stressed, "It's just not the thing to do. It'd be chaos." Another rural brothel owner also addressed the issue from a business perspective:

> When you start getting involved with the girls, it becomes a nightmare because the girls don't like it, first of all. And then the word spreads around in this business. It is a close society and everybody pretty soon knows what's going on and then you get a bad reputation and then you have problems getting people that will come to work for you. Because the good prostitutes want to make money. And, that's their interest.

Hof also expressed the notion that having sex with the women is a bad business decision. At the same time he has had multiple girlfriends over the years, some of whom have worked at the Moonlite Bunny Ranch. For Hof, blurring public and private life is part of his enigmatic persona as a high-profile brothel owner.

Workers' Thoughts on Managers

Sex workers themselves articulate the challenges of working with management in quite conventional ways: they make complaints about unfair fines, and how management deals with competition among the women. They rarely complained to us about the management of the brothel in which they were currently working. When they did, it was mostly about excessive or unwarranted application of fines. They also spoke of the level of camaraderie that can develop in a brothel.

Zoie communicated what many women told us: that the issue is as much about working with other independent contractors as it is working with management. "Every house has different girls. And once you've been around for a while you get to know the girls that are pretty much stationary in each house and you decide what kind of bullshit you want to put up with. Every house has different managers and it makes a difference." Many women move quite frequently from one brothel to another.

In the smaller brothels the women often refer to the brothel owners or management as family. For example, Angela at the Green Lantern talked about former owners of the Stardust where she had worked before, "I got really close to them. I'd never gone anywhere else. I loved it there. I got really super close to them. I call them mom and dad or mom and pop, and it's because they treated me with respect. You know they treated me like I was part of the family."

Mac and Sharon Moore self-consciously organized Angel's Ladies to be homely and casual, largely because there is little else that might attract a worker to Beatty. The owners, managers, and workers have dinner together, and managers encourage women to bring friends or even customers to dinner. One woman at Angel's Ladies talked about her relationship with the managers:

> It's a mind over matter job and it's more the mental stress. So he [George, the manager] understands that well. So he tries to make it easy on us, ya know. Other brothel owners, they just, "Make that money, make that money." That's how they are, ya know? They don't care about our feelings or how we're feeling, down low, sad, whatever, and such. Mac and Sharon do.

The women who work at these brothels, as with several of the small brothels, told us that they like to work there because they appreciate the sense of community, relaxed atmosphere, and slower pace a small house offers.

Bev, who worked at Miss Kitty's, told us that even at the larger brothels,

I think the girls stay in the houses because they feel loved, they bond, something they never get when they were working on the street. They don't want to leave here, they won't leave that love and companionship. And we do fun things together. We'll all get in groups and play games.

Nevertheless, many women articulated that the key differences between the rural and suburban brothels are the level of competition, inflexible and numerous rules, and the pace of work. One woman described the difference between a rural and suburban brothel's approach to dealing with relations between the women, an approach that seems to describe class differences in communication as much as anything else. At one point she was having problems with another woman and the manager of the rural brothel told her, as she recounted, to "just yell right back at her." But when she worked at Sheri's Ranch outside of Las Vegas,

There's no arguing in that place. If you argue, you have to go to the hostess in that place. Anybody arguing. It's very professional verbally on down. And that's why a lot of the girls don't like it because they have no self-expression, except with their customers and their parties. It's all polite or just stay to yourself. So I stayed to myself a lot, because then I didn't argue, you know.

CONCLUSION

The business of selling sex in Nevada's brothels is in many ways similar to leisure-oriented service work in restaurants, clothing stores, or hotels. The work itself is interactive; marketing is essential to capturing a wider client base; and, for suburban brothels especially, the business structure is becoming more corporate. All service businesses struggle to provide profitable, reproducible, and standardized services to consumers wanting individualized experiences. A growing tourist industry has driven dramatic growth in Nevada, with changing consumer incomes and tastes, and an increasing racial and class diversity of potential clientele, even in the rural areas. The business of sex is changing too, from ownership and marketing to business structure, organization of work, and management relations. Often, to what degree these changes take place is related to how close the brothel is to an urban resort city like Reno or Las Vegas.

Suburban brothels close to large travel destinations are bigger businesses with more capital and a broader customer base. These brothels have always been more likely to market to tourists, and bring in workers who conform more closely to conventional standards of attractiveness and charge more for services. These brothels are also more able to respond to changing consumer tastes, such as an increasingly sophisticated and modern male consumer who is willing to spend more money and travel further for relaxation and leisure services. The marketing of upscale individualized services has grown through the strategic cultivation of a singles bar atmosphere, the increasing number of fantasy rooms (hot tubs, dungeons, themes) and more resort- or spa-like packages, and the expansion of services to include massage, options for female customers (beyond just a heterosexual couple seeking a threesome), and on- and off-site dates. They are marketing to broad-ranging audiences, particularly since the advertising ban was lifted in 2007, using more mainstream business forms and generally diversifying as they try to integrate into Nevada's tourist economy in new ways.

The more isolated rural brothels used to market themselves as a sexual home away from home for men in traditionally masculine, working-class jobs—miners, farmers and farm hands, ranchers, and truckers. Marketing to this "bread-and-butter" client meant homey décor, discreet marketing tactics, and more affordable, less varied services. While this category of clientele is still the primary source of profit for small brothels, even the more remote small towns are seeing the effects of a globalized economy. Seasonal employees come from as far away as Chile, tourists travel to rural parts of the state, and small towns are experiencing major demographic changes.

Brothel management has been the subject of some debate. Brothels are highly gendered workplaces, and because they are stigmatized workplaces, workers are subject to rules that might not stand up to the scrutiny of labor laws, such as restrictions on mobility and residency, excessive fines, and 24-hour shifts. However, there are two very important trends to note here. The first trend is that, unlike what some critics may charge, we found absolutely no evidence that brothel workers were being held in the brothels against their will. We found no indication of trafficking. The only evidence of violence was one incident described by a worker who had been in the industry for over 15 years. We found no evidence that any worker who was not happy with her work situation could not leave. Because this is a legal business, workers and owners operate in the light of day. Brothels can be and have been shut down for violating laws, or even violating the norms of the community.

The second trend is that the demands of the marketplace are increasingly forcing owners to improve workplace conditions. Owners who want to be competitive for quality workers are changing their practices. The most competitive brothels allow women to work in regular-length shifts, have reasonable fines and fees, and are removing restrictions on mobility. The trend is toward improvement in these areas. Brothels are still businesses, however, and just as in any business, workers are subject to rules that are created to guarantee owner profit- ability and worker productivity. Independent contractors have even fewer rights than do regular employees in any service business. Add to that the stigma of being a sex worker and the worker's lack of connec- tions within the local community, and the playing field is tilted even more toward owners. Workers in Nevada brothels would benefit greatly from a union, or even a statewide ombudsman who could advocate on their behalf. Organizations like the Sin City Alternative Professional's Association (SCAPA, affiliated with the Las Vegas chapter of the national Sex Worker's Outreach Project) and the Desiree Alliance (a national sex workers' rights organization) have begun to publicly express concern about brothel workers' rights, including women's restricted mobility, their ability to receive phone calls from family or friends, and their right to collect all earnings at the end of a shift or contract.

5

PATHS TO BROTHEL WORK

How do women come to work in Nevada's brothels? In some ways, the answer to that question is the same reason thousands of residents have moved to Nevada since the 1950s—jobs in a booming leisure economy. The market for services such as escape, relaxation, and fantasy has drawn women from varied backgrounds to work in an array of sex-related jobs in Nevada since the days when mining was king. The state's tourist trade, as in other vacation destinations across the globe, draws workers from shrinking employment sectors in other regions who seek new opportunities. Global tourism generates all sorts of markets for sex, sexuality, and intimacy, and in Nevada's resort cities men and women seek employment in both formal and informal employment. Nevada's legal brothels provide one additional formal sector option in this array.

Nevada's legal brothels have always served as another choice for women who, for whatever reasons, choose to work as prostitutes. We find that today's legal brothels have a rotating door for women from illegal indoor and outdoor work in cities across the country. Women often come to the brothels from illegal work for a change in scene, or a break from the stress of hustling customers, or to escape the watchful eye of the law.

In addition, there is also a steady stream of women who have not routinely sold sex, but who come to the brothels to give it a try. In an increasingly unequal market, brothels draw women who are unable to make ends meet in service industry jobs who are willing to try sex for pay in a legal setting.

Finally, a growing global sex industry means more women make careers in legal sexual commerce. The profitable brothels in suburban areas that cater to upscale leisure-seeking tourists are a lucrative draw for high-end workers, from adult film to erotic dance.

This means there are significant differences in the social classes, resources, backgrounds, and motivations of women who work in Nevada's brothels. Indeed, the labor pools that brothels draw from have changed with transformations in the broader economy. We discuss the various paths women take into Nevada's legal brothels and how they lead to rural or suburban brothels in different ways. Also, we explore how brothels fit into women's larger work narratives and overall labor market careers. This chapter explores how the demographic and economic changes in a leisure economy affect the paths which women take into Nevada's brothels.

Talking about women's routes into the sex industry as a consequence of the demographic and economic changes in a growing leisure economy, rings counter to nearly a century of writing on why women become prostitutes. From journalistic accounts of white slave-traders stealing God-fearing women in the late 1800s, to tales of sex trafficking across today's permeable national borders, women's entrance into the sex industry has been wrapped in narratives of innocent women forced to do what no woman would ever do. Feminist debates often make it seem as if there are only two possible paths: women are either forced against their will, or freely choose prostitution.[1] However, a growing body of research is looking at women's entry into sex work as a consequence of shifting demographics and global economics. Some argue that even sex tourism needs to be understood as more than simply a form of victimization. Research is now showing that women's entrance into prostitution is more a consequence of labor market dynamics, migration patterns, and demographics, than individual experiences with abuse or violence.[2]

Indeed, none of the women we interviewed in the brothels told us stories of being forced into the brothels. Theirs were stories of the choices they made among their array of labor market options. To conclude that brothel workers are free from constraints, however, is just as naïve as to believe that women are shackled into sex work. The narratives of brothel workers' lives are so much more complex than a simple debate over coercion versus choice.

One woman's story illustrates the complexity of choice well. Ricki, 35, at Miss Kitty's, echoed popular notions when she told us: "I think I was pretty much programmed to be a prostitute" because she was sexually abused as a teenager. Her story stood out as the most traumatic of all our interviews. Yet the most striking element of her story was that she did not start selling sex until later in her life, despite how easily she explained her entrance into sex work in the context of abuse. Ricki told us of how her family got "screwed up" after her father, who was black, died when she was 5 years old. Her white mom had a lot of resentment about being left with two interracial kids. "I used to grow up feeling really ashamed that I was half black," Ricki explained. In high school she did a lot of drugs and later placed her two daughters for adoption with a couple she met at church because of her drug use. She blames sexual abuse from one of her mom's friends for the prostitution.

> I needed that attention so badly. So you know, it all falls into place . . . What he did to my head was a lot worse than what he did to me physically. Of course I did reach orgasm because the orifice performed and there was a lot of guilt behind that. You know, I felt very dirty. Every time, I felt really nasty. I felt bad. He'd always reward me. So there you go—prostitution. You do this, you get this, you know. And then I remember my mom telling me once that she had to live with this guy to pay the house payment. So I think, it's just something that I learned.

Yet Ricki did not start selling sex until around the age of 25. At the time when she first started selling sex, she had an unemployed, abusive husband. She began selling sex illegally to support him. Her husband began smoking crack cocaine with some pimps she had connected with, and all her money went to them to pay for it. Ricki left them and worked in Texas for a while when she heard about the Mustang Ranch. Moving to the brothel gave her independence from her husband and from her pimps. She worked at the Mustang for three years and then left to work for a large internet retail company in Nevada for $5.15 an hour. After working there for five years, she felt she was getting nowhere with that job. So she came back to the brothels and worked at Miss Kitty's for two years. Although Ricki told her story as being programmed to be a prostitute, she did leave an abusive husband and quit the illegal street sex industry. She worked for five years in the service industry, almost as long as she worked selling sex, but the work did not pay her enough to survive.

Changing labor markets tells a big part of the story of how women come to the brothels. The service sector has grown tremendously. Women comprise the vast majority of workers in this new economy.[3] Most service jobs are notoriously low paying. Indeed, much of the growth in the inter-mountain west has been in service jobs. Lower skilled service jobs (jobs that require some skill but not formal knowledge via college or specialized training) include call-center, retail, food service, financial services, care work, hospitality, sales, tourism, and public welfare jobs. The financial instability of working in lower paid service sector jobs creates a pool of women workers who may seek alternative ways to make ends meet. Many of the women working in Nevada brothels come from these types of jobs.

The characteristics of independent contract labor draw women to brothels. Work in the legal brothel is always temporary. The work is bound by ten-day to three-month contracts. Thus women's decisions to work in the brothels often involve short-term decisions—how many weeks they will work in the brothel and what they will do in between brothel contracts—and long-term goals—how long they plan to work in the industry before they move to another job completely or retire.

Women's choices are also affected by the fact that Nevada's brothels are legal, formal sector employment. Around half of the women we interviewed had never sold sex illegally. The most common story we heard was that the brothels were their first experience in direct sexual sales. A great many came straight to the legal brothels from service industry jobs. In other words, the majority of women were not career sex workers, or selling sex full-time. More than three-quarters of the women who we interviewed had worked in the service industry at some point in their work careers. These two facts alone make it clear that contrary to stereotypes, a woman who sells sex is not always a career prostitute, and often moves from job to job. Selling sex is often one form of labor among a variety of jobs.

In this chapter, we refer to women's primary occupation just prior to when we interviewed them in Nevada's brothels. So while over three-quarters of all the women who we interviewed have tried to earn a living in the service industry, only about one-third came directly from illegal prostitution to work in the brothels.

In general, the women with whom we spoke came to the brothels following one of three paths. First, about one-third of the women came to the brothels directly from non-sexual jobs in the service industry that were not paying them enough to survive. They needed money, and working in a brothel offered a higher paying option with little up-front training or capital investment; it was fast money.[4] Having come from a background in non-sexualized employment, they might consider this job temporary until they could get their income stabilized, or earn enough money to buy whatever, or go back to school.

Second, approximately one-third of women had come to the brothels from legal sex industries, mostly adult film or erotic dance. Legal prostitution offered a high-paying option, and some used brothel work to further their careers in the sex industry, often rotating brothel work between dance tours or films.

Finally, about one-third of our interviewees came to the brothels from illegal prostitution. They saw working in the brothels as a break, of sorts, from the stress of working illegally. Many of these illegal workers also had experience in service industries, often rotating between "straight" jobs and sex work.

Through our research, we can paint a general picture of the women who work in Nevada's brothels. Gathering precise demographic information on brothel workers is difficult. There is frequent turnover in the brothels; each one attracts women of different backgrounds and resources, and any one-shot interview or survey necessarily fails to capture a complete picture. Of the 38 women we interviewed, the vast majority work in the largest suburban brothels. These women worked at the Moonlite Bunny Ranch, Miss Kitty's, and the Old Bridge Ranch outside of Reno, and Sheri's Ranch outside of Las Vegas. A lesser number of interviewees came from five rural brothels in Carlin, Elko, Ely, and Beatty, and we observed brothel operations and conducted informal interviews in Winnemucca and Wells. None of the women were from the towns in which they worked. Based on these formal interviews and other informal observations and interviews we have gathered over the years, a reliable picture emerges. Women working in the brothels tend to range in age from 19 to 55, with the majority being in their late twenties to late thirties. The vast majority of the women identify themselves as heterosexual and a few identify as bisexual. About three-quarters of the women are white. The remaining participants are equally divided between Hispanic women and African American women. Around half of the women tend to be married or in a long-term intimate relationship. Most of the women have children; only about a quarter of the women do not. About two-thirds of the women have some education beyond high school. A few hold Bachelor's degrees, fewer still have done graduate work. About half of our interviewees volunteered information on the age they were when they began working in prostitution; the average age being 25. One had started illegal prostitution at age 15, one at 16, and four had begun at age 18 or 19. Six had started working as either illegal or legal prostitutes for the first time when they were over the age of 30.

COMING FROM THE SERVICE INDUSTRY

Almost all of the women we spoke with explained their initial decision to enter the sex industry as financial. As we said above, more than three-quarters of the women were rotating between sex industry work and straight work in some fashion. But what is most interesting is that about one-third of the women who we interviewed came directly to the brothels from non-sexual service work, never having regularly engaged in sexual labor before. These women were working in both rural and suburban brothels.[5]

They came from a diverse range of jobs: they had worked as pet shop owners, corporate trainers, animal trainers, teachers, nurses, librarians, and accountants, as well as in fields such as the military, real estate, publishing, restaurants, law enforcement, and emergency medicine. Some had worked in the service sector for only a few years. Others, like Strawberry Shortcake, 41, at rural Sharon's Ranch in Carlin, had worked in the restaurant industry for 13 years. Charli, in her thirties, who works at suburban Miss Kitty's, had been a secretary for 16 years. But working for low-wage service industry jobs could not

Figure 5.1 Brothel workers sit in the living area at Angel's Ladies while the managers George and Janet prepare dinner. Author photo.

sustain women through tough financial times. Brothel work is a way to make a lot of money quickly. For example, Shellie, a quiet woman in her thirties with short blonde hair, needed $1,000 to put her autistic son through an FDA drug trial. She told us how she did some research, quit her corporate marketing job, and came to suburban Sheri's Ranch the month before we met her. Shellie was planning to quit the brothel and go home as soon as she had the $1,000.

Sadie, at rural Angel's Ladies, was in her late twenties and had been working as a dancer in a southern city from the age of 17. At 24 she had a child, left dancing and got a job in real estate, but "found that I bit off a little more than I could chew." Then her house in Louisiana burned down. Six months before our interview, Sadie left her daughter with her mother and moved to Nevada, where she has been working at various brothels.

Charli began working at Miss Kitty's after a natural disaster destroyed her home.

> My house, I lived on the beach, it slid down the hill. I had a mudslide, so I was like homeless. And I had a card for a girl that worked here, and went there, because I really didn't have another place to go. I still have all my furniture and everything, but the house I lived in for 20 years just went right out to the front yard.

Dusty, in her mid-forties, first came to Miss Kitty's brothel two years earlier, stressing she had "never been a sex worker in my life. Never been a stripper, hooker, streetwalker . . ."

> I moved here almost three years ago and was working doing critical care, couldn't make a living. I'm a single mom. Started here [at the brothel] part-time, they let me come in a couple days a month. I'd built a new home here . . . I needed money and I needed it quick. I needed a little more for my down payment on my home. I initially worked six weekends in 1998, came in Friday night at six and left Sunday morning at six.

She got the money she needed in the first few weeks. She continued to work in her other job. A year later she decided to landscape the front yard. It was going to cost another $17,000.

> So I called up and they remembered me and said I wanna work

part-time. Usually there are no part-time girls and they said you come in and work whatever days, times. So I would work like two days, take four off, work two days, take three off, work two. And finally, I said I'm making more money doing this.

Dusty told us that she came to sex work with an open mind; she always liked sex, had an active sex life, and had played around with domination. In addition, she believes that with her medical training she knows a lot about male anatomy. But she never wanted to work illegally.

A lot of the girls have worked the street, they've worked the private hotels. I could never do that, I have too much to lose, you know. I'm scared to death. I'm very brave, but I'm not that brave. I think they need to legalize it, I really do.

She does not want to continue in sex work forever, mostly because she feels she cannot tell her children what she does. At the time of our interview, Dusty told us she had one more year of school to get credentials to be a physician's assistant and was planning to save enough in the next six months to get her through the last year of school.

Celeste at the Green Lantern was in her late forties at the time of our interview. She left an abusive relationship and a low-end service job in 1988 and moved to Nevada. Celeste describes her last stint in the service industry as a private investigator with a security firm, making $7.50 an hour as a surveillance expert.

The last gig I did for them they sent me 35 miles out into Puget Sound Bay at 3 o'clock in the morning . . . with over a million dollars handcuffed to my wrist . . . climbing the little rope up the ship because I had the payroll with two dudes in a rowboat. I can't swim a stroke. I'm thinking, it's going to take a lobbing off of this wrist right here then I'm overboard as fish food. And "see ya, bye bye" for $7.50 an hour?! I'll go back to hooking any day, you know. At least it's got tighter parameters of how my ass gets blown away.

She worked for a while as an outcall erotic dancer when she went to Nevada. She did not feel safe in that job and began to check into the brothels. When we met her, Celeste had been working in the brothels off and on for the past 13 years.

Jackie, in her early thirties, first came to work in the rural brothels of northern Nevada in 1988. She worked for a few years. Then she had a baby and decided to quit the brothels. For four and a half years she worked for a publishing company in Minnesota. Jackie said she hated the job, but kept it because it had good benefits. "I was making $9.78 an hour. But for a single woman, when you got a two-bedroom apartment for like $650 with the kid, you know it was, I wasn't going to go anywhere when they're giving 17 cents for one year raise, you know." So she came back to the brothels. At the time we spoke, Jackie's child lived with a friend in town, and Jackie was one of the few outside of the Reno area brothels who actually lived close to where she worked.

Joyce, 38, had worked as an erotic dancer for several years in her late teens and early twenties, but for the past seven years she had been working in a flower shop in Texas. A long-term relationship ended and she was left with no resources. Her daughter had been working in the brothels, and talked her into coming to Nevada. Joyce began to work at Angel's Ladies. She remarked, "This was the best option that I have to get me to another level. My goal is to have my own flower shop."

Some of the women have long term plans, such as gaining relative financial security before pursuing other careers. They want to build a financial cushion so that they can pursue other goals. For example, Charli, in addition to giving money to her own father who cares for her daughter, said she wants to save $10,000 for deposits for rent and savings in case she cannot get a job right away when she stops working at the brothel.

Twenty-nine-year-old Ginger, whom we met at the Old Bridge, had at that point only worked in the brothels for a few months. She told us that her plan was to work in the brothels long enough to earn enough money to buy a house and a car and to return to school.

> But I hope that when I'm done, I'm very well set, you know, in a different lifestyle where I have a home and a car and everything. To where you know it's like, if I'm going to school or if I have a regular job, I don't have to worry. But if I'm only making a certain amount of money, even if it is $10, $15 an hour, I don't have to worry that I am not making enough.

Alice, 19, who told us she was from a wealthy family in Nevada, had been working at the Moonlite Bunny Ranch for about six months when we interviewed her. She has never worked illegally. "The way that I see it, it's the fastest way to get money for my retirement," said Alice.

> My goals are a nice car, a couple of homes, some rental prop-
> erty and money in my savings account every month. When I
> am satisfied with that, hopefully by the time I am 35, I want to
> be done [. . .] I'd like to go back to school for a few things, and
> it's just if you utilize your time and you use your money wisely,
> I mean this is a wonderful business to do it in. It's quick money,
> it's good money, you know, it's all taxed, it's legal. If you do it
> the right way.

These women came directly from jobs in the service industry that did not pay enough to support families or realize their dreams. They saw brothels as quick money. Workers coming from the service sector worked in both rural and suburban brothels, depending on their connections, skills and resources. Those women who fit with prevailing standards of beauty and youth and who were willing to compete with large numbers of other women, went to the larger suburban brothels. Better working conditions, proximity to large cities, mobility, and more customers willing to spend more money made the suburban brothels appealing to some women. Others with fewer resources, perhaps less experience with or desire for competition, and who were willing to live in more isolated conditions went to the rural brothels.

COMING FROM ILLEGAL PROSTITUTION

Although Nevada's legal brothels attract a large number of women who have never worked illegally in the sex industry, about one-third of the women who we interviewed came to both suburban and rural brothels directly from illegal commercial sex. In other words, these were women whose main livelihood came from illegal sex work. Of the women who had done illegal work, most started selling sex in their late teens and early twenties, working in escort or outcall jobs. While one woman started selling sex at the age of 15, the majority of women started working in the illegal sex industry between the ages of 19 and 25, which is older than the portrayal of young teens tricked into prostitution often publicized in popular discourse. Many of these women talked about working occasional "straight" jobs in non-sexual legal sectors, but turned to illegal commercial sex because the pay was so much better.

Often, the women came to work in the brothels to take a break from the stress of working illegally. At the brothel, they explained, they can relax while the customers come to them. While the brothels were less stressful, they could also be less lucrative, depending on the kind of illegal work they had done. And for some women who were used to working independently, having a boss was an adjustment.

Carol, 22, at the Old Bridge Ranch, started working at an escort service at the age of 19 with her four girlfriends. She went through a number of pimps who arranged work for her in Hawaii and Las Vegas. She heard about the brothels from a taxi driver in Las Vegas, dumped her pimps, and came to work in the larger brothels in northern Nevada. When we met her, she said she was tired of working in the brothels, and was hoping to find work outside the sex industry.

Zoie, in her mid-thirties, was working at the Moonlite Bunny Ranch when we interviewed her. She had been selling sex for 16 years. She told us she first started selling sex in high school when she found out she was pregnant and needed money for the baby. From there she worked the streets in different cities, including working in casinos in Las Vegas and Reno. In her off-time she went to college for two years, majoring in accounting. At one point she worked as a file clerk. For the past six years she had been rotating among the suburban houses in northern Nevada, and working from home.

> I get tired of being in different houses, and I'll just say screw it and run an ad in the paper. You know, work from home for six months. And then I'll get tired of my world at home being invaded and my cell phone blasting and pagers going off in the middle of the night, and then I'll come back and work at a house for six months. Which, you know, it's just a matter of routine.

In addition to safety, routine, and predictability, the brothels provide a break from the legal risks of illegal work. For many women, fear of arrest is a big motivator for going to the brothels. Both Alysha and Jackie, workers who we met in two different small rural brothels in northern Nevada, told us how they had been working illegally in massage parlors until they were arrested.

Jackie's first job as a prostitute was in a massage parlor. However, she got busted after a short time there. She said she is terrified to be in jail and has only worked in legal brothels since.

Alysha worked in an illegal massage parlor for seven years and then got arrested, and that changed her attitude as well. She then came to work in the brothels because it took the pressure off of working illegally. She was not clear on whether or not she would go back to illegal prostitution.

Betty, 50, has worked in the sex industry since she was 34 years old. She came to the Moonlite Bunny Ranch after being arrested.

> I tried being a hooker at night, there's so much stress in worry-ing about being arrested. One time I did get arrested, a week before I made my plans to come out here ... Most of the houses in New York City, they have cameras, they're watching you on cameras. And you see the cops coming up and you know you're going to jail. But luckily it only happened to me once. But, the stress of worrying about it, you know you're constantly worrying about it. Even if there are no customers there, when the police come and they bust you, they are very mean. 'Cos I just had a stitch removed off my wrist when we got busted. And I was like, you can't touch my arm. They wanted $1,500 bail and five days in Rikers Island. For a first time being busted. You know what stress that puts on you? A lot. So being here is really stress-free.

Betty came for another reason; she was hopeful that being isolated at the brothel would help her sober up. "I would stay here until they kick me out. If it's two months, I don't care, just as long as I can stay alcohol-free."

Dallas, 28, who was working at Sheri's Ranch, commented, "Here you don't have the fear of being busted." When we talked to her, she alternated working as an escort and said,

> I'm in and out of limos all the time. I'm in and out of pent-house suites and, you know, the best of the best in town. But here I don't have to. I can lounge around and do nothing and the people come to me. So it's better money on the outside, but, safer here and less hustle, ya know?

Angela said she was at the Green Lantern because it is legal; she can avoid the hassle of the police. She told us that in some places you have protection from a bouncer: "But here it's very controlled. All you have to do if you have a problem in the room is yell and somebody is going to be listening and waiting and someone is going to tell."

At the Old Bridge Ranch we interviewed Ginger and Carol. Carol admits, "It's a big change. I worked on the streets of Hawaii and this is, I mean it was beautiful in Hawaii and the girls were all beautiful and it was like nothing that you'd even picture in your head, of like, a street walker. But it was scary. It was every second you're like scared too, you know?" Ginger added, "Like here, they care for us. You know what I mean? And they watch for our safety, so we're very safe here, which I think is a wonderful thing."

Misty, 34, started as an outcall dancer in Reno. She told us that she made good money, but when she refused to engage in sex it got dangerous. She wanted out of that. Her boss knew a brothel owner in the eastern part of Nevada, and they started talking. At first she did not want to work in a brothel, because "I thought it was going to be like this big orgy thing going on in the bar . . . everyone naked at once." But then money got tight and about a year prior to our interview she decided to try the Green Lantern brothel for three weeks and she stayed. "It wasn't what I thought it was. You are actually given respect, the customer; the girls respect you because they know how you feel . . . So it wasn't as bad as I thought."

Bev Waters, 21, had been an adult film star and had not worked illegally, but she thought a lot about the experiences of her colleagues at Miss Kitty's. As she saw it, "I think they just feel this is a comfortable home to them and they don't have to be walking up and down the street. They know it's safe, they are not going to be killed, raped or anything."

Many women choose to come to the legal brothels from illegal prostitution for a number of reasons. For some, the rules and organization provide an important structure to their work lives. It is safe, predictable, routine, and legal.

SEXUAL WOMEN IN SEXUAL CAREERS

About one-third of the women who we interviewed came to the brothels from work in the legal sex industry. Most of these were women working at the suburban Moonlite Bunny Ranch and Miss Kitty's. These brothels had hired the women as a part of owner Dennis Hof's increasingly successful efforts to recruit adult film stars. All of these women explained their job decision to us as part of their career in sex work. Almost all of them had worked legally in erotic dance or the adult film industry. These women had invested more resources in their careers, and had more experience with sexual commerce. Whether it was the resources, experience, or just the cachet from having made an adult film, these women tended to be high earners.

Ruby, 28, was a top earner at the Moonlite Bunny Ranch. She had one of the best rooms at the time, with lots of dark cherry wood furniture and a fireplace. When asked how she got into the field, she replied, "I was literally brought up in the American Dream. I have no abuse. None whatsoever . . . I'm just a highly sexed woman." Ruby's mother was a teacher and her dad was a lawyer; she recalls that she could be a "bad kid." But her parents are supportive of her work. Ruby started in the sex industry as a dancer and fairly quickly began to go on the road. After several years touring and doing the occasional magazine spread, she began making films as a way to boost her earnings potential as a dancer. She told us she liked making the films, and had made over 100 adult films at the time we interviewed her. She said she talked to Dennis Hof for a full year before she made the move to selling direct sexual service. She works for a month and a half, and then takes a month off. Ruby very explicitly told her story against the trope of abuse commonly held about women who sell sex.

> It's like sexual sovereignty over your own body. Ya know? And being able to do whatever I want with what God gave me . . . I never understood why women had to be nice. Why? You know, if it feels good, I mean why can't a woman go out and learn and sow her oats, like any other normal human being and have a good time. You know.

According to the IMDB (Internet Movie Database), Ruby was making adult movies as recently as 2008.

Princess, who was 18 years old when we interviewed her at Miss

Kitty's, came from a less privileged background. She was the one woman we interviewed who began working on the streets when she was 15 years old, after her dad put her out of the house. She worked in strip clubs at the age of 16 and in adult film at 18 before starting at the Moonlite Bunny Ranch eight months prior to our interview. However, Princess' narrative likewise rests on her enjoyment of sex. She finds brothel work to be "the easiest job you could have" and enjoys her work because "I like to have sex . . . I like to have sex with different people."

For many women who are successful, their work in the brothels is part of a career path, appealing particularly because brothels are legal businesses. Women who describe themselves as sexual defend their right to make money doing what they enjoy. For adult film star Annie Ander Sinn, this is a career, a calling of sorts. She told us how she first entered the sex industry while working in a Midwestern automotive plant.

> I lost a bet with a boyfriend, and the winner chose where to go out for the night. So, he chose to go to a strip club. So, when we were at the strip club I was getting into it, because I also like women. And then the following Saturday, I ended up going there and just started stripping on the weekends and working at my factory job during the week.

Annie cultivated a career as a headline dancer around the country. She was in her mid-twenties at the time of the interview and had been working at the Bunny Ranch for about four months.

> In August, I had a week in between dancing gigs, and I was out here on the West Coast, so I talked to an agent of mine and he said, "Why don't you on your week off go to the Bunny Ranch. Try that, you do adult movies." So I was like okay, so I tried it and I liked it, so now I'm doing this more than I am going on the road. I like it better.

She said she likes the freedom of working in a brothel compared to working in adult film. "It's a little more pleasurable because you don't have to cater to the film people. You can just do whatever." As of 2009, Annie continues to work at the Bunny Ranch and at other northern Nevada brothels.

Jane, 25, came to the brothels from San Francisco. She was a dark-haired, Goth-looking woman who did not wear makeup. Jane "discovered Annie Sprinkle, Betty Dodson, and all of my sex idols" while she was an undergraduate in college, where she trained to be an opera singer. "I really started to have a healthier view of sex and I started to be interested more in the sex industry, without necessarily being in it. I was sort of studying in the form of reading a lot." Jane has a Bachelor's degree in anthropology and almost got a certificate in women's studies, but stopped two credits short because of what she felt was the dominance of anti-sex feminism in most of the department.

> ... But I almost didn't finish the certificate because I discovered all these sex positive people, and I was like I can't really handle this [the women's studies program.]

She hopes to get a Master's in sexology. Jane had dabbled in a range of sexual jobs, including dancing, massage, adult film, professional submissive, and surrogate partnership. She became disenchanted with both strip clubs (the shoes hurt her feet) and adult film ("there's no way I would do condom-less work, and right now in the porn industry you can't make money unless you're doing that"). She asked herself, "What else can I do legally and have time for other stuff?" and came to the brothels. At the time of the interview she had been working at the Moonlite Bunny Ranch for six months, commuting to Los Angeles in between contracts.

Bev Waters, 21, had also been a stripper and came to Miss Kitty's after spending a year and a half in the adult film industry. She did some magazine work and had made more than 100 films at the time of our interview. She explained that she came to the brothels because she was trying to transition out of adult film and wanted to make about the same amount of money she had been making. There was also pressure to go without condoms.

> I wanted to get out of it. You know, you can only go so far in that industry before they want you to do anal, double penetration. And I was saying "I don't know." It was not that fun any more. It was fun at first . . . I wanted to get into something that was along the same amount of money that I was making. So I decided to come out here.

Bev was one of the higher earners. At the time of the interview she said she averaged about four customers a day for usually around $1,000 each. She lives in Carson City with her husband and works a 12-hour shift. She said her family is supportive and has even watched some of her films. She compared her work to the adult film industry by saying it is more secretive in the brothels. "You know how porn, you make a movie, it's gonna be up on the shelf. Here, you know, the gentleman can come in and know this is not gonna go out in their business, you know, they have lives, most of them."

Bev felt she was getting tired, " 'cos you can only enjoy the whole sex industry so long." Bev said she wanted to be out of the sex industry entirely by the time she was 24. "I'm gonna start having a baby by the time I'm 25." We don't know how much longer she worked in the brothels, but in terms of the adult movie business, Bev met her goal. According to the Internet Movie Database (IMDB), she made the last of 30 films in 2005, when she would have been 25 years old.[6]

For many of these women, work in the brothels was part of a career in the adult industry. Many women came to the brothels because work there is not as physically demanding as performing in adult movies, nor is there as much pressure to engage in acts they do not want to do, and they can make more money. Many of these women manage their own websites and, because brothel work is legal, could still remain visible in marketing and promotions for their films. The women seemed to have more resources as a group, both in education and other forms of social capital, than many other brothel workers.

CASH-IN-HAND: MANAGING FINANCES

Another issue that impacts a worker's career trajectory in the legal brothels is the fact that it is a cash business. Whether they choose to work in the brothels for the short term or long term, many find it hard to save their earnings. Even at very small rural brothels, women talk about the unprecedented amounts of money they can make in this job compared to service work. Although the money can be good, brothel income is unpredictable. Unlike getting a regular paycheck, it is not uncommon for even a top earner to make $10,000 one week and zero the next. Like other independent contractors and illegal sex workers, brothel workers get no health insurance or formal employee benefits, although a few houses bring in financial advisors or tax specialists to conduct seminars on handling money. In addition, brothel sex work requires a minimal capital investment from each woman (the cost of clothes and makeup, condoms if not provided by the house, room rent, etc.).

Because money comes quickly and sporadically, the concept of pay is very different for an independent contractor than for a worker who receives a steady paycheck. To save money, a woman has to be fairly diligent, and this is easier for some than others. The younger women in the houses often have a harder time managing money. Some women recognize that they simply will not be able to work in the industry forever, since age is a factor in success. One woman who had been in the industry for a while observed that about half of the women she works around have a savings plan and a strategy for getting out. The rest just spend the money they earn.

Many of the women interviewed were critical of others who were unable to save. Crystal, then manager/owner of the Stardust, said she knew of a woman who made millions, but blew the money on drugs and living in upscale hotels, and now has nothing. Lani said of some of the women, "They're like, 'oh! This money's gonna be here tomorrow.' So they'll just spend it. And then there are girls that some of them have worked awhile and they're like, 'Oh my God. I haven't been saving nothing, and now I have to save.' "

Dusty, in her forties, talked at length about the many women she has seen working without thinking about their future.

> I look at these girls. They live here. I say they have no education; they were done with school at 18. You're talking about girls who never worked for $2.12 an hour, or the minimum wage now is $5.15. Let's say, they're used to right off the bat getting $500 a week in their pocket. That's more than the average Joe Blow. Immediately. They don't think about having a car. We have a runner. They don't own their own apartment. They have a maid that cleans their room. Somebody cooks for them. Somebody does their laundry . . . It's very easy to fall prey to drinking, drugs.

She added that "the downfall of this job is no medical insurance, no financial advisement. And it's very hard. A lot of these girls haven't done their taxes in four or five years."

Dusty makes a lot of money at Miss Kitty's and says she finds it difficult to go back to service work. "I can see me starting to fall for it if I'm not careful. I make very good money. How do I wanna give this up?" As she continued, she said, "Well I can't do this forever. Looks fail, body fails, and you're through."

The women face different monetary challenges making money intermittently by working in brothels versus working in "straight" low-paying service industry jobs. Jane was new to prostitution and had only worked in legal sex businesses before coming to the brothels. She said she enjoys the work, "but I have a really hard time, I have never in my life had an irregular paycheck." Charli, in her mid-thirties, said she finds it hard to save; her daughter lives with Charli's dad, and she gives him money to care for her, including $4,000 for braces. Several owners told us it was typical for family members who were watching the workers' children to ask for extra money. The owners sometimes commented that this money was often proportionate to the worker's income.

Ricki, 35, who worked at the Mustang Ranch for nearly ten years and was out of the business for five years, thinks trying to survive in low-paying service industry jobs is not practical. When she returned to Miss Kitty's, she appreciated the money a lot more:

> Before I didn't have my kid and I was just blowing it. Of course, I hadn't had money like that. You know where I never thought about it, I never thought about money. For three years I did not think about money. And I blew it on buying that house for that guy and partying and just buying things that I really didn't need. So now I'm just struggling, and now having my daughter living with me, I have more responsibility, and I'm just more focused now. So now, I don't, and I know I'll miss it, I know once I get out of it, I'll really miss it.

Alice, 19, at the Moonlite Bunny Ranch, also learned to value her income:

> I got lucky because I was taught by the other girls, you know. I can't say I didn't blow my money because the first couple of months, I blew a few thousand dollars and I have nothing to show for it. But I learned quick and I was taught quick by experienced women. I'd say generally, a lot of the women in

here know that "I am not going to have this face forever and I am not going to work forever," but if I do it carefully now, then it won't matter later. I'll be set.

Because Dusty supports her family and drives a new car, she likes to give advice to the women:

I tell them that 10 percent of what you make today goes to you and the rest has to go in the bank and you learn to live with that 10 percent now. Ten percent can be $50 today and tomorrow it could be $300. You learn to live and that if you only made $50 today, you buy your carton of cigarettes, your condoms, and your lubes and then the next day if $300 is yours, then treat yourself to one outfit, one toy. We did have one gal who worked here. She did it and bought herself a car, went to school.

While some women worry about how to maintain household finances when they can no longer work at the brothel (due to age, burn-out, or some other reason), others worry about getting stuck. The money in prostitution is seductively good, notes Angela, who has worked as a receptionist, a nanny, a pizza chef, a gas station attendant, a video store clerk, and a health club employee. Since money in the sex industry is so much better, she did not see a reason to keep working in straight jobs. Now, at the age of 27, she works mostly in legal prostitution. As one prostitute stated of the service industry generally, "the wages suck." "I don't get it," said Angela, "not after you are used to making $400 a day." This kind of pay makes it hard to leave the sex industry for a low-paying service job.

Bev said, "There are some women who have been in it so long that they're kinda stuck. It's like an institution, it's like you are in prison." She sees many women who move from brothel to brothel or from brothel to the "track" (street) to escort services and just cannot save. As Bev explains, "I know when I was in the porn industry making that kind of money, there's no way. When you're used to making that kind of money, it is hard to say, okay, I've gotta stop and get a real job."

Even Ginger, who had the biggest plans after only six months into her goal of ten years in sex work, was circumspect on her ability to get out. "As far as getting out, I hope I can." Ginger uses her earnings to pay off debt, but she comments on how others cycle in and out without saving or spending practically.

> I have a lot of things to show for it, for my work, but I haven't really been saving a lot of money, 'cos I was very, very in debt when I first got here. Thousands and thousands of dollars. I'm no longer in debt, so that's, so I guess you could say, in a way, I've pulled myself out of debt, but, no I haven't really saved anything yet. But I do have a lot of things to show for my work ... I think the young ones come and go real quick. It's a hard thing. It's a vicious cycle. Some make good money and a lot of us just leave and spend it and come back with nothing.

Carol muses on the difficulty of going back to "straight" non-sexual jobs:

> It's just too hard to go back to straight life after, you know, living this lifestyle ... A lot of people are close minded and only think of you as one-way after you've worked this job. And so that's basically it. It's just really hard to live the straight life after doing this.

Magdalene comments that "it's easy to blow your money, but that's true for anyone. Even a waitress, it is easy to blow your money because you think you will have some tomorrow." She adds that young people typically have a problem with budgeting and saving. "You normally don't think about this stuff until you hit [your] thirties and you are almost at the end of your career. This is true of any cash business. Lots of straight jobs you can get, you just can't save." Over the past year she has been educating herself about investments. "I hit 33 or 34 and started worrying about the future. A bunch of us are helping each other." Magdalene helped sex workers share advice on stocks and finances via the internet.

MOBILITY IN BROTHEL WORK

Mobility is a key aspect of brothel work. Working in any of the legal brothels requires commuting from a nearby small town or, more often than not, from farther away, possibly leaving children or family behind.

Rarely do any local women in rural towns work in a brothel. One manager told us,

> I know a lot of women who grew up in this town and I've never had any of them want to go into the business. If they did, I would highly recommend that they went into the business someplace else. Because it's just a small town and they don't need to put up with the hassle.

The small towns tend to support the brothels, but still sometimes stigmatize the women.

Mobility serves to deny the women any sense of belonging to the community in which they work. The women do not act in response to an imagined community, and rarely interact with the town itself. Being away from one's home town offers a degree of anonymity for the brothel workers, lessening the immediate experiences of the social stigma around sex work.[7] The women tended to talk about the communities they came from, where they still have ties to family and home. Many women come to the brothels from other states. Joyce at Angel's Ladies moved to Nevada from Texas. Alysha and Angela at the Green Lantern came from Minnesota; several came from places on the West Coast. We did not meet any women from other countries.

The intersection of work and travel is not uncommon among sex workers, just as it is not uncommon among many workers in general.[8] Lani, 19, had worked as an escort in Hawaii before coming to Nevada to work at the Moonlite Bunny Ranch. She lives at the brothel when she is working there and either works in massage parlors in San Francisco or travels in her off-time. Charli often went to Virginia City or Reno, or other tourist destinations in neighboring states, during her off-time. This was true for many of the women we spoke to.

Women also tend to move from house to house. Crystal, then the owner/manager of the Stardust, first moved to Pahrump and started at Sheri's Ranch as a cook. When some of the working girls decided to check out the Sagebrush, Crystal went too. She worked ten days a month for one year at the Sagebrush as a sex worker, commuting from Pahrump. Then she worked a short while at the Moonlite Bunny Ranch, but left quickly because she felt there were too many women. Many women go back and forth between brothels. Celeste at the Green

Lantern in Ely had worked in nine different brothels in Carson City, Ely, and Elko in northern Nevada.

Women frequently move in and out of the sex industry, not only for the financial reasons discussed above but because of life changes. Some women told us that if they get a boyfriend or get married, or if they are pregnant or have a baby, they quit. Because of the temporary nature of the work, women are on the move from brothel house to brothel house, and also from city to whichever rural town the brothel is located in.

Women who have children must leave them with a family member or friend. These long-extended absences are difficult for the women, and pose particular challenges for both the family members who care for the children, and for the relationship between the woman and her family. Those who work in northern Nevada on shifts are able to rely on day care or family members for short-term care, and are much happier with this arrangement.

CONCLUSION

The leisure and tourist economy has had a profound effect on the shifting pools of workers who find their way to Nevada's legal brothels. The region's growing resort areas generate formal and informal markets for sex, sexuality, and intimacy. Workers from a variety of backgrounds see opportunities in Nevada's brothels for different reasons. Some women working illegally in informal markets choose the brothels as a break from the stress of illegal work. Some women working in the growing legal adult industry as dancers or in films see legal brothels as a complementary job option, especially as suburban brothels draw more consumers willing to spend on a sexual adventure, and as suburban brothels are able to provide quality work conditions. The service economy across the nation generates a pool of low-paid workers who come to the legal brothels for flexible, perhaps short-term, relatively high-paying jobs. All of these paths reflect changing demands and consequences of a growing leisure economy. These trends change the demographics of workers entering Nevada's brothels, and are likely to change them in legal and illegal sex sectors in other regions as well.

Nevada's shifting economy and demographics frame who comes to work in the legal brothels. Because the question of why women come to prostitution is so controversial, we need to reiterate several important points. First, as we have said, none of our interviewees told us, nor did we see evidence, that they had been coerced, forced, or trafficked into the brothels against their will. All of the women talked about the choices they made along the way. This is not to say that there are no societal structural constraints that limit women's work options or shape women's beliefs about sexual commerce. But analyzing broader social inequalities as they are embodied in prostitution is very different from arguing that prostitution is forced and is a form of violence against women. For the women who we interviewed, their labor market decisions were choices bracketed by structural inequalities, their class, and their relationships with the service industry and the sex industry.

Second, the legality of the work matters. Whether women come from other legal sex businesses, illegal prostitution, or the service industry, a part of what draws workers to Nevada's industry is that it is legal. For illegal workers it is a break from the stress of illegal work. For career legal sex workers and service workers they only want to do above-board work. Fewer than half of the women told us they had never worked illegally in prostitution. These were women who had either come directly from the service industry or from other parts of the legal sex industry. This tells us that the legal status of the brothels is important for making the industry a viable work option for women.

Third, brothel work is flexible, temporary, and part-time. Work in Nevada's brothels is always provisional since it is bounded by short-term contracts. Thus women's decisions to work involve short- and long-term goals.

The employment of independent contractors is increasing across many sectors of the economy, and this includes the sex industry. For some, this is an advantage—brothel work is so high paying that it affords more leisure time for vacations, family, or friends. On the other hand, for many, working as an independent contractor can be unstable. Much of the risk of the business, the fluctuating customer base, changes in profit margins, and planning for the costs of healthcare, retirement, and benefits falls on the workers, not employers. Independent contractors have few labor protections. There is rarely an opportunity to form unions. The irregular and unpredictable nature of payment makes it difficult to save. Even women who *can* save money worry about finding other jobs with similar earning potential. For many women in our sample, the mobility and flexibility of brothel work encourage a revolving door to prostitution that can span years or decades. While workers in other flexible service industry jobs talk about moving around, up, or out in their quest for more money, prestige, or stability, sex workers' narratives of moving are framed by the stigma of sexual labor. Their desire to "get out" and the fear of "getting stuck" are examples of the stigma of sex work that affects how women think about their ability to move between jobs.

Fourth, the labor market dynamics matter a great deal. More than three-quarters of the women to whom we spoke talked about selling sex because service industry jobs failed to provide economic stability. For those who come directly from the service industry, brothels are a monetary option available in times of financial need. For women who avoid working illegally, brothels offer an opportunity to make a lot more money quicker than in traditional service jobs. The ability to revolve in and out of a back up job like brothel work is significant to maintaining or improving a woman's economic standing. It is better to have something legal and paying than no options at all. Sex workers in Nevada's brothels work both sexual and non-sexual jobs in the service sector as they attempt to improve their economic standing.

Finally, social class and the resources that come with that are important. For lower middle- or working-class women, brothel labor presents a specific job opportunity that some find preferable, at least temporarily, to lower income service industry work or the stress of other forms of legal and illegal sex work. The women may come to the sex industry because of a lack of other job options or resources that could otherwise pull them through a financial crisis, like a family or social support system, savings, or a college degree.

Not all women come to the brothels out of financial need. They tell us they enter the brothels because of their interest in sexuality as a career choice. These women appear to have a wider range of available job options; sexuality has played a role in their decision to enter prostitution. Brothels thus provide a safe, legal option for an income.

6

BROTHEL LABOR:
MAKING FANTASIES AT WORK

In some ways, selling sex in Nevada's brothels is a lot like sex work in other venues of prostitution. It involves both bodily and emotional labor. It involves constructing sexual experiences that fit a customer's erotic, emotional, and monetary needs.

However, just how much body work or how intense the emotion work will be can vary greatly. On the one hand, indoor sex workers usually spend more time with a customer and do more emotional labor than the typical 15-minute encounter in street work. Like most indoor workers, Nevada brothel workers in more isolated rural areas are more likely to provide a 30- to 60-minute combination of one or two sexual acts to working-class customers.

On the other hand, as the tourist economy has grown in Nevada, legal sex workers who are able to construct more elaborate fantasy enactments or construct more convincing emotional connections earn much more money. They tend to work in the suburban brothels. Tapping into the growing market for high-dollar extended fantasy experiences while also meeting the demands of the more frequent working-class customer means that Nevada's workers must employ a wide variety of labor strategies. If, as Dennis Hof has said, "the guy is gonna get off in 30 seconds," it appears women strategically mix body and emotional labor in different ways as they attempt to sell a sexual fantasy experience. Women are diverse in how they do their job in the skills they possess. As selling feelings and fantasies becomes more central to a leisure economy, this has a profound effect on the work that legal prostitutes do.

Thinking of prostitution as labor has been quite controversial. The major debates surrounding prostitution generally revolve around two opposing lines of reasoning: one is "it is just work" and the other, "it involves her very being." Sex is so special, some argue, that to make it into work damages one's very selfhood and identity. Heterosexual relationships between men and women can be so unequal, this line of reasoning goes, that commodifying sex is inherently exploitative. Yet many of these concerns about exploitation, inequality, coercion, authenticity, selfhood, and psychological well-being have been addressed by studies of the labor process in other service industry jobs.

We pay close attention to the idea of *being* a prostitute as it connects with the idea of *doing* the paid labor of sex. Studies of emotional labor and body work show that it is rarely the work, in and of itself, that is good or bad for workers, but rather the social contexts, conditions of labor, and individual resources and control that matter. As such, the first part of this chapter will look at the different ways women describe the labor processes involved in selling sex in Nevada's legal brothels.

In addition, the identity of "prostitute" is a powerful image. In popular discourse, prostitution has become a metaphor for selling one's self in a job. How selling self might actually work, however, has been the subject of many studies of identity and emotional labor in a variety of service jobs that require interactions with customers. How do we reconcile our sense of ourselves with who we have to be at work? This can be even more complicated in a line of work that is highly gendered. The second section of this chapter will look at how sex workers reconcile selfhood and authenticity with their work. If authenticity is a component of a fantasy sexual exchange, how do workers negotiate their own sense of self both on the job and outside of work? Finally, we will also look at the impact of these constructions of self on well-being.

DOING SEX: LABOR STRATEGIES

"It's Not Just Sex"—Mind and Body in Sexual Labor

When the women explained what sex in the brothels is like, they almost always came around to this:

> It's not just sex. It's . . . you know. It's a lot more than that.
>
> Angela, the Green Lantern

> Everybody is under the conception that it's just all about spreading your legs. Wrong, wrong.
>
> Ricki, Miss Kitty's

> Straight humping and pumping, no, it's not going to work. [If] they just want to go hump and pump they can do that with their girlfriend, they can do that with their wife. They can pick a bitch up in a bar.
>
> Celeste, the Green Lantern

If it is not "just" about sex, what *is* it about?[1] These quotes reveal a narrative that equates "just" sex with the physical dimensions of sex.

The moral proscriptions around sex—that it must involve love and connection, that one must control the carnal desires of the flesh—draw on a Cartesian separation and superiority of the mind over the body. Good sex, according to prevailing norms, should involve a genuine, authentic connection between (only) two (heterosexual) people. In this moral framework, bad sex is that which lacks emotion. The market overrides the possibility of authentic exchange and sincerity. Sex without emotion turns the body into a thing and severs the body from one's sense of self.[2]

Indeed, our cultural understanding of work re-creates this mind–body dualism. Carol Wolkowitz writes that work incorporating the human body is increasingly central to post-industrial global economies. Yet there remains a stigma equating body work with "dirty work." Recent research on emotional labor elevates the psychological, associating the body with mindlessness or mechanical responses.[3]

Sex workers struggle with this mind–body dualism in a number of ways. Studies find low-income and street workers describe their work as wholly about the body to distinguish it from more intimate non-commodified sex.[4] This narrative of body often means disengaging the mind or emotions. However, other studies find upper-class and multi-hour workers just do a great deal of emotional labor as part of their work, stressing that sex work is not just about "selling bodies."[5]

Our interviews with women working in Nevada's brothels reveal that these are just different ways of selling sex, the relationship between mind and body was central to how the women talked about their work; yet not all of the women separated emotional and physical labor in the same way. Each Nevada brothel worker determines the amount of emotional connection and physical work she will use on the job. These labor practices vary depending on the kind and length of party, brothel location, and the personal resources she chooses to invest in her work.

We identify three different, sometimes overlapping, sets of practices women describe when talking about how they engage in the labor of commodified sex. These practices reflect different ways of thinking about their work. Workers often talked about employing any one of them at one time or another. On the whole, though, workers tend to subscribe to one practice more than to others, and sometimes distinguish themselves from other workers based on this. For some women, the practices are planned and intentional, part of a strategy for marketing to a particular kind of customer or a particular kind of service. For others, the practices are emotional management strategies, tried and true ways of coping with the demands of the job and avoiding burn-out. And for others, the practices are how they justify and make the work intelligible to themselves and to others. Either way, it shows us that there is no one way of reconciling body work and emotional labor in the practice of prostitution.

In the first set of practices, the women predominantly stress their physical performances, skills, and aesthetic appearance of their own or others' bodies in what we call "body practices." Body practices encourage visceral interactions where the body is used to sexually stimulate and arouse another person. Timed and categorized bodily acts are the main ways services are priced, so it makes sense that body practices constitute a major part of their vocabulary. Further, one of the key ways women rationalize the work of prostitution is by describing how they assign value in the negotiation process to both the packaged sexual, bodily services and to the aesthetic capital of the body itself. For the most part, this practice separates physical labor from emotional labor. It is not that emotional labor is absent, but the skills the women underscore are bodily skills orchestrated to create fantasy sex. In this case, the women comprehend the value of their labor to be a combination of physical appearance and physical skills.

In the second set of practices, women stress caring and emotional performances that we call "caring practices." The women articulate how they provide therapy, connect with clients and just talk with them, or play the role of a confidant. Using caring practices often evokes a gendered notion of women's roles in intimate heterosexual relationships. The most important feature of these practices is that they are constructed in opposition to the corporeal characterizations of "sex." Women describe caring practices as very distinct and separate from body practices and aesthetics. Caring practices are a particular kind of emotional labor (though not all emotional labor is implemented as caring practices).

In the third set of practices, women stress the integration of physical sex and sensual energy to form what we call "holistic practices." These types of interactions combine body labor with a high level of emotional labor. Workers describe striving for a kind of physical and emotional intimacy that both they and their clients experience. But the women do not necessarily define these practices as similar to the kind of heterosexual intimacy many think of in relational sex (by "relational" we mean sex outside of sexual commerce). Providing holistic experiences, nurturing a kind of synergy between feelings and flesh, is hard work. The physical sex and personal connection are mutually reinforcing. These women did not re-create the mind–body dualism at all, and in fact saw their sexual labor as a way to connect mind and body. These women's narratives echoed the holistic model in alternative medicine that self-consciously rejects the mind–body distinction.[6]

BODY PRACTICES

Prostitution involves intense amounts of physical contact. This is not all that unique, as many service industry workers need to provide a combination of personal and bodily interaction, from doctors and nurses, to masseuses, tattooists, and body piercers; from nannies and childcare workers with their wards to women pregnant as surrogates; from hospice workers to other caregivers. Sexual skills, shaping the body to meet physical standards of beauty, and adorning the body with makeup and clothes are all aspects of body practices that are an integral aspect of women's labor generally and in Nevada's brothels.

Packaging Timed Physical Interactions

Magdalene Meretrix, in her how-to advice book *Turning Pro*, describes two different styles of charging for parties: first is the "à la carte" method, where each act and/or position is negotiated; second is the "table d'hôte" style, where the customer purchases a period of time and a variety of sex acts that are apt to happen within that time frame.[7] In each method, it is largely the timed physical act that is the saleable and negotiable item. Almost all the women, regardless of labor strategy, talked about this as the predominant way sex is organized in the brothels. Ricki at Miss Kitty's explained how her services are packaged as physical acts bound by time:

> My minimum is $200. That's my minimum, and then it goes up from there. And then, depending on the individual, it's like if they want a blow job and they want sex, they can have those, but they're only get like 15, 20 minutes to do all that in.

Even women who earn top dollar by offering an holistic experience often talk about what they sell in terms of physical acts. "I'll take a $100 date and I'll give him a massage and I'll do a little hand job," said Princess at Miss Kitty's, "$2,000 per girl and you get your fetish party." Jane from the Moonlite Bunny Ranch starts at a higher rate: "I start at $500 for hand job, $600 for oral, $700 for deep throat, $800 for straight, $900 for half and half." These specifically categorized bodily interactions constitute the way brothel workers conceptualize the services they provide.

Three women at the Moonlite Bunny clarified time and acts that could be purchased for a $100:

Lani:	The majority of girls in this house will not take less than $100.
Interviewer:	For what? A half-hour?
Alice:	Oh God no!!
Lani:	Five or six minutes. Ten minutes at most!

Interviewer:	For what? Half-and-half? A blow job?
Lani:	Hand job.
Brenda:	Sweet, a five-minute hand job for a hundred bucks.
Lani:	A blow job would be $200.

Skill

The negotiation of prices is based on timed acts. Accordingly, some brothel workers create value in bodily interactions by highlighting their skills. As Celeste, 45, told us, it is more than just humping and pumping. She has been in the business for 13 years at various houses in northern Nevada after working in low-paying service jobs. She sat on a couch at the Green Lantern, a small brothel in Ely, next to Misty, 34, who had worked as a dancer and illegally as an escort, and the two women discussed with us the skill that is involved in their daily labor. Celeste explained, "Anyone can fuck and suck, let's see how much money *you* make at the end of the day. A lot of it, I'm sure you'll agree with me, is experience in finding out what works and what doesn't. Like when you pour on fast, then you pull back."

Celeste continued:

It's almost like choreographing a dance in bed . . . you have to pay attention, when you feel their buttocks tighten, or you feel a twitch here or a twitch there, what does that mean? Is that a good twitch or a bad twitch?

Misty told us that even a small thing like knowing whether to make eye contact or not, requires a lot of attention to detail. Celeste added to Misty's comment, "You've got to take stage directions well." For Celeste and Misty, body work was not just about tuning out or disassociating; rather it involved skill and attention.

Magdalene, who has worked in a number of northern Nevada brothels, reiterated this idea of taking stage directions. "Some guys have it down what they want to the last ooh and ahh. They come in and describe in great detail the fantasy they want enacted, when I do this you move that way and . . ." she laughs and continues:

Others come in and hem and haw and can't even say the words of what they want. Most people give off little signals, by hand gestures or the way they move. If they give no signals at all, then I just give them what people usually ask for, what is called a half and half.

The Significance of Looks

Looks matter a great deal in how many customers initially choose women with whom to party. Because suburban brothels draw more customers and workers, conformity to dominant standards of beauty is especially valued. Whether through a line-up or working the bar, all women recognize that how they look is what may get a customer to choose them. Different women value the importance of this in various ways depending on their labor strategies. Jackie at the Calico Club declared, "I get my money off my boobs, a lot of times." She remarked on men's attraction to her chest:

> The first thing they do is bury their heads in them. I'm wondering why this is such a fascination. You know. I just don't get it. Because it doesn't turn me on when they are doing that. I have to remember to make noises.

Women in the brothels do copious amounts of aesthetic labor, working on their appearance through exercise and beauty routines. The larger brothels often have exercise equipment on-site: Sheri's Ranch has a gym and a beauty salon. The women are likely to have extensive wardrobes, and may change several times a day. Sometimes an outside retail business comes to a brothel to sell clothing. Many women talked about the large amounts of money they spend on clothes.

Several women acknowledged the value in having physical characteristics that reflect the dominant standards of beauty. Large breasts are important; at the bigger suburban brothels many of the women had breast implants. Zoie, in her late thirties, who worked at the Moonlite Bunny Ranch, disclosed, "I'm already a triple D, a natural D." But when we spoke to her she was planning to have reduction surgery on her stomach and hips. "I know it's a $4,800 procedure, and I will make that back in the first month. I know I will." Zoie had worked for over 16 years at the brothels in northern Nevada in between working illegally as an escort and in casinos in larger cities. Indeed, in the larger brothels outside of Las Vegas and Reno, many women found it hard to compete unless they embodied dominant standards of beauty: youthful, slim bodies, large breasts, Caucasian features, and blonde hair.

Ricki, who had been working for ten years, most recently at Miss Kitty's, recalled the first time she was in a line-up at the Mustang Ranch.

> Oh my god, I walk in there and at that time I had no breasts. You know. It was like every woman in there had these boda-cious breasts and they had lashes and makeup. The clothes I brought, that I did buy, were nothing what I needed. What I thought I was doing good with wasn't at all. And the first three nights I did not make any money. The girls were nice but it was just very intimidating, very scary. Um, nothing I'd ever experi-enced before. And after about two months, it was like home.

Over a short period of time, she learned how to present herself. Aesthetic labor is an acquired skill that Ricki quickly picked up, and eventually she got breast implants.

For many of the women in the suburban brothels the primary value of looks comes in the competition in a line-up with other women. Betty, aged 50, who had come to the Moonlite Bunny Ranch from illegal work in New York four days before our interview, com-plained that the managers "should have told me I was going to be competing with 34 girls, ten triple-X porno movie stars and another 20 who are less than 21 years old." She had a $200 party on Monday and a $300 party the day she talked to us, and that was it. But she felt she was hitting a market for older women.

> I know the last guy I was with, he said, "how old are you?" So I said, "oh 50." So he said, "oh good, because I'm 49 and I only like older women." So, if I would have lied and said 45 or 40 then he would have said, oh you're too young for me.

Betty may not make the kind of money she had hoped for coming from the New York City escort industry, but her story illustrates another approach to body work that some women may take—develop-ing a personal style or niche. Particularly at the smaller brothels, many women talk about the diverse ways they market their bodies.

Angela at the rural Green Lantern brothel in the small town of Ely explained, "A lot of people think that just because I'm bigger that I don't make money. That's not true. I have plenty of men who don't want a skinny woman, they just want a woman who has meat. And I have meat." Angela worked illegally in sauna and outcall jobs before coming to the brothels.

Misty, who was also at the Green Lantern, clarified further:

We're not all a Barbie doll. We have our own little person-alities. We have our own look, our own body sizes and every-thing's always different. And for each guy that comes in that door, only one of us is going to look perfect to him. And it doesn't matter what the other girls say, do, will do or how much they charge. He's still going to think that one girl is perfect. Only one.

Even at the bigger brothels, women often successfully capitalize on certain aspects of their body that may be unique. Annie Ander Sinn, an adult film performer and high earner at the Moonlite Bunny Ranch, is six feet and one inch tall.

My look is more unique than theirs, because of my height factor. I tower over everybody so much more. So that's why if a guy likes me, he likes me. If he don't then he's going to pick someone else. So I don't feel any real competitiveness.

Both Celeste and Zoie talked about the importance of skill, as it distinguishes them from the younger women with more bodily capital. Zoie has been working on and off in prostitution for 16 years in various settings. She asserted, "I know what I'm doing. I've been doing it a long time. I'm pretty good at my job, even now with girls that are ten years younger than me."

Bev Waters, an adult film actress, and Precious both worked at Miss Kitty's and became friends. In separate interviews, they echoed each other's sentiment on dealing with the emotional consequences of socially defined beauty standards. Bev told us:

All the girls are different. Every gentleman that walks through the door knows exactly what he's looking for. So, if they are looking for a blonde hair, brown eyed, bigger lady, he's not going to pick me. He's not gonna pick whoever. He's gonna look for that type. If the girls are in that mindset, we all get along. But it's when they're feeling down or they're feeling low, it's like, they're not making money . . . I make the girls feel, you know, you're special too. It's just not your day. Everyone has their day.

Precious had been working illegally in massage parlors in the Bay Area in California for two and a half years before coming to the brothels two months earlier. She considers herself medium-sized, and found herself competing against all the "little petite girls who are really thin." But she said she never gets mad.

> Well, like, Bev Waters, she's a porn star and she gets picked a lot. Not only is she a porn star but her shape, her body and that. She's my friend you know. So I don't sit there and get mad at her 'cos she gets picked. It's like, "right on, go." You're doing good today. But each girl has those different days where one girl might do better that day than the next day. You know, I'll have my days where I'll be doing all right but then there's that day that I'm gonna make a lot of money.

Competition among women can be fierce, but women often diffuse these emotions by focusing on different aspects of brothel work. Some may work the bar while others prefer the line-up. Similarly, some may concentrate more on their aesthetic presentation.

Moreover, women's reflection on their bodily labor revealed a connection between how they look, how they present themselves at work, and how they feel. Their aesthetic labor is wrapped up in self-confidence and the emotional labor of self-presentation. Zoie indicated that her stomach and hip surgery was not just about selling the right body. "Having my tummy done will just increase my self-esteem, make me more outgoing." Dallas at Sheri's Ranch, who described herself as a successful escort who is very proud of her body, observed that "you can't walk into a place and think that 'I'm gonna bank beaucoup bank' when you think, 'God, I look like shit.' You can't do that."

Intimacy and Body Practices

The women for whom body practices were most central did not talk about selling intimacy. They referred to sex at work as "strictly business."

Emili at Sheri's Ranch had never sold sex before coming to the brothel seven weeks ago. She had much to share about what she was discovering regarding the sex itself:

> The hugging and familiarity is not there. The general feeling is, the compatibility, the love, the interchange, the emotion, all of it it's not there. It's strictly business. There's no glamor in it, ya know. You might think there's all this glitter and this glamor when you see us in a line-up and you see all these girls all frilled and propped up. And then you kind of close the doors, and all the frills and props come off, and it's just down to business, ya know. What do you want. How much will you pay or be willing to spend? I mean, there's no frills behind the door.

Misty, from the rural Green Lantern, thought that sex itself had no emotion in any circumstances, "I think sex is just sex. It has no meaning and it doesn't matter who you're with. It's the before and after. And there ain't no befores or afters in the brothel." For Misty, experiences like seduction, foreplay, and being together after sex are not a part of the saleable brothel experience.

For Zoie, the difference lies in the rational planning that she characterizes as something very distinct from more relational and spontaneous sex at home.

> With every man there's a plan in your head because your goal is to make them really happy. To "get them off and get them out," right? So as soon as you start touching them, or he's voiced to you what he likes, everything you do from that moment on is a calculated move to reach that goal.

Zoie continued, explaining that at the brothel, "basically I'm more worried about how I look and how I sound. At home it just comes naturally, whatever happens."

Although the women characterize sex at work as lacking intimate connections, they also acknowledge that some kind of emotional connection is important. Even Jackie, in comparing herself to a high-grossing colleague who looks like model Christie Brinkley, said in reference to herself, "I know I got boobs, I can make money. I'm not ugly, I can make money." For her, bodily practices seemed to be the primary commodity. Yet the very next words out of her mouth were, "And I can talk to people." Social interaction is a key part of the brothel transaction, however minimal or momentary it may be for these workers.

Women are also aware that how much they rely on body labor and emotional labor changes over time. Celeste said, "It just gets harder as you get older, the tools of the trade get a little rusty." She cannot get into the "buns of steel thing" any more, "I have to rely a lot more on humor these days and that's basically how I get most of my tricks."

CARING PRACTICES

While body practices are obviously critical to all brothel labor (everyone sets prices by physical acts and time), there are some workers who emphasize emotional labor as a significant feature in their transactions. Women in all of the brothels, regardless of whether they are rural or suburban, are very conscious of the fact that they have to perform routinized acts in ways that will not be seen as too cold, detached, or robotic. However, some women described how they deployed emotional work distinct from "the sex," and this work is what we label as caring practices. Workers who engaged in these practices are less likely to frame sex at work as an extremely instrumental process. They describe clients' needs as more than just sex. For them, this also justified the broad social value of their work. The workers add interactional or relational exchanges to the mix; they "care." Some see it as an extra component to the party; others see it as valuable within the party itself. Either way, women who utilize this practice value the care they provide their clients and the emotions their clients feel. The women who emphasized caring practices and distinguished caring from body practices work were more likely to work at smaller, more rural brothels.

When we interviewed her, Strawberry Shortcake worked at a small rural brothel in Carlin. For her, emotional labor was central to work at the brothel and her other customer service jobs. She insisted that "90 percent of any management job or any business, which is what this is, my business, is people management."

Joyce, who had been at Angel's Ladies for about nine months, maintained that, "Sometimes you've got to feel out your customer because sometimes what they need is, they don't need sex, they just need to be touched, held." Joyce, Sadie, and Dizyer, who all worked at Angel's, had a long conversation about the amount of physical, non-sexual touch their customers wanted. Joyce shared this anecdote:

> I had this one customer, he was real shy. He was very nervous and when I came back in I said, you know just let me give you a hug. And I held him and he held on to me. And I could just sense that he hadn't had the human touch. It had been a long time. Ya know?

Sadie added, "Believe it or not, there have been customers that will come in here and don't want sex at all. They just need to lie in your company." Joyce replied, "And those ones, you get paid the most, too." Sadie and Joyce believe caring is a valuable commodity. For Joyce, it actually earned her the most money.

Dizyer similarly emphasized caring, compassionate interaction, and also reflected on the excitement on the part of the customer.

> If you've ever been lonely and someone listens and just smiles and says, "Hi, how are you today?" I mean, they're [customers are] lookin' for a friend. I know it sounds like, oh, sure. But people can be very Christian, very compassionate and very mannerly. I mean just subservient down to "Can I move my arm? Can, can I tilt this way?" And they'll have a good party. And I love people like that, because they appreciate all the excitement and the attention.

Angela and Alysha at the rural Green Lantern talked at length about how their jobs seemed more about social connections than sexual ones. Angela observed,

> You get a lot of guys, just sitting at the bar, and they just want to sit there and have fun and joke around. They may not go in the back, they may just look, and we're just here to hang out and whatever. And that's good, that's fine, I don't have no problems with that. And sometimes when they go to a room they just want to lie down and give the girl a back massage or just get a back massage themselves.

Angela said about 30 to 40 percent of customers do not actually want to have sex; other women in different brothels made similar claims. One woman divulged that she had a customer who regularly paid for two hours of time to mostly just watch television with her.

Ricki at the suburban Miss Kitty's talked at length about the emotional labor she provides. She pours a great deal of herself into her work, and was very forthcoming about what it all means. Here she reflected on her "caring nature" and how it is an important part of her work:

> I think me being emotional and me being probably overly compassionate, and sometimes a doormat, but at the same time it benefits me in my job, because I truly care. And when I hear someone and they are telling me stuff, you know, I care. The older I get and the more trials that I have to go through in my life, the more I can relate sometimes to people that are coming in and they're going through stuff with their kids, or they're going through stuff with their parents, or they're going through stuff with their significant other. And, and I can relate, and I can listen and I can just be there. I'm there to just make you feel better.

In many ways these women's narratives reflect traditional gender roles. First, the brothels are very heteronormative spaces. As women, their job is to read their clients—men—and provide what they need. The women are sexually and emotionally attentive to men's needs, reifying modern notions of women's caretaking and nurturing responsibility toward men. Ostensibly, the customers come to the brothels for sex, but the women identify that what their clients really want and need are affection and intimate touch. This stereotypical heterosexual interaction is one of the cornerstones of Nevada's brothel industry.

Second, modern gender norms appear to affect these women's discussion of affection as a commodity. Caring is just what they do as women. Caring adds value to the exchange, but these women do not discuss the emotional connection as a part of their pricing. As Ricki noted,

> It doesn't take any time to do what they gotta do. Sure they can pay the time. You know. I'll take all the money you got. But I'll guarantee, more than likely you're gonna end up spending the rest of the time doing me, and massage and talking. You know. Which is cool with me.

HOLISTIC PRACTICES

The third type of practice combines physical sex and emotional interaction to provide an holistic sensual experience that engages body and mind, for both worker and client. There are two important characteristics of holistic practices. First, women who engage in holistic practices invoke a narrative that does not separate body and mind in the same way as in the other practices. Workers talk instead about combining sex and feelings into an intimate exchange. The value of sex at work is not something conceptualized as purely emotional, or purely physical. Physical and emotional connections are believed to mutually reinforce each other. Second, the women convey that there is reciprocity of emotions with their clients. The workers talk about self-consciously engaging their own emotions as well as arousing emotions in clients. Not that the women exercising caring practices are not emotionally invested, but holistic practitioners evoke emotions beyond just care and affection. Providing an holistic experience is less about some small token of caring and more about connection and intimacy. The women refer to an exchange of "sexual energy" or note the pleasurable feelings of their sexual encounters. This holistic approach is the foundation of the fantasy experience they are selling.

Magdalene Meretrix has worked in a variety of sex industry venues including Nevada's suburban brothels. She has written quite extensively about the more meditative side of her work in a book on how to become a sex worker. In a phone interview, she explained that what she is selling is not just detached physical contact.

> I am exchanging a certain kind of energy with them. Whether touching or talking, the bottom line is sexual energy. It's hard to explain, but I know it when I see it. It is an exchange of sexual energy . . . I have been a healing force in their life. I've given them healing, unconditional love. Whether they are fat, skinny, covered with scars or whatever. They get the same level of attention and compassion from me.

Bretney, 31, who worked at the suburban Moonlite Bunny, talked about how she works with her clients to awaken "the wonderful, fairy joy feeling that people don't always want to give themselves the permission to experience." She enjoys being very sexual, even exploring BDSM (bondage and discipline, sadism and masochism) with partners (not clients). She had been a stripper in Oregon before coming to the brothel industry and, with two exceptions, had not worked illegally. She sees her work as training others to enjoy their sexual selves. She had been working at the Moonlite Bunny Ranch on and off for three years.

Ruby, who rotated a career as an adult film actress with her work at the Moonlite Bunny Ranch, prided herself on the intense intimate labor she offers her customers. She was very careful to clarify that she does not view her work as "just her body."

> I don't know where they got, "selling your body," because, wow, wouldn't that be uncomfortable if somebody walked off with your vagina? Okay, I mean basically they are paying for my time and I perform what I am best at, what I'm good at, what my profession is. So to me it's, you know, I get very intimate with them. I get more intimate with my clients than most of these girls can even handle.

She even does what few brothel workers do: she kisses some of her clients, "because that's the art of being a courtesan. You have to sell intimacy as well. And it does exhaust you, which is why I'm not a high-traffic girl." For Ruby and all the other women who talked about holistic practices, the work is hard. They see themselves as engaging in high levels of emotional labor. At the time we interviewed her, Ruby had one of the better rooms at the Moonlite Bunny Ranch and was among the top earners.

Like women who engage in caring practices, Ruby implied that connecting with customers is an important skill. But at such high levels of emotional and physical labor, as she added, it is something more "than most of these girls can even handle." Even though there are plenty of incentives for sex workers to "get 'em in, off, and out," the majority of women who did holistic labor spoke with disdain about those who worked that way. Holistic workers consider their level of emotional investment to be more specialized and skilled than the other workers. Holistic workers distinguish themselves from other workers not by ignoring body work or interpreting care labor as separate from sex, but by correlating sexual pleasure with bodily and mental engagement.

Holistic experiences usually require more time, and so the women who engage in this practice tend to be higher earners, working at higher end brothels. This high level of emotional labor can be very tiring, so the women limit the number of customers they see (and can do so by charging more). Ruby, Bretney, Dusty, and Magdalene are all high earners at suburban brothels, spending more time with fewer clients. They will spend a whole day or more with a client, particularly with returning clients. Ruby said she was once paid over $8,000 for two days with a regular client. When clients spend a lot of money, she said, "I give 'em bonus, I give 'em extra time." Several years ago when we interviewed Magdalene, she said, "If they want a whole day it is at least $1,000." However, she does not always do a whole day, even if the customer requests it. "Usually I will require them to purchase a couple of hours first to make sure we will click." Thus workers with an holistic approach recognize the importance of establishing a connection with clients. If there is no connection, there is no party.

Dusty, in her forties, came to the brothels from a career in health. She described herself as one of Hof's higher earners at Miss Kitty's. Her work involves establishing a mental connection, and, she explained, "I pay a lot of attention to my clients." She has built up a large clientele and is able to pick and choose clients. She provides a wide range of services, all of them combining emotional connection and sexual experiences. Dusty, like others, believes that what many men want is "some TLC. You know, cuddling." She recounted a recent 24-hour out-date where she provided the classic "girlfriend" experience.

> We went out to dinner. We had all that snow and built a little teeny snowman. We went to the movies, sat and held hands, bought popcorn and coke, watched a very long movie, then we went back and played a little bit and then he was like, I wanna nightcap, so we walked out to one of the casinos, then we went back, played a little bit and slept the rest of the night. I have a lot of clients like that.

But Dusty added,

> A lot of men who have been married to their high school sweethearts a long time, not allowed to do anything, haven't experienced [something] and want to. And they can come in here and ask for certain things and not worry about being ridiculed for wanting to experiment or try something. So that's why they come.

Dusty also provides BDSM parties and told us how she likes to talk to customers for a while to find out their psychological motivation so she can better service them emotionally and sexually.[8]

Although it is work, all of the holistic workers talked about what they get out of the work. They usually underscored how they receive both sexual enjoyment and emotional fulfillment on the job. The women herald the combined bodily and mental aspects of their labor, and identify personal meaning in their interactions. Bretney said she is "forever combating that there is something wrong with me for being sexual." She reiterated, "I've always been very sexual. And I've always had it in my programming that I wanted to be as healthy sexually as I could be."

Bretney expressed how she enjoys time with her clients. She talked about younger snowboarders who come in and who are "a lot of fun." She explained excitedly, "I do five snowboarders! In a row! I have no problem with that, all these nice bodies." Bretney said to do so is challenging, "but I love to fuck. So it is fun for me and very athletic." She also said that she enjoys middle-aged customers, especially one client: "he's my tantric dude. I have my tantric customers that I like to party with because they like to use more yoga positions." In all, she felt, "That's one of the beautiful things about this place. Is to be able to see really how individual different people are, you know." In describing the body practices she was engaging in, it is clear that she works hard to provide an holistic sensual experience.

On the other hand, not all women see their holistic practices as work. Princess, at the suburban Miss Kitty's, captured this notion of personal sexual enjoyment, stating simply, "It's the easiest job that you could ever have. I don't have to do anything but what I like to do. I like to have sex. I like to have sex with different people."

Magdalene, Bretney, Dusty, and Ruby also spoke a great deal about providing a warm, even "healing" sexual experience. For example, Ruby expounded on her relationships with her customers:

> Nobody I bring back here is revolting to me in any way. So I'm kind of looking forward to it at that point in time. There are a lot of really super-business-minded girls and I, too, will do men that I wouldn't ordinarily do. But you know, to me that's also part of the job, being able to see something attractive in

somebody's eyes that other people don't see. In trying to find and focus on that one attractive quality that that person has. You know.

Labor Strategies, Resources, and the Leisure Economy

Nevada's legal brothels bring together a variety of women who rely on distinctive labor strategies to meet the needs of an increasingly diverse clientele. These three practices—body practices, caring practices, and holistic practices—demonstrate how women use a repertoire of skills to connect intimacy, emotions, and physical labor in different ways. At a micro level, these practices represent individual differences in expectations, resources, skills, and approaches to their body, sexuality, and emotions as they find strategies that work for them and that are profitable. At a macro level, these diverse practices show that sexual commerce is not just about selling rationalized bodily acts, but include selling the individualized fantasy experience that is increasingly demanded in brothel interactions. Yet some workers in the larger suburban brothels are responding to the demands of leisure consumers for more individualized interactions in ways that challenge how we have been thinking of sex work by incorporating both body and mind in the interactions. Studies of indoor work have always noted the emotional labor that sex workers provide. But documenting how workers deploy emotion and body work in diverse ways is new.

At one level, body practices are central in today's brothels and will continue to be so. Brothel labor is sold as discrete physical acts, and even those who used holistic practices determine price based on timed acts. Body appearance is important to determining value, and likely is even more important to upper-class customers. Many women believe physical skills are critical in distinguishing sex as work from sex as play. Emphasizing their work as bodily labor seemed particularly central for those who had come to the brothels from other venues of illegal prostitution. Workers who did not self-identify as high earners and/or who worked in rural areas seemed more likely to emphasize the corporeality of their work.

While physical appearance and skill are important determinants of value, emotional labor adds a great deal to the brothel encounter for many of the women. In other words, caring pays. Like women in other studies of sex work, many of Nevada's brothel workers used caring talk to emphasize that the work was not just about sex, thus adding some cultural value to the exchange, countering the stigma of bodily labor. This also serves to identify men's needs as more than just sex; some women identify that what customers really want is some kind of emotional care.

Those who combined body and mind in their work and who self-consciously used an holistic approach were the highest-earning women in the brothels where we interviewed. These women did not label and separate "caring" from the sexual service they sold. They referred to the combination of flesh and feeling as an erotic connection or sensual energy, and clearly saw it as part of what they were providing. Those who relied on holistic practices were more likely (though not exclusively) those who had worked legally in other sex work venues, such as adult film.

This has interesting implications for the enactment of femininity. On the one hand, rather traditional understandings of feminine caring add value to these heterosexual exchanges, whether or not women specifically "price" it. They talk about the caring component as outside the market exchange, something more akin to a gift exchange, even within a commodified setting. Thus they reproduce the idea of separate spheres between intimacy and the market.

On the other hand, in all three practices, there is a non-traditional understanding of gendered heterosexuality at work. These women do not take a passive approach to the enactment of sex, regardless of what practice they use. The women guide the sexual encounter, strategically deploying emotional and physical interaction to maximize the experience not only for the man, but for their own profit. They are the active partner in this sense. And men seek and participate in this emotional exchange. Even commodified sex, at this level, involves an emotional connection.

This strategic mix of body and emotional practices is a response to the changing markets surrounding sexual commerce. In suburban brothels that cater to upscale customers seeking touristic leisure experiences, women who use holistic practices have found a profitable niche. The larger suburban brothels seek to provide a more holistic experience to customers, though they are likely to employ women who use any combination of the three labor strategies. Suburban brothels are equipped both in staff and setting to meet customer demands for intimate experiences that go beyond physical gratification. The services requiring the most emotional labor are the most expensive commodities. Like the upscaling of strip clubs and the mainstreaming of adult sex toy stores throughout the country, the larger brothels are moving toward accommodating high levels of customer service and interpersonal exchanges.

While some women may still provide services as quick as a 15-minute hand job, workers in the suburban brothels are less likely to do so. Women in more isolated, small brothels talk mostly about the 60-minute half-and-half party (half oral sex, half vaginal penetration) as the most common party request. Workers in the larger brothels tend to book hourly or multi-hourly parties. The most high-end workers book parties that last for a day or two. Brothels like the Moonlite Bunny Ranch, Sheri's Ranch, and the Chicken Ranch have spacious, elaborate fantasy rooms and expensive VIP bungalows that accommodate multi-hourly parties. Many parties in these rooms include dinner or a massage. The women we interviewed who talked about holistic practices were those likely to book these types of parties. Nevada's larger brothels are attempting to capitalize on the broader leisure industry push for more experience-based exchanges that rely on mid- to high levels of emotional labor.

BEING A "PROSTITUTE"

What then does all this mean for the selfhood of women working in the brothels? How do women reconcile their own conceptions of themselves with what they do at work? To address these questions, we first need to understand how the growth of a leisure economy has profoundly changed the relationship between labor and identity for all interactive service workers. Because interactive service work requires the production of a range of emotions and identities, there is an undeniable tension between a worker's feelings of authenticity and having to manipulate oneself for a boss or a client. The production of fantasy in leisure often requires more sustained and complicated performances even farther outside one's normal routines as compared with those in typical sales or restaurant jobs. As workers are given more independence and suffer the consequences of unsuccessful performances more directly, questions of control, authenticity, and identity become more complex.

Understanding what selfhood means for sex workers involves two issues. One issue involves understanding how people think of identity and authentic interaction. Identity is typically understood as sets of signs and labels one gives to oneself. Identity creation and affirmation involve a process similar to looking at oneself in a social mirror, and assessing the self based on what that person perceives others to think. It is an interaction between self and the outside world, where both the labels a person assigns to herself/himself at an individual level, as well as social labels of race, class, gender, and ethnicity, all matter. Most researchers now talk about "identity work" to capture the efforts people use to construct a sense of self, or sense of selves.[9] Sociologist Erving Goffman says creating identity is best thought of as acting, where people's stage performances of selves vary in different arenas in a process of impression management.[10] Goffman's work, and the extensive research on the production of the self since then, undermines the idea that today's individual thinks of selfhood as one stable, core, unitary, or consistent self. Instead identities are multiple, flexible, situational, and discursive. In a consumer culture where selfhood is increasingly fluid and flexible, researchers find that the relation between work, structures of race, class, gender and ethnicity, and the construction of selves is a dynamic process.[11]

Another issue involves the consequences of those constructions for individual well-being. Given that much identity work is about flexible, fluid, and situational performances, research shows that there are no inevitable negative consequences from having to perform "who one is not" in interactive service jobs. Having to perform different selves at work can produce stress, emotional exhaustion, and feelings of alienation in certain circumstances, but not always. Performing a different identity at work can serve to provide a needed distinction between work and home. In some cases successful performances add to a worker's sense of accomplishment. The negative psychological consequences that do result from these performances have less to do with the frequency, type of interaction, or characteristics of the job and more to do with one's ability and available resources to manage emotions. Worker autonomy, whether or not someone is repressing negative emotions or performing positive ones, all affect a person's ability to deal with psychological distress resulting from not acting true to one's "self."[12]

Sex work seems no different. There is little evidence that there is something inherent in the act of selling sex that irreparably damages one's sense of self. Researcher Wendy Chapkis concludes: "sex work is no more a pact with the devil (in which the 'soul' is exchanged for worldly fortune) than any other form of emotional labor."[13] In a variety of studies that compare mental health problems in sex workers with other groups, it is the conditions of work, stigma, violence, role conflict, not having much, if any, choice to work, or lack of control in client interactions which are correlated with problems.[14]

What may distinguish sex work from other service work is the extent workers display high levels of distancing and depersonalization.[15] As we have seen earlier, studies of outdoor and lower income sex workers find that they disengage body and mind at work. Both indoor and outdoor sex workers tell researchers how they create various self-described boundaries between themselves and clients, including physical boundaries, disguising appearance, or avoiding emotional connections with clients.[16] However, rather than seeing any of this as a symptom or cause of psychological harm, studies show this to be a strategy for coping.[17] Indeed, studies find that role distance and detaching emotionally is an important strategy in a variety of occupations, including doctors, nurses, therapists, clergy, and waitresses.

Some sex workers also describe creating entire alternate identities separate from who they "really" are for work, complete with a pseudonym, new personality type, and a fictitious life story, family background, and childhood history. Teela Sanders calls this a "manufactured identity."[18] The performances of identity become part of the fantasy of sex work; "the prostitute" becomes one of an array of possible identities played out for a customer. Sanders sees this not as evidence of psychological harm, but a business strategy that not only helps manage emotions and their sense of self; it helps maximize their income in an era when customers demand individualized fantasy.

The sex workers we interviewed in Nevada's brothels echoed many of these themes in describing their identity formation on the job. What was different was the *variety* of ways they talked about reconciling their sense of self with who they were at work. Those who predominantly described body practices were much more likely to separate themselves emotionally from their work than others. Some women had complex ways of reconciling identity and work.

For example, Emili, 40, who had recently come to Sheri's Ranch in southern Nevada from a job as a convenience store clerk, explained to us what her job essentially was at the brothel: "How would I describe what I do? Um, I would describe what I do as offering sensual and sexual experiences designed to fit a personal need or a personal desire. A fantasy girl."

Ricki at Miss Kitty's told us, "You've got to be someone's fantasy. You basically have to manipulate yourself and be someone that you're not to entice them to go to your room." In some ways "being someone you are not" is very similar to other jobs. An insurance salesman interviewed by sociologist Robin Leidner said the same thing, "You have to learn to read people, to figure out what they want in a salesperson, and *be* that person."[19]

However, we found that many women talked about much more extended and intense roles that were played out in a customer's fantasy. Precious, 20, who has worked at a number of brothels in northern Nevada for the past two years and who had described much of her work as body work, told us, "It is acting, because a lot of guys, sometimes guys come in with a fantasy. They either want you to play like if you're in school, a high school girl, or you know, any kind of role they want." Zoie at the Moonlite Bunny Ranch, who talked in terms of body work, also described her work as acting.

> I just act really nasty with them . . . I know this man wants to hear me talk about this or my butthole, or some gross shit, or how I want to eat pussy, which I would never do . . . I would never say that shit to my husband. He would look at me like I'm totally insane. He'd like say, "Go wash out your mouth." My home life is way different than here.

Zoie and Ricki say they are not acting like themselves at all. Ricki says she has to become someone she is not. Zoie says things she would never say at home. In fact, Zoie is using the stereotypical image of prostitute as a bad girl, a nasty girl, to define who she is not.

In general, we found a correlation between how women talked about their labor practices and how they talked about a manipulation of self. Many of those who described their labor as body practices described their enactment of fantasies, when they did talk about it, as acting. On the one hand, we could think of this as an extension of the mind–body dualism. These workers accepted conventional notions of the lines between feelings and flesh, seeing work sex as disassociated from emotions. They drew boundaries around their emotional selves, disassociating their bodily performances from their inner selves. If they understand sex work as a form of labor performed by a depersonalized body, then it makes sense that they would see these as performances and not who they "really" were.

Indeed, many workers talked about the line they drew between sex at work and sex at home in these very ways. Like Charli at Miss Kitty's, many workers don't kiss clients because "that's personal. You don't get personal. Kissing is personal and romantic. You can act that way, but . . ." Like Princess at the Moonlite Bunny Ranch, they describe relationships with husbands or boyfriends where "I really put my feeling into it, and I give him all my love, you know, I'm giving him me."

We might also expect those who used caring practices to draw strong boundaries around their emotional selves at work. However, this was not the case.

Not all workers talk about their work as different from their "real selves." For example, Strawberry Shortcake, a long-term worker at the rural brothel Sharon's in Carlin, explicitly told us that her self at work *is* who she is. She told us that much of her work is about providing different fantasies. But, like others who drew on caring practices, this was not the same as *being* someone else.

> When I was first trained, they try to encourage the girls to take on another identity, take on another name. That lasted with me for about a week. It is harder to pretend to be somebody else than who you are. I gave that up real fast. It is too hard to do. You live here. And even with girls who do the three weeks on and one off, they are still spending more time on the premises of the job and three weeks of trying to be somebody else. That would be too confusing for me.

We asked her why she thought people suggested that. She replied,

> Because of the social stigma, I would assume. It is probably the

hardest part of the business, is dealing with that. And I just finally said, "Hey I am who I am."

To be sure, Strawberry Shortcake did take on a work name. But she, like others who talked about their work as caring practices, did not see her work self as separate and distinct from her "real" self.

To complicate things further, just because the women do talk about performing another identity at work does not mean their work self is not true to their values, transcendentally inauthentic, or completely estranged from how they really feel.

For example, Princess, 19, had worked for six months at the Moonlite Bunny when we spoke to her, and she had described her work as largely holistic. She described a wide array of rather stereotypical feminine identities she adopts in the course of doing her job in response to customer demands. She described the process as hard work.

Princess:	Princess is the freak, Princess is the whore, Princess is the baby, Princess is the little teenager, Princess is whatever you want her to be. Princess is the dominatrix that's spanking your ass, or Princess is the submissive that's letting you paddle her, you know?
Interviewer:	Now how do you know who to be?
Princess:	Well, however the guy comes off. You know, if the guy comes off as a sub[missive], you know, or he notices something that interests him and goes toward that, then you just go off your vibe or what they ask for or how they act you know.
Interviewer:	Is that easy to do?
Princess:	Sometimes, not all the time. Sometimes, I'm right, sometimes, I'm off. You know. There's always somebody for somebody else. If you don't like me, there's somebody else out there you might like. Find them, you know. Try everybody, you know. Experiment.

We asked her to tell us the difference between Princess and her non-work persona, and she said, "When I'm Princess, I'm not as real as when I'm Shellie." But she also said, "it's not too much different I guess." She performed an array of identities, but she considered this to

Figure 6.1 Strawberry Shortcake lives and works in her bedroom. Most women decorate their rooms with pictures of children, reminders from home, as well as items that reflect their personalities. Author photo.

be part of her job, and also did not see those identities as that much different from her off-work self.

Charli drew fairly strong boundaries between what she considered personal intimacy and her work. She had worked as a secretary for a number of years before becoming an erotic dancer and later, a brothel prostitute. She talks about creating a different identity for work.

> I think everybody does that. I think that's part of the reason they give you stage names, you know, when you're a dancer. You're not that person any more. Your inhibitions go with your name. It's just strange to have split personalities, but it really feels that way.

Charli sees her work identity as a way to help her get rid of inhibitions so she can do the job. Charli's split personality is not estranged from her values, or even something against which she defines herself. Indeed, the prostitute identity, she argues, may be inside every woman. "I think inside every woman there is something that says, 'Wow! What would it be like to be a stripper, showgirl, or courtesan?' And so Charli gets to do that."

Ricki, who talked about the work as "being someone you are not to entice a customer to come into your room," also said that she thinks her work self and her self outside of work are "basically the same person. It's just that one comes across a little more assertive, more confident, more vocal, you know?" In the second book of *The Internet Escort's Handbook Series*, author Amanda Brooks discusses how instead of an alternate persona, it can be easier to be a more polished version of yourself, "yourself on your best behavior in your Sunday clothes."[20] For Ricki, like Charli, her work requires her to act more confident, and at work she can do that when she has to.

> I just feel very compassionate and very warm because I have a lot more confidence. And I come across as "yeah baby I want you." When in reality I want to be in my sweats. I want to have my hiking boots on. I want to ride horses and be out in the desert.

Ricki was one of those workers who talked about her work predominantly in terms of caring practices. Like the others, she struggles to be genuine. "I care, I really care," she claimed. She thinks about her customers in terms of friendship potential.

> And, half the time, I can honestly say I could be friends with this person. I just couldn't do it, because you know the sex thing comes into play and I wouldn't necessarily want to have sex with this person on the outside, but I'd like to be their friend on the outside, but I wouldn't want to have sex with them. You know, that's just my job part.

Ricki feels a genuine connection with her customers, and the sex is "just the job part." She said that she believes the "reward of this business is that men can be just as vulnerable as women, and I don't think I ever believed that before." She shared stories of "sweet" customers.

Hochschild and other scholars, in analyzing emotional labor, draw a distinction between what they label surface acting and deep acting. Surface acting involves acting one way while feeling another, hiding one's true emotions or faking it. Deep acting is the effort to truly feel the emotion. It too is acting, but acting with good intentions. The distinction is important, as surface acting has been correlated with more burn-out and emotional distress at work. Deep acting has been associated with feelings of accomplishment and higher job satisfaction. The disjuncture between who one is expected to be at work and one's real self takes on a different meaning. One does not have to believe that a performance is true, real, or authentic in any transcendental sense for the interaction to be meaningful and emotionally satisfying. Identity is fluid, contextual, and flexible. Indeed, sociologist Rebecca Erickson, who researches emotional labor, calls for conceptualizing authenticity as being true to one's self-values, true to self in context or in particular relationships, and not true to self for all time. This seems a much better way of understanding how brothel workers who draw on caring and holistic practices reconcile authenticity and identity.

A lot of Ricki's struggles to be true to herself in context had to do with the stereotypes and labels of being a prostitute. Ricki left the brothels for five years to be a "normal everyday person." But she missed the sexual attention. Ricki told us she enjoys being a sexual person, but outside of work she felt judged, like "everyone thought I was a hooker." She hit a rough financial spot and decided to go back to the brothel where it is acceptable for her to be sexual and she can earn a living doing so. "I don't like to draw that kind of attention on the outside, you know. Now I get the attention I need and I do have a purpose in my life." Ricki takes pleasure in receiving sexual attention, but conceded that society at large tends not to approve of a woman's sexual expression. Her desire to express herself sexually is most strongly satiated through her work persona. As a result she feels a sense of accomplishment.

The Meaning of Authenticity in the Commodified Exchange

This issue of authenticity is an important one. In today's leisure economy it has become a key commodity as well as a way of doing identity work. Not only do today's brothel workers need to construct elaborate fantasies that are outside of what one encounters in daily life, they must construct fantasies that resemble those of day-to-day life. One such fantasy that reflects the complicated customer taste for a more everyday sexual encounter is the "girlfriend experience." If online brothel client discussion boards are any indication, a number of customers are seeking and willing to pay for this experience. It even gets its own initials—GFE. Authenticity is the most important commodity for a GFE. On a message board devoted to giving advice to potential customers seeking legal prostitution, a brothel customer known online as BunnyLover offers his definition of "the girlfriend experience."

> I'll use Speed Racer's definition with a few modifications. A session that includes activities that may make one forget that your party is a paid, professional encounter. It could include elements of the following: kissing (maybe DFK or Deep French Kissing), prolonged foreplay, cuddling, massage, and extensive conversation. A GFE session usually is an unrushed, relaxed atmosphere (within brothel limits, of course). In my opinion, someone that provides a GFE probably at least does some cuddling, has more extensive conversation, has an unrushed environment, and makes you forget your party is a paid encounter. A woman that provides a GFE may not provide the same or any of the same elements to another customer. It can often depend upon the chemistry between the client and the courtesan. You may experience inconsistencies in subsequent GFEs with the same provider.[21]

Chemistry and authenticity are central to the GFE. Twice in this long quote he says the experience will make you "forget your party is a paid professional encounter." This definition highlights the importance of an individualized experience and the possible incongruity between subsequent visits or among different customers. Thus, not only must the brothel workers draw on a number of skills and practices to create the girlfriend experience, they must create a moment of authentic interaction. Thus authenticity is a key component of a fantasy experience.

Ricki talked a great deal about feeling genuine, as we have noted, saying, "I care, I really care." Jane at the Moonlite Bunny Ranch, whose practices were largely holistic, explained that "I have this product that I really just want the customer to have, I mean, I believe in the quality of the product." Jane said she has trouble negotiating for larger sums of money for a party because she just wants "everyone to experience sexual pleasure." She disclosed that to help her negotiate for a higher price:

> I always offer a massage, I always say first thing, "So, do you like massages?" And nine out of ten will say, "Oh yes." And then I'll say, "Well I'll just throw that in with any party." And I just kind of hope that makes me more attractive to them. Because I just love to give massages, I always want to do that.

Jane earnestly wants customers to enjoy a pleasurable holistic experience. She sincerely loves to give massages. But these are also her strategies to make more money. A massage means less time actually having sex, which can be more physically wearing or tiring. A massage helps her connect with her client, a pragmatic business decision. For Jane, intimacy, genuine emotion, and her "product" are not incompatible.

Women like Jane who employ holistic practices are likely to be the most straightforward about how they connect authentic and commodified intimacy with their sense of self. Magdalene Meretrix affirmed that emotions, fantasy, sales, and sex are intertwined in complex ways.

> It is more intense at work. That seems weird, I know. But when a total stranger pays me for sex, it is not like they see me when I wake up in the morning, or when I am sick or in a bad mood.

> We have never had an argument over who takes out the gar-
> bage. So it is a special time out of time. It is a fantasy world
> insulated from the world so it is more intense.

Ruby at the Moonlite Bunny told us, "The idea that I could only
love one man, I mean, I love my man dearly, but he knows I have a huge
capacity of love and affection, you know?" Ruby is not just alluding to
sex, which she does enjoy, but she is asserting her ability to care for and
connect emotionally with many other people.

At this level, the women recognize a contractually bounded sense
of genuineness that sex work scholar Elizabeth Bernstein refers to as
"bounded authenticity." As one worker at Angel's Ladies told us, "For
me, I care about them about an hour. I care about them more than I
care about anyone else in that hour." In her interviews with customers,
Bernstein argues that what men describe that they want is emotional
connection and even intimacy, though bounded by a contract. The
market itself provides the emotional boundary between sex worker and
client, but that does not mean the exchange is emotionless. The men
wanted an erotic connection, to be pampered and dealt with emotionally as well as sexually, but bounded by a mutually negotiated market
agreement.[22] Katherine Frank similarly found that strip club regulars
value "real" and authentic exchange with erotic dancers while being
acutely aware of the monetary connections.[23] "Bounded authenticity"
actually cultivates an emotional connection between client and customer as an accepted product of the market. Bounded authenticity
makes sense in light of the notion that the self is fluid and contextual.
We also echo Bernstein's finding that bounded authenticity is central to
middle-class consumption of sexual commerce.[24] Nevada's suburban
brothels are attempting to garner a different customer base in just this
fashion.

For example, Ricki recounted a conversation she had with a happily
married customer who had a fantasy of visiting a prostitute. He and
his wife both agreed it was better to come to a brothel where it was
safe than to go to the girl next door and "end up with some '*Fatal
Attraction*' or disease or anything like that."

In fact, Crystal, a former prostitute and owner of Ely's Stardust
brothel, thinks the sex industry is more honest because it relies on the
market. She believes that in life there is a basic adversarial relationship
between men and women, particularly when people want to have

casual sex. "The guys go to bars, right? Pick up women. Go home, 'I'll call you in the morning' and never call. One great big lie." In social interactions, she thinks men feel they have to lie to a woman in order for her to agree to have sex.

> He meets someone at the bar, tells the whole truth that he just got a divorce. She knows he's on the rebound. So he knows he is not going to get whatever he wants because he just told the truth. He has to lie. Here, he tells the truth and it works.

At least in the brothel, she said, "it's cut and dry, the money changes hands, it's no more honest than this . . . nobody goes home ticked, you don't have to leave in the morning or sneak out and nobody has to call her or whatever. That's why I think it is honest." The market exchange of brothel prostitution can be a more honest exchange than a random one-night stand. Men do not have to lie, and women get paid for their labor. The morality of the market, according to Crystal, is easier to traverse than the morality of a one-night stand or casual sex because the terms of an exchange are explicit. In this way, brothels provide a commodified setting free from romantic confusion, hurt feelings, or expectations of continued interaction.

In the moment of bounded authenticity, sex worker and client agree that in this monetarily constrained time period, sex and some level of emotional labor will take place. The mixing of money, sex, and emotional sincerity is not incongruent to women's sense of identity at work or at home. Acting, in this sense, is not a disingenuous perform-ance; the creation of a commodified fantasy is not void of what women label as a genuine emotional connection. Self, for these women, is fluid and contextual.

Managing Stigma and Burn-out

What is the impact of this work on emotional well-being? We have already seen how many women talked about positive outcomes from their work, including a sense of accomplishment. Brothel workers also described negative consequences of working in the brothels. As with prior research, these discussions were not about the nature of the job, but about particular circumstances and their ability to deal with these circumstances.

The most common stressors women told us about were those around a lack of clients, not making enough money, and the inevitable self-esteem issues that result from not getting clients. Watching other women being picked out of a line-up while another worker is continually overlooked can wear on that woman's self-esteem. Earlier in the chapter, Misty, Precious, Air Force Amy, and Bev all talked about how they deal with not getting picked in a line-up. They recognized and supported each other by asserting that at the end of the day the customer is looking for the perfect woman for him. And it is just one woman. And that might not be her. Of course not all women are supportive, and there are days when it wears on a worker. Lani disclosed, "It does affect you, doing this type of stuff. It does affect. I know by the time I'm 35, I'll be certified, I believe it. 'Cos I deal with so much stress, and so many different problems. My mind goes so many different places. So, it is stressful." Misty said, "When your self-esteem starts going down sometimes, you have to know yourself, really believe in yourself, then they can't touch that."

Women talked frequently about specific problems with customers and how they dealt with them, but the women did not express negativity toward customers writ large. Indeed, many brothel workers talked a great deal about customers who were "sweethearts." Ricki, who claims to genuinely like her customers, said, "Sometimes, I don't like who I am dealing with." For many of the women, the drunken customers are the worst. For example, Lani, Brenda, and Alice recalled stories about customers who have had "one too many drinks, for instance. They can be loud and obnoxious and really hard to please." Misty told us that "it ain't gonna happen if they are too drunk." To deal with this, some brothels impose drink limits for customers. Emili at Sheri's Ranch explains that she believes alcohol impairs men's physical ability and emotional state:

> Because it is a depressant, a lot of times they can't get erect, and if they can't get erect, they can't come. And if they can't come, it's frustrating. And if it's frustrating, they turn angry. And if they turn angry, then they turn kind of abusive and then you pretty much got to take them to the curb anyway . . . if you're gonna spend $500 to $1,000, the last thing you need is somebody coming early, pissing their money down the tube and then getting angry about it. It's just easier to turn them away.

The women told us that the most effective way to deal with drunken customers is to just not party with them in the first place.

Sometimes drunk customers are rude to the women. Angela at the Green Lantern said that she learned to handle this by demanding a basic level of respect:

> If you don't want someone to touch you, or you don't want someone to talk to you in a certain way, just because this is the work that we do doesn't mean that you can sit and talk to me any kind of way, or disrespect me, or hurt me. No, I ain't having it.

Many women also describe having to act tough with customers who are not respectful. However, not all the women spoke of having to deal with bad customers. Those who did talk about troublesome customers made sure to explain that they were able to deal with these situations. The women added that they had the power to turn down customers. In reminiscing about her hesitant entry into the brothel industry, Misty recollected, "The customer has to respect you, they can't be calling you a whore or nothing or they have to leave." Strawberry Shortcake recalled how she handled customers who felt entitled to treat her in a way she did not like.

> You warn 'em, you give 'em another warning, and then you just say the party is over. All you have to do is open up that door, and if you need to scream, you can. If not, just walk out and say "You're outta here now. Would you like to get dressed or would you like to do it in the parking lot?"

She said the brothel management was always supportive, "Oh yeah, yeah. Oh yeah, they don't even ask questions."

Another stressful aspect of the job is living at the brothel and the subsequent limitations on a worker's mobility. Those who work in brothels that require workers to live on-site occasionally spoke about the negative consequences of the "lockdowns." But those who were there seemed to accept it as part of the job. Misty believes that some women who quit the brothel did so because they could not stand the lockdown. Celeste confirmed, "You go if you want, but it doesn't mean that you are going to have a job when you come back." Shellie, who works at Sheri's Ranch outside of Las Vegas, accepts the health rationale

for the restrictions on mobility. She is not pleased by it, but feels workers just have to look at it as a business thing. Rather surprisingly, the
women did not talk about the lockdown as being one of the most
stressful parts of the job. However, several who worked at brothels who
had shifts and could leave afterward were very happy with that practice.

Many of the women described burn-out as a very real consequence
of not managing her emotions, regardless of which of the three strategies she chooses. Jackie came back to the brothels just before our
interview after four years in a service industry job:

> If all of a sudden it gets really busy or something and the gold
> prices go up [which means more customers from mining], who
> knows, I might stay longer. Right now I'm hoping I don't have
> to be here. It's not that I hate it, but I get burned out, you know.

Ricki identified emotional labor as a major source of her experience with burn-out several years ago. She had lost the ability to draw
boundaries where she needed to and had difficulty managing her
multiple identities.

> I got to the point where when people call me by my real name,
> it didn't matter, I hardly could respond, everything that's when
> it got time to go and get the hell out. I just started losing who I
> was, who I was inside, you know. I lost myself . . . They became
> commodities, they became, you know, before I was the real nice
> hooker that wanted to hear what you had to talk about, I had
> great conversation. The guys are great guys . . . It got to the
> point that I could not service guys, and like, "I don't want to
> hear your story, I don't care if you're going through a divorce, I
> don't give a fuck . . . Tell me what you want and let's do it, and
> just get out of my sight." I never said it, but that's what I
> thought, you know what I mean. I became cold, I became
> bitter. I just became insensitive. And so, I quit.

After Ricki quit, she spent five years working in a warehouse for an
online retail company before going back to the brothel for mostly
financial reasons. She says she has a different attitude now because she
recognizes that men can be vulnerable, and she uses that to get repeat
customers.

When discussing negative aspects of the job, most of the women almost immediately followed that with a comparison to other service jobs they had. For them, brothel work is not that different in terms of frustration, burn-out, and bad customers than other jobs—it just pays better. Strawberry Shortcake managed restaurants for 13 years, and "several of those years were for corporations, so I sold a heck of a lot more than my body." Emili reflected on the positive aspects that help combat burn-out while living on-site at Sheri's Ranch: "I mean we've got a cook, we've got a sun deck back there, we have a garden, we have a Jacuzzi room, you know, we try to treat each other good."

Ricki conceded that while she mostly liked her customers, it was normal to not always like them. The only difference between this and other service sector jobs is that "I'm using my body, and other people are dealing with people on a mind level. That can be just as manipulative, just as disturbing, just as distasteful." She stressed that in both areas of work, "I don't want to kiss this person's ass, but I have to because it's my job, you know what I mean." She said that when she worked at a warehouse in Nevada for low pay, "I'm like walking around in sweats, no makeup, you know, really trying to be low key. And guys are still hitting on you and stuff."

While brothel workers talked of their problems on the job, stigma appeared to be the underlying source of most of their problems and negative emotions. Many of the women struggled with how sex work transgressed social norms around sex and femininity. Magdalene defended her work: "I come up against a lot of stigma. People have strange ideas about what a sex worker is or is not . . . It is a job like any other job. With sex work, you can treat it like a real job or not." Magdalene recognizes that even though brothel labor is legal work, it remains highly stigmatized. This is what scholar Gail Pheterson calls "whore stigma," a social backlash against women who exert economic and sexual initiative. The perniciousness of whore stigma extends to all women, regardless of whether or not they engage in sexual commerce: it is a type of gender policing meant to define and limit women's sexual expression and control. So even though the women have many workplace strategies to regulate the interaction and define their identities, resisting the internalization of whore stigma can be quite difficult.[25] As Celeste implied, it is a psychological struggle against social norms, "to be able to disjoint yourself from society and actually come into these places, and just hang as a solo project."

Most of the women strongly defended the work that they did against how they felt the world perceived them. For example, Angela responded to the stigma against exchanging sex for money: "My opinion is it's society that makes you think it's so wrong, you know . . . I feel like if Jesus Christ could sit there and bathe a prostitute's feet and make her feel like she was worthy . . ." Ruby extolled a positive social outcomes of sex work:

> Ya know, they'll criticize me for doing what I'm doing, but, you know, who's gonna take care of the guy in the wheelchair? Ya know? Who's going to do that? And make him feel special. You know, I just, to me it's very, very discouraging and frustrating dealing with the way society is.

Charm, at the Moonlite Bunny Ranch, proclaimed her sexual nature: "I am like over the fact that I'm being judged, pretty much. . . . It's a challenge, but get over it. It's been a challenge my whole life, 'cos I've always been highly sexual. And that is sort of how it is looked at in society's eyes." For women like Charm, brothel work validates their sexual expression. In brothels, women can be sexual and they can make money from it (joining the numbers of women who work in adult film and have sex on screen, or in sexualized industries like erotic dance, peep shows, and sex phone line operators), something rarely legally afforded to other groups of women.

For others, the struggle against stigma is more convoluted. Ginger at the Old Bridge outside of Reno found,

> It really is very hard to do this. At least with me, I start to feel like bad about myself, or just the thought of going back to a room with a total stranger and getting paid for sex. Sometimes it just almost makes me sick, you know. I mean, it really is a mind fuck. But you just kind of gotta get over it.

The construction of sex as special and romantic, something engaged in with a partner who they know, is at odds with the work women undertake in the brothels. The anxiety and negative emotions brothel workers feel seem to be a consequence of social ideologies that dictate proper sexual behavior for women. It is the idea of selling sex that is hard to embrace, more so than the actual practices. The women struggle with the idea of promiscuous sex or sex with multiple, fairly unfamiliar partners as a problem, but not the practice itself as harmful. Carol lamented,

> Well, I think it takes a piece of your soul and heart every time you have to go back to the room . . . It's not really the actual job, it's the everything outside of the job that messes with you.

It is important to note here that Carol identified the "outside" social pressure to conform as the reason for her negative feelings toward brothel work. For her, it is the general public community that skews brothel prostitution into something immoral and harmful. She continued,

> As far as I can tell, people look at you, how you're judged, how you're categorized and everything like that. But it also too is the job, and it's like, you can train yourself like it doesn't bother you. But deep down, once you take down the wall and really concentrate on what is going on, it messes with you.

The issue is a difficult one. At the time we talked to her, Carol was one of the few who conveyed that she was really burned out. She appeared to have lost her ability to draw the necessary lines she needs to maintain a sense of self. Yet she is not talking about customers who mistreat her or managers who exploit her as the source of her problems. It is the problem of burn-out that many emotional laborers have, but a burn-out intensified by the social stigma of selling sex.

One main strategy the women use to defy social stigma is to value their labor and their identities as prostitutes. Alysha talked about how she deals with stigma:

> That's a main thing that a lot of women lose in this business and I have lost it a time or two over the years. I lost respect for myself. I'm not even going to tell you that you don't lose respect. And that's where a lot of women go wrong. When you lose that respect, you ain't shit, you feel like you're not nothing. You feel like you're a worthless ass piece of shit and all you are is a piece of ass. But you know what? You're not, and you don't have to be that way. You can be in this business without being a worthless ass piece of shit.

Emili believes that only women who are strong in the face of transgressing cultural norms about femininity, sex, and money can sell sex:

> Mentally, physically, spiritually and emotionally, if you're not strong in every one of those facets, you won't make it in this business. This business is for very strong, open-minded women. And the kind of stuff that comes your way . . . I mean after it comes your way, ya know, you're okay with it, 'cos it's like a storm blows through and you're used to it, but, in the beginning it's not for shy people, it's not for the timid.

Celeste said that "if everybody could do this there would be a lot more people here." She affirmed that "either you're going to succeed or you're going to fail. And there's nobody to blame . . . there's no blame placing anywhere but on yourself, either you're going to shake and make it or you're not."

From all of this, we have two important observations. First, Nevada's brothel workers, like many interactive service workers, seem to have fluid, flexible, and situational identities that allow them to perform different "selves" for customers without feeling particularly estranged from some core sense of self. That said, the women do have different ways of doing identity work. Some women define their performance as a prostitute in opposition to who they are at home; while consciously enacting different identities at work, they see consistency or similarity in all of their performances. Other women see no inconsistencies at all between performing identity as a prostitute and who they may be while not at work.

Second, these commodified experiences are often framed by very strong gender dichotomies that limit women to the archetypal Madonna or whore identities: the modest, sexually passive, nurturing woman versus the sexually active, bold, inappropriate slut. Consequently the women in Nevada's brothels act in and around the constructed notion of who "a prostitute" is supposed to be.

What about the consequences of these performances? The women did not tell us that they thought the act of selling sex was itself somehow damaging to their sense of self. Some women did draw boundaries in different ways. In particular, women who talked about body practices were more likely to depersonalize their interactions at work. However, not all women disassociated, and in fact many relied on their caring or holistic practices for a sense of accomplishment and self-worth. Even those who talked about body practices did not always talk about these as a mechanism for withdrawing emotionally.

When women talked about negative feelings about work, they talked about specific conditions or incidences at their workplace, such as drunken customers, competition with certain women, or social stigma. In a few cases, women experienced burn-out or emotional distress, though this tended to be temporary. But like many interactive service workers, they talked about a number of emotional management strategies that helped them get through their work. It is very likely that legal brothels help provide workers with a number of resources to help combat emotional stress that other forms of sex work do not. For example, Nevada brothel workers did not experience violence in the brothels; instead they described it as a supportive workplace. As independent contractors they had a degree of workplace autonomy. In other words, the brothel context provided a number of resources that helped manage the consequences of emotional labor. However, competition and the lack of mobility did cause stress for a number of women.

CONCLUSION

Today Nevada's brothels have a diverse base of customers that includes sex tourists. We have found that Nevada's brothel workers sell sex in a wide variety of ways. They define their labor practices often in and against a mind–body dualism. We have shown how women talk about three broad practices when selling sex: body practices, caring practices, and holistic practices. These show not only that sex work is complex, involving both mental and physical labor, but that women employ different strategies for doing sexual labor. Not all women disassociate their emotions from their work. A number of high-earning sex workers have moved beyond the moral weight of mind–body dualism and conceive of their work in holistic ways.

Selling sex as an expensive fantasy experience to a sophisticated leisure consumer who is probably "gonna get off in 60 seconds" makes legal brothel prostitution more than about just selling one's body. Today's sexual tourist demands an experience of escape, relaxation, fantasy fulfillment, intimacy, and authentic connection beyond bodily gratification.[26] Popular discourse too often underplays or renders invisible the actual process of how sex is sold. Likewise, the concern about a prostitute's ability to manage her emotions or sense of self often means that the actual labor practices go unnoticed.

Arguably, as more middle-class customers with more disposable income are seeking sex, they can demand more sustained sexual interactions.[27] Indoor prostitution has always involved longer interactions and more emotional exchanges for a higher price. At the top end of the scale, the girlfriend experience may involve a date-like evening with dinner, conversation, and overnight sex play. At the lower end, it may involve simply providing extra attention, pampering, or even just a kiss at the end, in shorter periods of time. In a study of New York sex workers, Murphy and Venkatesh find that indoor workers are more likely to talk about personal connections with clients as important parts of their service, including providing clients with therapy, being friends, and having intellectual conversations.[28] As Nevada's brothels provide a wider range of services and encourage more extended services to attract more monied consumers, those women who provide even more emotional work, and, likely, more holistic services, will find a market.

While the prostitute identity is important, workers in Nevada's legal brothels seem to adopt several approaches to doing identity work, managing emotions, and dealing with the consequences of labor. Gergen argues that in today's culture an individual's selfhood is a continuous process of making and remaking multiple selves. The individual now maintains a "multiplicity of incoherent and disconnected relationships. These relationships pull us in myriad directions, inviting us to play such a variety of roles that the very concept of an "authentic self with knowable characteristics recedes from view."[29] This certainly seems as true for brothel workers, as for others in jobs where fantasy is sold.

What is different about sex work, however, is the social stigma around selling sex and the resulting extra demands on identity management. Much of the emotion and identity work that women undertake is a way to guard against social stigma.

Brothel work both challenges and reproduces powerful norms of gender, race, and heterosexuality at the macro and micro level. While brothel workers' vigorous sex lives may challenge norms of the sexually passive female, they also reproduce the idea that women are natural caregivers and nurturers as well as always sexually available to men. While brothel sex may allow women to exercise a higher degree of sexual freedom in the public space of a business, they are often paid to enact classic feminine and racial stereotypes—the nasty whore, the sexy schoolgirl, the blonde bombshell, the Asian submissive, or the dark-skinned exotic.

At the same time, brothel workers are getting paid well for caring and nurturing, unlike women in other traditionally feminine jobs, such as childcare workers. To the extent that sex workers profit handsomely from the cultural ideal of the emotional, caring woman by offering clients a moment of commodified authenticity, they arguably subvert traditional norms. To the extent that they sell what is supposed to be private intimacy subverts heterosexual norms dictating the rules of a sexual relationship. The important point here is that women use a variety of ways to negotiate these more or less stereotypical understandings of the place of caring, intimacy, and bodily skill in their work. Thus, women both embrace and resist traditional norms of femininity and sex on the job.

Overall, the labor practices that brothel workers utilize should be understood within the context of neoliberal, decentralized service work today. As independent contractors, brothel workers are self-regulating workers who manage their own work resources—their bodies (through clothing and possibly plastic surgery) and emotional investment (through their work practices). Not that the brothels are free of rules and norms, but the women are not controlled by a manager in the same way as an assembly-line worker. Women do their own branding.

As Carol Wolkowitz argues, instead of reproducing the notion of body work as mindless, we should recognize the centrality of body work to post-industrial global economies, and more closely examine the social relations and status distinctions where body work exists.[30] The modern hierarchy of mind/body separation is transforming. This transformation is about class and profit. Some service workers today integrate mind and body; and so we see holistic workers earning more money and suburban brothels pushing for the sale of experience and fantasy.

7

CONCLUSION

Learning from Nevada

You know it's been around since Jesus Christ. It's gonna be around 'til the day this world ends. You're not going to stop it because there's always going to be a man who wants to go somewhere and be with a woman or have a fantasy. Or there's going to be women who want to do this.

Angela, Green Lantern

I think it's my civil right to be a prostitute.

Jane, the Moonlite Bunny Ranch

I think prostitution should be legal everywhere. I think it's so much safer when you have the medical checkups and all of that.

Ricki, Miss Kitty's

I'd also like to do some lobbying and I'd like to speak to governments about setting up legalized prostitution. Like a federal program.

Ruby, Moonlite Bunny Ranch

Living in Nevada, we are always amazed at the gumption of policy-makers who seem to encourage every entrepreneur with a crazy idea. Two of us sat in a city council meeting once, trying to prevent an amusement ride from being constructed on a casino in our neighborhood—a 60-foot growling gorilla ascending the side of the 600-foot Stratosphere casino tower. One of the city councilmen said something along the lines of, "This is Las Vegas. We didn't become the fastest-growing city in the country by preventing things like King Kong from climbing a tower." However, for a variety of political reasons, the gorilla ride was not approved. The gorilla symbolized the one crazy thing the city would not do. It made the rest of it all look normal.

For almost every legislator, local official, or casino operator in Nevada, prostitution is the gorilla on the tower. The state's multi-billion-dollar leisure industry grew to what it is today by offering choices excluded by moral proscriptions in the rest of the country—easy divorce, easy marriage, gambling, abundant adult nightlife, and prostitution. Politicians and businesspeople are acutely aware that sanitized vice is the foundation of the state's billion-dollar leisure industry. Even though prostitution helped build the state's image, since the 1950s Nevada has used opposition to state-sanctioned prostitution as a sanitizer. State officials were backed into making prostitution legal in the first place. And even in the 2009 state legislative session, in the midst of a fiscal meltdown where everything was put on the table as a potential source of revenue, legislators refused to impose a state tax on brothels, or consider a red light district in downtown Las Vegas, largely because they feared the national attention that would result from yet again appearing to legitimize prostitution.

Nevada may be alone in the United States in having legalized prostitution. But in the new American heartland, the social relations and institutions that drive the sex industry in Nevada are increasingly vital to the rest of the nation. Sexuality is ever more fundamental to the leisure economy, evident in local, national, and international tourism industries and a large segment of service industries. Late capitalist consumer culture drives a changing political landscape where personal choice is seen as a moral right. In the market for intimacy, workplaces sell emotions and interactions, and companies want to profit from the growing consumer taste for fantasy. With leisure becoming a growing part of the economy in markets all around the world, prostitution is becoming arguably more prevalent, if not more visible.[1] Prostitution is already legal in other parts of the world. For U.S. policymakers it is only a matter of time before they look for criminalizing commercial sex.

As such, what can we learn from the state of sex in Nevada?

THE STATE OF SEX

The changes that have come about with the development of a leisure economy have profoundly shaped our society's relationship with intimacy. Prostitution has to be examined in this changing context. In the first half of the book, we looked at how our politics, our values, the organization of work, our sense of self, and our relationships have all been changed by the growth of a consumer and especially a leisure economy. This has spurred the growth and mainstreaming of sexual commerce generally. The history of prostitution in Nevada showed us the importance of tourism to the development of the brothel industry. Open prostitution played a key role in building the state's developing leisure industry up until the 1950s. Gender and class struggles channeled the diverse array of sexual leisure services in this early tourist economy into today's regulated legal brothels. In the second half of the twentieth century, the shift from mining to tourism meant a shift from selling sex to selling sexuality in the state's burgeoning resort cities. Independent working women in mining and railroad towns were pressed into working for someone else, forcing them to give up control of their work. Today, women work as independent contractors in brothels owned by entrepreneurs, corporations, or business partnerships. While the resort industry pushed brothels into the rural counties, it is clear that brothels would not be legal in Nevada without tourism.

The second half of the book explored how these demographic, social, and economic changes have affected what happens inside Nevada's brothels. Brothel businesses make sex into a service for sale in many of the same ways as other non-sex tourist businesses make fantasy and escape into a saleable service. Like other businesses in a leisure economy, brothels strive to provide reproducible and standardized services that are also (seemingly) personalized experiences. Suburban brothels that are near the growing tourist areas are upscaling, diversifying, corporatizing, and marketing to a wider range of potential clientele. They are attempting to tap into new leisure-seeking consumers, the modern male traveler with disposable income and a taste for fantasy sexual experiences. Rural brothels still market primarily to truckers, local and migrant workers who hold traditionally masculine working-class jobs. These brothels provide services that are discreet, affordable, and advertised as a home away from home. However, even rural brothels are changing as a globalized leisure industry reaches into all areas of the state. Rural areas are not economically and socially isolated, but are interwoven into the state's economy and culture.

Also typical of other leisure and tourist businesses, legal brothels are managed in highly gendered ways. Service industries often view women as a docile labor pool and as naturally possessing the characteristics necessary for good customer service: warmth, friendliness, and a knack for emotional interaction, and brothels are no different. Yet because legal brothel work is stigmatized, some rules, and the enforcement of these rules, are unique to brothel businesses. Legal sex workers are classified as independent contractors; however, house rules, restrictions on mobility, fines, and shifts often stretch the bounds of labor laws. The restrictions on mobility that exist in some of Nevada's brothels are especially hard on workers, and reflect the stigma associated with prostitution. Management practices within the brothels vary greatly, however. Some brothels now allow women to leave after their shift is over, signaling an important change in the treatment of workers. This seems to be a result of the further mainstreaming of the industry as suburban brothels must attract more laborers.

Today's leisure industries generate jobs in formal and informal sectors providing sexual and non-sexual leisure services. Brothels draw from these workers. Because brothels are legal, they attract both experienced workers who have sold sex illegally and workers who have never before sold sex. Women come from an expanding sex sector, including high-end workers who come from other legal adult industries. Brothels offer potentially well-paying employment for women facing intensifying inequality in low-paying service work.

Doing brothel labor must also be seen in the context of changing social relations in a growing leisure economy. Emotions are increasingly important commodities in a leisure economy. Much of what we know about how service workers manage emotions in interactions with customers also applies to brothel workers. The workers who we interviewed did not disassociate mentally when they did brothel labor. Brothel work involves both physical and emotional labor. Workers used different ways of combining these to meeting diverse needs of both traditional working-class customers and leisure consumers seeking sexual escape or adventure. They created complicated sexual fantasies, served as counselors to men who just wanted to talk, and managed male orgasms in set amounts of time. Women in rural brothels were more likely to talk about physical labor or caring practices, while some women in the suburban brothels had crafted successful careers providing extended and expensive holistic services. Indeed, even authenticity takes on different meanings for workers doing sexual labor. We found that brothel workers use strategies and techniques to manage intricate performances of self and combat emotional distress and burn-out just like workers in other interactive service jobs.

In sum, prostitution is not one thing. Our case study of Nevada teaches us several things about prostitution. First, context and legality matters. Not only do the historical and social circumstances affect what prostitution is—the fact that brothels are legal affects the way businesses are run as part of a legitimate, established industry in the state. It affects who contracts to work in the brothels, and what workplace practices are like. Second, being an industry in a region so heavily dependent on leisure and tourism matters. Prostitution was a core leisure industry in the mining West. As Nevada's economy moved to tourism, sexual labor remained. Sexual commerce in Nevada is legal today because it has been squeezed into the corset of law at the state and county levels. Likewise the forces of global capitalism, changing consumer tastes, changing conceptions of gender and class, changing labor markets, and changing labor processes affect the practices within the brothels.

THE SOCIAL RELATIONS OF SEXUAL COMMERCE

In this book, we purposefully took the focus off of individuals to explore larger social relations and institutions that shape the brothel industry and the people working in it. The stereotypical approaches to prostitution—as deviance, as the enduring power of men over women, as violence against women, or alternatively as sexual liberation and empowerment, are problematic because they frame prostitution as a universal, singular "other" sexual experience. We find that the social relations surrounding prostitution matter most in understanding commercial sex.

One long-enduring question about prostitution is whether or not the inequality of (sexual) relations between men and women means that women are harmed by the very fact of working in a business where they sell sex to men. Our research shows that gender inequality is clearly a part of the brothel industry, and affects the lives of men and women. However, we do not believe that selling sex itself is inherently harmful to women. Working conditions, the background and resources of the workers, and labor strategies vary considerably, and make a difference in terms of experiences of power and exploitation.

In Nevada's legal brothels, we saw no evidence of trafficking. What we found was that brothels successfully prevent violence and have working relationships with local police. Despite what some anti-prostitution abolitionists claim about Nevada's brothels and sex work in general, none of our interviewees were coerced or forced into the legal brothels, nor was there any indication that the women were there against their will. We found no signs of coercion or exploitation beyond what one might see in many workplaces, as owners push for profit and worker productivity. In some ways, the trend in the brothel industry seems to be toward improving workplace conditions, such as relaxing the restrictions on mobility, as brothels compete for quality workers.

The structures that constrain life for sex workers in Nevada's brothels are the same structures that constrain all of us—structures of gender, race, sexual orientation, ethnicity, and social class. Women's job choices, owners' business practices, and customers' desires must all be seen in the context of these changing and intersecting structures of inequality. The belief that women are free from constraints when it comes to work is unrealistic, just as the belief that women are all shackled into sex work is ideological and misguided. Gendered expectations of appropriate sexual behavior for men and women attach a stigma to prostitution even in a legal industry. This affects the brothel owners, customers, and citizens of these small towns as well as the workers.

Brothels are heterosexual, masculine, commercial spaces that cater to male sexual fantasies and demand particular performances of masculinity and femininity. However, masculinity and femininity are not stable and static categories, but rather malleable experiences that adjust to changes in the organization of economic and social life. We see this in how the type of customer that brothels cater to is changing. A working-class masculinity that puts a premium on clandestine encounters in a sexualized, bawdy home away from home is slowly giving way to a masculinity that relies on consumption to form identity. Heterosexuality is affirmed through the purchase and consumption of brothel sex, and the suburban brothels advertise a classier image of urbane living and style. And femininity is performed both as the empathetic caregiver as well as the sexually charged, always sexually available whore. Managers perform a paternalistic, protective masculinity, particularly salient in their imaginings of, and dealings with, pimps. These displays of gender in the search for profit and consumption exemplify new forms of femininity and masculinity that have developed in relationship with the growth of a consumer economy.

Inequalities based on class, race, ethnicity, sexual identities, and sexual practices that are found in our society at large explain much of what we see in Nevada's brothels. Commercial sex does not create cultural norms; rather it reflects them. Society itself is racist, classist, sexist, and heterosexist; blaming prostitution for being oppressive and discriminatory creates a sense that a utopian fairness does exist in other businesses, sexual or otherwise. Yet we know that this is simply untrue. The inequalities in the brothel industry have less to do with the work itself than with the larger social relations that shape it. This is the underlying and unspoken root of the discomfort around commercial sex. Identifying the sex industry as the origin of gender and sexual inequality relieves the general population of any accountability for being part of the problem, for maintaining gender and sexual categories that limit our experiences of ourselves. In truth, gender and sexual norms are glaringly apparent in the sex industry, but they are not created by the sale of sex. The sex industry does not hold that much power.

Understanding social inequalities is complicated by the fact that markets exist within cultural, social, and politically influenced regulatory frameworks. First, today's leisure and service industries merge economic activity with common aspects of personal life, such as how we see ourselves and our relationships, and who we are and who we want to be. Second, regulating the economy is regulating morality, and vice versa. Third, the line between what is genuine and what is fake has always been a struggle in consumer culture. This promises to be an even greater challenge as we turn more and more human emotions into services for sale. This struggle has implications for how we think about work and how we think about regulating the ever-expanding reach of capitalism. Nowhere is this struggle more played out than in the sex industry. Examining how something as intimate as sex can be turned into a service for sale is quite telling of the ever-evolving market in emotions.

As sociologists, the lessons we learn from the state of sex are lessons about the purchase of intimacy in late capitalism. Viviana Zelizer's argument about the mutually constitutive relationship between intimacy and the market holds true here: they are not separate, hostile spheres, but interconnected ways of relating. Brothels, like other service industries, are redefining work to contain a commercialized emotional element. In even the most intimate of commercial settings, workers and consumers find ways to create both moments of genuine connection and profitable interactions. Yet the tensions in commodified interaction are numerous: from identity at work and the self, to caring for the customer while maintaining physical and emotional boundaries, to making money and acting the part. Workers use various strategies to deal with these tensions, but there are not inherent contradictions to these strategies that diminish the workers' sense of self.

Nevada politics and libertarian political culture reflects changes evident across the United States. Nevada's politics reflects a neoliberal economic philosophy. The state's approach to values politics exemplifies a market morality in the selling of leisure, escape, intimacy, and transgression. The market is the arbiter of acceptability rather than government regulation of appropriateness. This neoliberalism and market morality has allowed cities like Las Vegas to become paradigmatic meccas of the postmodern tourist/touristic economy. It has cultivated the type of economic shift that has earned Nevada's place in the new American heartland. This market morality has also, in somewhat paradoxical ways, supported the existence of the brothel industry. We see evidence of this in several areas: the women are active, public sexual entrepreneurs who provide rationalized and experiential services, as do other touristic service industry workers. Heterosexuality is the dominant sexual orientation; the transgressive characteristic of brothel sex is not the sex itself but rather the sale of it. The sale of sex is still legal in parts of Nevada because it fits nicely within pre-existing heteronormative beliefs that privilege heterosexual sex over other sexual orientations. In this sense, a market actor is reproducing cultural norms. The bounded authenticity enacted within the brothels, and the market morality that reigns over it, means that brothel sex is actually not subversive. Brothels may be a sign of liberalized sexual norms, but they do not challenge inequalities.

In late capitalist society that increasingly commercializes and commodifies sexuality, the market helps regulate morality.[2] Market morality simultaneously drives acceptance of sexual diversity but also fuels a backlash by the religious Right and other conservative groups. Nevada's market morality is widely embraced especially by those who reject government imposition of values on individuals, urban and rural citizens alike.

That sex is rendered public via the market removes some of the specialness. Brothels (and other forms of commercial sex) expose the specialness of sex as something socially constructed; sex is diverse and fractured, made up of many acts and thoughts. The authenticity of sex as "natural" is challenged by the very existence of legal brothels. The lines between public and private are blurred, and there is growing acceptance of both the buying and selling of commodified intimacy; the general public is more accepting of the convergence of sex work and service work. This convergence is fueled by a sexualization of mainstream jobs and the centrality of service to tourist economies.

NEVADA'S LEGAL BROTHELS AS A MODEL?

Is the Nevada model of legalized prostitution a "good" model? And what does "good" mean—does it refer to (as sex workers' activists argue for) bettering working conditions, ensuring worker safety, increasing the availability of non-discriminatory health, legal, and financial services for workers, or does it refer to (as policymakers and citizens often assert) protecting communities, reducing crime control costs, and maintaining order?[3] There are several approaches which governments around the world take to prostitution policies. These include: (1) prohibitionist policies where all forms of the sale of sex are illegal and the prostitute is criminalized; (2) abolitionist policies, where laws punish third parties and not sex workers, banning pimping, pandering, brothel keeping, or soliciting; (3) legalization, where governments control certain conditions, and may institute licensing, registration, health checks, and so on, and (4) decriminalization, where all criminal statutes are removed and sex work is regulated like other independent businesses. In actual practice, many countries, including the United States, criminalize prostitution by combining prohibitionist and abolitionist policies. In governments that enact regulations, the line between decriminalization and legalization is largely a matter of degree.

Across the globe, the regulation of prostitution has shifted in the late twentieth and early twenty-first centuries to reflect a new set of sexual norms, and a new economic climate. There has been a significant trend across the globe away from prohibition toward legalization and decriminalization.[4] New South Wales in Australia decriminalized prostitution in 1995; New Zealand decriminalized prostitution in 2003. The Netherlands legalized brothels in 2000, Germany in 2002. Iceland decriminalized some aspects of prostitution in 2007. Most of Western Europe has decriminalized the act of prostitution, but certain activities surrounding prostitution, such as pimping or operating brothels, are illegal. Parts of Australia, Germany, Austria, the Netherlands, Switzerland, Turkey, Senegal, Denmark, Greece, and Hungary have forms of regulated brothels, including brothels. Austria and Germany have granted sex workers social security and equitable taxation. While Sweden and Norway recently enacted policies to criminalize clients, in general the trend has been toward reducing regulations.[5] The United States has remained outside the norm in clinging to prohibitionist policies.

Today, most U.S. laws criminalize the sex act as well as associated activities such as pimping and pandering. In practice, most enforcement is uneven and selective, and serves to confine illegal activities to, or displace them from, particular areas. Informal mandates and enforcement patterns de facto serve many of the same functions as zoning and registration, attempting to render prostitution invisible and at the same time criminalizing the women who practice it. For the most part, street prostitutes are disproportionately the target of police raids because they are the most visible, while indoor workers are targeted less frequently. This results in the arrest and conviction of mostly poor women of color. Recently, however, controversy about workers who advertise online through websites like Craigslist has brought increased police and political attention to indoor workers.

There are two important ideological trends in the United States. In reviewing recent poll data and newspaper articles on opponents of prostitution, sociologist Ronald Weitzer has argued that while the public is still predominantly opposed to prostitution, the majority of attacks are framed against the assumed secondary effects that impact neighborhood image, reputation, and property values. Regulators target disorderly conduct, health risks, *visible* drug use, violence, and public sexual displays that threaten the perceived values of heterosexual families and children. It is defined as a quality-of-life crime. Further, the objection is largely to more public and visible forms of street prostitution. Commercial sex in private, as long as it has no spillover in public, tends to escape social judgment and much legal attention.[6] Thus, in some respects, police and even the public are less concerned about people engaging in non-monogamous, non-procreative consensual adult sex.

Second, there has been a concerted effort by some anti-prostitution groups to frame the primary issue with prostitution as the exploitation of women by either drawing attention to the clients as victimizers, or by focusing on trafficking. In addition, feminists have critiqued prostitution policy for mainly controlling and penalizing women. As a result, there has been increasing political and media attention on the clients of prostitution. There has been a shift away from punishing prostitutes and a push toward punishing clients. For example, in San Francisco, studies find a 25 percent increase in client arrest rates.[7] In the 1990s, more cities instituted programs to discourage male consumers' demand. These include john schools, first offender programs, client re-education projects, and vehicle impoundment, along with revoking the driving licenses of clients and publicizing their names.

Moreover, the discourse has shifted from talking about the coerciveness of prostitution to talking about all prostitution as sex trafficking. There has been growing attention to sex trafficking since 2000, when the Trafficking Victims Protection Act (TVPA) was enacted at the federal level. For years, feminists internationally have struggled with the problems of forced migration and slavery, working to separate consensual from non-consensual sex, tighten laws, and establish services to rescue and rehabilitate those forced into sex work. Since the TVPA, many scholars note that the sex-trafficking issue has been elevated to a kind of moral panic. Fundamentalist feminists, Christian organizations, anti-immigration groups, and conservative political leaders are capitalizing and mobilizing around escalating moral outrage over sex trafficking. These groups equate all prostitution with trafficking, and define all forms of sexual labor as inherently exploitative and non-consensual.[8]

From our analysis of Nevada brothels, we conclude that Nevada's legal model is a better solution than criminalization. In Nevada's legal brothels, there are structures in place that have successfully prevented violence, disease, and severe exploitation. The rural communities where prostitution is legal do not experience problems typically assumed to be associated with illegal prostitution—underage prostitution, trafficking, drugs, littering (of used condoms, drug paraphernalia), violence, disease, and a general increase in crime.[9]

Given today's consumer-based leisure economy, changing attitudes toward sex and sexual relations, and the pervasiveness of low-paying, unskilled jobs for poor and lower class women, prohibiting the sale of sex seems to be fighting against the momentum of our culture. The cost of continuing to try to prohibit prostitution will only rise as our economic system drives it forward. Prohibition and abolitionist policies fail to accomplish what they set out to do: curb prostitution. In their attempts to do so, these approaches push illegal work further underground. Illegal laborers are more likely to be vulnerable to violent or petty crimes as they may feel that they have no legal recourse. They may experience exploitation by police, social discrimination and stigma, and an inability or difficulty in transitioning to other legal jobs. Further, such policies increase the number of women (and men and transgender people) with criminal records, and create other negative consequences that do nothing to increase the quality of life for the worker, the client, or the local community.

Nevada's specific policies may not easily transfer to other communities. The current brothel system in the state has been in development since the early 1900s. We also would not advocate a brothel-only approach, and indeed we would encourage jurisdictions to consider ways to allow women to work independently or in collectives. Nevada's brothels are problematic in many ways, from restrictions on mobility to frequent health checks of workers but not clients, to liberties taken with independent contractor laws, to discriminating against men and transgender workers who might otherwise seek a legal venue in which to work. However, ignorance of the lessons of Nevada's model is sure to further obscure the discussion. The following principles are worth ongoing analysis and further consideration by scholars, policymakers, and advocates.

First, licensing that occurs at the local level allows small counties and incorporated cities to respond to perceived needs and interests— economic, sexual, and otherwise—in their own communities. This decentralized model of legalization is flexible, with minimal state over-sight. Local officials are free to regulate as they see fit. Certainly one of the major arguments against changing these policies at the state level in Nevada is that politicians do not want to go against local governments. At the same time, local governments often maintain informal norms which, as we have seen, are often sexist, racist, and homophobic. It is imperative to balance this with more centralized civil protections from discriminatory practices.

Second, both the workers and owners should be offered the same legal rights and protections as the owners and workers in other legally operated and licensed businesses. Most of Nevada's counties have added due process clauses to regulations that help protect the business owners. However, we find that protections for the independent con-tractor are minimal and/or rarely enforced. Guidelines on the legal rights of independent contractors ought to be distributed to workers. Ideally, some state agency or, even better, a workers' union with politi-cal clout, ought to be involved in monitoring practices at brothels to make sure workplace policies and practices fall within the law. Jurisdic-tions should at least review any codified restrictions on women's mobility. There is no evidence to suggest that limiting mobility helps protect customers from disease. Allowing women to leave after shifts in the northern Nevada brothels has had no effect on health test results. Informal limitations that are placed on workers and owners fail to protect their interests and establish independent contractors as second-tier members of their communities. Good working conditions are essential for brothels to be able to recruit good workers.

Third, the confidential health-testing practices and mandatory condom use are effective and widely accepted among members of Nevada's brothel culture.[10] Minimal standards are imposed at the state level. The health regulations in Nevada's brothels, however, currently focus on a limited range of STIs and could be expanded and updated. Legal systems ought to make sure that there are mechanisms in place to easily update policies as health officials see fit, outside of the realm of politics. Testing is also expensive, and the cost is currently borne by the workers. Further, the assumption that women are vectors of disease is problematic, but potentially unavoidable in a legalized system.

Fourth, the privilege licenses and application processes allow local governments a great deal of leeway in screening potential owners. They allow local governments to keep owners with questionable backgrounds out of the industry, much as licenses have functioned in cleaning up the gaming industry in the state. This has proven to be a source of power for communities who permit brothel prostitution in Nevada, as well as a source of comfort. However, without proper oversight, this system also allows unstructured and unspoken rules and even discriminatory screening of owners whose rights may be violated as legal business owners. The merits and drawbacks of privilege licenses should be investigated further to establish their legality and their role in developing community-based, flexible but fair systems of legalized prostitution.

Fifth, legal brothels can be mainstream businesses. Legalizing this industry allows it to be subject to the norms and practices of other non-sex industries and other legal sexually oriented businesses. In Nevada, brothels have become respectable and well-integrated members of local communities where they have made the effort to do so.

If Nevada's brothels tell us anything, it is that you can never fully understand prostitution unless you look at it within the larger picture of social norms and market demands. Other states and communities around the United States can learn valuable policy lessons about the structures and experiences of prostitution today by paying attention to Nevada as a model, not as a social oddity. Social, cultural, and political meanings influence the process of governing bodies, sexuality, and commercial sexual exchanges. By recognizing the similarities and differences sex work has with other forms of labor, it is possible to frame, define, legislate, and regulate commercial sex in ways that are more empowering for sex workers and healthier for communities.

> It seems to me like you people have more important issues to talk about and do something about than brothels. They never bothered anybody. And they do bring business to town. You have more important issues to address.
>
> Bob, Ely citizen, at a public hearing on legal brothels

APPENDIX A

Nevada Brothel Guide

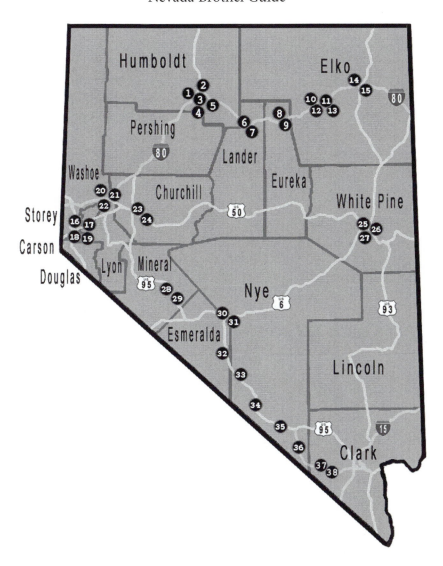

Winnemucca, Humboldt County

1. Wild West Saloon (formerly the Cozy Corner)
2. The Pussycat Ranch (closed for remodel)
3. The Villa Joy Ranch
4. My Place (demolished 2008)
5. Simone's de Paris (demolished 2008)

Battle Mountain, Lander County

6. Donna's Battle Mountain Ranch (formerly the Calico Club)
7. Desert Club (closed)

Carlin, Elko County

8. Dovetail Ranch
9. Sharon's Bar and Brothel

Elko, Elko County

10. Sue's Fantasy Club
11. No. 1 Geisha (formerly Mona Lisa's; before that, Chardon's Club)
12. Mona's Ranch
13. Inez's D&D Bar

Wells, Elko County

14. Bella's Gentleman's Club (formerly Hacienda Club)
15. Donna's Ranch

Lyon County (outside Carson City)

16. The Moonlite Bunny Ranch
17. The Kit Kat Ranch
18. Sagebrush Ranch
19. The Love Ranch (formerly Miss Kitty's)

Sparks, Storey County (outside Reno)

20. Wild Horse Ranch
21. The World Famous Mustang Ranch
22. Old Bridge Ranch

Fallon, Churchill County

23. Salt Wells Villa (closed)
24. Lazy B Ranch (closed)

ELY, WHITE PINE COUNTY

25. Stardust Ranch
26. Big 4 Ranch
27. Green Lantern (closed)

MINERAL COUNTY (HWY 95 BETWEEN TONOPAH & HAWTHORNE)

28. Playmate Ranch (closed)
29. Wild Kat Ranch

TONOPAH, NYE COUNTY

30. Billie's Day and Night (closed)
31. Bobbie's Buckeye Bar (closed)

LIDA JUNCTION, ESMERALDA COUNTY

32. Cottontail Ranch (closed)

SCOTTY'S JUNCTION, NYE COUNTY (HWY 95 BETWEEN BEATTY & TONOPAH)

33. Shady Lady Ranch

BEATTY, NYE COUNTY

34. Angel's Ladies Ranch (closed)

ARMARGOSA VALLEY, NYE COUNTY

35. Cherry Patch II
36. Mabel's Whorehouse

PAHRUMP, NYE COUNTY

37. Chicken Ranch
38. The Resort and Spa at Sheri's Ranch

APPENDIX B

Table A.1 Nevada county brothel laws and income (2007)

Counties	Currently operating brothels	Within one-hour's drive of major metro area	Population per square mile, 2006*	County law prohibits in unincorporated areas	Towns with licensing ordinances	Total yearly income from license fees, room, and liquor taxes	Total yearly income from work cards
Carson City	prohibited by county law	yes	386.6	yes			
Clark	prohibited by state law	yes	224.7	yes			
Douglas	prohibited by county law	yes	64.7	yes			
Washoe	prohibited by county law	yes	62.5	yes			
Lincoln	prohibited by county law	no	0.4	yes			
Pershing	prohibited by county law	no	1.1	yes			
Eureka	no written ordinance	no	0.4				
Churchill	none open	yes	5.1				
Elko	two in Carlin	no	2.7	yes	Carlin	$3,000	$1,200
	four in Elko	no			Elko	$12,960	$7,800
	two in Wells	no			Wells	$10,600[2]	$7,500[1]
Esmeralda	none open	no	0.2			$0	$0
Humboldt	three in Winnemucca (including one closed for renovation)	no	1.8	yes	Winnemucca	$25,500	$2,600[1]
Lander	two in Battle Mountain	no	1.0			$1,200	$1,100[1]
Lyon	four outside Carson City	yes	25.7			$327,500	$26,300
Mineral	two in/near Mina (including one unopened)	no	1.3			$4,560	$1,525[3]

Nye	four near Pahrump	yes	2.4			$114,375	$34,938
	one near Beatty	no					
Storey	two in Sparks	yes	15.7	yes		$160,000	$18,750
White Pine	two in Ely	no	1.0	yes	Ely	$1,490	$1,275

Notes

1 Income from prostitutes' work cards is estimated, as the county issues the same work cards as for other workers.

2 Income from license fees, room, and liquor taxes is estimated and does not reflect additional merchandise fees determined on sales volume.

3 Estimated total based on 35 work cards issued, an unknown number were renewals ($15), and the remaining were new issues ($65). Calculated 15 as renewals.

* Determined using data on 2006 Nevada County Demographics, from *US Census Bureau State & County QuickFacts*, http://quickfacts.census.gov/qfd/states/32000.html. Last revised: July 25, 2008.

APPENDIX C
Sex Workers Interviewed

RURAL BROTHELS

Angel's Ladies, Beatty

Dizyer, in her forties
Mia, in her early thirties
Sadie, in her late twenties
Joyce, 38 years old

Calico Club, Battle Mountain

Jackie, in her early thirties

Green Lantern, Ely

Alysha, in her late twenties
Angela, 27 years old
Celeste, around 45 years old
Misty, 34 years old

Mona's, Elko

Kitten, age unknown
Lisa, age unknown
Lisa L., age unknown
Valerie, age unknown

Sharon's Place, Carlin

Strawberry Shortcake, 41 years old

Stardust, Ely

Crystal, co-owner, former sex worker, 29 years old

Suburban Brothels

Miss Kitty's, outside Carson City

Charli, in her thirties
Dusty, in her forties
Bev Waters, 21 years old
Precious, 20 years old
Ricki, 35 years old
Zoie, in her thirties

Moonlite Bunny Ranch, outside Carson City

Amy, in her twenties
Alice, 19 years old
Annie Ander Sinn, in her twenties
Betty, 50 years old
Brenda, in her twenties
Bretney, 31 years old
Jane, in her twenties
Lani, 19 years old
Princess, 19 years old
Ruby, in her twenties

Mustang Ranch, outside Reno

Maria, age unknown
Sandra, age unknown

Old Bridge, outside Reno

Carol, 22 years old
Ginger, 29 years old

Sheri's Ranch, Pahrump

Dallas, 28 years old
Emili, 40 years old
Shellie, in her twenties

Magdalene Mertrix, in her twenties, worked at several brothels in northern Nevada.

NOTES

Chapter 1

1 Nevada has the only legal system of prostitution. Technically, prostitution that occurs indoors is legal in Rhode Island, but associated activities are illegal; for example, pimping, owning a brothel, loitering in public places for prostitution, and soliciting prostitution services in a vehicle. And Rhode Island does not license, monitor, or otherwise regulate prostitution in the state.

2 In 2008, Las Vegas ranked 12th globally on the number of air passengers and is the 48th most visited city in the world. Caroline Bremner, "Top 150 City Destinations: London Leads the Way" (2007), http://www.euromonitor.com/Top_150_City_ Destinations_London_Leads_the_Way. In 2008, Nevada tourism also brought in $41.6 billion a year. Las Vegas Visitors and Convention Authority, "Vegas Faqs," http://www.lvcva.com/getfile/2008%20Vegas%20FAQs.pdf?fileID=106.

3 Despite the significance of male and transgendered workers in prostitution, in this book we refer to brothel workers as women because there are no male prostitutes in Nevada. Medical testing policies and various local codes, formal and informal, prevent males from selling sex in the brothels. Allowing men and transgendered individuals to work as legal prostitutes in Nevada would require a change in state law which currently requires that all prostitutes undergo regular health screenings for HIV/AIDS and provide a "cervical specimen" to test for gonorrhea, Chlamydia, and other sexually transmitted infections (Nevada Administrative Code 441A.800). The Code's specific references to "her work card" and a "cervical specimen" de jure exclude other genders from legal sex work in Nevada.

4 Mark Gottdiener, Claudia C. Collins, and David R. Dickens, *Las Vegas: The Social Production of an All-American City* (Malden, MA: Blackwell, 1999), Hal Rothman, *Neon Metropolis: How Las Vegas Started the Twenty-first Century* (New York: Routledge, 2002), xix.

5 The Las Vegas Convention and Visitors Authority (LVCVA) marketing campaign used the slogan for years (2005–2008), and unveiled a new slogan in 2008, "Your Vegas is Showing," in a slew of national television and print advertisements. The LVCVA's website in 2009 featured an interactive component where you could create your own identity for your trip, complete with a personalized business card and certificate of achievement. Las Vegas Convention and Visitors Authority, "Be Any-one in Las Vegas," http://www.visitlasvegas.com/vegas/features/be-anyone/. For

visitor statistics, see Las Vegas Convention and Visitors Authority, "2008 Las Vegas Year to Date Executive Summary," Las Vegas Convention and Visitors Authority, http://www.lvcva.com/getfile/ES-YTD2008%20Revised.pdf?fileID=571.

6 See Viviana A. Rotman Zelizer, *The Purchase of Intimacy* (Princeton, NJ: Princeton University Press, 2005).

7 Lynn Comella, "It's Sexy. It's Big Business. And It's Not Just for Men," *Contexts* 7, no. 3 (2008).

8 According to a U.S. Census Press Release in January 2008, Nevada's population of 2.5 million grew 28.4 percent between 2000 and 2007, making it the nation's fastest-growing state. The U.S. population grew by 7.2 percent during that same period. Public Information Office U.S. Census Bureau, "U.S. Census Bureau News Press Release: Nevada in Focus: Census Bureau Pre-Caucus Snapshot, Jan. 16," ed. Department of Commerce (Washington, D.C.: U.S. Census Bureau, 2008). In 2005, statewide, 23 percent of all jobs were in accommodations, food service, entertainment, and recreation. Elizabeth Fadali, Thomas R. Harris, and Kynda R. Curtis, "Factors Affecting Agritourism Potential in Rural Nevada." In *Fact Sheet* (Reno: University of Nevada Cooperative Extension, 2007). The economic downturn that began in 2008 slowed Nevada's tourism and growth. However, there are few indications that the larger trend toward dramatic population growth in the western United States will change. Economic boom and bust has been typical of Nevada's economy since statehood.

9 The Brookings Institution targeted the southern part of the Intermountain West because of its dramatic population growth and rapidly changing economy. The area's growth far outpaces the rest of the country and the trend is expected to continue through 2030. The Intermountain West's far-flung urban cores are converging into five super-regions combining development, economic, and social trends to make it the most dynamic part of the country. Robert E. Lang, Andrea Sarzynski, and Mark Muro, "Mountain Megas: America's Newest Metropolitan Places and a Federal Partnership to Help Them Prosper." In *Metropolitan Policy Program* (Washington, D.C.: The Brookings Institution, 2008), 20–21.

10 Traded industries are industries in regional economies that sell products and services across regions and often to other countries. They locate in a particular region based not on local resources as much as on broader competitive considerations or employment concentrations.

11 According to the Brookings Institute study, the Intermountain West saw employment grow 291 percent between 1970 and 2006, while the U.S. average was 91 percent. Las Vegas led the way at 671 percent. Population growth between 2000 and 2006 was 17.9 percent in the Intermountain West, 6.4 percent in the U.S., and Las Vegas grew by 28.1 percent. Lang, Sarzynski, and Muro, "Mountain Megas: America's Newest Metropolitan Places and a Federal Partnership to Help Them Prosper."

12 Ibid., 14–15.

13 Thomas Frank has written about the inconsistency of the trend in the middle-income, central states in the United States to vote Republican when their pro-business policies often favor the wealthiest. Frank argues that "red state" politics seem based on the perception of the authenticity of conservative values as against the liberal "blue state" urbane, intellectual elite. In Nevada's libertarian

communities, we see this same critique of inauthenticity launched against some politicians who seek to impose their social values on others. Thomas Frank, *What's the Matter with Kansas?* (New York: Henry Holt & Company, 2004).

14 U.S. Census Bureau, "State and County Quick Facts," http://quickfacts.census.gov/qfd/states/32000.html, Lang, Sarzynski, and Muro, "Mountain Megas: America's Newest Metropolitan Places and a Federal Partnership to Help Them Prosper," U.S. Census Bureau American FactFinder, "Tm-M2. Persons Per Square Mile: 2008 Nevada by County," U.S. Census Bureau, http://factfinder.census.gov/.

15 In 2001, 60 million acres in Nevada were federally managed. The U.S. Department of Energy owns 1.1 percent (3 million acres), the Department of Defense owns 4.7 percent, and the Department of the Interior owns 71 percent of the state's land. It is the country's highest percentage of state land managed by the federal government. Alaska is next. About 50 percent of the U.S. West is federally managed. Nevada Natural Resources Plan Technical Working Group, "Nevada Natural Resources Status Report: Land and Management Status," Nevada Department of Conservation and Natural Resources, http://dcnr.nv.gov/nrp01/land01.htm.

16 Pahrump's population was 7,463 in 1990, 24,631 in 2000, and 39,351 in 2008. It has grown 59 percent since 2000. U.S. Census Bureau, "State and County Quick Facts." Center for Regional Studies, "Geodemographic Analysis—Pahrump Area Census Tracts." In *2008 Business Activity Report, Pahrump, Nye County, Nevada* (Reno, NV: University of Nevada, Reno, 2009).

17 Brothels change names and go in and out of business fairly frequently. Throughout the book we will use the name of the brothel at the time we visited it.

18 For an in-depth discussion of brothel laws, see Barbara G. Brents and Kathryn Hausbeck, "State Sanctioned Sex: Negotiating Informal and Formal Regulatory Practices in Nevada Brothels," *Sociological Perspectives* 44, no. 3 (2001).

19 Nevada Revised Statute 201.354, NRS 201.380, and NRS 201.390.

20 Nevada Administrative Code Chapter 441A010 to A325 and 441A775 to A815.

21 Exact wording for Lander County Code 5.16.080, Churchill County Code 5.20.100 E 7, City of Carlin Code 5-9-8 (E) 6, Ely City Code Sec 10A-7 (e) 6), Wells, 3-6-9, close wording for Storey, Storey County Code 5.16.090. "Associates Considered by the Board to be Inappropriate" is from the Carlin City Code 5-9-8-E 8.

22 Richard Synmanski conducted an extensive examination of the legal brothel system in 1970. He found that while there was a lot of local support for brothels in the rural areas, legal and many quasi-legal rules restricted women's civil rights, particularly those rules that required women workers to live at the brothel. Zoning regulations and other informal rules treated brothels unlike other businesses. Richard Synmanski, "Prostitution in Nevada," *Annuals of the Association of American Geographers* 65, no. 3 (1974). Ellen Pillard found that local governments regulated brothels as a privilege license, which meant they were subject to all sorts of discriminative practices. Ellen Pillard, "Legal Prostitution: Is It Just?," *Nevada Public Affairs Review* 2 (1983), Pillard, "Rethinking Prostitution: A Case for Uniform Regulations," *Nevada Public Affairs Review* 1 (1991). Helen Reynolds included a chapter on Nevada's legal brothels in a book on the economics of prostitution. She was less critical, arguing that Nevada's unusual laws resulted from a "live-and-let-live" attitude combined with capitalist political power and push for profit. Helen Reynolds, *The Economics of Prostitution* (Springfield, Ill.: C. C. Thomas, 1986). Alexa Albert

(2001) lived at one of the brothels, the Mustang Ranch, to conduct a public health study on the effectiveness of the mandatory condom law and ended up publishing a book on life in the brothel. Alexa Albert, *Brothel: Mustang Ranch and Its Women*, 1st ed. (New York: Random House, 2001). Lenore Kuo visited several Nevada brothels as part of a larger study on prostitution laws. She concluded, like others, that as Nevada's brothels were currently organized, they disempowered workers and further stigmatized prostitution. However, she echoed Pillard's view that Nevada laws could be modernized, and felt that with reforms, legalized prostitution could work. Lenore Kuo, *Prostitution Policy: Revolutionizing Practice through a Gendered Perspective* (New York: New York University Press, 2002).

23 See, for example, Barbara Meil Hobson, *Uneasy Virtue: The Politics of Prostitution and the American Reform Tradition* (Chicago: University of Chicago Press, 1990), Wendy Chapkis, *Live Sex Acts: Women Performing Erotic Labor* (New York: Routledge, 1997). In 2007, Melissa Farley distributed findings of a study on trafficking and Nevada brothels, funded by the U.S. Department of Justice. However, her interviews with the workers found no direct evidence of trafficking and indeed she found that most of the workers were not dissatisfied with their experience. Despite this she concluded that the brothels were oppressive. Most of her conclusions were drawn from selective reading of the studies of Kuo, Albert, and Brents and Hausbeck.

24 Ronald Weitzer, "New Directions in Research on Prostitution," *Crime, Law and Social Change* 43, no. 4 (2005), Weitzer, "Flawed Theory and Method in Studies of Prostitution," *Violence Against Women* 11, no. 7 (2005).

25 Kathleen Barry, *Female Sexual Slavery* (New York: New York University Press, 1984), Andrea Dworkin, *Pornography: Men Possessing Women* (New York: E.P. Dutton, 1989), Catharine A. MacKinnon, *Feminism Unmodified: Discourses on Life and Law* (Cambridge, MA: Harvard University Press, 1987), Carole Pateman, *The Sexual Contract* (Stanford, CA: Stanford University Press, 1988).

26 Frederique Delacoste and Priscilla Alexander, *Sex Work: Writings by Women in the Sex Industry*, 2nd ed. (San Francisco, CA: Cleis Press, 1998), Jill Nagle, *Whores and Other Feminists* (New York: Routledge, 1997).

27 Chapkis, *Live Sex Acts: Women Performing Erotic Labor*, Teela Sanders, " 'It's Just Acting': Sex Workers' Strategies for Capitalizing on Sexuality," *Gender, Work and Organization* 12, no. 4 (2005), Sanders, *Sex Work: A Risky Business* (Cullompton: Willan Publishing, 2005), Sanders, "Controllable Laughter: Managing Sex Work through Humor," *Sociology* 38, no. 2 (2004), Joanna Brewis and Stephen Linstead, " 'The Worst Thing Is the Screwing' (1): Consumption and the Management of Identity in Sex Work," *Gender, Work and Organization* 7, no. 2 (2000), Brewis and Linstead, *Sex, Work and Sex Work: Eroticizing Organization* (New York: Routledge, 2000), Ine Vanwesenbeeck, "Burnout among Female Indoor Sex Workers," *Archives of Sexual Behavior* 34, no. 6 (2005), Jacqueline Lewis, Eleanor Maticka-Tyndale, and Frances M. Shaver, "Managing Risk and Safety on the Job: The Experiences of Canadian Sex Workers," *Contemporary Research On Sex Work* (2005).

28 Laura M. Agustín, "A Migrant World of Services," *Social Politics* 10, no. 3 (2003), Laura M. Agustín, *Sex at the Margins: Migration, Labour Markets and the Rescue Industry* (New York: Zed Books, 2007), Laura María Agustín, "Migrants in the Mistress's House: Other Voices in The "Trafficking" Debate," *Social Politics* 12, no. 1

(2005), Kamala Kempadoo, *Sexing the Caribbean: Gender, Race, and Sexual Labor* (New York: Routledge, 2004), Kamala Kempadoo and Jo Doezema, *Global Sex Workers: Rights, Resistance, and Redefinition* (New York: Routledge, 1998), Joyce Outshoorn, *The Politics of Prostitution: Women's Movements, Democratic States, and the Globalisation of Sex Commerce* (New York: Cambridge University Press, 2004).

Work specifically on the issue of the regulation of trafficking includes Julia O'Connell Davidson, "Will the Real Sex Slave Please Stand Up?," *Feminist Review* 83, no. 1 (2006), Gail Kligman and Stephanie Limoncelli, "Trafficking Women after Socialism: To, through, and from Eastern Europe," *Social Politics* 12, no. 1 (2005), Kamala Kempadoo, Jyoti Sanghera, and Bandana Pattanaik, *Trafficking and Prostitution Reconsidered: New Perspectives on Migration, Sex Work, and Human Rights,* 1st ed. (Boulder, Colo.: Paradigm Publishers, 2005), Wendy Chapkis, "Trafficking, Migration, and the Law: Protecting Innocents, Punishing Immigrants," *Gender and Society* 17, no. 6 (2003), Jo Doezema, "Loose Women or Lost Women? The Re-emergence of the Myth of White Slavery in Contemporary Discourses of Trafficking in Women," *Gender Issues* 18, no. 1 (2000), Vanessa E. Munro, "Stopping Traffic? A Comparative Study of Responses to the Trafficking in Women for Prostitution," *British Journal of Criminology* 46, no. 2 (2006), Munro, "Exploring Exploitation: Trafficking in Sex, Work and Sex Work." In *Demanding Sex: Critical Reflections on the Regulation of Prostitution,* ed. Vanessa Munro and Marina Della Giusta (London: Ashgate Publishing, 2008), Joyce Outshoorn, "The Political Debates on Prostitution and Trafficking of Women," *Social Politics* 12, no. 1 (2005), Ronald Weitzer, "The Social Construction of Sex Trafficking: Ideology and Institutionalization of a Moral Crusade," *Politics and Society* 35, no. 3 (2007).

29 Teela Sanders, *Paying for Pleasure: Men Who Buy Sex* (Cullompton: Willan Publishers, 2008), Kerwin Kay, Jill Nagle, and Baruch Gould, *Male Lust: Pleasure, Power, and Transformation* (New York: Harrington Park Press, 2000), Peter Aggleton, ed., *Men Who Sell Sex: International Perspectives on Male Prostitution and HIV/AIDS* (Philadelphia: Temple University Press, 1999), Martin A. Monto, "Female Prostitution, Customers, and Violence," *Violence Against Women* 10, no. 2 (2004), John Scott et al., "Understanding the New Context of the Male Sex Work Industry," *Journal of Interpersonal Violence* 20, no. 3 (2005), Vincent Minichiello, P.G. Harvey, and R. Marino, "Sexual Intentions of Male Sex Workers: An International Study of Escorts Who Advertise on the Web." In *Sex as Crime?,* ed. Gayle Letherby et al. (Cullompton: Willan, 2008).

30 Patty Kelly, *Lydia's Open Door: Inside Mexico's Most Modern Brothel* (Berkeley: University of California Press, 2008), Prabha Kotiswaran, "Born Unto Brothels: Towards a Legal Ethnography of Sonagachi's Sex Industry," *Law & Social Inquiry* 33, no. 3 (2008), Ronald Weitzer, "Legalizing Prostitution: Morality Politics in Western Australia," *British Journal of Criminology* (2008).

31 Phil Hubbard and Mary Whowell, "Revisiting the Red Light District: Still Neglected, Immoral and Marginal?," *Geoforum* 39, no. 5 (2008), Phil Hubbard, Roger Matthews, and Jane Scoular, "Legal Geographies—Controlling Sexually Oriented Businesses: Law, Licensing, and the Geographies of a Controversial Land Use," *Urban Geography* 30, no. 2 (2009), Hubbard, "Regulating Sex Work in the European Union: Prostitute Women and the New Spaces of Exclusion," Scott et al., "Sex Outside the City: Sex Work in Rural and Regional New South Wales," Elizabeth

Bernstein, *Temporarily Yours: Intimacy, Authenticity and the Commerce of Sex* (Chicago: University of Chicago Press, 2007), Samuel Cameron, "Space, Risk and Opportunity: The Evolution of Paid Sex Markets," *Urban Studies* 41, no. 9 (2004).

32 Ryan Bishop and Lillian S. Robinson, *Night Market: Sexual Cultures and the Thai Economic Miracle* (New York: Routledge, 1998), Kamala Kempadoo, *Sun, Sex, and Gold: Tourism and Sex Work in the Caribbean* (Lanham, MD: Rowman & Littlefield Publishers, 1999), Martin Oppermann, "Sex Tourism," *Annals of Tourism Research* 26, no. 2 (1999), Chris Ryan, "Sex Tourism: Paradigms of Confusion." In *Tourism and Sex: Culture, Commerce and Coercion*, ed. Stephen Clift and Simon Carter (London: Cassell, 2000), Chris Ryan and C. Michael Hall, *Sex Tourism: Marginal People and Liminalities* (New York: Routledge, 2001), Julia O'Connell Davidson, *Prostitution, Power, and Freedom* (Ann Arbor: University of Michigan Press, 1998), Jacqueline Sanchez Taylor, "Tourism and 'Embodied' Commodities: Sex Tourism in the Caribbean." In *Tourism and Sex: Culture, Commerce and Coercion*, ed. Stephen Clift and Simon Carter (Cassell, 2000), Amalia L. Cabezas, "Between Love and Money: Sex, Tourism, and Citizenship in Cuba and the Dominican Republic," *Signs* 29, no. 4 (2004).

33 Throughout the book we refer to all the sex workers using pseudonyms. We refer to managers, owners, and others we interviewed using the names they indicated on informed consents (either their real names or a pseudonym). We are aware that as a result we often refer to workers by their first names only, and to managers and owners by their first and last names.

34 Laura María Agustín, "The Cultural Study of Commercial Sex," *Sexualities* 8, no. 5 (2005).

Chapter 2

1 For an additional discussion of how the consumer economy has altered the social relations around selling sex, see Barbara G. Brents and Kathryn Hausbeck, "Marketing Sex: U.S. Legal Brothels and Late Capitalist Consumption," *Sexualities* 10, no. 4 (2007).

2 Many scholars have documented a diversity of experiences within sex work, and question the wisdom of putting all categories of commodified sex together. Sex work is not experienced similarly across cultural contexts or various venues. Stephanie Wahab, "Guest Editor's Introduction," *Journal of Interpersonal Violence* 20, no. 3 (2005). Even the stigma against prostitution varies across time, culture, and locale. Helga K. Hallgrimsdottir et al., "Sporting Girls, Streetwalkers, and Inmates of Houses of Ill Repute: Media Narratives and the Historical Mutability of Prostitution Stigmas," *Sociological Perspectives* 51, no. 1 (2008). Studies of job satisfaction, self-esteem, physical and psychological health, and occupational practices show differences between street prostitutes, escorts, and brothel workers. For example, see John E. Exner Jr. et al., "Some Psychological Characteristics of Prostitutes," *Journal of Personality Assessment* 41, no. 5 (1977), Janet Lever and Deanne Dolnick, "Clients and Call Girls: Seeking Sex and Intimacy." In *Sex for Sale: Prostitution, Pornography and the Sex Industry*, ed. Ronald Weitzer (New York: Routledge, 2009), Roberta Perkins and Frances Lovejoy, *Call Girls: Private Sex Workers in Australia* (University of Western Australia Press, 2007), Perkins and Lovejoy,

"Healthy and Unhealthy Life Styles of Female Brothel Workers and Call Girls (Private Sex Workers) in Sydney," *Australia and New Zealand Journal of Public Health* 20, no. 5 (1996), Deborah R. Brock, *Making Work, Making Trouble: Prostitution as a Social Problem* (Toronto; Buffalo: University of Toronto Press, 1998), J. E. Lewis et al., "Managing Risk and Safety on the Job: The Experiences of Canadian Sex Workers," *Journal of Psychology and Human Sexuality* 17, nos. 1/2 (2005), Rachel Phillips and Cecilia Benoit, "Social Determinants of Health Care Access among Sex Industry Workers in Canada" (2005), Martin A. Monto, "Female Prostitution, Customers, and Violence," *Violence Against Women* 10, no. 2 (2004), Charlotte Seib, Jane Fischer, and Jakob M. Najman, "The Health of Female Sex Workers from Three Industry Sectors in Queensland, Australia," *Social Science & Medicine* 68, no. 3 (2009). See also reviews of the prostitution literature by Ronald Weitzer, "Flawed Theory and Method in Studies of Prostitution," *Violence Against Women* 11, no. 7 (2005), Weitzer, "New Directions in Research on Prostitution," *Crime, Law and Social Change* 43, no. 4 (2005), Cecilia Benoit and Frances M. Shaver, "Critical Issues and New Directions in Sex Work Research," *Canadian Review of Sociology and Anthropology* 43, no. 3 (2006), Lynn Sharon Chancer, "Prostitution, Feminist Theory, and Ambivalence: Notes from the Sociological Underground," *Social Text* 37, Winter (1993), Ine Vanwesenbeeck, "Another Decade of Social Scientific Work on Sex Work: A Review of Research 1990–2000," *Annual Review of Sex Research* 12 (2001).

3 Changes in the process of production, the nature of commodities, advertising, and consumption have been analyzed by writers such as Ernest Mandel, *Late Capitalism*, Revised ed. (London: Humanities Press, 1975), Fredric Jameson, *Postmodernism, or, the Cultural Logic of Late Capitalism*, Post-Contemporary Interventions (Durham: Duke University Press, 1991), Daniel Bell, *The Cultural Contradictions of Capitalism* (New York: Basic Books, 1976), Alvin Toffler, *Powershift: Knowledge, Wealth, and Violence at the Edge of the 21st Century* (New York: Bantam Books, 1990), Manuel Castells, *The Rise of the Network Society, Information Age*, 2nd ed., (Oxford: Blackwell, 2000).

4 According to the World Travel and Tourism Council (WTTC), in 2009 travel and tourism generated 7.6 percent of total employment globally. In spite of a global recession, real growth in GDP for travel and tourism is expected to average 4 percent per year over the next ten years. World Travel and Tourism Council, "Travel & Tourism Economic Impact: Executive Summary," (London: World Travel & Tourism Council, 2009). See also Nancy Wonders and Raymond Michalowski, "Bodies, Borders, and Sex Tourism in a Globalized World: A Tale of Two Cities—Amsterdam and Havana," *Social Problems* 48, no. 4 (2001): 549.

5 Personal, business, educational, and health services are a large part of current markets, but according to David Harvey and others, the market in spectacle and distractions has become increasingly larger. David Harvey, *The Condition of Postmodernity: An Enquiry into the Origins of Cultural Change* (Cambridge, MA: Blackwell, 1989), 285.

6 See John Urry, *The Tourist Gaze*, 2nd ed. (London; Thousand Oaks, CA: Sage, 2002), Scott Lash and John Urry, *Economies of Signs and Space* (London; Thousand Oaks, CA: Sage, 1994), Chris Rojek, *Ways of Escape: Modern Transformations in Leisure and Travel*, Postmodern Social Futures (Lanham, MD: Rowman &

Littlefield, 1994), Chris Rojek and John Urry, *Touring Cultures: Transformations of Travel and Theory* (New York: Routledge, 1997), George Ritzer and Allen Liska, " 'McDisneyization' and 'Post Tourism': Complementary Perspectives on Contemporary Tourism." In *Touring Cultures: Transformations of Travel and Theory*, ed. Chris Rojek and John Urry (New York: Routledge, 1997). For other examples of what constitutes touristic experiences, see Ulrich Beck, *Risk Society: Towards a New Modernity* (London; Newbury Park, CA: Sage, 1992), Lori Holyfield, "Manufacturing Adventure: The Buying and Selling of Emotions," *Journal of Contemporary Ethnography* 28, no. 1 (1999), Eric Sharpe, " 'Going Above and Beyond:' The Emotional Labor of Adventure Guides," *Journal of Leisure Research* 37, no. 1 (2005).

7 These touristic services play into masculinity and femininity. For discussions of masculine experiences in sports, see Garry Crawford, *Consuming Sport: Fans, Sport and Culture* (New York: Routledge, 2004). For discussion of heterosexual sexualized spaces for male consumers, see Anne Allison, *Nightwork: Sexuality, Pleasure, and Corporate Masculinity in a Tokyo Hostess Club* (Chicago, IL: University of Chicago Press, 1994), Katherine Frank, *G-strings and Sympathy: Strip Club Regulars and Male Desire* (Durham, NC: Duke University Press, 2002).

8 By a variety of measures, global income inequality is on the rise. In the United States, the hourly wage of average workers, when adjusted for inflation, is lower than it was in 1970. At the same time, between 1970 and 2006 the average CEO salary has gone from 30 times greater to 300 times for the typical worker. Nobel Prize-winning economist Paul Krugman argues that income inequality in the United States is higher now than at any point since the late nineteenth century. Paul R. Krugman, *The Conscience of a Liberal*, 1st ed. (New York: W. W. Norton & Co., 2007). See also Martina Morris and Bruce Western, "Inequality in Earnings at the Close of the Twentieth Century," *Annual Review of Sociology* 25, no. 1 (1999).

9 Luxury consumption is a trend not only among the increasingly wealthy upper class, but reflects what many call a democratization of luxury for the middle classes. James B. Twitchell, *Living It Up: Our Love Affair with Luxury* (New York: Columbia University Press, 2002), Michael Silverstein, Neil Fiske, and John Butman, *Trading Up: Why Consumers Want New Luxury Goods—and How Companies Create Them*, Revised ed. (New York: Portfolio, 2005), Rachel Sherman, *Class Acts: Service and Inequality in Luxury Hotels* (Berkeley: University of California Press, 2007).

10 Barbara Ehrenreich and Arlie Russell Hochschild, *Global Woman: Nannies, Maids, and Sex Workers in the New Economy*, 1st ed. (New York: Metropolitan Books, 2003).

11 Edith Kuiper and Drucilla K. Barker, *Feminist Economics and the World Bank: History, Theory and Policy* (London; New York: Routledge, 2006), David Harvey, *Spaces of Hope* (Berkeley: University of California Press, 2000).

12 John Urry, *Mobilities* (Cambridge, UK, and Malden, MA: Polity Press, 2007), Stephen Crook, Jan Pakulski, and Malcolm Waters, *Postmodernization: Change in Advanced Society* (London; Newbury Park, CA: Sage, 1992).

13 Beck, *Risk Society: Towards a New Modernity*, Zygmunt Bauman, *Liquid Modernity* (Cambridge, UK: Polity Press, 2000), 31–32, Lash and Urry, *Economies of Signs and Space*.

14 See Michael Burawoy, *Manufacturing Consent* (Chicago: University of Chicago Press, 1982), Richard C. Edwards, *Contested Terrain: The Transformation of the*

Workplace in the Twentieth Century (New York: Basic Books, 1979), Holly J. McCammon and Larry J. Griffin, "Workers and Their Customers and Clients," *Work and Occupations* 27, no. 3 (2000).

15 Jennifer Pierce, *Gender Trials: Emotional Lives in Contemporary Law Firms* (Los Angeles: University of California Press, 1996), Joan Acker, "Hierarchies, Jobs, Bodies: A Theory of Gendered Organizations," *Gender and Society* (1990).

16 Karla Erickson and Jennifer L. Pierce, "Farewell to the Organization Man: The Feminization of Loyalty in High-end and Low-end Service Jobs," *Ethnography* 6, no. 3 (2005), Cameron L. Macdonald and Carmen Sirianni, *Working in the Service Economy* (Philadelphia, PA: Temple Univervity Press, 1996), Robin Leidner, *Fast Food, Fast Talk: Service Work and the Routinization of Everyday Life* (Berkeley: University of California Press, 1993).

17 Ritzer and Liska have argued that an assembly-line model has been used in modern tourism to provide rationalized, safe, efficient, standardized, calculable, and predictable experiences in inauthentic environments. Ritzer and Liska, " 'McDisney-ization' and 'Post Tourism': Complementary Perspectives on Contemporary Tourism." These McTourist sites, such as Disneyland, use set prices, regulated tourist routes, and other techniques to render tourist behavior predictable and controllable. This removes the novelty, but also, they argue, the excitement. See also Harry Braverman, *Labor and Monopoly Capital* (New York: Monthly Review Press, 1974), Leidner, *Fast Food, Fast Talk: Service Work and the Routinization of Everyday Life*, George Ritzer, *The McDonaldization of Society* (Thousand Oaks, CA: Pine Forge Press, 1996).

18 Molly George, "Interactions in Expert Service Work: Demonstrating Professionalism in Personal Training," *Journal of Contemporary Ethnography* 37, no. 1 (2008), McCammon and Griffin, "Workers and Their Customers and Clients," David E. Bowen and Edward E. Lawler III, "Empowering Service Employees," *Sloan Management Review* 36, no. 4 (1995).

19 Marianne A. Ferber and Julie A. Nelson, *Feminist Economics Today: Beyond Economic Man* (Chicago: University of Chicago Press, 2003), Chris Tilly, *Half a Job: Bad and Good Part-time Jobs in a Changing Labor Market* (Philadelphia: Temple University Press, 1996), Patricia A. Adler and Peter Adler, *Paradise Laborers: Hotel Work in the Global Economy* (ILR Press, 2004), Arne L. Kalleberg, "Nonstandard Employment Relations: Part-time, Temporary and Contract Work," *Annual Review of Sociology* 26, no. 1 (2000).

20 For discussions of interactive service work and its effects on emotions, see Arlie Russell Hochschild, *The Managed Heart: Commercialization of Human Feeling* (Berkeley: University of California Press, 1983), Greta Foff Paules, *Dishing It Out: Power and Resistance among Waitresses in a New Jersey Restaurant* (Philadelphia: Temple University Press, 1991), Leidner, *Fast Food, Fast Talk: Service Work and the Routinization of Everyday Life*, Amy S. Wharton, "The Affective Consequences of Service Work: Managing Emotions on the Job," *Work and Occupations* 20, no. 2 (1993), Rebecca J. Erickson and Amy S. Wharton, "Inauthenticity and Depression: Assessing the Consequences of Interactive Service Work," *Work and Occupations* 24, no. 2 (1997), Amy S. Wharton, "The Sociology of Emotional Labor," *Annual Review of Sociology* 35, no. 1 (2009).

21 Kristina Abiala, "Customer Orientation and Sales Situations: Variations in Inter-

active Service Work," *Acta Sociologica* 42, no. 3 (1999), Wharton, "The Affective Consequences of Service Work: Managing Emotions on the Job," Heather Ferguson Bulan, Rebecca J. Erickson, and Amy S. Wharton, "Doing for Others on the Job: The Affective Requirements of Service Work, Gender, and Emotional Well-being," *Social Problems* 44, no. 2 (1997), Wharton, "The Sociology of Emotional Labor," Celeste M. Brotheridge and Alicia A. Grandey, "Emotional Labor and Burnout: Comparing Two Perspectives of 'People Work'," *Journal of Vocational Behavior* 60, no. 1 (2002), Dieter Zapf and Melanie Holz, "On the Positive and Negative Effects of Emotion Work in Organizations," *European Journal of Work and Organizational Psychology* 15, no. 1 (2006).

22 Kenneth J. Gergen, *The Saturated Self: Dilemmas of Identity in Contemporary Life* (New York: Basic Books, 1991). See also J. A. Holstein and Jaber F. Gubrium, "The Self We Live By: Narrative Identity in a Postmodern World," *Symbolic Interaction* 23, no. 4 (2000).

23 Sharpe, " 'Going Above and Beyond:' The Emotional Labor of Adventure Guides," Holyfield, "Manufacturing Adventure: The Buying and Selling of Emotions."

24 Leidner, *Fast Food, Fast Talk: Service Work and the Routinization of Everyday Life*, 2.

25 Ibid., 184.

26 Joanne Entwistle and Elizabeth Wissinger, "Keeping up Appearances: Aesthetic Labour in the Fashion Modelling Industries of London and New York," *Sociological Review* 54, no. 4 (2006), Chris Warhurst and Dennis Nickson, "Employee Experience of Aesthetic Labour in Retail and Hospitality," *Work, Employment & Society* 21, no. 1 (2007), Chris Warhurst et al., "Aesthetic Labour in Interactive Service Work: Some Case Study Evidence from the 'New' Glasgow," *The Service Industries Journal* 20, no. 3 (2000), Anne Witz, Chris Warhurst, and Dennis Nickson, "The Labour of Aesthetics and the Aesthetics of Organization," *Organization* 10, no. 1 (2003).

27 Entwistle and Wissinger, "Keeping up Appearances: Aesthetic Labour in the Fashion Modelling Industries of London and New York."

28 Linda McDowell, "Bodywork: Heterosexual Gender Performances in City Workspaces." In *Mapping Desire*, edited by David Bell and Gill Valentine, 75–95, New York: Routledge, 1995, 78.

29 Witz, Warhurst, and Nickson, "The Labour of Aesthetics and the Aesthetics of Organization," Warhurst et al., "Aesthetic Labour in Interactive Service Work: Some Case Study Evidence from the 'New' Glasgow."

30 Sarah Oerton, "Bodywork Boundaries: Power, Politics and Professionalism in Therapeutic Massage," *Gender Work and Organization* 11, no. 5 (2004), George, "Interactions in Expert Service Work: Demonstrating Professionalism in Personal Training," Carol Wolkowitz, *Bodies at Work* (Thousand Oaks, CA: Sage, 2006). Wolkowitz, "The Social Relations of Body Work," *Work, Employment & Society* 16, no. 3 (2002).

31 David Harvey argues that the search for new markets, rapid turnover of goods, and advertising's manipulation of taste has created a culture of ephemerality, surface images, and juxtaposition of styles rather than authenticity. Harvey, *The Condition of Postmodernity: An Enquiry into the Origins of Cultural Change*, 286.

32 Lash and Urry, *Economies of Signs and Space*, Anthony Giddens, *Modernity and Self-identity: Self and Society in the Late Modern Age* (Stanford, CA: Stanford University

Press, 1991), Gergen, *The Saturated Self: Dilemmas of Identity in Contemporary Life*.

33 Kondo's study of the shop floor in family-owned factories in Japan finds that female part-time employees see boundaries between self and other to be fluid, changing, contextual, multiple, and layered, in distinct contrast with Western notions of a unitary "I." Her work promotes the idea that in modern work contexts, it is no longer useful to see the self as bounded and filled with "real feelings" that are threatened by the modern workplace. Instead, selves are crafted and created in gendered contexts of power. Dorinne K. Kondo, *Crafting Selves: Power, Gender, and Discourses of Identity in a Japanese Workplace* (Chicago: University of Chicago Press, 1990).

34 Guy Debord, *The Society of the Spectacle* (New York: Zone Books, 1994), Marshall McLuhan and Quentin Fiore, *The Medium is the Message* (NY: Penguin, 2008).

35 Anthony Giddens terms this "pure relationships" and argues that late capitalism has allowed the possibility of relationships for their own sake, freely entered into, freely exited from, with no bonding characteristics other than the relationship itself. Although Giddens talks about intimacy, it is unclear how commodified sexual gratification fits with this. Anthony Giddens, *The Transformation of Intimacy: Sexuality, Love, and Eroticism in Modern Societies* (Stanford, CA: Stanford University Press, 1992).

36 It has encouraged, according to some, more liberal and egalitarian attitudes toward intimacy and sex: Stevi Jackson and Sue Scott, "Sexual Antinomies in Late Modernity," *Sexualities* 7, no. 2 (2004), Linda Singer, *Erotic Welfare: Sexual Theory and Politics in the Age of Epidemic*, Thinking Gender (New York: Routledge, 1992) and, an increasing commercialization or commodification of intimacy: Viviana A. Rotman Zelizer, *The Purchase of Intimacy* (Princeton, NJ: Princeton University Press, 2005), Kathryn Hausbeck and Barbara G. Brents, "McDonaldization of the Sex Industries? The Business of Sex." In *McDonaldization: The Reader*, ed. George Ritzer (Thousand Oaks, CA: Pine Forge Press, 2002), Arlie Russell Hochschild, *The Managed Heart: Commercialization of Human Feeling*, Hochschild, *The Commercialization of Intimate Life: Notes from Home and Work*, Eva Illouz, *Consuming the Romantic Utopia: Love and the Cultural Contradictions of Capitalism* (Berkeley: University of California Press, 1997), and an acceptance of fleeting, temporary relationships: Zygmunt Bauman, *Liquid Love: On the Frailty of Human Bonds* (Malden, MA: Blackwell Publishers, 2003), Giddens, *The Transformation of Intimacy: Sexuality, Love, and Eroticism in Modern Societies*, Castells, *The Rise of the Network Society*. See also discussion in Elizabeth Bernstein, "The Meaning of the Purchase: Desire, Demand and the Commerce of Sex," *Ethnography* 2, no. 3 (2001): 414, note 13.

37 The General Social Survey shows increasing acceptance of premarital sex and homosexual sex between 1972 and 2004. James A. Davis, Tom W. Smith, and Peter V. Marsden, *General Social Surveys, 1972–2004 [Cumulative File]*, vol. ICPSR04295-v2, General Social Survey Series (Chicago, IL, Storrs, CT: National Opinion Research Center [producer], Roper Center for Public Opinion Research, University of Connecticut/Ann Arbor, MI: Inter-university Consortium for Political and Social Research [distributors], 2006–04–05.). The U.S. Supreme Court repealed the sodomy laws in 2003 and since 1999 same-sex unions in some form have been

legalized in a number of European countries, Canada, South Africa, and a few U.S. states. See also Robert Andersen and Tina Fetner, "Cohort Differences in Tolerance of Homosexuality: Attitudinal Change in Canada and the United States, 1981–2000," *Public Opinion Quarterly* 72, no. 2 (2008), Paul R. Brewer, "Values, Political Knowledge, and Public Opinion About Gay Rights: A Framing-based Account," *Public Opinion Quarterly* 67, no. 2 (2003), Jeni Loftus, "America's Liberalization in Attitudes toward Homosexuality, 1973 to 1998," *American Sociological Review* 66, no. 5 (2001).

38 Steven Seidman, *Beyond the Closet: The Transformation of Gay and Lesbian Life* (New York: Routledge, 2003), Sasha Roseneil, "Queer Frameworks and Queer Tendencies: Toward an Understanding of Postmodern Transformations of Sexuality," *Sociological Research Online* 5, no. 3 (2000), Judith Stacey, *In the Name of the Family: Rethinking Family Values in the Postmodern Age* (Boston, MA: Beacon Press, 1996), Gail Hawkes, *A Sociology of Sex and Sexuality* (Philadelphia: Open University Press, 1996), Jeffrey Weeks, *The World We Have Won: The Remaking of Erotic and Intimate Life* (Routledge, 2007).

39 Giddens argues that there is a reflexive project of the self whereby "a person's identity is not to be found in behaviour, nor—important though this is—in the reactions of others, but in the capacity to keep a particular narrative going. The individual's biography, if she is to maintain regular interaction with others in the day-to-day world, cannot be wholly fictive. It must continually integrate events which occur in the external world, and sort them into the ongoing 'story' about the self" (Giddens, *Modernity and Self-identity: Self and Society in the Late Modern Age*, 54).

40 Jackson and Scott, "Sexual Antinomies in Late Modernity," 238.

41 Neoliberalism is a political philosophy that emphasizes private property rights, free trade, free markets, and minimal state action. Ehrenreich and Hochschild, *Global Woman: Nannies, Maids, and Sex Workers in the New Economy*, Krugman, *The Conscience of a Liberal*, David Harvey, *A Brief History of Neoliberalism* (New York: Oxford University Press, 2007).

42 David Harvey and others argue that neoliberal political thought fosters an ethic that elevates contractual relations in the market to a guiding human value. Hawkes argues that consumer capitalism itself encourages a value of free choice that has affected sexual attitudes as well as consumption. Hawkes, *A Sociology of Sex and Sexuality*, Harvey, *A Brief History of Neoliberalism*. A good example of this is in interviews with clients of prostitution who express great joy in being freed from what they see as the hypocrisy of gift exchange. Bernstein, "The Meaning of the Purchase: Desire, Demand and the Commerce of Sex," Allison, *Nightwork: Sexuality, Pleasure, and Corporate Masculinity in a Tokyo Hostess Club*, Monica Prasad, "The Morality of Market Exchange: Love, Money, and Contractual Justice," *Sociological Perspectives* 42, no. 2 (1999).

43 While the U.S. government periodically attempts crack-downs on pornography, the trend has been toward more relaxed laws. Since the 1970s in the United States the Supreme Court ruled many anti-sexuality laws unconstitutional, including the 1986 McKinnon-Dworkin anti-porn laws and, most recently, many attempts to regulate the internet. Organizations like the Adult Film and Video Association of America and the Free Speech Coalition remain important players on the national

scene, and in states like California. Sex worker organizations since the early 1970s have challenged selective enforcement and discrimination in criminal law and reframed prostitution as work. Ronald Weitzer, "Prostitutes' Rights in the United States: The Failure of a Movement," *Sociological Quarterly* 32, no. 1 (1991), Valerie Jenness, *Making It Work: The Prostitute's Rights Movement in Perspective*, Social Problems and Social Issues (New York: Aldine de Gruyter, 1993).

44 Barbara G. Brents and Kathryn Hausbeck, "Sex Work Now: What the Blurring Boundaries Around the Sex Industry Means for Sex Work, Research and Activism." In *Sex Work Matters: Exploring Money, Power and Intimacy in the Global Sex Industry*, ed. Melissa Ditmore, Antonia Levy, and Alys Willman (London: Zed Books, forthcoming 2010).

45 *The Economist*, "Giving the Customer What He Wants," *The Economist*, February 14, 1998, Lin Lean Lim, *The Sex Sector: The Economic and Social Bases of Prostitution in Southeast Asia* (Geneva: International Labour Organization, 1998).

46 Eric Schlosser, "The Business of Pornography," *U.S. News & World Report*, February 10, 1997, ABC News, "Porn Profits: Corporate America's Secret: Corporate America is Profiting from Porn—Quietly," *ABC News Primetime*, May 27, 2004, Dan Ackman, "How Big is Porn?," *Forbes*, May 25, 2001, Free Speech Coalition. In *Adult Entertainment in America: A State of the Industry Report*, ed. Michelle L. Freridge (Canoga Park: Free Speech Coalition, 2006), William Spain, "Strip Clubs go Mainstream," *MSN Money MarketWatch* (2007), http://articles.moneycentral.msn.com/Investing/Extra/StripClubsGoMainstream.aspx.

47 Teela Sanders, *Sex Work: A Risky Business* (Cullompton: Willan Publishing, 2005), 11.

48 Stephen Castle, "Passports and Panic Buttons in the Brothel of the Future," *Independent*, September 23, 2006, Barbara G. Brents and Teela Sanders, "Mainstreaming the Sex Industry: Economic Inclusion and Social Ambivalence," *Journal of Law and Society* (forthcoming, 2010).

49 Elizabeth Bernstein, *Temporarily Yours: Intimacy, Authenticity and the Commerce of Sex* (Chicago: University of Chicago Press, 2007), Lynn Comella, "Selling Sexual Liberation: Women-owned Sex Toy Stores and the Business of Social Change" (University of Massachusetts Amherst, 2004).

50 Beth Montemurro, "Strippers and Screamers: The Emergence of Social Control in a Noninstitutionalized Setting," *Journal of Contemporary Ethnography* 30, no. 3 (2001), E. A. Wood, "Working in the Fantasy Factory: The Attention Hypothesis and the Enacting of Masculine Power in Strip Clubs," *Journal of Contemporary Ethnography* 29, no. 1 (2000), Frank, *G-strings and Sympathy: Strip Club Regulars and Male Desire*, Bernadette Barton, *Stripped: Inside the Lives of Exotic Dancers* (New York: New York University Press, 2006).

51 Laura María Agustín, "A Migrant World of Services," *Social Politics* 10, no. 3 (2003), Joanna Brewis and Stephen Linstead, *Sex, Work and Sex Work: Eroticizing Organization* (London; New York: Routledge, 2000), Brewis and Linstead, " 'The Worst Thing Is the Screwing': Context and Career in Sex Work," *Gender, Work and Organization* 7, no. 3 (2000), Wendy Chapkis, *Live Sex Acts: Women Performing Erotic Labor* (New York: Routledge, 1997), Lever and Dolnick, "Clients and Call Girls: Seeking Sex and Intimacy." Teela Sanders, " 'It's Just Acting': Sex Workers' Strategies for Capitalizing on Sexuality," *Gender, Work and Organization* 12, no. 4

(2005), Sanders, *Sex Work: A Risky Business*, Candice Michelle Seppa Arroyo, "Labor Violations and Discrimination in the Clark County Outcall Entertainment Industry" (MA Thesis, University of Nevada, Las Vegas, 2003), Ine Vanwesenbeeck, "Burnout among Female Indoor Sex Workers," *Archives of Sexual Behavior* 34, no. 6 (2005), Teela Sanders, "Controllable Laughter: Managing Sex Work Through Humor," *Sociology* 38, no. 2 (2004).

52 Martin A. Monto, "Why Men Seek out Prostitutes." In *Sex for Sale: Prostitution, Pornography and the Sex Industry*, ed. Ronald Weitzer (New York: Routledge, 2009), Prasad, "The Morality of Market Exchange: Love, Money, and Contractual Justice," Bernstein, "The Meaning of the Purchase: Desire, Demand and the Commerce of Sex." Martin Monto argues that while fellatio is the predominant service sought out by clients of street prostitutes, it is not just that they are not getting fellatio in their other relationships. The nature of the encounter, the fact that it is on the streets, in a car, in a much more monitored situation, requires a quick exchange.

53 Bernstein, *Temporarily Yours: Intimacy, Authenticity and the Commerce of Sex*, 402. Bernstein argues that street prostitution is a relatively small sector of prostitution and is in decline.

54 See Bernstein's (401) discussion of "bounded authenticity" in Bernstein, *Temporarily Yours*.

55 Katherine Frank, "The Production of Identity and the Negotiation of Intimacy in a 'Gentleman's Club'," *Sexualities* 1, no. 2 (1998): 197, Frank, *G-strings and Sympathy: Strip Club Regulars and Male Desire*.

56 Danielle Egan, *Dancing for Dollars and Paying for Love: The Relationships between Exotic Dancers and Their Regulars* (New York: Palgrave Macmillan, 2006).

57 Wahab, "Guest Editor's Introduction."

58 Sociologist Elizabeth Bernstein and other scholars have noted that late capitalism's features have affected the sale of sex: the merging of public and private, the growth of services, the preference for the market over diffuse non-market exchanges, and the simultaneous normalization and problematization of sexual consumption. Bernstein, *Temporarily Yours: Intimacy, Authenticity and the Commerce of Sex*, Allison, *Nightwork: Sexuality, Pleasure, and Corporate Masculinity in a Tokyo Hostess Club*, Prasad, "The Morality of Market Exchange: Love, Money, and Contractual Justice," Kamala Kempadoo and Jo Doezema, *Global Sex Workers: Rights, Resistance, and Redefinition* (New York: Routledge, 1998).

Chapter 3

1 Timothy J. Gilfoyle, "Prostitutes in History: From Parables of Pornography to Metaphors of Modernity," *The American Historical Review* 104, no. 1 (1999): 135.

2 Historian Timothy Gilfoyle reviewed a number of studies situating prostitution in the changing politics and economics of modernizing societies. He argues that these studies collectively show that with modernity, prostitution expanded, services emphasized sexual offerings and less companionship, and evangelical Christianity was highly influential in eliminating tolerated prostitution in societies with expanding states. Ibid.: 130. This research includes studies of France, e.g., Alain Corbin, *Women for Hire: Prostitution and Sexuality in France after 1850* (Cambridge, MA: Harvard University Press, 1990), Shanghai, e.g., Gail Hershatter, *Dangerous*

Pleasures: Prostitution and Modernity in Twentieth-Century Shanghai (Berkeley: University of California Press, 1997), Buenos Aires, e.g., Donna J. Guy, *Sex & Danger in Buenos Aires: Prostitution, Family, and Nation in Argentina*, V. 1 (Lincoln: University of Nebraska Press, 1991), England, e.g., Judith R. Walkowitz, *City of Dreadful Delight: Narratives of Sexual Danger in Late-Victorian London* (Chicago: University of Chicago Press, 1992), Nairobi, e.g., Luise White, *The Comforts of Home: Prostitution in Colonial Nairobi* (Chicago: University of Chicago Press, 1990), and Tsarist Russia, e.g., Laurie Bernstein, *Sonia's Daughters: Prostitutes and Their Regulation in Imperial Russia* (Berkeley: University of California Press, 1995).

3 The relation between the development of Anglo-Saxon bourgeois class identity and the social control of women's sexuality has been documented in a number of studies, including Nicola Beisel and Tamara Kay, "Abortion, Race, and Gender in Nineteenth-Century America," *American Sociological Review* 69, no. 4 (2004), Nicola Kay Beisel, *Imperiled Innocents: Anthony Comstock and Family Reproduction in Victorian America* (Princeton, NJ: Princeton University Press, 1997), Gail Hawkes, *A Sociology of Sex and Sexuality* (Philadelphia: Open University Press, 1996), Judith R. Walkowitz, *Prostitution and Victorian Society: Women, Class, and the State* (Cambridge; New York: Cambridge University Press, 1980). Prior to the 1800s, throughout Europe, efforts to regulate sex so that ideally it was reproductive, coital, monogamous, and heterosexual was largely accomplished by church or ecclesiastical courts, and, in the American colonies, through local codes, censure and neighborhood surveillance. As laboring classes filled cities in the U.S. and Europe, sexuality came under government surveillance. Kristin Luker, "Sex, Social Hygiene, and the State: The Double-edged Sword of Social Reform," *Theory and Society* 27, no. 5 (1998): 622, Guy Rocha, "Brothel Prostitution in Nevada: A Unique American Cultural Phenomenon" (San Diego State University, 1975), Walkowitz, *Prostitution and Victorian Society: Women, Class, and the State,* Joel Best, *Controlling Vice: Regulating Brothel Prostitution in St. Paul, 1865–1883,* The History of Crime and Criminal Justice Series (Columbus: Ohio State University Press, 1998), Timothy J. Gilfoyle, *City of Eros: New York City, Prostitution, and the Commercialization of Sex, 1790–1920,* 1st ed. (New York: W. W. Norton, 1992), Jo Doezema, "Loose Women or Lost Women? The Re-emergence of the Myth of White Slavery in Contemporary Discourses of Trafficking in Women," *Gender Issues* 18, no. 1 (2000), Priscilla Alexander, "Feminism, Sex Workers and Human Rights." In *Whores and Other Feminists,* ed. Jill Nagle (New York: Routledge, 1997), Barbara Meil Hobson, *Uneasy Virtue: The Politics of Prostitution and the American Reform Tradition* (Chicago: University of Chicago Press, 1990).

4 Luker, "Sex, Social Hygiene, and the State: The Double-edged Sword of Social Reform," Gilfoyle, "Prostitutes in History: From Parables of Pornography to Metaphors of Modernity," 134.

5 The discovery of the Comstock Lode in 1859 along the eastern slopes of the Sierra Nevada mountains near what is now Reno founded Nevada's economic, political, and cultural history. During its twenty-year life span the Comstock mineral vein produced nearly $300 million in gold and silver. This made Nevada the number one contributor to the United States' gold and silver stocks. Nevada's wealth provided capital for California's railroads, telegraph companies, hotels, banks, and other

buildings. The U.S. took 62 percent of its gold and silver from the mines outside of Virginia City in 1875. Russell R. Elliott, *Nevada's Twentieth-Century Mining Boom: Tonopah, Goldfield, Ely* (Reno: University of Nevada Press, 1966; reprinted 1988), 3, Rocha, "Brothel Prostitution in Nevada: A Unique American Cultural Phenomenon."

6 Sally Zanjani, *Goldfield: The Last Gold Rush on the Western Frontier* (Athens: Ohio University Press, 1992), 95, Mona Reno, "Nevada Place Names Population 1860–2000," Nevada Department of Cultural Affairs, http://nevadaculture.org/nsla/index.php?option=com_content&task=view&id=1036&Itemid=1.

7 Sally S. Zanjani, *Devils Will Reign: How Nevada Began* (Reno: University of Nevada Press, 2006), Ronald M. James, *The Roar and the Silence: A History of the Virginia City and the Comstock Lode* (Reno: University of Nevada Press, 1998), Sally S. Zanjani and Guy Louis Rocha, *The Ignoble Conspiracy: Radicalism on Trial in Nevada* (Reno: University of Nevada Press, 1986).

8 See Appendix 1.1, p. 304 in Ronald M. and James C. Elizabeth Raymond, eds, *Comstock Women: The Making of a Mining Community* (Reno: University of Nevada Press, 1998), 304.

9 Jon M. Kingsdale, "The 'Poor Man's Club': Social Functions of the Urban Working-class Saloon," *American Quarterly* 25, no. 4 (1973).

10 Zanjani, *Goldfield: The Last Gold Rush on the Western Frontier*, 159–62.

11 Raymond M. Smith, *Saloons of Old & New Nevada* (Minden, NV: R.M. Smith, 1992), 1–5.

12 James, *The Roar and the Silence: A History of the Virginia City and the Comstock Lode*, 169.

13 Mark Twain, *Roughing It* (New York: Harper and Brothers Publishers, 1871; reprinted 1913), 76.

14 Paula Petrik, *No Step Backward: Women and Men on the Western Mining Frontier, Helena Montana 1865–1900* (Helena: Montana Historical Society Press, 1987), 25–58.

15 The majority of the first women in Virginia City were there with their husbands. In 1860, 5 percent of residents were women, and 83 of these 111 accompanied their spouses. Half of them came with their children. James, ed. *Comstock Women: The Making of a Mining Community.*

16 This figure includes what census enumerators listed as prostitutes (109) and harlots (48) in the 1870 census. See Appendix III.2, p. 318 in ibid., 318. James and Fleiss argue that in 1870 prostitution was the most common profession listed in the census for women, and in 1880 it was the third most common profession. Ronald M. James and Kenneth H. Fliess, "Women of the Mining West: Virginia City Revisited." In *Comstock Women: The Making of a Mining Community*, ed. Ronald M. and James C. Elizabeth Raymond (Reno: University of Nevada Press, 1998), 29–31.

17 Mary McNair Matthews, who wrote her memoirs of living in Virginia City in the 1870s, was a widowed middle-class woman who working as a seamstress, school-teacher, laundress, lodging house operator, nurse, businesswoman, and entre-preneur investing in mining stocks and real estate. James and Fliess, "Women of the Mining West: Virginia City Revisited," Mary McNair Mathews, *Ten Years on the Comstock. Or Life on the Pacific Coast* (Lincoln: University of Nebraska Press, 1880;

reprinted 1985), Petrik, *No Step Backward: Women and Men on the Western Mining Frontier, Helena Montana 1865–1900*, 25–58.

18 James and Fliess, "Women of the Mining West: Virginia City Revisited," 176, Marion Goldman, *Gold Diggers & Silver Minors: Prostitution and Social Life on the Comstock Lode* (Ann Arbor: University of Michigan Press, 1981), Rocha, "Brothel Prostitution in Nevada: A Unique American Cultural Phenomenon," 4, George Williams III, *The Redlight Ladies of Virginia City, Nevada* (Riverside, CA: Tree by the River Publishers, 1984).

19 Donald L. Hardesty, "Gender and Archaelology on the Comstock." James and Raymond, eds, *Comstock Women: The Making of a Mining Community* (1998), Alexy Simmons, "Red Light Ladies: Settlement Patterns and Material Culture of the Mining Frontier," *Anthropological Northwest No. 4* (Corvallis: Department of Anthropology Oregon State University, 1989).

20 Sue Fawn Chung, "Their Changing World: Chinese Women on the Comstock 1860–1910," in *Comstock Women: The Making of a Mining Community*, ed. Ronald M. James and C. Elizabeth Raymond (Reno: University of Nevada Press, 1998), 208.

21 James and Fliess, "Women of the Mining West: Virginia City Revisited," 31.

22 Doug McMillan, "From a Miner's Friend to a Nevada Way of Life," *Reno Gazette-Journal*, November 9, 1986.

23 Zanjani, *Goldfield: The Last Gold Rush on the Western Frontier*, 163.

24 Ibid., 107.

25 David Spanier, *Welcome to Pleasuredome: Inside Las Vegas* (Reno: University of Nevada Press, 1992), 138–89. Scrugham was not a native Nevadan, and did not live on the Comstock at the time. He appears to have based some of what he said on a report from Eliot Lord, who did spend some time in Virginia City, according to an email exchange one of the authors had with Guy Rocha. Lord wrote, "The working miners had few pleasures except the unfailing resources of gambling and drinking. Prostitution flourished, as in all large camps, and courtesans promenaded the streets slowly, decked out in gay dresses and showy jewelry, and drifting about with the restless tide which set to and fro through the city." Elliott Lord, *Comstock Mining and Miners* (Washington, DC: United States Government Printing Office, 1880).

26 Donald R. Abbe, *Austin and the Reese River Mining District: Nevada's Forgotten Frontier* (Reno: University of Nevada Press, 1985), 74.

27 As the story of the frontier prostitute became embellished in later years, male writers drew the line between the prostitutes and the wives even more distinctly. There is the oft-told story of Julia Bulette, a prostitute who was murdered in 1867. The legend may be found in many books of Nevada history, but the story is the same: the men adored her and the respectable women hated her. Local firefighters named an engine after her, "a fact which enraged the virtuous females of the social set," according to Lucius Morris Beebe and Charles Clegg, *Legends of the Comstock Lode* (Oakland, CA: G. H. Hardy, 1950), 15.

28 Zanjani, *Goldfield: The Last Gold Rush on the Western Frontier*, 104–105.

29 Rocha, "Brothel Prostitution in Nevada: A Unique American Cultural Phenomenon," 8, Zanjani, *Goldfield: The Last Gold Rush on the Western Frontier*, 193.

30 Michael Wayne Bowers, *The Sagebrush State: Nevada's History, Government, and Politics* (Reno: University of Nevada Press, 1996), 15–16, James W. Hulse, *The Silver*

State: Nevada's Heritage Reinterpreted (Reno: University of Nevada Press, 1991), 80.

31 Luker, "Sex, Social Hygiene, and the State: The Double-edged Sword of Social Reform."

32 Rocha, "Brothel Prostitution in Nevada: A Unique American Cultural Phenomenon," 9.

33 Abbe, *Austin and the Reese River Mining District: Nevada's Forgotten Frontier*, 78.

34 Sally and Roger Morris Denton, *The Money and the Power: The Making of Las Vegas and Its Hold on America 1947–2000* (New York: Alfred A. Knopf, 2001), 39.

35 Elliott, *Nevada's Twentieth-Century Mining Boom: Tonopah, Goldfield, Ely*, 238–239.

36 Quotes are from the *Ely Record*, February 5 and June 25, 1909, cited in ibid., 233–237.

37 Reno, "Nevada Place Names Population 1860–2000."

38 Cindy Sondik Aron, *Working at Play: A History of Vacations in the United States* (New York: Oxford University Press, 1999).

39 T. Jackson Lears, *No Place of Grace: Antimodernism and the Transformation of American Culture 1880–1920* (New York: Pantheon, 1981).

40 See Taylor's discussion of the making of the images of the Comstock. Andria Daley Taylor, "Girls of the Golden West," in *Comstock Women: The Making of a Mining Community*, ed. Ronald M. James and Elizabeth C. Raymond (Reno: University of Nevada Press, 1998).

41 Bret Harte, founder of the *Overland Monthly*, and briefly a reporter for the *Territorial Enterprise*, Virginia City's newspaper, wrote *The Luck of Roaring Camp and Other Sketches* in 1870, a series of short stories painting the wild and woolly, rugged, and violent lawlessness of the Gold Rush. Bret Harte and Gary Scharnhorst, *The Luck of Roaring Camp and Other Writings*, Penguin Classics (New York: Penguin Books, 2001). Mark Twain's brief experience with gold mining from 1861 to 1864 led to the publication of *Roughing It* in 1872, a collection of stories of his work on the mining frontier. Twain, *Roughing It*. He too was a resident of Virginia City and worked briefly for the *Territorial Enterprise*.

42 Bernard DeVoto, *Across the Wide Missouri* (Boston, MA: Houghton Mifflin Company, 1947), 11. DeVoto won a Pulitzer prize in 1947 for his history of the west, *Across the Wide Missouri*.

43 McMillan, "From a Miner's Friend to a Nevada Way of Life," Barbara Land and Myrick Land, *A Short History of Reno* (Reno: University of Nevada Press, 1995), 42–43. It is worth noting here that there are very few histories written specifically about Nevada's legal brothels. In this chapter we rely heavily on several key sources. Guy Rocha's 1975 master's thesis was for years the definitive work on the history of the legal brothels: Rocha, "Brothel Prostitution in Nevada: A Unique American Cultural Phenomenon." Rocha served as the Nevada State Archivist for 28 years and wrote several short informational pieces about Nevada's brothels. Sarah Washburn's master's thesis is a detailed history of the closing of Block 16 in Las Vegas in the 1930s through to the end of 1950s. Sarah Hall Washburn, "Changing Images: The End of Legalized Prostitution in Las Vegas" (University of Nevada, Las Vegas, 1999). Finally, *Reno Gazette-Journal* reporter Doug McMillan wrote an excellent, detailed, eight-part series for the paper in November, 1986 on the history and contemporary state of the brothels. John Galliher also graciously shared data

gathered for his and John Cross' book on the Nevada brothels. John Galliher and John Cross, *Morals Legislation without Morals: The Case of Nevada* (New Brunswick, NJ: Rutgers University Press, 1983).

44 Land and Land, *A Short History of Reno*, 42.

45 James, ed. *Comstock Women: The Making of a Mining Community*, 263.

46 Many of these literati were financed in the post-World War II years by the silver fortune made by San Francisco publishing magnate William Randolf Hearst's father, George Hearst, in Virginia City. Taylor, "Girls of the Golden West."

47 Land and Land, *A Short History of Reno*, 41.

48 Doug McMillan, "The Reno Stockade," *Reno Gazette-Journal*, November 9, 1986.

49 Reno, "Nevada Place Names Population 1860–2000."

50 Washburn, "Changing Images: The End of Legalized Prostitution in Las Vegas," 7.

51 McMillan, "From a Miner's Friend to a Nevada Way of Life," McMillan, "The Reno Stockade."

52 Eugene P. Moehring, *Resort City in the Sunbelt: Las Vegas, 1930–2000*, 2nd ed., Wilbur S. Shepperson Series in History and Humanities (Reno: University of Nevada Press, 2000), 13–14.

53 Ibid., 17–18.

54 David G. Schwartz, *Suburban Xanadu: The Casino Resort on the Las Vegas Strip and Beyond* (New York: Routledge, 2003), 45, Washburn, "Changing Images: The End of Legalized Prostitution in Las Vegas."

55 Washburn, "Changing Images: The End of Legalized Prostitution in Las Vegas," 13–21.

56 Ibid., 35.

57 Ibid., 29.

58 Guy Rocha, "Myth #105—the Mississippi of the West," Nevada Department of Cultural Affairs, http://nevadaculture.org/nsla/index.php?option=com_content&task=view&id=786&Itemid=95, Washburn, "Changing Images: The End of Legalized Prostitution in Las Vegas," 7. In the 1940 census, Las Vegas was 97 percent white and 2 percent black. By 1950 the census shows that in Las Vegas 11.1 percent of the population was black.

59 Washburn, "Changing Images: The End of Legalized Prostitution in Las Vegas," 44.

60 Luker, "Sex, Social Hygiene, and the State: The Double-edged Sword of Social Reform," 622, Hobson, *Uneasy Virtue: The Politics of Prostitution and the American Reform Tradition*, 180.

61 Rocha, "Brothel Prostitution in Nevada: A Unique American Cultural Phenomenon."

62 If any region refused, the Federal Security Agency could authorize military enforcement of prostitution law in a local area.

63 McMillan, "From a Miner's Friend to a Nevada Way of Life."

64 Ibid.

65 Rocha, "Brothel Prostitution in Nevada: A Unique American Cultural Phenomenon," 14.

66 Richard Synmanski, "Prostitution in Nevada," *Annuals of the Association of American Geographers* 65, no. 3 (1974): 363.

67 Washburn, "Changing Images: The End of Legalized Prostitution in Las Vegas," 50.

68 Rocha, "Brothel Prostitution in Nevada: A Unique American Cultural Phenomenon," 13–14.

69 Reno, "Nevada Place Names Population 1860–2000," Schwartz, *Suburban Xanadu: The Casino Resort on the Las Vegas Strip and Beyond*, 77.

70 Moehring, *Resort City in the Sunbelt: Las Vegas, 1930–2000*, 65.

71 McMillan, "From a Miner's Friend to a Nevada Way of Life."

72 A. D. Hopkins and K. J. Evans, *The First 100: Portraits of the Men and Women Who Shaped Las Vegas*, 1st ed. (Las Vegas: Huntington Press, 1999).

73 Between 1945 and 1946 they were able to hire one of the nation's largest advertising firms, J. Walter Thompson, to market Las Vegas. In 1948 they hired the publicity agency of Steve Hannagan and Associates, which had packaged Miami Beach and Sun Valley, Idaho as resort destinations. Moehring, *Resort City in the Sunbelt: Las Vegas, 1930–2000*, 66–67.

74 David Schwartz, "Suburban Xanadu: The Casino Resort on the Las Vegas Strip 1945–1978" (UCLA, 2000), 108–109, Schwartz, *Suburban Xanadu: The Casino Resort on the Las Vegas Strip and Beyond*, 58.

75 Denton, *The Money and the Power: The Making of Las Vegas and Its Hold on America 1947–2000*, 102.

76 Barbara Ehrenreich outlines the growth of a new male consumer around the image of the playboy. Barbara Ehrenreich, *The Hearts of Men: American Dreams and the Flight from Commitment* (Garden City, NY: Anchor Press/Doubleday, 1983).

77 Moehring, *Resort City in the Sunbelt: Las Vegas, 1930–2000*, 76, Barbara Land and Myrick Land, *A Short History of Las Vegas* (Reno: University of Nevada Press, 1999), 141.

78 Schwartz, "Suburban Xanadu: The Casino Resort on the Las Vegas Strip 1945–1978," 182, Schwartz, *Suburban Xanadu: The Casino Resort on the Las Vegas Strip and Beyond*, 58–59.

79 Rocha, "Brothel Prostitution in Nevada: A Unique American Cultural Phenomenon," 15, Doug McMillan, "Brothels: From Public Nuisances to Licensed Businesses," *Reno Gazette Journal*, November 15, 1986.

80 The group made a three-point demand: "1—The county wants no part of 'legalized' prostitution today, tomorrow, or ever; 2—The citizens want ordinances, both city and county, drawn up which will bar for today, tomorrow and forever, all houses of prostitution in the city and county. 3—A morals squad shall be formed in both the sheriff's office and city police departments, which will operate in harmony to run all known prostitutes out of the city and county." This was reported in the *Las Vegas Evening Review Journal*, January 5, 1946. Washburn, "Changing Images: The End of Legalized Prostitution in Las Vegas."

81 Ibid., 67–69, Moehring, *Resort City in the Sunbelt: Las Vegas, 1930–2000*, 60.

82 Moehring, *Resort City in the Sunbelt: Las Vegas, 1930–2000*, 61.

83 Washburn, "Changing Images: The End of Legalized Prostitution in Las Vegas," 69–70.

84 Moehring, *Resort City in the Sunbelt: Las Vegas, 1930–2000*, 54, Russell Elliott, *History of Nevada* (Lincoln: University of Nebraska Press, 1973), 329, Ronald A. Farrell and Carole Case, *The Black Book and the Mob: The Untold Story of the Control of Nevada's Casinos* (Madison: University of Wisconsin Press, 1995), Schwartz, *Suburban Xanadu: The Casino Resort on the Las Vegas Strip and Beyond*.

85 Schwartz, "Suburban Xanadu: The Casino Resort on the Las Vegas Strip 1945–1978," 310–312.

86 Rocha, "Brothel Prostitution in Nevada: A Unique American Cultural Phenomenon," 15, Washburn, "Changing Images: The End of Legalized Prostitution in Las Vegas," 71, McMillan, "Brothels: From Public Nuisances to Licensed Businesses," Synmanski, "Prostitution in Nevada," Gabriel Vogliotti, *The Girls of Nevada* (Secaucus, NJ: Citadel Press, 1975).

87 McMillan, "Brothels: From Public Nuisances to Licensed Businesses."

88 Rocha, "Brothel Prostitution in Nevada: A Unique American Cultural Phenomenon," 16.

89 McMillan, "Brothels: From Public Nuisances to Licensed Businesses."

90 Ibid.

91 Ibid.

92 From a *Los Angeles Times* article, Suzanne Sonnier, "The Mustang Ranch and the Politics of Nevada Brothel Prostitution," *Nevada Women's History Working Papers* no. 2 (1994): 7.

93 Ken Miller, "Conforte Parlayed Mustang into Fame, Fortune, Trouble," *Reno Gazette-Journal*, November 14, 1986, Mike Sion, "Conforte Changed the Face of Nevada Bordellos," *Reno Gazette-Journal*, January 20, 1995.

94 A newspaper photo documented a smiling Raggio with other officials when Sparks Fire Chief Bill Farr put a match to it. Raggio later explained to a Reno reporter, "You have to understand, Conforte had flaunted the law and it was necessary to do what was done. I was the DA here and I was bound and determined that the laws of the county would be upheld. Look, nobody else would take this guy on. We had police getting cigars with $20 bills wrapped around them. Things were getting out of hand." Ken Miller, "Raggio Has Been Nemesis for More Than 25 Years," *Reno Gazette-Journal*, November 14, 1986.

95 Sonnier, "The Mustang Ranch and the Politics of Nevada Brothel Prostitution."

96 Ibid.: 18. Many of Conforte's escapades were told to us over the years, and to other reporters, by Nevada brothel lobbyist George Flint.

97 Conforte could not hold the license because of his felony conviction. McMillan, "Brothels: From Public Nuisances to Licensed Businesses," Sion, "Conforte Changed the Face of Nevada Bordellos," Vogliotti, *The Girls of Nevada.*

98 Gerald Astor, "Legal Prostitution Spreads in Nevada," *Look*, June 29, 1971.

99 McMillan, "Brothels: From Public Nuisances to Licensed Businesses."

100 Galliher, *Morals Legislation without Morals: The Case of Nevada*, 71.

101 Doug McMillan, "Nevada's Sex-for-Sale Dilemma," *Reno Gazette-Journal*, November 9, 1986, Rocha, "Brothel Prostitution in Nevada: A Unique American Cultural Phenomenon," 24.

102 Jeanie Kasindorf, *The Nye County Brothel: A Tale of the New West* (New York: Linden Press/Simon & Schuster, 1985), 29–33.

103 Galliher, *Morals Legislation without Morals: The Case of Nevada.*

104 Ibid., 73.

105 Doug McMillan, "A Tale of Two Counties," *Reno Gazette-Journal*, November 13, 1986.

106 Rocha, "Brothel Prostitution in Nevada: A Unique American Cultural Phenomenon," 18.

107 McMillan, "A Tale of Two Counties."

108 Rocha, "Brothel Prostitution in Nevada: A Unique American Cultural Phenomenon," 25–26.

109 Astor, "Legal Prostitution Spreads in Nevada."

110 Kasindorf, *The Nye County Brothel: A Tale of the New West*, 202–216.

111 Doug McMillan, "While Legislators Ducked the Issue, Courts Set Brothel Law," *Reno Gazette-Journal*, November 15, 1986.

112 Kasindorf, *The Nye County Brothel: A Tale of the New West*, 10.

113 Ibid., 30.

114 Ibid., 33.

115 McMillan, "While Legislators Ducked the Issue, Courts Set Brothel Law."

116 Ibid.

117 Doug McMillan, "Rural Nevada Reluctant to Abolish Legal Brothels," *Reno Gazette-Journal*, November 13, 1986.

118 His contributions to certain Washoe and Storey County officials, and the mysterious death of Argentine heavyweight boxer Oscar Bonavena who was killed outside the ranch, were all subject to investigations. But no charges would stick. Meanwhile, District Attorney Bill Raggio was elected state senator in 1973, held various Senate leadership positions in the late 1970s and 1980s, and became the Senate Majority leader in 1993. Miller, "Raggio Has Been Nemesis for More Than 25 Years."

119 Ibid.

120 Reno, "Nevada Place Names Population 1860–2000."

121 Doug McMillan, "Lawmakers: Brothel Issue Likely Topic for '87 Session," *Reno Gazette-Journal*, November 13, 1986.

122 Susan Taylor Martin, "Nevada Brothels Battle for Business Amid AIDS Scare," *St. Petersburg Times*, November 1, 1987.

123 Cheryl L. Radeloff, "Vectors, Polluters and Murderers: HIV Testing Policies toward Prostitutes in Nevada" (University of Nevada, Las Vegas, 2004), 102–103. Cheryl Radeloff's Ph.D. dissertation is the definitive work on the development of Nevada's HIV testing policies. Cheryl has also graciously allowed the authors to use the interviews and data she gathered in the process of doing her research.

124 Ibid., 111.

125 McMillan, "Nevada's Sex-for-Sale Dilemma."

126 Information on the development of the Nevada Brothel Association comes from several interviews with George Flint, in 1997, 1998, and 2002.

127 These and subsequent quotes are from an interview with Larry Matheis by Cheryl Radeloff, January 21, 2002.

128 Radeloff, "Vectors, Polluters and Murderers: HIV Testing Policies toward Prostitutes in Nevada," 112–33.

129 Ibid., 115.

130 McMillan, "Nevada's Sex-for-Sale Dilemma."

131 William Darrow, "Prostitution, Intravenous Drug Use, and HIV-1 in the United States." In *AIDS, Drugs, and Prostitution*, ed. Martin A. Plant (New York: Routledge, 1990), Doug McMillan, "AIDS Brings Fear, Uncertainty to Brothels," *Reno Gazette-Journal*, November 12, 1986.

132 "Legalized Prostitution Debate Transcript #112–2." on *Larry King Live* (1990). This

study was presented at the 6th international conference on AIDS. The Nevada legal brothel system was a model for AIDS prevention among female sex industry workers. Russ Reade, Gary A. Richwald, and N. Williams, "The Nevada Legal Brothel System as a Model for AIDS Prevention among Female Sex Industry Workers" (1990).

133   UPI, "Regional News," *Regional newswire*, November 12, 1987.

134   Letters from Steve Wynn and Richard Bryan are from the files of Cheryl Radeloff.

135   Pat Harrison, *Gannett News Service*, March 24, 1989.

136   Barbara G. Brents and Kathryn Hausbeck, "State Sanctioned Sex: Negotiating Informal and Formal Regulatory Practices in Nevada Brothels," *Sociological Perspectives* 44, no. 3 (2001), Kathryn Hausbeck and Barbara G. Brents, "Inside Nevada's Brothel Industry." In *Sex for Sale*, ed. Ronald Weitzer (New York: Routledge, 2009).

Chapter 4

1   Robert E. Lang, Andrea Sarzynski, and Mark Muro, "Mountain Megas: America's Newest Metropolitan Places and a Federal Partnership to Help Them Prosper." In *Metropolitan Policy Program* (Washington, DC: The Brookings Institution, 2008).

2   In rural Nevada 20 percent of all jobs were tourism-related jobs, and in Elko County it was 31 percent. Elizabeth Fadali, Thomas R. Harris, and Kynda R. Curtis, "Factors Affecting Agritourism Potential in Rural Nevada." In *Fact Sheet* (Reno: University of Nevada Cooperative Extension, 2007).

3   These trends toward more diversity in rural areas will likely continue at some level in spite of an economic crisis that began in 2008.

4   Lang, Sarzynski, and Muro, "Mountain Megas: America's Newest Metropolitan Places and a Federal Partnership to Help Them Prosper," William F. Theobald, *Global Tourism*, 2nd ed. (Boston, MA: Butterworth-Heinemann, 1998), William Riebsame, "Atlas of the New West: Portrait of a Changing Region," Center of the American West (University of Colorado at Boulder, 1997), Andrew J. Hansen et al., "Ecological Causes and Consequences of Demographic Change in the New West," *BioScience* 52, no. 2 (2002).

5   Thomas C. Wright, "Immigration and Ethnic Diversity in Nevada," Center for Democratic Culture, University of Nevada, Las Vegas, http://www.unlv.edu/centers/cdclv/healthnv/immigration.html.

6   "Brothel World Famous Chicken Ranch Pahrump, NV," BizQuest, http://www.bizquest.com/buy/852847.html.

7   Becky Bosshart, "NV50 Mixes Drinks and Fine Food," *Nevada Appeal*, January 21, 2005.

8   Kit Kat Guest Ranch, "Sheila and Jacie Caramella," Kit Kat Ranch, http://www.cathouselovers.com/welcome_owners.html.

9   Mineral County mandates that signs only say "Guest Ranch—Men Only." See Barbara G. Brents and Kathryn Hausbeck, "State Sanctioned Sex: Negotiating Informal and Formal Regulatory Practices in Nevada Brothels," *Sociological Perspectives* 44, no. 3 (2001) for more information on advertising laws prior to the ban being lifted.

10   The Sin City Chamber of Commerce is a chamber of commerce formed in Las

Vegas that brings together adult and non-adult businesses. It was founded in 2004.

11 Donna's Ranch, "Where the Wild West Still Lives," Donnasranch.net, http://www.donnasranch.net/.

12 Rita Cosby, "Bunny Ranch." In *Rita Cosby Live and Direct*, ed. MSNBC (MSNBC, 2005).

13 Adam Tanner, "Nevada's Legal Brothels Given Timid Embrace," *Washington Post*, March 12, 2006.

14 Lynnette Curtis, "ACLU Joins Fight against Limits on Brothel Ads," *Las Vegas Review Journal*, March 18, 2006.

15 Although these taxi services are advertised as free, women whose customers come by limousine must usually tip the drivers. They add this to their negotiated prices if they can.

16 Barbara G. Brents and Kathryn Hausbeck, "Marketing Sex: U.S. Legal Brothels and Late Capitalist Consumption," *Sexualities* 10, no. 4 (2007).

17 Richard Abowitz, "Cathouse Dreams: A Day in the Life of a Ranch—Nevada Style," *Las Vegas Weekly*, May 31, 2001.

18 Cosby, "Bunny Ranch."

19 S. Kruhse-Mount Burton, "Sex Tourism and Traditional Australian Male Identity." In *International Tourism: Identity and Change*, ed. Marie-Françoise Lanfant, John B. Allcock, and Edward M. Bruner (Thousand Oaks, CA: Sage, 1995), 193.

20 Amalia L. Cabezas, "Between Love and Money: Sex, Tourism, and Citizenship in Cuba and the Dominican Republic," *Signs* 29, no. 4 (2004), Martin Oppermann, "Sex Tourism," *Annals of Tourism Research* 26, no. 2 (1999), Chris Ryan, "Sex Tourism: Paradigms of Confusion." In *Tourism and Sex: Culture, Commerce and Coercion*, ed. Stephen Clift and Simon Carter (London: Cassell, 2000), Chris Ryan and C. Michael Hall, *Sex Tourism: Marginal People and Liminalities* (New York: Routledge, 2001), Chris Ryan and Rachel Kinder, "Sex, Tourism and Sex Tourism: Fulfilling Similar Needs?," *Tourism Management* 17, no. 7 (1996).

21 Rebecca Mead, "Letter from Nevada: American Pimp, How to Make a Living from the Oldest Profession," *New Yorker*, April 23, 2001.

22 Alexa Albert, *Brothel: Mustang Ranch and Its Women*, 1st ed. (New York: Random House, 2001), 20.

23 http://www.airforceamy.com/, retrieved Feb. 11, 2009.

24 Much of the material in this section is also discussed in Barbara G. Brents and Kathryn Hausbeck, "Violence and Legalized Brothel Prostitution in Nevada: Examining Safety, Risk and Prostitution Policy," *Journal of Interpersonal Violence* 20, no. 3 (2005).

25 In 2000, the Moonlite Bunny Ranch charged $19 a day for room and board and Sheri's Ranch charged $30 a day.

26 Barbara Ann Sullivan, *The Politics of Sex: Prostitution and Pornography in Australia since 1945* (Cambridge, MA: Cambridge University Press, 1997).

Chapter 5

1 The debate over whether prostitution is choice or coercion is an old one. Works include Kathleen Barry, *Female Sexual Slavery* (New York: New York University

Press, 1984), Wendy Chapkis, *Live Sex Acts: Women Performing Erotic Labor* (New York: Routledge, 1997), Laurie Shrage, *Moral Dilemmas of Feminism: Prostitution, Adultery, and Abortion* (New York: Routledge, 1994), Christine Overall, "What's Wrong with Prostitution? Evaluating Sex Work," *Signs* 17, no. 4 (1992). Barbara Heyl is one of the few who have looked at career trajectories of sex workers. See Barbara S. Heyl, *The Madam as Entrepreneur: Career Management in House Prostitution* (New Brunswick, NJ: Transaction Books, 1979).

2 Amalia L. Cabezas, "Between Love and Money: Sex, Tourism, and Citizenship in Cuba and the Dominican Republic," *Signs* 29, no. 4 (2004), Laura M. Agustín, *Sex at the Margins: Migration, Labour Markets and the Rescue Industry* (New York: Zed Books, 2007), Barbara G. Brents and Teela Sanders, "Mainstreaming the Sex Industry: Economic Inclusion and Social Ambivalence," *Journal of Law and Society* forthcoming 2010, Teela Sanders, *Paying for Pleasure: Men Who Buy Sex* (Cullompton: Willan Publishers, 2008), Martin Oppermann, "Sex Tourism," *Annals of Tourism Research* 26, no. 2 (1999), Chris Ryan, "Sex Tourism: Paradigms of Confusion." In *Tourism and Sex: Culture, Commerce and Coercion*, ed. Stephen Clift and Simon Carter (London: Cassell, 2000), Agustín, *Sex at the Margins: Migration, Labour Markets and the Rescue Industry*.

3 From Rebecca. J. Erickson and Amy S. Wharton, "Inauthenticity and Depression: Assessing the Consequences of Interactive Service Work," *Work and Occupations* 24, no. 2 (1997).

4 The question of how much up-front training or capital investment one needs to be a successful worker is a complex issue. One can certainly come into a brothel with little of either. Other workers often informally provide the training the women receive at the brothel. Women are often surprised at the amount of money they need to spend on requirements of the job—health testing, licenses, or tipping the other brothel employees such as the cook. And many found that the more one spends on other things the more successful she is—clothes, makeup, hair, body modifications like cosmetic surgery, etc.

5 A few of these women told us that they had sold sex once or twice before coming to the brothels, but not on a regular or ongoing basis. A few had worked in erotic dance, but described it as casual employment: either they had tried it once or twice, or had done it for a while in their youth.

6 The film career for Bev Waters (not her real name or her adult film name) was found in the *Internet Movie Database* (IMDb.com, Inc., 2009).

7 For more on the characteristics of rural prostitution, see John Scott et al., "Sex Outside the City: Sex Work in Rural and Regional New South Wales," *Rural Society* 16, no. 2 (2006). When women do not live in the same town they work in, it makes it possible to "avoid the stigmatization associated with communities exhibiting gemeinshaft characteristics" of rural life (164).

8 Agustín, *Sex at the Margins: Migration, Labour Markets and the Rescue Industry*.

Chapter 6

1 It is not all that surprising that these women downplay the sexual aspects of the job. Researchers have found that other body workers, including gynecologists, massage therapists, other female and male prostitutes, desexualize their work to avoid

the stigma of (potential or actual) sexualized interactions on the job. J. Henslin and M. Biggs, "Dramaturgical Desexualisation: The Sociology of the Vaginal Examination." In *The Sociology of Sex: An Introductory Reader* (1978), Sarah Oerton and Joanna Phoenix, "Sex/Bodywork: Discourses and Practices," *Sexualities* 4, no. 4 (2001), Albert J. Reiss, "Sex Offenses: The Marginal Status of the Adolescent," *Law and Contemporary Problems* 25 (1960).

2　See, for example, Carole Pateman, *The Sexual Contract* (Stanford, CA: Stanford University Press, 1988), Kathleen Barry, *Female Sexual Slavery* (New York: New York University Press, 1984), Julia O'Connell Davidson, *Prostitution, Power, and Freedom* (Ann Arbor: University of Michigan Press, 1998), Sheila Jeffreys, *The Industrial Vagina: The Political Economy of the Global Sex Trade* (New York: Routledge, 2008), Melissa Farley, " 'Bad for the Body, Bad for the Heart': Prostitution Harms Women Even If Legalized or Decriminalized," *Violence Against Women* 10, no. 10 (2004). For a review of these debates about prostitution, see Laurie Shrage, *Moral Dilemmas of Feminism: Prostitution, Adultery, and Abortion*, Thinking Gender (New York: Routledge, 1994).

3　Carol Wolkowitz, "The Social Relations of Body Work," *Work, Employment & Society* 16, no. 3 (2002): 499.

4　Oerton and Phoenix, "Sex/Bodywork: Discourses and Practices." Neil P. McKeganey and Marina Barnard, *Sex Work on the Streets: Prostitutes and Their Clients* (Philadelphia: Open University Press, 1996), Jan Browne and Victor Minichiello, "The Social Meanings Behind Male Sex Work: Implications for Sexual Interactions," *British Journal of Sociology* 46, no. 4 (1995), Cecilie Hoigard and Liv Finstad, *Backstreets: Prostitution, Money, and Love* (University Park: Pennsylvania State University Press, 1992). Graham Scambler and Annette Scambler, *Rethinking Prostitution: Purchasing Sex in the 1990s* (London; New York: Routledge, 1997), Maggie O'Neill, *Prostitution and Feminism* (Cambridge: Polity Press, 2001).

5　See, for example, Wendy Chapkis, *Live Sex Acts: Women Performing Erotic Labor* (New York: Routledge, 1997), Ine Vanwesenbeeck, "Burnout among Female Indoor Sex Workers," *Archives of Sexual Behavior* 34, no. 6 (2005).

6　Rejecting the mind/body dualism is an important part of alternative and holistic medicine. While some studies find that workers in alternative medicine do positively value body work because of its connection with caring, others find that nurses and even massage therapists distance themselves from the body in subtle ways. Oerton and Phoenix did a study comparing therapeutic massage practitioners with sex workers and how they defined body practices and affective connections. They found that both sets of workers created a mind–body dualism in different ways. The massage workers talked about their work in ways that had little to do with corporeality; the body was just a path to the spirit. Likewise, sex workers talked about distinguishing sex from work and saw sex as utterly embodied, with no affective connection involved. Yet, Oerton and Phoenix found these distinctions were unstable. Oerton and Phoenix, "Sex/Bodywork: Discourses and Practices," Wolkowitz, "The Social Relations of Body Work."

7　Magdalene Meretrix, *Turning Pro: A Guide to Sex Work for the Ambitious and the Intrigued* (Emeryville, CA: Greenery Press, 2001). We also spoke with her by phone.

8　For BDSM players, sex itself may be secondary or inconsequential (many BDSM players engage in no sex at all). The enjoyment comes from temporarily handing over large amounts of physical, emotional, and sexual control to another person, and playing with boundaries between pain and pleasure, in the safety of BDSM rules. For more information on power play and BDSM, see Dossie Easton and Janet W. Hardy, *The New Bottoming Book* (Emeryville, CA: Greenery Press, 2001), Easton and Hardy, *The Ethical Slut: A Roadmap for Relationship Pioneers*, 2nd ed. (Berkeley, CA: Celestial Arts, 2009).

9 Michael L. Schwalbe and Douglas Mason-Schrock, "Identity Work as Group Process," *Advances in Group Processes* 13 (1996).

10 Erving Goffman, *The Presentation of Self in Everyday Life* (New York: Anchor Books, 1959).

11 For a review of identity and work see Robin Leidner, "Identity and Work." In *Social Theory at Work*, ed. Marek Korczynski, Randy Hodson, and Paul Edwards (New York: Oxford University Press, 2006). For other excellent ethnographies on the construction of identity at work see Timothy Diamond, *Making Gray Gold: Narratives of Nursing Home Care* (Chicago: University of Chicago Press, 1992), Robin Leidner, *Fast Food, Fast Talk: Service Work and the Routinization of Everyday Life* (Berkeley: University of California Press, 1993), Jennifer Pierce, *Gender Trials: Emotional Lives in Contemporary Law Firms* (Los Angeles: University of California Press, 1996).

12 There is an extensive literature on the effects of emotional labor on service work. See Chapter 2. Amy S. Wharton, "The Sociology of Emotional Labor," *Annual Review of Sociology* 35, no. 1 (2009) for an excellent review. See also Rebecca. J. Erickson and Amy S. Wharton, "Inauthenticity and Depression: Assessing the Consequences of Interactive Service Work," *Work and Occupations* 24, no. 2 (1997), Rebecca J. Erickson and C. Ritter, "Emotional Labor, Burnout, and Inauthenticity: Does Gender Matter?," *Social Psychology Quarterly* (2001), Amy S. Wharton, "The Affective Consequences of Service Work: Managing Emotions on the Job," *Work and Occupations* 20, no. 2 (1993), Heather Ferguson Bulan, Rebecca J. Erickson, and Amy S. Wharton, "Doing for Others on the Job: The Affective Requirements of Service Work, Gender, and Emotional Well-being," *Social Problems* 44, no. 2 (1997), Celeste M. Brotheridge and Alicia A. Grandey, "Emotional Labor and Burnout: Comparing Two Perspectives of 'People Work'," *Journal of Vocational Behavior* 60, no. 1 (2002), Alicia A. Grandey, "Emotion Regulation in the Workplace: A New Way to Conceptualize Emotional Labor," *Journal of Occupational Health Psychology* 5, no. 1 (2000), Dieter Zapf and Melanie Holz, "On the Positive and Negative Effects of Emotion Work in Organizations," *European Journal of Work and Organizational Psychology* 15, no. 1 (2006).

13 Chapkis, *Live Sex Acts: Women Performing Erotic Labor*, 78.

14 One multi-country study found that two-thirds of sex workers interviewed met the diagnostic criteria for post-traumatic stress disorder. While the authors concluded that prostitution itself was intrinsically harmful, the authors did not test other intervening variables that they found in this population, including the high prevalence of homelessness, violence, and drug addiction. Melissa Farley et al., "Prostitution in Five Countries," *Feminism and Psychology* 8, no. 4 (1998). Studies comparing sex workers with other groups show that childhood abuse, experiences of violence, drug abuse, and stigma cause more mental health problems than does sex work itself. Ine Vanwesenbeeck et al., "Professional HIV Risk Taking, Levels of

Victimization, and Well-being in Female Prostitutes in the Netherlands," *Archives of Sexual Behavior* 24, no. 5 (1995), Nabila El-Bassel et al., "Sex Trading and Psychological Distress among Women Recruited from the Streets of Harlem," *American Journal of Public Health* 87, no. 1 (1997).

15 Ine Vanwesenbeeck studied burn-out in indoor sex workers against a comparison group of nurses and people in a treatment program for work-related psychological problems in the Netherlands. She found that of three measures of burn-out, the sex workers were comparable to those in treatment on only one, depersonalization. Half of the variance on this measure was explained by not working by choice, negative social reactions, experiences of violence, and lack of control in interaction with clients. She concludes that psychological stress was not related to sex work per se, but sex work under certain conditions, particularly where workers experienced more stigma, violence, role conflict, and lack of a worker-supportive workplace. Vanwesenbeeck, "Burnout among Female Indoor Sex Workers."

16 Joanna Brewis and Stephen Linstead, " 'The Worst Thing Is the Screwing'(1): Consumption and the Management of Identity in Sex Work," *Gender, Work and Organization* 7, no. 2 (2000), Browne and Minichiello, "The Social Meanings Behind Male Sex Work: Implications for Sexual Interactions," Teela Sanders, "The Condom as Psychological Barrier: Female Sex Workers and Emotional Management," *Feminism and Psychology* 12, no. 4 (2002), Hoigard and Finstad, *Backstreets: Prostitution, Money, and Love*, McKeganey and Barnard, *Sex Work on the Streets: Prostitutes and Their Clients*, Teela Sanders, " 'It's Just Acting': Sex Workers' Strategies for Capitalizing on Sexuality," *Gender, Work and Organization* 12, no. 4 (2005), Oerton and Phoenix, "Sex/Bodywork: Discourses and Practices."

17 Vanwesenbeeck, "Burnout among Female Indoor Sex Workers."

18 Sanders, " 'It's Just Acting': Sex Workers' Strategies for Capitalizing on Sexuality." See also O'Neill, *Prostitution and Feminism*.

19 Leidner, *Fast Food, Fast Talk: Service Work and the Routinization of Everyday Life*, 184.

20 Amanda Brooks, *The Internet Escort's Handbook Book 2: Advertising and Marketing* (Golden Girl Press, 2009).

21 BunnyLover posted on a message board devoted to fans of Nevada brothels called NVBrothels.net, at http://mysite.verizon.net/res1dzs0/messageboards/id15.html retrieved Nov 22, 2008. He refers to Speed Racer, the online moniker of a brothel customer who has posted information about the brothels on another website, www.sex-in-nevada.com.

22 Elizabeth Bernstein, "The Meaning of the Purchase: Desire, Demand and the Commerce of Sex," *Ethnography* 2, no. 3 (2001).

23 Katherine Frank, *G-strings and Sympathy: Strip Club Regulars and Male Desire* (Durham, NC: Duke University Press, 2002).

24 Elizabeth Bernstein, *Temporarily Yours: Intimacy, Authenticity and the Commerce of Sex* (Chicago: University of Chicago Press, 2007).

25 Gail Pheterson, *The Prostitution Prism* (Amsterdam: Amsterdam University Press, 1996).

26 Martin Oppermann, "Sex Tourism," *Annals of Tourism Research* 26, no. 2 (1999). See also Amalia L. Cabezas, "Between Love and Money: Sex, Tourism, and Citizenship in Cuba and the Dominican Republic," *Signs* 29, no. 4 (2004), Chris Ryan, "Sex

Tourism: Paradigms of Confusion." In *Tourism and Sex: Culture, Commerce and Coercion*, ed. Stephen Clift and Simon Carter (London: Cassell, 2000), Chris Ryan and C. Michael Hall, *Sex Tourism: Marginal People and Liminalities* (New York: Routledge, 2001).

27 Bernstein, *Temporarily Yours: Intimacy, Authenticity and the Commerce of Sex*, 482.

28 Alexandra K. Murphy and Sudhir A. Venkatesh, "Vice Careers: The Changing Contours of Sex Work in New York City," *Qualitative Sociology* 29, no. 2 (2006).

29 Kenneth J. Gergen, *The Saturated Self: Dilemmas of Identity in Contemporary Life* (New York: Basic Books, 1991), 7, Eric Sharpe, " 'Going Above and Beyond:' The Emotional Labor of Adventure Guides," *Journal of Leisure Research* 37, no. 1 (2005).

30 Carol Wolkowitz, *Bodies at Work* (Thousand Oaks, CA: Sage, 2006).

Chapter 7

1 Tracy Swartz, "Prostitution Arrests Go up 4.5% in City," *Chicago Tribune*, March 20, 2009.

2 Viviana A. Rotman Zelizer, *The Purchase of Intimacy* (Princeton, NJ: Princeton University Press, 2005), Kathryn Hausbeck and Barbara G. Brents, "McDonaldization of the Sex Industries? The Business of Sex." In *McDonaldization: The Reader*, ed. George Ritzer (Thousand Oaks, CA: Pine Forge Press, 2002), Eva Illouz, *Consuming the Romantic Utopia: Love and the Cultural Contradictions of Capitalism* (Berkeley: University of California Press, 1997), Gail Hawkes, *A Sociology of Sex and Sexuality* (Philadelphia: Open University Press, 1996).

3 See the Bay Area Sex Worker Advocacy Network, www.bayswan.org/, Best Practices Policy Project, www.bestpracticespolicy.org/index.html, Desiree Alliance, www.desireealliance.org/, and Sex Workers' Outreach Project, www.swop-usa.org for more information on rights from organizations run by and for sex workers.

4 Prostitution Law Review Committee, "Report of the Prostitution Law Review Committee on the Operation of the Prostitution Reform Act 2003" (Wellington, NZ: Ministry of Justice, 2008).

5 However, research on the experiences of sex workers in Australia, the Netherlands, and Germany shows that legalization alone does not always change the stigma associated with prostitution. See Joyce Outshoorn, *The Politics of Prostitution: Women's Movements, Democratic States, and the Globalisation of Sex Commerce* (Cambridge; New York: Cambridge University Press, 2004), Outshoorn, "The Political Debates on Prostitution and Trafficking of Women," *Social Politics* 12, no. 1 (2005), Barbara Ann Sullivan, *The Politics of Sex: Prostitution and Pornography in Australia since 1945* (Cambridge, MA: Cambridge University Press, 1997), Alison Arnot, "Legalisation of the Sex Industry in the State of Victoria, Australia: The Impact of Prostitution Law Reform on the Working and Private Lives of Women in the Legal Victoria Sex Industry" (University of Melbourne, 2002), Chrisje Brants, "The Fine Art of Regulated Tolerance: Prostitution in Amsterdam," *Journal of Law and Society* 25, no. 4 (1998), Ine Vanwesenbeeck, "Another Decade of Social Scientific Work on Sex Work: A Review of Research 1990–2000," *Annual Review of Sex Research* 12 (2001), Nancy A. Wonders and Raymond Michalowski, "Bodies, Borders, and Sex Tourism in a Globalized World: A Tale of Two Cities—Amsterdam and Havana," *Social Problems* 48, no. 4 (2001), Elaine Mossman, "International

Approaches to Decriminalising or Legalising Prostitution" (Wellington, NZ: Ministry of Justice, 2007), Ronald Weitzer, "Legalizing Prostitution: Morality Politics in Western Australia," *British Journal of Criminology* (2008).

6 A 1996 general social survey found 45 percent of respondents agreeing with the statement that "There is nothing inherently wrong with prostitution, so long as the health risks can be minimized. If consenting adults agree to exchange money for sex, that is their business"; 52 percent disagreed. Ronald Weitzer, "The Politics of Prostitution in America." In *Sex for Sale*, ed. Ronald Weitzer (New York: Routledge, 2000), 165. However, by 2006, the U.S. General Social Survey found that only 34 percent of the population strongly disagreed when asked the same question.

7 Elizabeth Bernstein, "The Meaning of the Purchase: Desire, Demand and the Commerce of Sex," *Ethnography* 2, no. 3 (2001).

8 Wendy Chapkis, "Trafficking, Migration, and the Law: Protecting Innocents, Punishing Immigrants," *Gender and Society* 17, no. 6 (2003), Chapkis, "Soft Glove, Punishing Fist: The Trafficking Victims Protection Act of 2000." In *Regulating Sex: The Politics of Intimacy and Identity*, ed. Elizabeth Bernstein and Laurie Schaffner (New York: Routledge, 2005), Laura M. Agustín, *Sex at the Margins: Migration, Labour Markets and the Rescue Industry* (New York: Zed Books, 2007), Ronald Weitzer, "The Social Construction of Sex Trafficking: Ideology and Institutionalization of a Moral Crusade," *Politics and Society* 35, no. 3 (2007), Kamala Kempadoo, *Sun, Sex, and Gold: Tourism and Sex Work in the Caribbean* (Lanham, MD: Rowman & Littlefield, 1999), Kamala Kempadoo and Jo Doezema, *Global Sex Workers: Rights, Resistance, and Redefinition* (New York: Routledge, 1998), Kamala Kempadoo, Jyoti Sanghera, and Bandana Pattanaik, *Trafficking and Prostitution Reconsidered: New Perspectives on Migration, Sex Work, and Human Rights* (Boulder, CO: Paradigm, 2005).

9 The assumption that sexually oriented adult businesses are linked to an increase in crime have been debunked by looking at erotic dance establishments and adult video and book stores. See Harold P. Fahringer, "Zoning out Free Expression: An Analysis of New York City's Adult Zoning Resolution," *Buffalo Law Review* 46 (1998), Judith L. Hanna, "Exotic Dance Adult Entertainment: A Guide for Planners and Policy Makers," *Journal of Planning Literature* 20, no. 2 (2005), Daniel Linz et al., "Testing Legal Assumptions Regarding the Effects of Dancer Nudity and Proximity to Patron on Erotic Expression," *Law and Human Behavior* 24, no. 5 (2000), Linz et al, "An Examination of the Assumption That Adult Businesses Are Associated with Crime in Surrounding Areas: A Secondary Effects Study in Charlotte, North Carolina," *Law and Society Review* 38, no. 1 (2004), Bryant Paul, Bradley J. Shafer, and Daniel Linz, "Government Regulation Of 'Adult' Businesses through Zoning and Anti-nudity Ordinances: Debunking the Legal Myth of Negative Secondary Effects," *Communication Law and Policy* 6, no. 2 (2001).

10 Studies of condom use in Nevada's brothels are easier to conduct due to the legal nature of the work. In 1987, condom use in the brothels became law, although usage was already high. In the late 1980s, the UCLA Medical Center conducted a study of women working at the Chicken Ranch brothel in Pahrump, Nye County, about an hour outside of Las Vegas. They found no sero-transmission of HIV and a very low 1 percent positive gonorrhea rate. The researchers determined that the regulations around brothel prostitution, like licensing requirements, mandatory

condom use, on-site AIDS prevention education for workers and promotion of low-risk, non-penetrative sexual practices, help ensure safe sex practices in the brothels. Russ Reade, Gary A. Richwald, and N. Williams, "The Nevada Legal Brothel System as a Model for AIDS Prevention among Female Sex Industry Workers" (1990).

Further, in 1995, Albert et al. found that rates of STIs and HIV were very low among Nevada's legal brothel workers, and that instances of condom slippage or breakage were also low. In 1998, Albert reported that compliance with the condom use requirement was quite high. The study found that few clients (2.7 percent) asked to not use condoms, and the women either convinced them to use a condom or had non-penetrative sex without a condom. (A small percentage of clients left without services.) However, women did not always use condoms with their boy-friends, husbands, or non-paying partners. The study concluded that women are at more of a risk for acquiring HIV and STIs from their personal lives than at work. Alexa Albert et al., "Condom Use among Female Commercial Sex Workers in Nevada's Legal Brothels," *American Journal of Public Health* 85, no. 11 (1995), Alexa E. Albert, "Facilitating Condom Use with Clients During Commercial Sex in Nevada's Legal Brothels," *American Journal of Public Health* 88, no. 4 (1998).

BIBLIOGRAPHY

Abbe, Donald R. *Austin and the Reese River Mining District: Nevada's Forgotten Frontier.* Reno: University of Nevada Press, 1985.

ABC News. "Porn Profits: Corporate America's Secret: Corporate America is Profiting from Porn—Quietly." *ABC News Primetime*, May 27, 2004, http://abcnews.go.com/Primetime/story?id=132370&page=1.

Abiala, Kristina. "Customer Orientation and Sales Situations: Variations in Interactive Service Work." *Acta Sociologica* 42, no. 3 (1999): 207–222.

Abowitz, Richard. "Cathouse Dreams: A Day in the Life of a Ranch—Nevada Style." *Las Vegas Weekly*, May 31, 2001, 19–22.

Acker, Joan. "Hierarchies, Jobs, Bodies: A Theory of Gendered Organizations." *Gender and Society* (1990): 139–158.

Ackman, Dan. "How Big Is Porn?" *Forbes*, May 25, 2001.

Adler, Patricia A. and Peter Adler. *Paradise Laborers: Hotel Work in the Global Economy.* Ithaca, NY: Cornell University Press, 2004.

Aggleton, Peter, ed. *Men Who Sell Sex: International Perspectives on Male Prostitution and HIV/AIDS.* Philadelphia: Temple University Press, 1999.

Agustín, Laura María. *Sex at the Margins: Migration, Labour Markets and the Rescue Industry.* New York: Zed Books, 2007.

——— . "The Cultural Study of Commercial Sex." *Sexualities* 8, no. 5 (2005): 618–631.

——— . "Migrants in the Mistress's House: Other Voices in The 'Trafficking' Debate." *Social Politics* 12, no. 1 (2005): 96–117.

——— . "A Migrant World of Services." *Social Politics* 10, no. 3 (2003): 377–396.

Albert, Alexa E. *Brothel: Mustang Ranch and Its Women.* 1st ed. New York: Random House, 2001.

Albert, Alexa E. "Facilitating Condom Use with Clients During Commercial Sex in Nevada's Legal Brothels." *American Journal of Public Health* 88, no. 4 (1998): 643–647.

Albert, Alexa E., David Lee Warner, Robert A. Hatcher, James Trussell, and Charles Bennett. "Condom Use among Female Commercial Sex Workers in Nevada's Legal Brothels." *American Journal of Public Health* 85, no. 11 (1995): 1514–1520.

Alexander, Priscilla. "Feminism, Sex Workers and Human Rights." In *Whores and Other Feminists*, ed. Jill Nagle, 83–97. New York: Routledge, 1997.

Allison, Anne. *Nightwork: Sexuality, Pleasure, and Corporate Masculinity in a Tokyo Hostess Club.* Chicago, IL: University of Chicago Press, 1994.

Andersen, Robert and Tina Fetner. "Cohort Differences in Tolerance of Homosexuality: Attitudinal Change in Canada and the United States, 1981–2000." *Public Opinion Quarterly* 72, no. 2 (2008): 311.

Arnot, Alison. "Legalisation of the Sex Industry in the State of Victoria, Australia: The Impact of Prostitution Law Reform on the Working and Private Lives of Women in the Legal Victoria Sex Industry," Ph.D dissertation, University of Melbourne, 2002.

Aron, Cindy Sondik. *Working at Play: A History of Vacations in the United States.* New York: Oxford University Press, 1999.

Astor, Gerald. "Legal Prostitution Spreads in Nevada." *Look*, June 29, 1971, 34–36.

Barry, Kathleen. *Female Sexual Slavery.* New York: New York University Press, 1984.

Barton, Bernadette. *Stripped: Inside the Lives of Exotic Dancers.* New York: New York University Press, 2006.

Bauman, Zygmunt. *Liquid Love: On the Frailty of Human Bonds.* Malden, MA: Blackwell Publishers, 2003.

——. *Liquid Modernity.* Cambridge, UK: Polity Press, 2000.

Beck, Ulrich. *Risk Society: Towards a New Modernity.* London: Sage, 1992.

Beebe, Lucius Morris and Charles Clegg. *Legends of the Comstock Lode.* Oakland, CA: G. H. Hardy, 1950.

Beisel, Nicola Kay. *Imperiled Innocents: Anthony Comstock and Family Reproduction in Victorian America.* Princeton, NJ: Princeton University Press, 1997.

Beisel, Nicola and Tamara Kay. "Abortion, Race, and Gender in Nineteenth-Century America." *American Sociological Review* 69, no. 4 (2004): 498–518.

Bell, Daniel. *The Cultural Contradictions of Capitalism.* New York: Basic Books, 1976.

Benoit, Cecilia and Frances M Shaver. "Critical Issues and New Directions in Sex Work Research." *Canadian Review of Sociology and Anthropology* 43, no. 3 (2006): 243.

Bernstein, Elizabeth. *Temporarily Yours: Intimacy, Authenticity and the Commerce of Sex.* Chicago: University of Chicago Press, 2007.

——. "The Meaning of the Purchase: Desire, Demand and the Commerce of Sex." *Ethnography* 2, no. 3 (2001): 389–420.

Bernstein, Laurie. *Sonia's Daughters: Prostitutes and Their Regulation in Imperial Russia.* Berkeley: University of California Press, 1995.

Best, Joel. *Controlling Vice: Regulating Brothel Prostitution in St. Paul, 1865–1883.* Columbus: Ohio State University Press, 1998.

Bishop, Ryan, and Lillian S. Robinson. *Night Market: Sexual Cultures and the Thai Economic Miracle.* New York: Routledge, 1998.

Bosshart, Becky. "NV50 Mixes Drinks and Fine Food." *Nevada Appeal*, January 21, 2005, http://www.nevadaappeal.com/article/20050121/DAYTON/101210040.

Bowen, David E. and Edward E. Lawler III. "Empowering Service Employees." *Sloan Management Review* 36, no. 4 (1995): 73.

Bowers, Michael Wayne. *The Sagebrush State: Nevada's History, Government, and Politics.* Reno: University of Nevada Press, 1996.

Brants, Chrisje. "The Fine Art of Regulated Tolerance: Prostitution in Amsterdam." *Journal of Law and Society* 25, no. 4 (1998): 6211–6235.

Braverman, Harry. *Labor and Monopoly Capital.* New York: Monthly Review Press, 1974.

Bremner, Caroline. "Top 150 City Destinations: London Leads the Way" (2007), http://www.euromonitor.com/Top_150_City_Destinations_London_Leads_the_Way.

Brents, Barbara G. and Kathryn Hausbeck. "Sex Work Now: What the Blurring Boundaries Around the Sex Industry Mean for Sex Work, Research and Activism." In *Sex Work Matters: Exploring Money, Power and Intimacy in the Global Sex Industry*, ed. Melissa Ditmore, Antonia Levy, and Alys Willman. London: Zed Books, forthcoming 2010.

——. "Marketing Sex: U.S. Legal Brothels and Late Capitalist Consumption." *Sexualities* 10, no. 4 (2007): 425–439.

——. "Violence and Legalized Brothel Prostitution in Nevada: Examining Safety, Risk and Prostitution Policy." *Journal of Interpersonal Violence* 20, no. 3 (2005): 270–295.

——. "State Sanctioned Sex: Negotiating Informal and Formal Regulatory Practices in Nevada Brothels." *Sociological Perspectives* 44, no. 3 (2001): 307–332.

Brents, Barbara G. and Teela Sanders. "Mainstreaming the Sex Industry: Economic Inclusion and Social Ambivalence." *Journal of Law and Society*, forthcoming 2010.

Brewer, Paul R. "Values, Political Knowledge, and Public Opinion About Gay Rights: A Framing-based Account." *Public Opinion Quarterly* 67, no. 2 (2003): 173–201.

Brewis, Joanna and Stephen Linstead. " 'The Worst Thing Is the Screwing'(1): Consumption and the Management of Identity in Sex Work." *Gender, Work and Organization* 7, no. 2 (2000): 84–97.

——. *Sex, Work and Sex Work: Eroticizing Organization*. London; New York: Routledge, 2000.

——. " 'The Worst Thing Is the Screwing': Context and Career in Sex Work." *Gender, Work and Organization* 7, no. 3 (2000): 168–180.

Brock, Deborah R. *Making Work, Making Trouble: Prostitution as a Social Problem*. Toronto; Buffalo: University of Toronto Press, 1998.

Brooks, Amanda. *The Internet Escort's Handbook Book 2: Advertising and Marketing*. Reno, Nevada: Golden Girl Press, 2009.

"Brothel World Famous Chicken Ranch Pahrump, NV." BizQuest, http://www.bizquest.com/buy/852847.html.

Brotheridge, Celeste M. and Alicia A. Grandey. "Emotional Labor and Burnout: Comparing Two Perspectives of 'People Work'." *Journal of Vocational Behavior* 60, no. 1 (2002): 17–39.

Browne, Jan and Victor Minichiello. "The Social Meanings Behind Male Sex Work: Implications for Sexual Interactions." *British Journal of Sociology* 46, no. 4 (1995): 598–622.

Bulan, Heather Ferguson, Rebecca J. Erickson, and Amy S. Wharton. "Doing for Others on the Job: The Affective Requirements of Service Work, Gender, and Emotional Well-being." *Social Problems* 44, no. 2 (1997): 235–256.

Burawoy, Michael. *Manufacturing Consent*. Chicago: University of Chicago Press, 1982.

Cabezas, Amalia L. "Between Love and Money: Sex, Tourism, and Citizenship in Cuba and the Dominican Republic." *Signs* 29, no. 4 (2004): 987–1015.

Cameron, Samuel. "Space, Risk and Opportunity: The Evolution of Paid Sex Markets." *Urban Studies* 41, no. 9 (2004): 1643–1657.

Castells, Manuel. *The Rise of the Network Society*. 2nd ed, Information Age. Oxford: Blackwell, 2000.

Castle, Stephen. "Passports and Panic Buttons in the Brothel of the Future." *Independent*, September 23, 2006, 34.

Center for Regional Studies. "Geodemographic Analysis—Pahrump Area Census Tracts." In *2008 Business Activity Report, Pahrump, Nye County, Nevada*. Reno, NV: University of Nevada, Reno, 2009.

Chancer, Lynn Sharon. "Prostitution, Feminist Theory, and Ambivalence: Notes from the Sociological Underground." *Social Text* 37, Winter (1993): 143–171.

Chapkis, Wendy. "Soft Glove, Punishing Fist: The Trafficking Victims Protection Act of 2000." In *Regulating Sex: The Politics of Intimacy and Identity*, ed. Elizabeth Bernstein and Laurie Schaffner, 51–65. New York: Routledge, 2005.

——. "Trafficking, Migration, and the Law: Protecting Innocents, Punishing Immigrants." *Gender and Society* 17, no. 6 (2003): 923–937.

——. *Live Sex Acts: Women Performing Erotic Labor*. New York: Routledge, 1997.

Chung, Sue Fawn. "Their Changing World: Chinese Women on the Comstock 1860–1910." In *Comstock Women: The Making of a Mining Community*, ed. Ronald M. James and C. Elizabeth Raymond, 203–228. Reno: University of Nevada Press, 1998.

Comella, Lynn. "It's Sexy. It's Big Business. And It's Not Just for Men." *Contexts* 7, no. 3 (2008): 61–63.

——. "Selling Sexual Liberation: Women-owned Sex Toy Stores and the Business of Social Change." University of Massachusetts, Amherst, 2004.

Corbin, Alain. *Women for Hire: Prostitution and Sexuality in France after 1850*. Cambridge, MA: Harvard University Press, 1990.

Cosby, Rita. "Bunny Ranch." In *Rita Cosby Live and Direct*, ed. MSNBC, 11 minute episode on MSNBC-TV: MSNBC, 2005.

Crawford, Garry. *Consuming Sport: Fans, Sport and Culture*. New York: Routledge, 2004.

Crook, Stephen, Jan Pakulski, and Malcolm Waters. *Postmodernization: Change in Advanced Society*. Newbury Park, CA: Sage, 1992.

Curtis, Lynnette. "ACLU Joins Fight against Limits on Brothel Ads." *Las Vegas Review Journal*, March 18, 2006.

Darrow, William. "Prostitution, Intravenous Drug Use, and HIV-1 in the United States." In *AIDS, Drugs, and Prostitution*, ed. Martin A. Plant, 18–40. New York: Routledge, 1990.

Davidson, Julia O'Connell. "Will the Real Sex Slave Please Stand Up?" *Feminist Review* 83, no. 1 (2006): 4–22.

——. *Prostitution, Power, and Freedom*. Ann Arbor: University of Michigan Press, 1998.

Davis, James A., Tom W. Smith, and Peter V. Marsden. *General Social Surveys, 1972–2004 [Cumulative File]*. Vol. ICPSR04295-v2., General Social Survey Series. Chicago, IL, Storrs, CT: National Opinion Research Center [producer], Roper Center for Public Opinion Research, University of Connecticut/Ann Arbor, MI: Inter-university Consortium for Political and Social Research [distributors], 2006-04-05.

Debord, Guy. *The Society of the Spectacle*. New York: Zone Books, 1994.

Delacoste, Frederique, and Priscilla Alexander. *Sex Work: Writings by Women in the Sex Industry*. 2nd ed. San Francisco, CA: Cleis Press, 1998.

Denton, Sally and Roger Morris. *The Money and the Power: The Making of Las Vegas and Its Hold on America 1947–2000.* New York: Alfred A. Knopf, 2001.

DeVoto, Bernard. *Across the Wide Missouri.* Boston, MA: Houghton Mifflin Company, 1947.

Diamond, Timothy. *Making Gray Gold: Narratives of Nursing Home Care.* Chicago: University of Chicago Press, 1992.

Doezema, Jo. "Loose Women or Lost Women? The Re-emergence of the Myth of White Slavery in Contemporary Discourses of Trafficking in Women." *Gender Issues* 18, no. 1 (2000): 23–50.

Donna's Ranch. "Where the Wild West Still Lives." Donnasranch.net, http://www.donnasranch.net/.

Dworkin, Andrea. *Pornography: Men Possessing Women.* New York: E. P. Dutton, 1989.

Easton, Dossie and Janet W. Hardy. *The Ethical Slut: A Roadmap for Relationship Pioneers.* 2nd ed. Berkeley, CA: Celestial Arts, 2009.

——— . *The New Bottoming Book.* Emeryville, CA: Greenery Press, 2001.

Edwards, Richard C. *Contested Terrain: The Transformation of the Workplace in the Twentieth Century.* New York: Basic Books, 1979.

Egan, Danielle. *Dancing for Dollars and Paying for Love: The Relationships between Exotic Dancers and Their Regulars.* New York: Palgrave Macmillan, 2006.

Ehrenreich, Barbara. *The Hearts of Men: American Dreams and the Flight from Commitment.* Garden City, NY: Anchor Press/Doubleday, 1983.

Ehrenreich, Barbara and Arlie Russell Hochschild. *Global Woman: Nannies, Maids, and Sex Workers in the New Economy.* 1st ed. New York: Metropolitan Books, 2003.

El-Bassel, Nabila, Robert F. Schilling, Kathleen L. Irwin, Sarius Faruque, Louisa Gilbert, Jennifer Von Bargen, Yolanda Serrano, and Brian R. Edlin. "Sex Trading and Psychological Distress among Women Recruited from the Streets of Harlem." *American Journal of Public Health* 87, no. 1 (1997): 66–70.

Elliott, Russell. *History of Nevada.* Lincoln: University of Nebraska Press, 1973.

——— . *Nevada's Twentieth-Century Mining Boom: Tonopah, Goldfield, Ely.* Reno: University of Nevada Press, 1966. Reprinted 1988.

Entwistle, Joanne and Elizabeth Wissinger. "Keeping up Appearances: Aesthetic Labour in the Fashion Modelling Industries of London and New York." *Sociological Review* 54, no. 4 (2006): 774–794.

Erickson, Karla and Jennifer L. Pierce. "Farewell to the Organization Man: The Feminization of Loyalty in High-end and Low-end Service Jobs." *Ethnography* 6, no. 3 (2005): 283.

Erickson, Rebecca J. and C. Ritter. "Emotional Labor, Burnout, and Inauthenticity: Does Gender Matter?" *Social Psychology Quarterly* (2001): 146–163.

Erickson, Rebecca. J. and Amy S. Wharton. "Inauthenticity and Depression: Assessing the Consequences of Interactive Service Work." *Work and Occupations* 24, no. 2 (1997): 188.

Exner Jr, John E., Joyce Wylie, Antonnia Laura, and Tracey Parrill. "Some Psychological Characteristics of Prostitutes." *Journal of Personality Assessment* 41, no. 5 (1977): 474.

Fadali, Elizabeth, Thomas R. Harris, and Kynda R. Curtis. "Factors Affecting Agritourism Potential in Rural Nevada." In *Fact Sheet.* Reno: University of Nevada Cooperative Extension, 2007.

Fahringer, Harold P. "Zoning out Free Expression: An Analysis of New York City's Adult Zoning Resolution." *Buffalo Law Review* 46 (1998): 403.

Farley, Melissa. " 'Bad for the Body, Bad for the Heart': Prostitution Harms Women Even If Legalized or Decriminalized." *Violence Against Women* 10, no. 10 (2004): 1087.

Farley, Melissa, Isin Baral, Merab Kiremire, and Ufuk Sezgin. "Prostitution in Five Countries." *Feminism and Psychology* 8, no. 4 (1998): 405–426.

Farrell, Ronald A. and Carole Case. *The Black Book and the Mob: The Untold Story of the Control of Nevada's Casinos.* Madison: University of Wisconsin Press, 1995.

Ferber, Marianne A. and Julie A. Nelson. *Feminist Economics Today: Beyond Economic Man.* Chicago: University of Chicago Press, 2003.

Frank, Katherine. *G-strings and Sympathy: Strip Club Regulars and Male Desire.* Durham, NC: Duke University Press, 2002.

——. "The Production of Identity and the Negotiation of Intimacy in a 'Gentleman's Club'." *Sexualities* 1, no. 2 (1998): 175–201.

Frank, Thomas. *What's the Matter with Kansas?* New York: Henry Holt & Company, 2004.

Free Speech Coalition. *Adult Entertainment in America: A State of the Industry Report,* ed. Michelle L. Freridge. Canoga Park: Free Speech Coalition, 2006.

Galliher, John and John Cross. *Morals Legislation without Morals: The Case of Nevada.* New Brunswick, NJ: Rutgers University Press, 1983.

George, Molly. "Interactions in Expert Service Work: Demonstrating Professionalism in Personal Training." *Journal of Contemporary Ethnography* 37, no. 1 (2008): 108.

Gergen, Kenneth J. *The Saturated Self: Dilemmas of Identity in Contemporary Life.* New York: Basic Books, 1991.

Giddens, Anthony. *The Transformation of Intimacy: Sexuality, Love, and Eroticism in Modern Societies.* Stanford, CA: Stanford University Press, 1992.

——. *Modernity and Self-identity: Self and Society in the Late Modern Age.* Stanford, CA: Stanford University Press, 1991.

Gilfoyle, Timothy J. "Prostitutes in History: From Parables of Pornography to Metaphors of Modernity." *The American Historical Review* 104, no. 1 (1999): 117–141.

——. *City of Eros: New York City, Prostitution, and the Commercialization of Sex, 1790–1920.* 1st ed. New York: W. W. Norton, 1992.

Goffman, Erving. *The Presentation of Self in Everyday Life.* New York: Anchor Books, 1959.

Goldman, Marion. *Gold Diggers & Silver Minors: Prostitution and Social Life on the Comstock Lode.* Ann Arbor: University of Michigan Press, 1981.

Gottdiener, Mark, Claudia C. Collins, and David R. Dickens. *Las Vegas: The Social Production of an All-American City.* Malden, MA: Blackwell, 1999.

Grandey, Alicia A. "Emotion Regulation in the Workplace: A New Way to Conceptualize Emotional Labor." *Journal of Occupational Health Psychology* 5, no. 1 (2000): 95–110.

Guy, Donna J. *Sex & Danger in Buenos Aires: Prostitution, Family, and Nation in Argentina.* Lincoln: University of Nebraska Press, 1991.

Hallgrimsdottir, Helga K., Rachel Phillips, Cecilia Benoit, and Kevin Walby. "Sporting Girls, Streetwalkers, and Inmates of Houses of Ill Repute: Media Narratives and the Historical Mutability of Prostitution Stigmas." *Sociological Perspectives* 51, no. 1 (2008): 119–138.

Hanna, Judith L. "Exotic Dance Adult Entertainment: A Guide for Planners and Policy Makers." *Journal of Planning Literature* 20, no. 2 (2005): 116.

Hansen, Andrew J., Ray Rasker, Bruce Maxwell, Jay J. Rotella, Jerry D. Johnson, Andrea W. Parmenter, Ute Langner, Warren B. Cohen, Rick L. Lawrence, and Matthew P.V. Kraska. "Ecological Causes and Consequences of Demographic Change in the New West." *BioScience* 52, no. 2 (2002): 151–162.

Hardesty, Donald L. "Gender and Archaelology on the Comstock." In *Comstock Women: The Making of a Mining Community*, ed. Ronald M. James and C. Elizabeth Raymond, 283–302. Reno: University of Nevada Press, 1998.

Harrison, Pat. *Gannett News Service*, March 24, 1989, newswire.

Harte, Bret and Gary Scharnhorst. *The Luck of Roaring Camp and Other Writings*, Penguin Classics. New York: Penguin Books, 2001.

Harvey, David. *A Brief History of Neoliberalism*. New York: Oxford University Press, 2007.

——. *Spaces of Hope*. Berkeley: University of California Press, 2000.

——. *The Condition of Postmodernity: An Enquiry into the Origins of Cultural Change*. Cambridge, MA: Blackwell, 1989.

Hausbeck, Kathryn and Barbara G. Brents. "Inside Nevada's Brothel Industry." In *Sex for Sale*, ed. Ronald Weitzer, 255–281. New York: Routledge, 2009.

——. "McDonaldization of the Sex Industries? The Business of Sex." In *McDonaldization: The Reader*, ed. George Ritzer, 91–106. Thousand Oaks, CA: Pine Forge Press, 2002.

Hawkes, Gail. *A Sociology of Sex and Sexuality*. Philadelphia, PA: Open University Press, 1996.

Henslin, J. and M. Biggs. "Dramaturgical Desexualisation: The Sociology of the Vaginal Examination." *The Sociology of Sex: An Introductory Reader* (1978): 141–170.

Hershatter, Gail. *Dangerous Pleasures: Prostitution and Modernity in Twentieth-Century Shanghai*. Berkeley: University of California Press, 1997.

Heyl, Barbara S. *The Madam as Entrepreneur: Career Management in House Prostitution*. New Brunswick, NJ: Transaction Books, 1979.

Hobson, Barbara Meil. *Uneasy Virtue: The Politics of Prostitution and the American Reform Tradition*. Chicago: University of Chicago Press, 1990.

Hochschild, Arlie Russell. *The Commercialization of Intimate Life: Notes from Home and Work*. Berkeley: University of California Press, 2003.

——. *The Managed Heart: Commercialization of Human Feeling*. Berkeley: University of California Press, 1983.

Hoigard, Cecilie and Liv Finstad. *Backstreets: Prostitution, Money, and Love*. University Park: Pennsylvania State University Press, 1992.

Holstein, J. A. and Jaber F. Gubrium. "The Self We Live By: Narrative Identity in a Postmodern World." *Symbolic Interaction* 23, no. 4 (2000).

Holyfield, Lori. "Manufacturing Adventure: The Buying and Selling of Emotions." *Journal of Contemporary Ethnography* 28, no. 1 (1999): 3–32.

Hopkins, A. D. and K. J. Evans. *The First 100: Portraits of the Men and Women Who Shaped Las Vegas*. 1st ed. Las Vegas: Huntington Press, 1999.

Hubbard, Phil. "Regulating Sex Work in the European Union: Prostitute Women and the New Spaces of Exclusion." *Gender, Place & Culture* 15, no. 2 (2008): 137–152.

Hubbard, Phil and Mary Whowell. "Revisiting the Red Light District: Still Neglected, Immoral and Marginal?" *Geoforum* 39, no. 5 (2008): 1743–1755.

Hubbard, Phil, Roger Matthews, and Jane Scoular. "Legal Geographies—Controlling Sexually Oriented Businesses: Law, Licensing, and the Geographies of a Controversial Land Use." *Urban Geography* 30, no. 2 (2009): 185–205.

Hulse, James W. *The Silver State: Nevada's Heritage Reinterpreted.* Reno: University of Nevada Press, 1991.

Illouz, Eva. *Consuming the Romantic Utopia: Love and the Cultural Contradictions of Capitalism.* Berkeley: University of California Press, 1997.

Jackson, Stevi and Sue Scott. "Sexual Antinomies in Late Modernity." *Sexualities* 7, no. 2 (2004): 233–248.

James, Ronald M. *The Roar and the Silence: A History of the Virginia City and the Comstock Lode.* Reno: University of Nevada Press, 1998.

James, Ronald M. and C. Elizabeth Raymond, eds. *Comstock Women: The Making of a Mining Community.* Reno: University of Nevada Press, 1998.

James, Ronald M. and Kenneth H. Fliess. "Women of the Mining West: Virginia City Revisited." In *Comstock Women: The Making of a Mining Community,* ed. Ronald M. James and C. Elizabeth Raymond, 17–39. Reno: University of Nevada Press, 1998.

Jameson, Fredric. *Postmodernism, or, the Cultural Logic of Late Capitalism,* Postcontemporary Interventions. Durham, NC: Duke University Press, 1991.

Jeffreys, Sheila. *The Industrial Vagina: The Political Economy of the Global Sex Trade.* New York: Routledge, 2008.

Jenness, Valerie. *Making It Work: The Prostitute's Rights Movement in Perspective.* New York: Aldine de Gruyter, 1993.

Kalleberg, Arne L. "Nonstandard Employment Relations: Part-time, Temporary and Contract Work." *Annual Review of Sociology* 26, no. 1 (2000): 341–365.

Kasindorf, Jeanie. *The Nye County Brothel: A Tale of the New West.* New York: Linden Press/Simon & Schuster, 1985.

Kay, Kerwin, Jill Nagle, and Baruch Gould. *Male Lust: Pleasure, Power, and Transformation.* New York: Harrington Park Press, 2000.

Kelly, Patty. *Lydia's Open Door: Inside Mexico's Most Modern Brothel.* Berkeley: University of California Press, 2008.

Kempadoo, Kamala and Jo Doezema. *Global Sex Workers: Rights, Resistance, and Redefinition.* New York: Routledge, 1998.

Kempadoo, Kamala, Jyoti Sanghera, and Bandana Pattanaik. *Trafficking and Prostitution Reconsidered: New Perspectives on Migration, Sex Work, and Human Rights.* 1st ed. Boulder, Colo.: Paradigm Publishers, 2005.

Kempadoo, Kamala. *Sexing the Caribbean: Gender, Race, and Sexual Labor.* New York: Routledge, 2004.

——— . *Sun, Sex, and Gold: Tourism and Sex Work in the Caribbean.* Lanham, Md.: Rowman & Littlefield Publishers, 1999.

Kingsdale, Jon M. "The 'Poor Man's Club': Social Functions of the Urban Working-class Saloon." *American Quarterly* 25, no. 4 (1973): 472–489.

Kit Kat Guest Ranch. "Sheila and Jacie Caramella." Kit Kat Ranch, http://www.cathouselovers.com/welcome_owners.html.

Kligman, Gail, and Stephanie Limoncelli. "Trafficking Women after Socialism: To, Through, and From Eastern Europe." *Social Politics* 12, no. 1 (2005): 118–140.

Kondo, Dorinne K. *Crafting Selves: Power, Gender, and Discourses of Identity in a Japanese Workplace.* Chicago: University of Chicago Press, 1990.

Kotiswaran, Prabha. "Born Unto Brothels: Towards a Legal Ethnography of Sonagachi's Sex Industry." *Law & Social Inquiry* 33, no. 3 (2008).

Krugman, Paul R. *The Conscience of a Liberal.* New York: W. W. Norton & Co., 2007.

Kruhse-Mount Burton, S. "Sex Tourism and Traditional Australian Male Identity." In *International Tourism: Identity and Change,* ed. Marie-Françoise Lanfant, John B. Allcock, and Edward M. Bruner, 192–204. Thousand Oaks, CA: Sage, 1995.

Kuiper, Edith and Drucilla K. Barker. *Feminist Economics and the World Bank: History, Theory and Policy.* London; New York: Routledge, 2006.

Kuo, Lenore. *Prostitution Policy: Revolutionizing Practice through a Gendered Perspective.* New York: New York University Press, 2002.

Land, Barbara and Myrick Land. *A Short History of Las Vegas.* Reno: University of Nevada Press, 1999.

——. *A Short History of Reno.* Reno: University of Nevada Press, 1995.

Lang, Robert E., Andrea Sarzynski, and Mark Muro. "Mountain Megas: America's Newest Metropolitan Places and a Federal Partnership to Help Them Prosper." In *Metropolitan Policy Program,* 64. Washington, DC: The Brookings Institution, 2008.

Las Vegas Convention and Visitors Authority. "2008 Las Vegas Year to Date Executive Summary." http://www.lvcva.com/getfile/ES-YTD2008%20Revised.pdf?fileID=571.

——. "Be Anyone in Las Vegas." Las Vegas Convention and Visitors Authority, http://www.visitlasvegas.com/vegas/features/be-anyone/.

——. "Vegas Faqs." http://www.lvcva.com/getfile/2008%20Vegas%20FAQs.pdf?fileID=106.

Lash, Scott and John Urry. *Economies of Signs and Space.* London; Thousand Oaks, CA: Sage, 1994.

Lears, T. Jackson. *No Place of Grace: Antimodernism and the Transformation of American Culture 1880–1920.* New York: Pantheon, 1981.

"Legalized Prostitution Debate Transcript #112–2." On *Larry King Live,* 1990.

Leidner, Robin. "Identity and Work." In *Social Theory at Work,* ed. Marek Korczynski, Randy Hodson, and Paul Edwards, 424. New York: Oxford University Press, 2006.

——. *Fast Food, Fast Talk: Service Work and the Routinization of Everyday Life.* Berkeley: University of California Press, 1993.

Lever, Janet and Deanne Dolnick. "Clients and Call Girls: Seeking Sex and Intimacy." In *Sex for Sale: Prostitution, Pornography and the Sex Industry,* ed. Ronald Weitzer, 187–209. New York: Routledge, 2009.

Lewis, Jacqueline, Eleanor Maticka-Tyndale, Frances M. Shaver and Heather Schramm. "Managing Risk and Safety on the Job: The Experiences of Canadian Sex Workers." *Journal of Psychology and Human Sexuality* 17, nos 1/2 (2005): 147–167.

Lim, Lin Lean. *The Sex Sector: The Economic and Social Bases of Prostitution in Southeast Asia.* Geneva: International Labour Organization, 1998.

Linz, Daniel, Eva Blumenthal, Edward Donnerstein, Dale Kunkel, Bradley J. Shafer, and Allen Lichtenstein. "Testing Legal Assumptions Regarding the Effects of Dancer

Nudity and Proximity to Patron on Erotic Expression." *Law and Human Behavior* 24, no. 5 (2000): 507–533.

Linz, Daniel, Kenneth C. Land, Jay R. Williams, Bryant Paul, and Michael E. Ezell. "An Examination of the Assumption That Adult Businesses Are Associated with Crime in Surrounding Areas: A Secondary Effects Study in Charlotte, North Carolina." *Law and Society Review* 38, no. 1 (2004): 69–104.

Loftus, Jeni. "America's Liberalization in Attitudes Toward Homosexuality, 1973 to 1998." *American Sociological Review* 66, no. 5 (2001): 762–782.

Lord, Elliott. *Comstock Mining and Miners.* Washington, DC: United States Government Printing Office, 1880.

Luker, Kristin. "Sex, Social Hygiene, and the State: The Double-edged Sword of Social Reform." *Theory and Society* 27, no. 5 (1998): 601–634.

MacDonald, Cameron L. and Carmen Sirianni. *Working in the Service Economy.* Philadelphia: Temple University Press, 1996.

MacKinnon, Catharine A. *Feminism Unmodified: Discourses on Life and Law.* Cambridge, MA: Harvard University Press, 1987.

Mandel, Ernest. *Late Capitalism.* Revised ed. London: Humanities Press, 1975.

Martin, Susan Taylor. "Nevada Brothels Battle for Business Amid AIDS Scare." *St. Petersburg Times,* November 1, 1987, 1.

Mathews, Mary McNair. *Ten Years on the Comstock. Or Life on the Pacific Coast.* Lincoln: University of Nebraska Press, 1880. Reprinted 1985.

McCammon, Holly J. and Larry J. Griffin. "Workers and Their Customers and Clients." *Work and Occupations* 27, no. 3 (2000): 278–293.

McDowell, Linda. "Bodywork: Heterosexual Gender Performances in City Workspaces." In *Mapping Desire,* ed. David Bell and Gill Valentine, 75–95, New York: Routledge, 1995.

McKeganey, Neil P. and Marina Barnard. *Sex Work on the Streets: Prostitutes and Their Clients.* Philadelphia, PA: Open University Press, 1996.

McLuhan, Marshall, and Quentin Fiore. *The Medium is the Message.* New York: Penguin, 2008.

——. "Brothels: From Public Nuisances to Licensed Businesses." *Reno Gazette-Journal,* November 15, 1986.

——. "While Legislators Ducked the Issue, Courts Set Brothel Law." *Reno Gazette-Journal,* November 15, 1986.

——. "A Tale of Two Counties." *Reno Gazette-Journal,* November 13, 1986.

——. "Lawmakers: Brothel Issue Likely Topic for '87 Session." *Reno Gazette-Journal,* November 13, 1986.

——. "Rural Nevada Reluctant to Abolish Legal Brothels." *Reno Gazette-Journal,* November 13, 1986.

——. "AIDS Brings Fear, Uncertainty to Brothels." *Reno Gazette-Journal,* November 12, 1986.

——. "Nevada's Sex-for-Sale Dilemma." *Reno Gazette-Journal,* November 9, 1986.

——. "The Reno Stockade." *Reno Gazette-Journal,* November 9, 1986.

McMillan, Doug. "From a Miner's Friend to a Nevada Way of Life." *Reno Gazette-Journal,* November 9, 1986.

Mead, Rebecca. "Letter from Nevada: American Pimp, How to Make a Living from the Oldest Profession." *New Yorker,* April 23, 2001.

Meretrix, Magdalene. *Turning Pro: A Guide to Sex Work for the Ambitious and the Intrigued.* Emeryville, CA: Greenery Press, 2001.

Miller, Ken. "Conforte Parlayed Mustang into Fame, Fortune, Trouble." *Reno Gazette-Journal,* November 14, 1986.

——. "Raggio Has Been Nemesis for More Than 25 Years." *Reno Gazette-Journal,* November 14, 1986.

Minichiello, Vincent, P. G. Harvey, and R. Marino. "Sexual Intentions of Male Sex Workers: An International Study of Escorts Who Advertise on the Web." In *Sex as Crime?,* edited by Gayle Letherby, Kate Williams, Philip Birch and Maureen Cain, 156–171. Cullompton: Willan Publishers, 2008.

Moehring, Eugene P. *Resort City in the Sunbelt: Las Vegas, 1930–2000.* 2nd ed. Wilbur S. Shepperson Series in History and Humanities. Reno: University of Nevada Press, 2000.

Montemurro, Beth. "Strippers and Screamers: The Emergence of Social Control in a Noninstitutionalized Setting." *Journal of Contemporary Ethnography* 30, no. 3 (2001): 275–304.

——. "Why Men Seek out Prostitutes." In *Sex for Sale: Prostitution, Pornography and the Sex Industry,* ed. Ronald Weitzer, 233–254. New York: Routledge, 2009.

Monto, Martin A. "Female Prostitution, Customers, and Violence." *Violence Against Women* 10, no. 2 (2004): 160.

Morris, Martina and Bruce Western. "Inequality in Earnings at the Close of the Twentieth Century." *Annual Review of Sociology* 25, no. 1 (1999): 623–657.

Mossman, Elaine. "International Approaches to Decriminalising or Legalising Prostitution." Wellington, NZ: Ministry of Justice, 2007.

Munro, Vanessa E. "Exploring Exploitation: Trafficking in Sex, Work and Sex Work." In *Demanding Sex: Critical Reflections on the Regulation of Prostitution,* edited by Vanessa Munro and Marina Della Giusta, 83–98. London: Ashgate Publishing, 2008.

——. "Stopping Traffic? A Comparative Study of Responses to the Trafficking in Women for Prostitution." *British Journal of Criminology* 46, no. 2 (2006): 318–333.

Murphy, Alexandra K. and Sudhir A. Venkatesh. "Vice Careers: The Changing Contours of Sex Work in New York City." *Qualitative Sociology* 29, no. 2 (2006): 129–154.

Nagle, Jill. *Whores and Other Feminists.* New York: Routledge, 1997.

Nevada Natural Resources Plan Technical Working Group. "Nevada Natural Resources Status Report: Land and Management Status." Nevada Department of Conservation and Natural Resources, http://dcnr.nv.gov/nrp01/land01.htm.

Oerton, Sarah. "Bodywork Boundaries: Power, Politics and Professionalism in Therapeutic Massage." *Gender Work and Organization* 11, no. 5 (2004): 544–565.

Oerton, Sarah and Joanna Phoenix. "Sex/Bodywork: Discourses and Practices." *Sexualities* 4, no. 4 (2001): 387.

O'Neill, Maggie. *Prostitution and Feminism.* Cambridge: Polity Press, 2001.

Oppermann, Martin. "Sex Tourism." *Annals of Tourism Research* 26, no. 2 (1999): 251–266.

Outshoorn, Joyce. "The Political Debates on Prostitution and Trafficking of Women." *Social Politics* 12, no. 1 (2005): 141.

——. *The Politics of Prostitution: Women's Movements, Democratic States, and the Globalisation of Sex Commerce.* Cambridge, UK; New York: Cambridge University Press, 2004.

Overall, Christine. "What's Wrong with Prostitution? Evaluating Sex Work." *Signs* 17, no. 4 (1992): 705–725.

Pateman, Carole. *The Sexual Contract.* Stanford, CA: Stanford University Press, 1988.

Paul, Bryant, Bradley J. Shafer, and Daniel Linz. "Government Regulation Of 'Adult' Businesses through Zoning and Anti-nudity Ordinances: Debunking the Legal Myth of Negative Secondary Effects." *Communication Law and Policy* 6, no. 2 (2001): 355–391.

Paules, Greta Foff. *Dishing it Out: Power and Resistance Among Waitresses in a New Jersey Restaurant.* Philadelphia: Temple University Press, 1991.

Perkins, Roberta and Frances Lovejoy. *Call Girls: Private Sex Workers in Australia.* Perth: University of Western Australia Press, 2007.

——. "Healthy and Unhealthy Life Styles of Female Brothel Workers and Call Girls (Private Sex Workers) in Sydney." *Australia and New Zealand Journal of Public Health* 20, no. 5 (1996): 512–516.

Petrik, Paula. *No Step Backward: Women and Men on the Western Mining Frontier, Helena Montana 1865–1900.* Helena: Montana Historical Society Press, 1987.

Pheterson, Gail. *The Prostitution Prism.* Amsterdam: Amsterdam University Press, 1996.

Phillips, Rachel and Cecilia Benoit. "Social Determinants of Health Care Access Among Sex Industry Workers in Canada." *Research in the Sociology of Health Care* 23 (2005) 79–104.

Pierce, Jennifer. *Gender Trials: Emotional Lives in Contemporary Law Firms.* Los Angeles: University of California Press, 1996.

Pillard, Ellen. "Rethinking Prostitution: A Case for Uniform Regulations." *Nevada Public Affairs Review* 1 (1991): 45–49.

——. "Legal Prostitution: Is It Just?" *Nevada Public Affairs Review* 2, (1983): 43–47.

Prasad, Monica. "The Morality of Market Exchange: Love, Money, and Contractual Justice." *Sociological Perspectives* 42, no. 2 (1999): 181–214.

Prostitution Law Review Committee. "Report of the Prostitution Law Review Committee on the Operation of the Prostitution Reform Act 2003." Wellington, New Zealand: Ministry of Justice, 2008.

Radeloff, Cheryl L. "Vectors, Polluters and Murderers: HIV Testing Policies toward Prostitutes in Nevada," Ph.D. dissertation, University of Nevada, Las Vegas, 2004.

Reade, Russ, Gary A. Richwald, and N. Williams. "The Nevada Legal Brothel System as a Model for AIDS Prevention among Female Sex Industry Workers." Paper presented at the Sixth International Conference on AIDS, San Francisco, CA, June, 1990.

Reiss, Albert J. "Sex Offenses: The Marginal Status of the Adolescent." *Law and Contemporary Problems* 25, (1960): 309.

Reno, Mona. "Nevada Place Names Population 1860–2000." Nevada Department of Cultural Affairs, http://nevadaculture.org/nsla/index.php?option=com_content&task=view&id=1036&Itemid=1.

Reynolds, Helen. *The Economics of Prostitution.* Springfield, Ill.: C. C. Thomas, 1986.

Riebsame, William. "Atlas of the New West: Portrait of a Changing Region." In Center of the American West. *University of Colorado at Boulder,* 1997.

Ritzer, George and Allen Liska. " 'McDisneyization' and 'Post Tourism': Complementary Perspectives on Contemporary Tourism." In *Touring Cultures: Transform-*

ations of Travel and Theory, ed. Chris Rojek and John Urry, 96–112. London; New York: Routledge, 1997.

Ritzer, George. *The McDonaldization of Society*. Thousand Oaks, CA: Pine Forge Press, 1996.

Rocha, Guy. "Myth #105—the Mississippi of the West." Nevada Department of Cultural Affairs (2008): http://nevadaculture.org/nsla/index.php?option=com_content &task=view&id=786&Itemid=95.

———. "Brothel Prostitution in Nevada: A Unique American Cultural Phenomenon," Master's thesis, San Diego State University, 1975.

Rojek, Chris. *Ways of Escape: Modern Transformations in Leisure and Travel*, Postmodern Social Futures. Lanham, MD: Rowman & Littlefield, 1994.

Rojek, Chris and John Urry. *Touring Cultures: Transformations of Travel and Theory*. New York: Routledge, 1997.

Roseneil, Sasha. "Queer Frameworks and Queer Tendencies: Toward an Understanding of Postmodern Transformations of Sexuality." *Sociological Research Online* 5, no. 3 (2000): <http://www.socresonline.org.uk/5/3/roseneil.html>.

Rothman, Hal. *Neon Metropolis: How Las Vegas Started the Twenty-first Century*. New York: Routledge, 2002.

Ryan, Chris and C. Michael Hall. *Sex Tourism: Marginal People and Liminalities*. New York: Routledge, 2001.

Ryan, Chris and Rachel Kinder. "Sex, Tourism and Sex Tourism: Fulfilling Similar Needs?" *Tourism Management* 17, no. 7 (1996): 507–518.

Ryan, Chris. "Sex Tourism: Paradigms of Confusion." In *Tourism and Sex: Culture, Commerce and Coercion*, edited by Stephen Clift and Simon Carter (23–40). London: Cassell, 2000.

Sanders, Teela. *Paying for Pleasure: Men Who Buy Sex*. Cullompton: Willan Publishers, 2008.

———. " 'It's Just Acting': Sex Workers' Strategies for Capitalizing on Sexuality." *Gender, Work and Organization* 12, no. 4 (2005): 319–342.

———. *Sex Work: A Risky Business*. Cullompton: Willan Publishing, 2005.

———. "Controllable Laughter: Managing Sex Work through Humor." *Sociology* 38, no. 2 (2004): 273–291.

———. "The Condom as Psychological Barrier: Female Sex Workers and Emotional Management." *Feminism and Psychology* 12, no. 4 (2002): 561–566.

Scambler, Graham and Annette Scambler. *Rethinking Prostitution: Purchasing Sex in the 1990s*. London; New York: Routledge, 1997.

Schlosser, Eric. "The Business of Pornography." *U.S. News & World Report*, February 10, 1997.

Schwalbe, Michael L. and Douglas Mason-Schrock. "Identity Work as Group Process." *Advances in Group Processes* 13 (1996): 113–147.

Schwartz, David. "Suburban Xanadu: The Casino Resort on the Las Vegas Strip 1945–1978," Ph.D dissertation, UCLA, 2000.

———. *Suburban Xanadu: The Casino Resort on the Las Vegas Strip and Beyond*. New York: Routledge, 2003.

Scott, John, John T. Hunter, Vanessa H. Hunter, and Angela T. Ragusa. "Sex Outside the City: Sex Work in Rural and Regional New South Wales." *Rural Society* 16, no. 2 (2006): 151–168.

Scott, John, Victor Minichiello, Rodrigo Marino, Glenn P. Harvey, Maggie Jamieson, and Jan Browne. "Understanding the New Context of the Male Sex Work Industry." *Journal of Interpersonal Violence* 20, no. 3 (2005): 320.

Seib, Charlotte, Jane Fischer, and Jakob M. Najman. "The Health of Female Sex Workers from Three Industry Sectors in Queensland, Australia." *Social Science & Medicine* 68, no. 3 (2009): 473–478.

Seidman, Steven. *Beyond the Closet: The Transformation of Gay and Lesbian Life*. New York: Routledge, 2003.

Seppa Arroyo, Candice Michelle. "Labor Violations and Discrimination in the Clark County Outcall Entertainment Industry." MA thesis, University of Nevada, Las Vegas, 2003.

Sharpe, Eric. " 'Going Above and Beyond:' The Emotional Labor of Adventure Guides." *Journal of Leisure Research* 37, no. 1 (2005): 29–50.

Sherman, Rachel. *Class Acts: Service and Inequality in Luxury Hotels*. Berkeley: University of California Press, 2007.

Shrage, Laurie. *Moral Dilemmas of Feminism: Prostitution, Adultery, and Abortion*. New York: Routledge, 1994.

Silverstein, Michael, Neil Fiske, and John Butman. *Trading Up: Why Consumers Want New Luxury Goods—and How Companies Create Them*. Revised ed. New York: Portfolio, 2005.

Simmons, Alexy. "Red Light Ladies: Settlement Patterns and Material Culture of the Mining Frontier." *Anthropological Northwest No. 4.* Corvallis: Department of Anthropology Oregon State University (1989).

Singer, Linda. *Erotic Welfare: Sexual Theory and Politics in the Age of Epidemic*, Thinking Gender. New York: Routledge, 1992.

Sion, Mike. "Conforte Changed the Face of Nevada Bordellos." *Reno Gazette-Journal*, January 20, 1995.

Smith, Raymond M. *Saloons of Old & New Nevada*. Minden, NV: R.M. Smith, 1992.

Sonnier, Suzanne. "The Mustang Ranch and the Politics of Nevada Brothel Prostitution." *Nevada Women's History Working Papers* no. 2 (1994).

Spain, William. "Strip Clubs Go Mainstream." *MSN Money MarketWatch* (2007), http://articles.moneycentral.msn.com/Investing/Extra/StripClubsGoMainstream.aspx.

Spanier, David. *Welcome to the Pleasuredome: Inside Las Vegas*. Reno: University of Nevada Press, 1992.

Stacey, Judith. *In the Name of the Family: Rethinking Family Values in the Postmodern Age*. Boston, MA: Beacon Press, 1996.

Sullivan, Barbara Ann. *The Politics of Sex: Prostitution and Pornography in Australia since 1945*. Cambridge: Cambridge University Press, 1997.

Swartz, Tracy. "Prostitution Arrests Go up 4.5% in City." *Chicago Tribune*, March 20, 2009, 2.

Synmanski, Richard. "Prostitution in Nevada." *Annuals of the Association of American Geographers* 65, no. 3 (1974): 357–377.

Tanner, Adam. "Nevada's Legal Brothels Given Timid Embrace." *Washington Post*, March 12, 2006, A08.

Taylor, Andria Daley. "Girls of the Golden West." In *Comstock Women: The Making of a*

Mining Community, ed. Ronald M. James and C. Elizabeth Raymond, 265–282. Reno: University of Nevada Press, 1998.

Taylor, Jacqueline Sanchez. "Tourism and 'Embodied' Commodities: Sex Tourism in the Caribbean." In *Tourism and Sex: Culture, Commerce and Coercion*, edited by Stephen Clift and Simon Carter, 41. New York: Cassell, 2000.

The Economist. "Giving the Customer What He Wants." *The Economist*, February 14, 1998, 21–24.

Theobald, William F. *Global Tourism*. 2nd ed. Boston, MA: Butterworth-Heinemann, 1998.

Tilly, Chris. *Half a Job: Bad and Good Part-time Jobs in a Changing Labor Market*. Philadelphia: Temple University Press, 1996.

Toffler, Alvin. *Powershift: Knowledge, Wealth, and Violence at the Edge of the 21st Century*. New York: Bantam Books, 1990.

Twain, Mark. *Roughing It*. New York: Harper and Brothers Publishers, 1871. Reprinted 1913.

Twitchell, James B. *Living It Up: Our Love Affair with Luxury*. New York: Columbia University Press, 2002.

U.S. Census Bureau American FactFinder. "Tm-M2. Persons Per Square Mile: 2008 Nevada by County." U.S. Census Bureau, http://factfinder.census.gov/.

U.S. Census Bureau, Public Information Office. "U.S. Census Bureau News Press Release: Nevada in Focus: Census Bureau Pre-Caucus Snapshot, Jan. 16." edited by Department of Commerce. Washington, D.C.: U.S. Census Bureau, 2008.

U.S. Census Bureau. "State and County Quick Facts." http://quickfacts.census.gov/qfd/states/32000.html.

UPI. "Regional News." *Regional Newswire*, November 12, 1987.

Urry, John. *Mobilities*. Malden, MA: Polity Press, 2007.

——— . *The Tourist Gaze*. 2nd ed. London; Thousand Oaks, CA: Sage, 2002.

Vanwesenbeeck, Ine. "Burnout Among Female Indoor Sex Workers." *Archives of Sexual Behavior* 34, no. 6 (2005): 627–39.

——— . "Another Decade of Social Scientific Work on Sex Work: A Review of Research 1990–2000." *Annual Review of Sex Research* 12 (2001): 242–289.

Vanwesenbeeck, Ine, Ron de Graaf, Gertjan van Zessen, Cees J. Straver, and Jan H. Visser. "Professional HIV Risk Taking, Levels of Victimization, and Well-being in Female Prostitutes in the Netherlands." *Archives of Sexual Behavior* 24, no. 5 (1995): 503–515.

Vogliotti, Gabriel. *The Girls of Nevada*. Secaucus, NJ: Citadel Press, 1975.

Wahab, Stephanie. "Guest Editor's Introduction." *Journal of Interpersonal Violence* 20, no. 3 (2005): 263–269.

Walkowitz, Judith R. *City of Dreadful Delight: Narratives of Sexual Danger in Late-Victorian London*. Chicago: University of Chicago Press, 1992.

——— . *Prostitution and Victorian Society: Women, Class, and the State*. Cambridge; New York: Cambridge University Press, 1980.

Warhurst, Chris and Dennis Nickson. "Employee Experience of Aesthetic Labour in Retail and Hospitality." *Work, Employment & Society* 21, no. 1 (2007): 103.

Warhurst, Chris, Dennis Nickson, Anne Witz, and Anne-Marie Cullen. "Aesthetic Labour in Interactive Service Work: Some Case Study Evidence from the 'New' Glasgow." *The Service Industries Journal* 20, no. 3 (2000): 1–18.

Washburn, Sarah Hall. "Changing Images: The End of Legalized Prostitution in Las Vegas," Master's thesis, University of Nevada, Las Vegas, 1999.

Weeks, Jeffrey. *The World We Have Won: The Remaking of Erotic and Intimate Life.* New York: Routledge, 2007.

Weitzer, Ronald, ed. *Sex for Sale.* New York: Routledge, 2010.

——. "Paradigms and Policies." In *Sex for Sale*, ed. Ronald Weitzer, 1–43. New York: Routledge, 2009.

——. "Legalizing Prostitution: Morality Politics in Western Australia." *British Journal of Criminology* (2008).

——. "The Social Construction of Sex Trafficking: Ideology and Institutionalization of a Moral Crusade." *Politics and Society* 35, no. 3 (2007): 447–475.

——. "Flawed Theory and Method in Studies of Prostitution." *Violence Against Women* 11, no. 7 (2005): 934.

——. "New Directions in Research on Prostitution." *Crime, Law and Social Change* 43, no. 4 (2005): 211–235.

——. "Prostitutes' Rights in the United States: The Failure of a Movement." *Sociological Quarterly* 32, no. 1 (1991): 23–41.

Wharton, Amy S. "The Sociology of Emotional Labor." *Annual Review of Sociology* 35, no. 1 (2009).

——. "The Affective Consequences of Service Work: Managing Emotions on the Job." *Work and Occupations* 20, no. 2 (1993): 205.

White, Luise. *The Comforts of Home: Prostitution in Colonial Nairobi.* Chicago: University of Chicago Press, 1990.

Williams, George III. *The Redlight Ladies of Virginia City, Nevada.* Riverside, CA: Tree by the River Publishers, 1984.

Witz, Anne, Chris Warhurst, and Dennis Nickson. "The Labour of Aesthetics and the Aesthetics of Organization." *Organization* 10, no. 1 (2003): 33.

Wolkowitz, Carol. *Bodies at Work.* Thousand Oaks, CA: Sage, 2006.

——. "The Social Relations of Body Work." *Work, Employment & Society* 16, no. 3 (2002): 497.

Wonders, Nancy A. and Raymond Michalowski. "Bodies, Borders, and Sex Tourism in a Globalized World: A Tale of Two Cities—Amsterdam and Havana." *Social Problems* 48, no. 4 (2001): 545–571.

Wood, E. A. "Working in the Fantasy Factory: The Attention Hypothesis and the Enacting of Masculine Power in Strip Clubs." *Journal of Contemporary Ethnography* 29, no. 1 (2000): 5–31.

World Travel and Tourism Council. "Travel & Tourism Economic Impact: Executive Summary." http://www.wttc.org/eng/Tourism_Research/Tourism_Economic_ Research. London: World Travel & Tourism Council, 2009.

Wright, Thomas C. "Immigration and Ethnic Diversity in Nevada." Center for Democratic Culture, University of Nevada, Las Vegas (2006): http://www.unlv.edu/ centers/cdclv/healthnv/immigration.html.

Zanjani, Sally S. *Devils Will Reign: How Nevada Began.* Reno: University of Nevada Press, 2006.

——. *Goldfield: The Last Gold Rush on the Western Frontier.* Athens: Ohio University Press, 1992.

Zanjani, Sally S. and Guy Louis Rocha. *The Ignoble Conspiracy: Radicalism on Trial in Nevada.* Reno, Nevada: University of Nevada Press, 1986.

Zapf, Dieter, and Melanie Holz. "On the Positive and Negative Effects of Emotion Work in Organizations." *European Journal of Work and Organizational Psychology* 15, no. 1 (2006): 1–28.

Zelizer, Viviana A. Rotman. *The Purchase of Intimacy.* Princeton, NJ: Princeton University Press, 2005.

INDEX